School-Based
Play Therapy

Second Edition

School-Based Play Therapy

Second Edition

Edited by
Athena A. Drewes
Charles E. Schaefer

WILEY

John Wiley & Sons, Inc.

Copyright © 2010 by John Wiley & Sons, Inc. All rights reserved.

Published by John Wiley & Sons, Inc., Hoboken, New Jersey.
Published simultaneously in Canada.

Library of Congress Cataloging-in-Publication Data:

School-based play therapy/Athena A. Drewes, Charles E. Schaefer [editors]. – 2nd ed.
    p. cm.
Includes bibliographical references and index.

  ISBN 978-0-470-37140-4 (cloth)

 1. School psychology–United States. 2. Play therapy–United States.
I. Drewes, Athena A., 1948- II. Schaefer, Charles E.
LB1027.55.S34 2010

155.4′18–dc22   2009020117

Printed in the United States of America

10 9 8 7 6 5 4 3 2 1

This book is dedicated to

Scott Richard Drewes Bridges and Seth Andrew Bridges
and
Irene and Eric Schaefer

Contents

Preface

I F EVER WE needed play therapy in the schools, it is now! With the rapid increase in school violence, bullying, homeless children and families, angry and aggressive children, and children exposed to chronic trauma situations, both human-made and by nature, play therapy is needed more than ever in the schools. Schools are the place where children spend a majority of their day, learning, socializing, and having their self-esteem shaped. It makes sense that in this environment, school clinicians would be able to have a significant impact in helping to heal children and adolescents suffering from emotional and behavioral difficulties. The healing powers of play *as* a treatment modality and play *in* therapy or counseling can significantly help children and adolescents decrease their emotional and behavioral difficulties. With the growth of play therapy as a respected modality, many school counselors, psychologists, teachers, and social workers have been searching for techniques that could be incorporated into their school settings.

This second edition is born out of our desire to help meet school clinicians' needs. The invited authors in this text have many years of expertise working in school settings, both in the public and private sectors, and have a broad range of experience with the age groups that they serve. They bring a wealth of knowledge on how to use play therapy to work with children and adolescents in individual and group settings and with a variety of tools.

Two-thirds of the chapters in this volume are new chapters focusing on up-to-date approaches. The remaining one-third are chapters from the first edition that we felt were important to include. These chapters have been updated to include recent developments over the last ten years. This volume is divided into six parts. Part I addresses the therapeutic power of play and offers a review of the outcome research of school-based play therapy. Part II gives the school clinician practical information on how to incorporate play therapy in the schools, along with the concomittant challenges and barriers that are encountered.

Part III addresses play-based assessments for the primary years and for elementary and intermediate school settings. Part IV addresses play-based prevention programs using paraprofessionals and teachers. Part V focuses on individual and group play therapy approaches that specifically target children with autism, anger management difficulties, ADHD, and trauma. Part VI addresses special populations and special issues encountered when using play therapy in the school setting, such as parental alcoholism, selective mutism, homelessness, and bereavement issues. All chapters are meant to be applicable to the school or classroom setting. There are clear descriptions of each approach with suggestions as to how they might be implemented.

We hope that school clinicians and teachers will find this second edition a useful resource for helping the children and adolescents they serve.

Athena A. Drewes
Charles E. Schaefer
November, 2009

Contributors

Brittney Bixby, EdS candidate
University of Denver
Morgridge College of Education
Denver, Colorado

Sue C. Bratton, PhD, LPC, RPT-S
Associate Professor
Director, Center for Play Therapy
University of North Texas
Denton, Texas

Judy Doran, MS, LPC, RPT
Elementary School Counselor
Springfield Public Schools
Springfield, Missouri

Athena A. Drewes, PsyD, RPT-S
Director of Clinical Training and
APA-Accredited Doctoral
   Internship
Astor Services for Children &
   Families
Poughkeepsie, New York
Adjunct Professor
Marist College, Poughkeepsie,
   NY
Sage College, Albany, NY

James G. Emshoff, PhD
Associate Professor of Psychology
Georgia State University
Atlanta, Georgia

**Barbara Fischetti, DEd, NCSP,
   ABPP, RPT**
Diplomate in School Psychology
Coordinator of Psychological
   Services
Westport Public Schools
Westport, Connecticut

**Ruthellen Griffin, MEd, MA,
   ADTR**
Friends of Hospice, Litchfield and
   New Milford
Visiting Nursing Association,
   New Milford
Visiting Nurses Services of
   Connecticut
Torrington, West Cornwall,
   Connecticut

**Wendy Pretz Helker, PhD, LPC-S,
   NCC, RPT**
Professional Counseling
   Program
Texas State University
San Marcos, Texas

A. Dirk Hightower, PhD
Children's Institute
Rochester, New York

Laura L. Jacobus-Kantor, PhD
Assistant Research Professor
Center for Integrated Behavioral
   Health Policy
George Washington University
   Medical Center
Washington, DC

Deborah Johnson
Children's Institute
Rochester, New York

Theresa Kestly, PhD
Director, Program Development
   and Training
Sand Tray Training Institute of
   New Mexico
Corrales, New Mexico

G.W. Krauss, MA
Widener University
Department of Psychology
Chester, Pennsylvania

Daniel B. LeGoff, PhD, LP
Director of Neuropsychology
Adjunct Associate Professor
The Center for Neurological and
   Neurodevelopmental Health
Voorhees, New Jersey

Sarah Allen Levin, MA
Drexel University
Department of Psychology
Philadelphia, Pennsylvania

Toni Linder, EdD
Professor
Child, Family, and School
   Psychology
University of Denver
Morgridge College of Education
Denver, Colorado

David E. McIntosh, PhD
Department of Special Education
Ball State University
Muncie, Indiana

Mary O. Morrison, PhD, LPC-S,
   NCC, RPT-S
Assistant Professor
Professional Counseling Program
Texas State University
San Marcos, Texas

Mary Anne Peabody, LCSW,
   RPT-S
Interim Director of National
   Services
Children's Institute
Rochester, New York

Kristi L. Perryman, PhD, LPC,
   RPT
Assistant Professor
Counseling Program
Internship Coordinator
Missouri State University
Springfield, Missouri

Dee C. Ray, PhD, LPC-S, NCC, RPTS
Associate Professor, Counseling Program
Director, Child and Family Resource Clinic
University of North Texas
Denton, Texas

Linda A. Reddy, PhD
Associate Professor
Rutgers University
Director, Child and Adolescent ADHD-Related Disorders Clinic
The Graduate School of Applied and Professional Psychology
Piscataway, New Jersey

Charles E. Schaefer, PhD, RPT-S
Professor Emeritus
Director Emeritus of the Association for Play Therapy
Fairleigh Dickinson University
Teaneck, New Jersey

Mary May Schmidt, MS, MA, LMHC, RPT-S
Nationally Certified Counselor
Registered Play Therapist-Supervisor
American Board of School Neuropsychology, Diplomate
Monticello, New York

Yih-Jiun Shen, DEd, NCC, CSC
Assistant Professor
Department of Educational Psychology
The University of Texas-Pan American
Edinburg, Texas

Karen Stagnitti, PhD
Associate Professor
School of Health and Social Development
Deakin University
Australia

Ana Maria Sutton, MA
Founder, Director of Clinical Services
Nana's Children Mental Health Foundation
Phoenix, Arizona

Geraldine Thomas, MSc, MA
Play Therapist, Supervisor, Certified Filial Therapist-Instructor
Member CAMHS Outreach Team
Associate Researcher with Lifespan Research
United Kingdom

Alison Woolf, BEd
Master's in Play Therapy
Director of Care-Northwest
United Kingdon

Laurie Zelinger, MS, PhD, RPT-S
Child Psychologist
Oceanside Public Schools
Oceanside, New York
Private Practice
Cedarhurst, New York

PART I

PLAY THERAPY: ITS THERAPEUTIC POWER AND RESEARCH EFFECTS

CHAPTER 1

The Therapeutic Powers of Play and Play Therapy

CHARLES E. SCHAEFER and
ATHENA A. DREWES

PLAY IS AS natural to children as breathing. It is a universal expression of children, and it can transcend differences in ethnicity, language, or other aspects of culture (Drewes, 2006). Play has been observed in virtually every culture since the beginning of recorded history. It is inextricably linked to how the culture develops poetry, music, dance, philosophy, social structures—all linked through the society's view of play (Huizinga, 1949). But how play looks and is valued differs across and within cultures (Sutton-Smith, 1974, 1999).

The use of fantasy, symbolic play, and make-believe is a developmentally natural activity in children's play (Russ, 2007). Play is not only central but critical to childhood development (Roopnarine & Johnson, 1994). For a variety of species, including humans, play can be nearly as important as food and sleep. The intense sensory and physical stimulation that comes with playing helps to form the brain's circuits and prevents loss of neurons (Perry, 1997). Play is so critical to a child's development that it is promoted by the United Nations 1989 Convention on the Rights of the Child, Article 31.1, which recognizes "the right of the child to rest and leisure, to engage in play and recreational activities appropriate to the age of the child and to participate freely in cultural life and the arts." Play is perhaps the most developmentally appropriate and powerful medium for young children to build adult-child relationships, develop cause-effect thinking critical to impulse control, process stressful experiences, and learn social skills (Chaloner,

2001). Play can provide a child the sense of power and control that comes from solving problems and mastering new experiences, ideas, and concerns. As a result, it can help build feelings of confidence and accomplishment (Drewes, 2005). Through play and play-based interventions children can communicate nonverbally, symbolically, and in an action-oriented manner.

Play is not only essential for promoting normal child development, but it has many therapeutic powers as well. All therapies require, among other factors, the formation of a therapeutic relationship, along with the use of a medium of exchange (Drewes, 2001). The use of play helps establish a working relationship with children, especially those who lack verbal self-expression, and even with older children who show resistance or an inability to articulate their feelings and issues (Haworth, 1964). The presence of toys and play materials in the room sends a message to the child that this space and time is different from all others. It indicates to the child that they are given permission to be children and to feel free to be fully themselves (Landreth, 1993).

Play is used in therapy by play therapists and child clinicians as a means of helping children deal with emotional and behavioral issues. Play therapy and the use of play-based interventions is by no means a new school of thought (Drewes, 2006). The use of play to treat children dates back to the 1930s to Hermione Hug-Hellmuth, Anna Freud, and Melanie Klein. Several adult therapies have since been adapted for use with children, such as child-centered play therapy adapted by Virginia Axline (1947), sandplay therapy evolving out of Jungian theory through Margaret Lowenfeld (1979) and Dora Kalff (1980), and cognitive-behavioral play therapy by Susan Knell (1993).

In the safe, emotionally supportive setting of a therapy room, the child can play out concerns and issues, which may be too horrific or anxiety producing to directly confront or talk about in the presence of a therapist who can help them feel heard and understood. The toys become the child's words and play becomes his or her language (Landreth, 1991), which the therapist then reflects back to the child to foster greater understanding.

CURATIVE FACTORS OF PLAY

Therapists from differing theoretical orientations have long been interested in the healing or curative factors of psychotherapy. It is only over the past 25 years that child clinicians and researchers have looked more closely at the specific qualities inherent in play behavior that makes it a therapeutic agent for change (Russ, 2004). The goal is to understand what invisible but powerful forces resulting from the therapist-client play interactions are successful in helping the client overcome and heal psychosocial difficulties. A greater understanding of these change mechanisms enables the clinician to apply them more effectively to meet the particular needs of a client (Schaefer, 1999).

Freud wrote of insight, facilitated by the therapist's interpretations and analysis of transference (Schaefer, 1999), as the key component toward curing a client in psychoanalysis.

Yalom (1985) wrote about "therapeutic factors" or change mechanisms that he believed were inherent in group psychotherapy (Schaefer, 1999). They included acceptance, altruism, catharsis, instillation of hope, interpersonal learning, self-disclosure, self-understanding, universality, vicarious learning, and guidance (Schaefer, 1999). Bergin and Strupp (1972) offered critical factors that transcended theoretical schools of thought: counterconditioning, extinction, cognitive learning, reward and punishment, transfer and generalization, imitation and identification, persuasion, empathy, warmth, and interpretation (Schaefer, 1999).

Schaefer (1999) was the first to describe the therapeutic powers of play. Based upon a review of the literature, he identified 25 therapeutic factors that will be discussed below.

SELF-EXPRESSION

Developmental limitations in expressive and receptive language skills, limited vocabulary repertoire, and limitations in abstract thinking ability contribute to young children's difficulty in communicating effectively. Perhaps the major therapeutic power of play that has been described in the literature (Schaefer, 1995, 1999) is its communication power. In play, children are able to express their conscious thoughts and feelings better through play activities than by words alone. Children are naturally comfortable with expression through concrete play activities and materials (Landreth, 1995). Use of symbolic representation and expression through dolls and puppets provides emotional distance from emotionally charged experiences, thoughts, and feelings. Through indirect expression in play the child can gain awareness of troublesome affects and memories and begin the process of healing.

ACCESS TO THE UNCONSCIOUS

Through the specially chosen toys, games, and materials for their therapeutic and neutral stimulus qualities, the child can reveal unconscious conflicts via the defense mechanisms of projection, displacement, and symbolization (Klein, 1955). With the support of the play therapist in a safe environment, the child can begin to transform and integrate unconscious wishes and impulses into conscious play and actions (Schaefer, 1999).

DIRECT AND INDIRECT TEACHING

Play allows you to overcome knowledge and skills deficits in clients by direct instruction. For example, when you teach social skills to children using dolls, puppets, and role-plays, the children are more likely to learn and remember the lessons. The use of fun and games captures children's attention and increases their motivation to learn.

Story telling and the use of play narratives allow the child to join in interactive fantasy play with the therapist (Schaefer, 1999). This in turn can result in the child learning a lesson or solution to his or her problem (Gardner, 1971). This is a gradually paced, indirect method with room for repetition that allows for less emotional arousal than direct confrontation (Frey, 1993). Play narratives enable clients to organize their fragmented memories and experiences into a cohesive, meaningful story (Pennebaker, 2002).

ABREACTION

Through the use of play, children reenact and relive stressful and traumatic experiences and thus gain a sense of power and control over them (Schaefer, 1999). Through repetitive play reenactments, the child is able to gradually mentally digest and gain mastery over horrific thoughts and feelings (Waelder, 1932). Children show a natural tendency to cope with external events and traumas through play. After the horror of 9/11, many children were observed building towers with blocks and crashing toy airplanes into them. "Post-traumatic play can be effectively used therapeutically. It is, in fact, the most potent way to effect internal change in young traumatized children" (Terr, 1990, p. 299).

STRESS INOCULATION

The anticipatory anxiety of upcoming stressful life events, such as a family move, starting school, birth of a sibling, or visit to a doctor or dentist, can be lessened by playing out the event in advance (Wohl & Hightower, 2001). By playing out with miniature toys exactly what to expect and using a doll to model coping skills, the strange can be made familiar and less scary to the child.

COUNTERCONDITIONING OF NEGATIVE AFFECT

Two mutually exclusive internal states are not able to simultaneously co-exist, such as anxiety and relaxation or depression and playfulness (Schaefer, 1999). Thus, allowing a child to play hide-and-seek in a darkened room can help in conquering fear of the dark. Or dramatic play with hospital-related toys can help to significantly reduce hospital-specific fears. Rea et al. (1989) found hospitalized children's adjustment was significantly improved (anxiety significantly reduced) for the randomly assigned group that was encouraged to engage in fantasy play with both medical and non-medical materials.

Fantasy play allows the child to move from a passive to an active role; for example, the child can role-play giving an injection to a doll patient. Fantasy play also facilitates the expression of several defense mechanisms such as projection, displacement, repetition, and identification (Schaefer, 1999).

CATHARSIS

Catharsis allows for the release and completion of previously restrained or interrupted affective release via emotional expression (e.g., crying) or activity (e.g., bursting balloons, pounding clay, or punching an inflated punching bag) (Schaefer, 1999). Emotional release is a critical element in psychotherapy (Ginsberg, 1993).

POSITIVE AFFECT

While involved in play, children tend to feel less anxious or depressed. Enjoyable activities contribute to a greater sense of well-being and to less distress (Aborn, 1993). In play, both children and adults are likely to elevate their mood and sense of well-being (Schaefer, 1999). Sustained high levels of the stress hormone cortisol can damage the hippocampus, an area of the brain responsible for learning and memory, which results in cognitive deficits that can continue into adulthood (Middlebrooks & Audage, 2008). Laughter and positive affects help to create the opposite effect, releasing mood-boosting hormones or endorphins, lowering serum cortisol levels, and stimulating the immune system (Berk, 1989). Play and playfulness and its potential for mirth and laughter become an antidote to negative affects such as anxiety and depression (Schaefer, 1999).

SUBLIMATION

Sublimation allows the channeling of unacceptable impulses into substitute activities that are socially acceptable (Schaefer, 1999). The child who physically hits another may be re-directed, helped to practice and learn through repetition alternative means of expressing negative feelings by using "warlike" board games (chess, checkers), card games (War), or competitive sports activities (Fine, 1956; Schaefer, 1999).

ATTACHMENT AND RELATIONSHIP ENHANCEMENT

Play has been found to facilitate the positive emotional bond between parent and child. Studies of filial therapy (Ray, Bratton, Rhine, & Jones, 2001; Van Fleet & Guerney, 2003), Theraplay, and Parent-Child Inter-action Therapy (Brinkmeyer & Eyberg, 2003; Hood & Eyberg, 2003) have shown success in promoting parent-child attachment and rela-tionship enhancement (Drewes, 2006). Through step-by-step, live-coached sessions, the parent/caregiver and child create positive affec-tive experiences, such as playing together, which results in a secure, nurturing relationship. Gains are reflected, via research, in improve-ments in parental empathy, increased perception of positive changes in the family environment, self-esteem, perception of child-adjustment, perception of the child's behavioral problems, along with the child's self-concept, and changes in the child's play behavior (Rennie & Landreth, 2000).

MORAL JUDGMENT

Piaget (1932) first asserted that children's spontaneous rule-making and rule-enforcing play in informal and unsupervised play situations was a critical experience for the development of mature moral judg-ment. Game play experiences help children move beyond the early stage of moral realism, in which rules are seen as external restrictions arbitrarily imposed by adults in authority, to the concept of morality that is based on the principles of cooperation and consent among equals (Schaefer, 1999).

EMPATHY

Through role-play, children are able to develop their capacity for empathy, the ability to see things from another's perspective. Role-playing different characters in social play has been found to increase altruism (Iannotti, 1978) and empathy (Strayer & Roberts, 1989), as well as social competence (Connolly & Doyle, 1984).

POWER/CONTROL

Children feel powerful and in control during their play. They can make the play world conform to their wishes and needs (Schaefer, 1999). In marked contrast with the sense of helplessness children experience during a disaster, play affords them a strong sense of power and control. The child towers over the play materials and determines what and how to play during the therapy session. Eventually, this competing response (power) helps overcome the child's feelings of insecurity and vulnerability.

COMPETENCE AND SELF-CONTROL

Play provides children with unlimited opportunities to create, such as through stories, worlds constructed in a sandtray, or drawings, whereby they can gain a sense of competence and self-efficacy that boosts their self-esteem (Schaefer, 1999). In addition, by engaging in activities such as game playing or construction play, children can learn self-control through thought and behavior stopping that can help them to stop and think and plan ahead. As a result the child can anticipate the consequences of various potential behaviors and actions. These skills can be mastered through practice opportunities and positive re-inforcement and can consequently then generalize into any number of settings (e.g., school, home, social settings).

SENSE OF SELF

Through the play and child therapist's use of a child-led, child-centered approach (Axline, 1947), a child can begin to experience complete acceptance and permission to be himself without the fear of judgment, evaluation, or pressure to change. Through a commentary on the child's play, the therapist provides a mirror, figuratively speaking, by which the child can understand inner thoughts and feelings and develop an inner self-awareness (Schaefer, 1999). Play can also provide the opportunity for the child to realize the power within to be an individual in one's own right, to think for oneself, make one's own decisions, and discover oneself (Winnicott, 1971). Since this is often a unique experience, Meares (1993) noted that the field of play is where, to a large extent, a sense of self is generated. He concluded that play with an attuned adult present is where experiences are generated that become the core of what we mean by personal selves (Schaefer, 1999).

Accelerated Development

Preschool children's levels of development can advance in play beyond the ordinary accomplishments of their age period and function at a level of thinking that will only become characteristic later on (Schaefer, 1999). Vygotsky (1967) observed that children at play are always above their average age and their daily behavior.

Creative Problem Solving

Numerous studies have demonstrated that play and playfulness are associated with increased creativity and divergent thinking in children (Feitelson & Ross, 1973; Schaefer, 1999). Since in play the process is more important than the end product, children can freely, without fear of consequences, come up with novel combinations and discoveries that can aid them in solving their own problems and social problems (Schaefer, 1999; Sawyers & Horn-Wingerd, 1993). Indeed there is "something about play itself that acts as a vehicle for change" (Russ, 2007, p. 15). Divergent thinking has been thought to be a mediating link between pretend play and coping strategies (Russ, 2007), whereby children who are good at pretend play (use of affect and fantasy) are better divergent thinkers, have more coping strategies, and could more readily shift from one strategy to another (Christiano & Russ, 1996). Goldstein and Russ (2009) found in a study with first grade children that there was a positive and significant relationship between imagination in play and the frequency of coping responses and variety of strategies used, even when the sample was controlled for IQ. Russ (2007) and Singer (1995) speculate that it is divergent thinking that underlies children's pretend play, a notion that has received empirical support. Being able to think up and find different uses for objects (e.g., clay, blocks), to create different endings to stories, or to devise scenarios of action can increase divergent thinking (Dansky, 1999).

FANTASY COMPENSATION

In play, children can get immediate substitute gratification of their wishes. A fearful child can be courageous, or a weak child can be strong. Robinson (1970) saw play as essentially a compensatory mechanism operating much like a daydream. Impulses and needs that cannot find expression in real life find an outlet through fantasy.

REALITY TESTING

Play experiences allow children to practice reading cues in social situations and can help differentiate fantasy from reality. In social pretend play, children often switch back and forth between the roles they are playing and their real selves (Schaefer, 1999). Frequent engagement in pretend play allows for better discrimination between reality and fantasy (Singer & Singer, 1990).

BEHAVIORAL REHEARSAL

In the safe environment of play, socially acceptable behaviors, such as assertiveness versus aggressiveness, can be rehearsed and practiced. The play and child therapist can model in play new behaviors that are more adaptive for the child through use of puppets and role-play, which the child can then repeatedly practice to ensure skill development and mastery (Schaefer, 1999; Jones, Ollendick, & Shenskl, 1989).

RAPPORT BUILDING

One of the most potent therapeutic powers of play is the relational component of rapport building. This occurs when the client responds positively to the playful and fun-loving therapist. Since most children do not come willingly to therapy, they need to be initially engaged in the process through therapist/child play interactions. Also, since "play is the language of the child," it provides a natural medium for communicating with, and establishing a relationship with, the child (Landreth, 1983, p. 202).

PRESCRIPTIVE PLAY THERAPY

Each of the well-known schools of play therapy (e.g., client-centered, cognitive-behavioral, and psychodynamic) emphasizes one or more of the curative powers of play. The prescriptive eclectic approach

(Kaduson, Cangelosi, & Schaefer, 1997) advocates that play therapists become skilled in numerous therapeutic powers and differentially apply them to meet the individual needs of clients. The prescriptive approach is based on the individualized, differential, and focused matching of curative powers to the specific causative forces underlying the problem of a client (Kaduson, Cangelosi, & Schaefer, 1997). When therapists have a greater understanding of these change mechanisms, they can then become more effective in meeting the particular needs of the client.

Norcross (2002) also advocates a prescriptive approach to treatment whereby techniques are modified to match the client's diagnosis or presenting problem. Moreover, therapists should change their interpersonal style of interaction to match the client's style in order to improve treatment outcome.

FUTURE RESEARCH

Although there are numerous outcome studies now attesting to the efficacy of play therapy with children, there are few, if any, process studies of play therapy. Process studies seek to identify the specific mediators, that is, the therapeutic factors that produced the desired change in the clients' behavior. Play therapists also need to look at which change agents in play can be combined to optimize treatment effectiveness. A clearer knowledge of the array of therapeutic factors underlying play therapy will allow child clinicians to borrow flexibly from available theoretical positions to tailor their treatment to a particular child (Kaduson, Cangelosi, & Schaefer, 1997).

CONCLUSION

This chapter has briefly highlighted the various therapeutic change mechanisms within play that can help clients overcome their psychosocial difficulties. The therapeutic factors within play should not be viewed as mysterious but as capable of being understood, altered, and even fully controlled. The use of individualized treatment goals facilitates and guides the therapist in deciding which therapeutic powers to apply. Further research is needed to elucidate the specific therapeutic powers of play that are most effective with the specific presenting problems of clients.

This prescriptive matching of change agents with underlying causes will result in the most cost-effective play interventions.

REFERENCES

Aborn, A. I. (1993). Play and positive emotion. In C. E. Schaefer (Ed.), *Therapeutic powers of play* (pp. 291–308). Northvale, NJ: Jason Aronson.

Axline, V. M. (1947). *Play therapy: The inner dynamics of childhood*. Boston: Houghton Mifflin.

Bergin, A. E., & Strupp, H. H. (1972). *Changing frontiers in the science of psychotherapy*. Chicago: Aldine.

Berk, L. S. (1989). Eustress of mirthful laughter modified natural killer cell activity. *American Journal of Medical Science, 298*, 390–396.

Brinkmeyer, M. Y., & Eyberg, S. M. (2003). Parent-child interaction therapy for oppositional children. In A. E. Kazdin & J. R. Weisz (Eds.), *Evidence-based psychotherapies for children and adolescents* (pp. 204–223). New York: Guilford Press.

Chaloner, W. B. (2001). Counselors coaching teachers to use play therapy in classrooms: The Play and Language to Succeed (PALS) early, school-based intervention for behaviorally at-risk children. In A. A. Drewes, L. J. Carey, & C. E. Schaefer (Eds.), *School-based play therapy* (pp. 368–390). New York: John Wiley & Sons.

Christiano, B., & Russ, S. (1996). Play as a predictor of coping and distress in children during an invasive dental procedure. *Journal of Clinical Child Psychology, 25*, 130–138.

Connolly, J. A., & Doyle, A. (1984). Relation of social fantasy play to social competence in preschoolers. *Developmental Psychology, 20*, 797–806.

Dansky, J. (1999). Play. In M. Runco & S. Pritzker (Eds.), *Encyclopedia of creativity* (pp. 393–408). San Diego, CA: Academic Press.

Drewes, A. A. (2001). The possibilities and challenges in using play therapy in schools. In A. A. Drewes, L. J. Carey, & C. E. Schaefer (Eds.), *School-based play therapy* (pp. 41–61). New York: John Wiley & Sons.

Drewes, A. A. (2005). Play in selected cultures. In E. Gil & A. A. Drewes (Eds.), *Cultural issues in play therapy* (pp. 26–71). New York: Guilford Press.

Drewes, A. A. (2006). Play-based interventions. *Journal of Early Childhood and Infant Psychology, 2*, 139–156.

Feitelson, D., & Ross, G. (1973). The neglected factor—play. *Human Development, 16*, 202–223.

Fine, R. (1956). Psychoanalytic observations on chess and chess masters [monograph]. *Psychoanalysis, 4*, 1.

Frey, D. (1993). Learning by metaphor. In C. E. Schaefer (Ed.), *The therapeutic powers of play* (pp. 223–237). Northvale, NJ: Jason Aronson.

Gardner, R. (1971). *Therapeutic communication with children. The mutual story-telling technique*. New York: Science House.

Ginsberg, B. G. (1993). Catharsis. In C. E. Schaefer (Ed.), *The therapeutic powers of play* (pp. 107–141). Northvale, NJ: Jason Aronson.

Goldstein, A. B., & Russ, S. W. (2000–2001). Understanding children's literature and its relationship to fantasy ability and coping. *Imagination, Cognition, and Personality, 20,* 105–126.

Haworth, M. R. (1964). *Child psychotherapy: Practice and theory.* Northvale, NJ: Jason Aronson.

Hood, K. K., & Eyberg, S. M. (2003). Outcomes of parent-child interaction therapy: New directions in research. *Cognitive and Behavioral Practice, 9,* 9–16.

Huizinga, J. (1949). *Homo ludens.* London: Routledge & Kegan Paul.

Iannotti, R. (1978). Effects of role-taking experiences on emotion, altruism and aggression. *Developmental Psychology, 14,* 119–124.

Jones, R. T., Ollendick, T. H., & Shenskl, F. (1989). The role of behavioral versus cognitive variables in skill acquisition. *Behavioral Therapy, 29,* 293–302.

Kaduson, H., Cangelosi, D., & Schaefer, C. (1997). *The playing cure: Individualized play therapy for specific childhood problems.* Northvale, NJ: Jason Aronson.

Kalff, D. (1980). *Sandplay: A psychotherapeutic approach to the psyche.* Santa Monica, CA: Sigo Press.

Klein, M. (1955). The psychoanalytic play technique. *American Journal of Orthopsychiatry, 35,* 223–237.

Knell, S. M. (1993). *Cognitive-behavioral play therapy.* Northvale, NJ: Jason Aronson.

Landreth, G. (1991). *The art of the relationship.* Muncie, IN: Accelerated Development.

Landreth, G. (1995). Self-expressive communication. In C. E. Schaefer (Ed.), *The therapeutic powers of play* (pp. 41–63). Northvale, NJ: Jason Aronson.

Landreth, G. L. (1983). Play therapy in elementary school settings. In C. E. Schaefer & K. J. O'Connor (Eds.), *Handbook of play therapy* (pp. 202–212). New York: John Wiley & Sons.

Lowenfeld, M. (1979). *The world technique.* London: Allen & Unwin.

Meares, R. (1993). *The metaphor of play.* Northvale, NJ: Jason Aronson.

Middlebrooks, J. S., & Audage, N. C. (2008). *The effects of childhood stress on health across the lifespan.* Atlanta, GA: Centers for Disease Control and Prevention, National Center for Injury Prevention and Control.

Norcross, J. C. (Ed.). (2002). *Psychotherapy relationships that work.* New York: Oxford University Press.

Pennebaker, J. W. (2002, January/February). What our words can say about us: Toward a broader language psychology. *APA Monitor,* 8–9.

Perry, B. D. (1997). Incubated in terror: Neurodevelopmental factors in the "cycle of violence." In J. Osofsky (Ed.), *Children in a violent society* (pp. 124–149). New York: Guilford Press.

Piaget, J. (1932). *The moral judgment of the child.* New York: Harcourt.

Ray, D., Bratton, S., Rhine, T., & Jones, L. (2001). The effectiveness of play therapy: Responding to the critics. *International Journal of Play Therapy, 10,* 85–108.

Rea, W., Worchel, R., Upchurch, J., Sanner, J., & Daniel, C. (1989). The psychosocial impact of play on hospitalized children. *Journal of Pediatric Psychology, 14,* 617–627.

Rennie, R., & Landreth, G. (2000). Effects of filial therapy on parent and child behaviors. *International Journal of Play Therapy, 9*(2), 19–37.

Robinson, E. S. (1970). The compensatory function of make-believe play. *Psychological Review, 27,* 429–439.

Roopnarine, J., & Johnson, J. (1994). A need to look at play in diverse cultural settings. In J. Roopnarine, J. Johnson, & F. Hooper (Eds.), *Children's play in diverse cultures* (pp. 1-8). Albany: State University of New York Press.

Russ, S. (2004). *Play in child development and psychotherapy. Toward empirically supported practice.* Mahwah, NJ: Lawrence Erlbaum Associates.

Russ, S. W. (2007). Pretend Play: A resource for children who are coping with stress and managing anxiety. *NYS Psychologist, XIX, 5,* 13–17.

Sawyers, J. K., & Horn-Wingerd, D. M. (1993). Creative problem-solving. In C. E. Schaefer (Ed.), *The therapeutic powers of play* (pp. 309–322). Northvale, NJ: Jason Aronson.

Schaefer, C. E. (1995). *The therapeutic powers of play.* Northvale, NJ: Jason Aronson.

Schaefer, C. E. (1999). Curative factors in play therapy. *Journal for the Professional Counselor, 14,* 1, 7–16.

Singer, D. G., & Singer, J. L. (1990). *The house of make-believe: Play and the developing imagination.* Cambridge, MA: Harvard University Press.

Singer, J. L. (1995). Imaginative play in childhood. Precursor of subjunctive thoughts, daydreaming, and adult pretending games. In A. Pellegrini (Ed.), *The future of play theory* (pp. 187–219). Albany: State University of New York Press.

Strayer, J., & Roberts, W. (1989). The association of empathy, ego resiliency, and prosocial behavior in children. *Journal of Applied Developmental Psychology, 10,* 227–239.

Sutton-Smith, B. (1974). The anthropology of play. *Association for the Anthropological Study of Play, 2,* 8–12.

Sutton-Smith, B. (1999). Evolving a consilience of play definitions: Playfully. In S. Reifel (Ed.), *Play and culture studies* (Vol. 2; pp. 239–256). Stamford, CT: Ablex.

Terr, L. (1990). *Too scared to cry: Psychic trauma in childhood.* New York: HarperCollins.

United Nations Convention on the Rights of the Child (1989). Article 31.1. Retreived April 20, 2008, from http://ww2.ohchr.org/English/law/crc.htm.

VanFleet, R., & Guerney, L. (Eds.). (2003). *Casebook of Filial Therapy.* Boiling Springs, PA: Play Therapy Press.

Vygotsky, L. S. (1967). Play and its role in the mental development of the child. *Soviet Psychology, 17,* 66–72.

Waelder, R. (1932). The psychoanalytic theory of play. *Psychoanalytic Quarterly, 2*, 208–224.

Winnicott, D. W. (1971). *Playing and reality*. New York: Basic Books.

Wohl, N., & Hightower, D. (2001). Primary Mental Health Project: A School-based prevention program. In A. A. Drewes, L. J. Carey, & C. E. Schaefer (Eds.), *School-based play therapy* (pp. 277–296). New York: John Wiley & Sons.

Yalom, I. D. (1985). *The theory and practice of group psychotherapy*. New York: Basic Books.

CHAPTER 2

Meeting the Early Mental Health Needs of Children Through School-Based Play Therapy

A Review of Outcome Research

SUE C. BRATTON

T HE 2000 NATIONAL Conference on Children's Mental Health brought attention to the urgent need to identify effective interventions for children who suffer from emotional and behavioral disorders, estimating that one fifth of America's children have diagnosable disorders that require mental health treatment (U.S. Public Health Service, 2000). The report highlighted the fact that less than half of the children in need receive any treatment and described the lack of appropriate services as a major "crisis" in children's healthcare. In response, former Surgeon General David Satcher stated that "growing numbers of children are suffering needlessly because their emotional, behavioral, and developmental needs are not being met by those very institutions which were explicitly created to take care of them" (Satcher, 2000, p. 11). The national action agenda that was developed as a result of the conference emphasized the vital role of schools in

Correspondence concerning this chapter should be addressed to Sue C. Bratton, Center for Play Therapy, Department of Counseling and Higher Education, University of North Texas, 1155 Union Circle #310829, Denton, TX 76203, sue.bratton@unt.edu.

The author would like to give special thanks to Sheila Soslow, Katie Purswell, Yung-Wei Linn, and Yulia Proncheko for their assistance in retrieval of studies.

addressing this "crisis" and further called for 1) early identification and treatment and 2) research to identify developmentally and culturally sensitive interventions targeted for young children and their families.

The significant unmet mental health needs of children continued to receive national focus in 2003, with a report generated by the President's New Freedom Commission on Mental Health. The report acknowledged that a substantial number of children most in need are not receiving services due to a myriad of factors, including poverty, lack of health insurance, parental negligence, social stigma, and lack of culturally relevant services. As a result a special subcommittee was formed to specifically address the complex issues and needs of children. Their report reiterated the critical role of schools in early mental health care, recognizing that for many children with significant emotional and behavioral problems, schools are the only location in which they are likely to receive services. Other recommendations included the need for early interventions that are empirically validated; that are responsive to the unique developmental needs of children; and that involve caregivers/families in a culturally relevant manner (Subcommittee on Children and Family, 2003). While a review of the literature revealed a growing interest in school-based mental health over the past decade, no evidence was found to support that schools are increasing mental health services for children with significant need.

Clearly, schools have been issued a challenge—one that they appear ill-prepared to meet. School mental health professionals are typically underrepresented in schools and are often assigned numerous non-counseling tasks, leaving them insufficient time to meet the mental health needs of the children in their care (Berkowitz, 2005; Ray, Armstrong, Warren, & Balkin, 2005). The current strategy for referring children with significant emotional and behavioral difficulties to community agencies is not working for the numerous reasons cited above. Children who need mental health services the most are not receiving any help and will continue to suffer needlessly unless schools make significant changes in their approach to providing for the mental health needs of their young charges.

Nowhere is the need greater than for the increasing number of minority and low-income preschool children attending Head Start and other public school programs designed to provide early remediation for preschool children considered at-risk for school achievement. Nationally, there is a growing thrust to identify early mental health interventions, not only to respond to early onset behavioral problems, but to also mediate the impact of early risk factors such as poverty and other societal problems that have been shown to negatively impact the social-emotional and academic development of children (Duncan, Brooks-Gunn, & Klebanov, 1994; Evans, 2004; Knitzer, 2000). The importance of early intervention cannot be overstated. Children's early school experiences establish future behavior patterns and interactions with others. Particularly for children identified as at-risk, early interventions can counteract risk factors while enhancing personal strengths, thereby altering a trajectory of increased behavioral problems, low self-esteem, and academic failure (Ackerman, Brown, & Izard, 2003; Keiley, Bates, Dodge, & Pettit, 2000; Knitzer, 2000; Webster-Stratton & Reed, 2003). The evidence overwhelmingly points to the need to identify and utilize interventions such as play therapy that are proven responsive to the unique needs of children, particularly preschool-age populations. However, university preparation programs for school mental health professionals seldom include curricular experiences that require working with young children (Galassi, Griffin, & Akos, 2008). Galassi et al. advocated for school-based services targeted at preschool populations in response to the growth in early education programs and further proposed that school counselor training be expanded to include working with this increasingly diverse population of young children.

PLAY THERAPY IN THE SCHOOLS

Play therapy is a culturally responsive intervention (Bratton, Ray, & Landreth, 2008; Gil & Drewes, 2005) that uses the therapeutic and developmental properties of play to help children achieve optimal growth and development. Play therapy has a long history of use in elementary schools. Seeman (1954), while not the first to research play therapy in the schools, was among the first to describe its rationale and use in school settings. School-based play therapy literature and research increased dramatically in the 1970s (see Table 2.1), most likely due to the establishment of guidance and counseling programs in elementary schools in the 1960s and the introduction of play therapy training at the university level (Landreth, 1987).

The use of play therapy is based on a developmental understanding of children and the role of play in their growth and development (Erickson, 1963; Piaget, 1962; Vygotsky, 1966). Play provides children a nonverbal means of expression that crosses language and cultural barriers. Experts in the field maintain that play therapy is the only intervention uniquely suited to respond to the needs of young children

Table 2.1

Summary of School-Based Play Therapy Publications and Research Studies by Decade

Decade	All School-Based Play Therapy Publications	No. of Outcome Research Studies		
		Professional	Paraprofessional	Total
1940	3	2	0	2
1950	6	4	1	5
1960	5	3	0	3
1970	24	13	1	14
1980	17	8	1	9
1990	28	7	4	11
2000	82	23	17	40
Total	165	60	24	84

(Landreth, 2002; Oaklander, 2003; O'Connor, 2001; Schaefer, 2001). In play therapy children are provided toys and materials that allow symbolic expression of complex thoughts and feelings that they are unable to fully express through words alone. Most elementary-aged children are functioning in the preoperational (2–7 years) or concrete operational (8–11 years) stages of cognitive development (Piaget, 1962). In contrast to talk therapy and other primarily cognitive/educational activities, play therapy helps children bridge the gap between concrete experience and abstract thought, allowing them to make sense of and express troubling experiences. Through this mechanism children are able to develop mastery over these experiences and/or learn coping strategies that allow them to more fully benefit from their academic experience.

Training parents to use play therapy with their children has a long history of use, beginning with the development of filial therapy by Bernard and Louise Guerney in the 1960s (Guerney, 1964). The involvement of parents and other significant caregivers, especially teachers, in mental health interventions for young children has gained wide acceptance over the last two decades, primarily because of the significance of the caregiver-child relationship (Baker, 2006; Eyberg, Boggs, & Algina, 1995; Hamre & Pianta, 2001; Landreth & Bratton, 2006; Pianta & Stuhlman, 2004; VanFleet, 2005; Webster-Stratton & Reid, 2003). More recently, there has been an increase in literature and research focusing on involving parents and teachers in play therapy–based early mental health interventions in the schools (see Table 2.1).

While play therapy has been the treatment of choice for children since the early 1900s and today is widely used among practitioners to successfully treat a variety of emotional and behavioral problems (Bratton & Ray, 2000), the majority of school mental health professionals do not use play therapy (Berkowitz, 2005; Ray et al., 2005). The significant increase in publications on school-based play therapy since 2000 (see Table 2.1), and the fact that the only book to date focused entirely on the use of play therapy in schools was published in this decade (Drewes, Carey, & Schaefer, 2001), shows a dramatic increase in interest in this topic. However, Berkowitz and Ray et al. conducted national surveys of school psychologists and school counselors, respectively, and found that both groups of professionals supported the use of play therapy in the schools and believed it was effective, but that insufficient time and a lack of training during their professional preparation prevented the majority from using play therapy in their setting.

EMPIRICAL SUPPORT FOR SCHOOL-BASED PLAY THERAPY INTERVENTIONS

In the current school climate of accountability, providing evidence for the effects of school-based play therapy on children's social-emotional and academic development is critical in order to expand its use to meet the mental health needs of children in a developmentally and culturally responsive manner. Counselors in all settings are ethically bound to use interventions that are proven most effective; however, since the Task Force on Promotion and Dissemination of Psychological Procedures (Task Force, 1995) published criteria for establishing the efficacy of interventions, there has been greater emphasis on identifying evidence-based treatments (EBT) for specific childhood disorders (Society of Clinical and Child and Adolescent Psychology & Network on Youth Mental Health, 2009). School mental health professionals of all disciplines, including school counselors (Galassi, Griffin, & Akos, 2008), school psychologists (Kratochwill, 2004), and school social workers (Raines, 2004) are being directed by their licensing and credentialing bodies and by practice standards to utilize empirically supported interventions. Further, administrators are demanding accountability from school mental health professionals, challenging them to use proven interventions that also meet the needs of an increasingly diverse population of students. To begin to meet the crisis in children's mental health in this country will require significant financial resources targeted for schools. More and more, federal and state funding is allotted to only those interventions with empirical support. While play therapy has not been identified as evidence-based according to the most stringent criteria (Society of Clinical Child and Adolescent Psychology & Network on Youth Mental Health, 2009), it is widely used by practitioners (Lambert et al., 2005) and has a solid empirical base to support its use (Bratton et al., 2005).

While providing play therapy in the school setting seems like an obvious solution to responding to the crisis in providing appropriate psychological services for our nation's children, several barriers exist: lack of professional training, lack of administrative "buy-in," and lack of financial resources in schools (Berkowitz, 2005; Ray et al., 2005). School mental health professionals are in a unique position to address these barriers by: 1) educating administrators about the current crisis in adequate early mental health services for children and the resulting impact on their academic potential; 2) advocating for the use of play therapy (and play-based interventions utilizing teachers and parents) as a developmentally and culturally responsive intervention for children; 3) educating administrators, school board members, and legislators about the considerable body of empirical evidence to support the effects of play therapy; and 4) using research findings to collaborate with district grant writers to secure federal and state funding to hire additional school professionals specifically trained in play therapy. As the demand for specialized training in play therapy increases, along with research to support its efficacy in school settings, it is reasonable to expect that universities will respond by requiring school counselors, psychologists, and social workers to be trained in play therapy to respond to the current mental health needs of our nation's children.

While substantial empirical evidence exists for the benefits of school-based play therapy on the academic, social, and emotional development of children across cultures, a comprehensive examination of the literature revealed no systematic review of the body of play therapy research conducted in school settings. Thus, the purpose of this chapter is to provide school mental health professionals, and academicians who prepare them, with a comprehensive overview and summary of contemporary research, including meta-analytic findings and individual outcome research studies. Although many school-based case studies describing play therapy's effect with various presenting issues have been published, they are not included in this chapter. While their results are compelling, case studies are rarely accepted as scientific research and certainly do not provide generalizable results. Specific inclusion criteria for individual studies examined in this chapter are included in a later section.

Meta-analytic Support for Play Therapy in the Schools

As in most psychotherapy research, play therapy studies are limited by small sample size, resulting in the inability to draw conclusions or generalize results (Ray, Bratton, Rhine, & Jones, 2001). Meta-analytic reviews of research have made it possible to overcome this limitation by combining findings from individual studies to compute an overall treatment effect to assess the effectiveness of an intervention. Treatment effect size (ES) calculations reported in this section use Cohen's *d* and are interpreted according to his guidelines (.20 = small; .50 = medium; .80 = large). Only meta-analyses that focused exclusively on play therapy were reviewed. While a few other meta-analyses and systemic reviews of child psychotherapy have reported favorable outcomes for play therapy, they included only a handful of play therapy studies and made only minimal note of its effects (Allin, Wathan, & MacMillan, 2005; Beelmann & Schneider, 2003; Eyeberg, Nelson, & Bogs, 2008; Hetzel-Riggin, Brausch, & Montgomery, 2007; Wethington et al., 2008). A review of the literature found no meta-analysis focusing exclusively on school-based play therapy, but did reveal two meta-analytic reviews of play therapy that included several studies conducted in school settings. These reviews are summarized below.

LeBlanc and Ritchie (2001) conducted the first meta-analysis to focus exclusively on play therapy studies and reported a moderate treatment effect size of .66 for the 42 controlled studies they included in their analysis. Their findings were consistent with effect sizes found in other child psychotherapy meta-analyses (Casey & Berman, 1985, ES = .71; Weisz et al., 1995, ES = .71). LeBlanc and Ritchie further noted that benefits of play therapy appeared to increase with the inclusion of parents. While the researchers did not specifically analyze the effects of play therapy in school settings, their findings support the utility of play therapy in remediating children's problems that can negatively impact school success.

Bratton, Ray, Rhine, and Jones (2005) conducted the largest meta-analysis on play therapy outcome research to date. Their meta-analysis included the review of 180 documents that appeared to measure the effectiveness of play therapy dated 1942 to 2000. Based on stringent criteria for inclusion, such as designating use of a controlled research design, sufficient data for computing effect size, and the identification by the author of a labeled "play therapy" intervention, 93 studies were included in the final calculation of effect size. The overall effect size was calculated at .80 standard deviations interpreted as a large treatment effect, indicating that children receiving play therapy interventions performed .80 standard deviations above children who did not receive play therapy. The average age of study participants was 7.0, reduced to 6.7 years when play therapy was conducted by paraprofessionals (primarily parents). Their findings contrasted meta-analytic findings conducted on a broad range of child psychotherapies that reported mean ages of 10.2 years (Kazdin, Bass, Ayers, & Rodgers,1990) and 10.5 years (Weisz et al., 1995). Brestan and Eyberg (1998) reviewed studies focused on conduct-disordered children and reported a similar mean age of 9.8 years. Bratton et al. (2005) emphasized the implication of their finding regarding the mean-age of children helped by play therapy in light of the national priority to identify effective early interventions that allow children to receive help when problems first arise (U.S. Public Health Service, 2000) and concluded that because play therapy can be used with young children, it has the potential to prevent more severe and costly mental health problems that can develop over time.

Bratton et al. (2005) coded specific study characteristics to investigate their impact on play therapy outcome, including the effects of play therapy by setting. Of the 93 studies coded for analysis, the largest number of studies (n = 36) were conducted in a school setting, followed by outpatient clinic (n = 34). The treatment effect for clinic-based investigations were consistent with the overall effect size for play therapy (ES = .81), while school-based studies demonstrated a treatment effect of .69 standard deviations. Studies conducted in residential or crises settings produced significantly greater treatment effects (ES = 1.05) than those carried out in schools or clinics, indicating that the location in which play therapy is conducted impacts treatment outcome. However, it is important to note that the average number of sessions for play therapy in school settings was 8.4, approximately one-third the length of treatment in clinical settings (22.4 sessions). The authors noted the lower number of sessions in schools might have accounted for the lower treatment effect, explaining that school counselors and other mental health professionals must often limit sessions per child in order to reach more students. Hence, treatment length in school settings may be less likely to depend on severity of presenting issue and problem resolution. Still, the intervention effect for school-based play therapy is considered a moderate treatment effect and is consistent with the effect size for child psychotherapy reported in the meta-analytic reviews cited earlier in this chapter.

Additional findings from Bratton et al. (2005) indicated that play therapy had a moderate to large beneficial effect for internalizing (ES = .81), externalizing (ES = .79), and combined problem types (ES = .93). Treatment effects on outcomes for measures of self-concept, social adjustment, personality, anxiety, adaptive functioning, and family functioning, including quality of the parent-child relationship, were also reported in the moderate to large range. Effect sizes for humanistic (ES = .92) and nonhumanistic/behavioral play therapy (ES = .71) interventions were considered to be effective regardless of theoretical approach. However, the effect size reported for humanistic approaches, including child-centered and nondirective play therapy, was in the large effect category, while nonhumanistic was in the moderate category. This difference in effect may be attributed to a larger number of calculated humanistic studies (n = 73) compared to nonhumanistic studies (n = 12). Regardless, the findings for humanistic interventions is encouraging in light of a recent survey of Association for Play Therapy members that indicated the majority of its members subscribed to the child-centered play therapy (CCPT) approach (Lambert et al., 2005).

Meta-analytic findings on play therapy (Bratton et al., 2005; Leblanc & Ritchie, 2002) provide empirical support for its use in school settings as an early intervention to ameliorate a variety of children's mental health problems that can negatively impact children's ability to benefit from their academic experiences and, if untreated, can ultimately diminish their capacity to reach their full potential.

Outcome Research Studies to Support Play Therapy in the Schools

Play therapy has a long history of research, dating back to the early 1940s (Dulsky, 1942). School-based play therapy research dates almost as far back. Virginia Axline, considered the originator of what is now generally referred to in North America as CCPT, can also be considered the pioneer in school-based play therapy research. Her training and experience as an elementary teacher influenced her early attempts to extend credibility to play therapy by studying its impact on second graders identified with reading problems (Axline, 1947) and its effect on the intelligence of children identified with emotional, behavioral, and speech problems (Axline, 1949). Bills (1950a, 1950b) followed

Axline's line of research by examining the impact of play therapy on students with reading delays. Although their groundbreaking research would not meet the rigors of today's standards, their pioneering work set the stage for further research in the schools and added to play therapy's acceptance as a viable intervention for children.

Results from a comprehensive search spanning over six decades identified a total of 84 outcome research studies examining the efficacy of play therapy in the schools (see Table 2.1) that met criteria specified below. Of these, 24 studies focused on the effects of paraprofessional (parents, teachers, and mentors) specially trained to provide therapeutic play sessions with children, while 60 studies examined the outcome of professionals employed to deliver play therapy directly to children. Studies were included that clearly identified a play therapy intervention and utilized pre and post measures. Results revealed a noticeable difference between decades regarding the number of studies conducted. Published research in the schools dramatically increased in the 21st century, doubling the total number of research studies conducted from 1947 to 1999. The pattern of the number of studies conducted across decades prior to 2000 is interesting and similar to what Bratton and Ray (2000) reported in their article summarizing all play therapy outcome studies from 1940 to 2000. Research peaked in the 1970s and showed a decline in the 1980s and 1990s.

For the purpose of this chapter, *play therapy* was defined as ''an approach that uses play as the principal means for facilitating the expression, understanding, and control of experiences, and not simply a way of facilitating communication (Wetherington et al., 2008). While a variety of play-based interventions that failed to meet this definition have been used successfully in schools to remediate a broad range of social, emotional, and behavioral problems in children (Reddy, Files-Hall, & Schaefer, 2005), their inclusion was beyond the scope of this chapter. For example, play-based interventions conducted by non-mental health personnel (e.g., games used by teachers to promote pro-social behavior), were omitted from this review. Play therapy outcome studies that met the specified definition and were conducted in a school setting (preschool through junior high school) were reviewed and grouped according to play therapy delivery method: 1) studies in which play therapy was delivered directly to children by a mental health professional, and 2) studies in which a specially trained paraprofessional (parent, teacher, mentor, coach) provided therapeutic play sessions to children, under the direct supervision of a mental health professional.

Difficulty in discerning the use of play therapy according to the aforementioned definition may have resulted in the omission of qualified studies. In some cases because the author was familiar with the intervention, studies were included that did not appear to meet the criteria. For example, Parent-Child Interaction Therapy (PCIT) studies were included, although the term *play therapy*, or *play intervention*, was not included in the study, and in many cases, there was no mention of play. Another program used with parents, teachers, and children in school settings, Incredible Years (IY; Webster-Stratton & Reid, 2003), was omitted after much deliberation, because it failed to meet the criteria for parent/teacher use of play therapy procedures under the direct supervision of a mental health professional. An additional challenge in identifying studies was researchers' lack of clarity in describing the study setting. For example, the term *preschool children* was often used to describe subjects in PCIT studies, but it was unclear if the study was conducted in a school setting. Systemic reviews of PCIT research were helpful in making that distinction, which resulted in the omission of a few PCIT outcome studies originally included in the present review (Gallagher, 2003). Gallagher specifically acknowledged that the lack of real world settings was a limitation of PCIT research.

Finally, while early research on play therapy is not to be dismissed and laid the groundwork for more contemporary studies, research rigor has substantially improved over the past two decades. Hence, only studies conducted from 1990 to the present are reviewed.

SUMMARY OF OUTCOME RESEARCH 1990 TO PRESENT

A comprehensive search of school-based play therapy research over the past two decades found 51 studies that met criteria. As revealed in Table 2.1, approximately 75 percent of studies retrieved were conducted in the present decade (through 2008). Outcome studies in which a mental health professional delivered play therapy directly to children numbered 30, representing a 100 percent increase in the total of studies conducted during the five decades prior to 1990. The number of studies where parents, teachers, and mentors were trained and supervised to conduct play sessions with children increased the most dramatically, with 21 studies since 1990 with only 3 studies conducted in school settings prior to that time.

Of the 51 studies reviewed from 1990 to present, 43 were controlled studies, with over 50 percent using random assignment to treatment groups (see Tables 2.2 and 2.3). The vast majority of studies compared play therapy to a no-treatment wait-list control group, but a few utilized comparison treatments to investigate the effects of play therapy. Seven well-designed, pre-post single-group design studies were included, along with one single case study (Schottelkorb, 2008) that demonstrated exceptional rigor by including multiple baseline measures, repeated measurements throughout the treatment and three sources of data. While play therapy research continues to be plagued by small sample sizes, the mean sample size across all 51 studies reviewed was 44 participants. When the data was examined according to treatment provider (professional versus paraprofessional), the mean sample size was 50 for studies in which a mental health professional provided the intervention with the child versus 37 for studies when the intervention was conducted by a supervised paraprofessional (parent, teacher, or mentor).

Table 2.2
School-Based Play Therapy Research 1990 to
Present—Professional-Child Interventions

Author/Year/Title	Participants, *Treatment groups, # Sessions	Findings
Baggerly, J., & Jenkins, W. (2009). The effectiveness of child-centered play therapy on developmental and diagnostic factors in children who are homeless.	n = 36 K–5th grade, homeless no control group 11–25 sessions CCPT (1/wk, 45 min)	Findings show a statistically significant improvement for homeless children receiving CCPT in one of two developmental stands and one of three diagnostic profiles as measured by the Boxall Profile. Specifically, participants improved in internalization of controls and self-limiting features.
Crow, J. (1990). Play therapy with low achievers in reading.	n = 24 1st-graders E = 12 CCPT C = 12 no-treatment control 10 sessions (1/wk, 30 min)	Poor readers who received 10 nondirective individual play therapy sessions demonstrated statistically significant gains in self-concept and internal locus of control, when compared to a nonintervention control group. Both the experimental and control groups made gains in reading ability.

Danger, S., & Landreth, G. (2005). Child-centered group play therapy with children with speech difficulties.

n = 21 Pre-K to K referred for speech problems
E = 12 group CCPT
C = 10 no-treatment control
Random drawing to groups
25 sessions (1/wk, 30 min)

Child-centered group play therapy demonstrated a large treatment effect on improving young, speech-delayed children's expressive language skills and a moderate treatment effect on their receptive skills when compared to a group of children receiving traditional speech therapy. Differences between groups were not statistically significant.

Fall, M., Balvanz, J., Johnson, L., & Nelson, L. (1999). A play therapy intervention and its relationship to self-efficacy and learning behaviors.

n = 62 5–9-yr.-olds
E = 31 CCPT
C = 31 no-treatment control
Random drawing to groups
6 sessions (1/wk, 30 min)

While between-group differences were not statistically significant, children receiving play therapy demonstrated improvement in self-efficacy, while the control group worsened slightly. Both groups showed a reduction in classroom behavior problems, with teachers reporting greater gains for the experimental group. Classroom observations did not support the teachers' report.

Fall, M., Navelski, L., & Welch, K. (2002). Outcomes of a play intervention for children identified for special education services.

n = 66 Elem. Special Ed.
E = 43 CCPT
C = 23 no-treatment control
Random drawing to groups
6 sessions (1/wk, 30 min)

Results from teacher ratings revealed greater decreases in problematic behaviors and less social problems for the experimental group compared to the control group. Case manager ratings showed a significant decrease in anxiety for children receiving play therapy, but not for the control group. No significant differences were found

(Continued)

Table 2.2
(Continued)

Author/Year/Title	Participants, *Treatment groups, # Sessions	Findings
		between the play therapy and control group in self-efficacy.
Flahive, M., & Ray, D. (2007). Effect of group sandtray therapy with preadolescents.	n = 56 4th- & 5th-graders E = 28 group Jungian sandtray C = 28 no-treatment control Random drawing to groups 10 sessions (1/wk, 45 min)	Results from teacher report revealed statistically significant differences in total, externalizing, and internalizing problems between the experimental (sandtray) group and control group over time. Parent report indicated a statistically significant between-group difference on externalizing problems.
Garza, Y., & Bratton, S. C. (2005). School-based child-centered play therapy with Hispanic children: Outcomes and cultural considerations.	n = 29 K–5th grade Hispanic children, identified at-risk E = 15 CCPT C = 14 small-group guidance curriculum Random drawing to groups 15 sessions (1/wk, 30 min) Both groups were facilitated by bilingual counselors.	According to parent reports, from pre- to post-testing, Hispanic children receiving CCPT from a bilingual counselor showed statistically significant decreases in externalizing behavior problems compared to the curriculum-based treatment group. Between-group differences showed that CCPT demonstrated a large treatment effect on externalizing behavior problems and a moderate treatment effect on internalized problems.
Hull, S. (2008). The effects of weekly child-centered play therapy on the behavioral problems of elementary students.	n = 30 Elem. students E = 15 CCPT C = 15 no-treatment control Random drawing to groups 8 sessions (1/wk, 30 min)	There was no statistical significance between the groups; however, compared to the control group, more children in the experimental group showed a decrease in office referrals.

Kostina, L. (2004). Adjustment of first-year schoolchildren to school by means of lowering their anxiety level.

Study details unknown because article published in Russian
No control group

Results show the positive effect of play therapy on preschooler anxiety and improvement in school adjustment and performance.

McGuire, D. (2001). Child-centered group play therapy with children experiencing adjustment difficulties.

n = 29 Kindergartners
E = 15 group CCPT
C = 14 no-treatment control
Nonrandomized groups
12 sessions (1/wk, 40 min)

Children receiving child-centered group play therapy showed improved behavior and self-concept, although between-group differences were not statistically significant. Parents of CCPT children also reported a reduction in parent-child relationship stress.

Muro, J., Ray, D., Schottelkorb, A., Smith, M., & Blanco, P. (2006). Quantitative analysis of long-term child-centered play therapy.

n = 23 at-risk Pre-K–5th
No control group
Phase 1 CCPT
16 sessions (2/wk, 30 min)
Phase 2 CCPT
16 sessions (1/wk, 30 min)

Results indicated that from pre- to mid- to post-testing, children who participated in 32 sessions of CCPT demonstrated statistically significant improvement on the Total Problem Scale of the CBCL. Further analysis revealed nonstatistically significant differences between pre- to mid- and mid- to post-testing, indicating that children showed consis-tent improvement over the entire treatment period.

Ogawa, Y. (2007). Effectiveness of child-centered play therapy with Japanese children in the United States.

n = 10 K–3rd (Japanese school)
No control group
Repeated measures w/ baseline
8 sessions (1/wk, 30 min)

While results were not statistically significant, CCPT demonstrated moderate to large effect sizes on the CBCL and PSI, across 3 points of measure. Individual analysis provided further information on environmental, developmental, and cultural factors that may have impacted individual change in children.

(Continued)

Table 2.2
(Continued)

Author/Year/Title	Participants, *Treatment groups, # Sessions	Findings
Packman, J., & Bratton, S. (2003). A school-based group play/activity therapy intervention with learning disabled preadolescents exhibiting behavior problems.	n = 24 4th- & 5th-graders w/LD E = 12 group play/activity therapy C = 12 no-treatment control Random drawing to groups 12 sessions (1/wk, 1 hr)	Preadolescents receiving group play/activity therapy showed statistically significant decreases, from pre- to post-test, in total behavior problems and internalizing problems compared to the no-treatment control group. Practical significance of findings revealed that play therapy demonstrated a large treatment effect on internalizing and total problem behaviors and a moderate treatment effect on externalizing problems.
Paone, T., Packman, J., Maddux, C., & Rothman, T. (2008). A school-based group activity therapy intervention with at-risk high school students as it relates to their moral reasoning.	n = 61 9th-graders, at-risk E1 = 27 group activity therapy E2 = 34 group talk therapy 10 sessions (1/wk, 50 min)	Findings showed a statistically significant difference over time between group activity therapy and group talk therapy on moral reasoning, indicating that group activity therapy may be more effective than talk therapy to enhance moral reasoning in adolescents.
Post, P. (1999). Impact of child-centered play therapy on the self-esteem, locus of control, and anxiety of at-risk 4th, 5th, and 6th grade students.	n = 168 at-risk 4th–6th-graders E = 77 CCPT C = 91 no-treatment control 1–25 (m = 4) sessions (1/wk)	Results indicated a statistically significant difference between the experimental group and the control group over time. Children receiving no treatment showed deterioration in self-esteem and locus of control, while children receiving play therapy neither worsened nor improved.

Ray, D. (2007). Two counseling interventions to reduce teacher-child relationship stress.

$n = 93$ at-risk Pre-K–5th-graders, $n = 59$ teachers
E1 = 32 CCPT
E2 = 29 Teacher Consult (TC)
E3 = 32 CCPT + TC
Random drawing to groups
CCPT = 16 sessions (2/wk, 30 min)
TC = 8 (1/wk, 10 min)

A 3 (group) x 2 (time) split-plot analysis revealed a statistically significant main effect for time (pre to post) and a large effect size, but interaction effect for group x time was not statistically significant. Post hoc analysis revealed statistically significant reductions in teacher-child relationship stress (total stress and teacher and student problem characteristics) for all three treatment groups.

Ray, D., Blanco, P., Sullivan, J., & Holliman, R. (in press). An exploratory study of child-centered play therapy with aggressive children.

$n = 41$ Elementary-age, aggressive children
E = 21 CCPT
C = 20 wait-list control group
14 sessions (30 min)

Teachers ($n = 41$) reported that both groups improved aggressive behaviors at a statistically significant level. Post hoc analysis revealed that the within-group improvement for the CCPT group was statistically significant, while the control group's improvement was not statistically significant. Parents ($n = 32$) reported a moderate decrease in aggressive behavior for the CCPT group over the control group, according to effect size calculations.

Ray, D., Henson, R., Schottelkorb, A., Brown, A., & Muro, J. (2008). Effects of short- and long-term play therapy services of teacher-child relationship stress.

$n = 58$ Pre-K–5th-graders
T1 = 30 (Intensive CCPT)
T2 = 28 (Long-term CCPT),
Random assignment
T1 = 16 sessions over 8 weeks
T2 = 16 sessions over 16 weeks
(all sessions were 30 min)

A 2 (group) x 2 (time) split-plot analysis revealed a statistically significant main effect for time (pre to post) for total stress and student characteristics; effect sizes were moderate. Post hoc analysis revealed that from pre to post, the Intensive CCPT group

(Continued)

Table 2.2

(Continued)

Author/Year/Title	Participants, *Treatment groups, # Sessions	Findings
		demonstrated a statistically significant reduction in total stress (large effect) and in student characteristics (large effect). The long-term CCPT group did not demonstrate statistically significant reductions in either dependent variable, and treatment effects were small. While findings revealed no statistically significant between-group differences on any dependent variable, the intensive CCPT showed a moderate treatment effect over time on total stress compared to the 16-week CCPT model.
Ray, D., Schottelkorb, A., & Tsai, M. (2007). Play therapy with children exhibiting symptoms of attention deficit hyperactivity disorder.	n = 60 K–5th-graders E = 31 CCPT C = 29 Reading Mentoring (RM) Random assignment 16 sessions (1/wk, 30 min)	A 2 (group) x 2 (time) split-plot analysis revealed a statistically significant main effect for time (pre to post); effect size was large. Post hoc analysis revealed 1) both the CCPT and RM interventions demonstrated a statistically significant improvement in ADHD symptoms, and 2) the experimental group showed statistically significant within-group improvement on three subscales of the Index of Teaching Stress: student characteristics domain (moderate effect), emotional lability

(moderate effect) and anxiety-withdrawal (moderate effect), while the RM group did not. No statistically significant differences between groups over time were found.

Reams, R., & Fridrich, W. (1994). The efficacy of time-limited play therapy with maltreated preschoolers.	n = 36 preschoolers who were victims of abuse and had been attending therapeutic preschool for 1 year prior to study E = 24 directed play therapy C = 12 no-treatment control 15 sessions (1/wk, 50 min)	Results indicated that children receiving 15 weeks of directed play therapy demonstrated a statistically significant reduction in isolated play as compared to the control group. No other statistically significant findings were reported.
Rennie, R. (2003). A comparison study of the effectiveness of individual and group play therapy in treating kindergarten children with adjustment problems.	n = 42 Kindergartners w/ adjustment problems E1 = 14 Individual CCPT (30 min) E2 = 15 Group CCPT (45 min) C = 13 (nonrandom control) avg. of 12 sessions (1/wk)	Experimental group children receiving individual CCPT exhibited a significant reduction in CBCL Total Problems and Externalizing Problems subscale, compared to the nonrandomized no-treatment control group. Although not statistically significant, individual CCPT demonstrated a moderate to large treatment effect when compared to group CCPT.
Schottelkorb, A. (2008). Effectiveness of child-centered play therapy and person-centered teacher consultation on ADHD behavioral problems of elementary school children: A single case design.	n = 5 5–10-yr.-olds with ADHD Single-case design—repeated measures with baseline. Children received different doses and timing of interventions, including CCPT, Reading Mentoring (RM), and Teacher Consultation (TC). 3 children received 24 sessions of CCPT (2/wk,	Utilizing baseline measures from direct observation by objective raters, teacher data, and parent data, 3 of the 5 students demonstrated substantial improvement in observed ADHD behaviors in the classroom. Two students' observational data indicated improvement in on-task behaviors over time. One child's parents

(*Continued*)

Table 2.2
(Continued)

Author/Year/Title	Participants, *Treatment groups, # Sessions	Findings
	30 min) and 6 sessions of TC (1/wk, 10 min); 2 children received 10 sessions of RM (2/wk, 30 min), followed by 14 sessions of CCPT (2/wk, 30 min)	no longer had clinical levels of concern for the child. Teaching stress was reduced substantially for one teacher, and one teacher was not positively affected.
Schumann, B. (2005). Effects of child-centered play therapy and curriculum-based small-group guidance on the behaviors of children referred for aggression.	n = 37 Aggressive K–4th-graders E = 20 Individual CCPT C = 17 Second Step curriculum, delivered in small-group format Random drawing to group assignment 12–15 sessions (1/wk, 30 min)	Results revealed that children receiving CCPT and children receiving Second Step, a SAMSA "Model" anti-violence program, demonstrated statistically significant improvement on the Aggressive subscale of the BASC. Informal parent ratings revealed that more children in the CCPT group than the Second Step group showed improvement following the interventions.
Shen, Y. (2002). Short-term group play therapy with Chinese earthquake victims: Effects on anxiety, depression, and adjustment.	n = 30 3rd–6th-graders E = 15 group CCPT C = 15 no-treatment control Random drawing to groups 8–12 sessions (2–3/wk, 40 min)	Children in the experimental group demonstrated statistically significant reductions in anxiety and suicide risk after receiving an average of 10 group sessions of CCPT as compared to a control group. According to parents, children's life adjustment was improved, although not at a statistically significant level.
Shen, Y. (2007). Developmental model using gestalt-play versus cognitive-verbal group with Chinese adolescents.	n = 81 7th–8th-graders E1 = 26 Gestalt-play groups E2 = 26 Cognitive-Verbal groups	Teachers reported significantly greater increases in overall behavior and emotional strengths for the gestalt

C = 29 no-treatment control
10 sessions (1/wk, 40 min)

play therapy group over the control group, but not over the cognitive-verbal group. On the measure of school and social adjustment, teachers and peers reported the intervention had a weak impact.

Shen, Y. P., & Armstrong, S. (2008). Impact of group sandtray therapy on the self-esteem of young adolescent girls.	n = 37 7th-grade girls
E = 20 group sandtray
C = 17 nonrandomized control
9 sessions (2/wk, 50 min)	Results revealed statistically significant between-group differences from pre- to post-test on 5 of the 6 subscales of a self-esteem measure. An examination of group means showed that the self-esteem of control group girls worsened over time, while girls participating in group sandtray improved in all 6 areas of self-esteem after 4.5 weeks of group sandtray.
Utay, J. (1992). Effectiveness of a cognitive-behavioral group play therapy intervention on selected aspects of social skills of third through sixth grade students with learning disabilities.	66 3rd–6th graders with learning disabilities
E = 20 group play therapy
C1 = 18 placebo control
C2 = 28 no-treatment control
E = 8 sessions, (1/wk, 50 min) of The Social Skills Game
C1 = 8 sessions of educational games (1/wk, 50 min)	Children receiving group play therapy/social skills game made statistically significant gains on teacher preferred social skills and a school adjustment measure, compared to the other 2 groups. Play therapy and placebo groups both performed better on peer preferred social behavior as compared to the control group. The placebo group also demonstrated statistical gains in school adjustment over the control group.
Watson, D. (2007). An early intervention approach for students	n = 30 Pre-K–1st grade
E = 15 Group PT
C = 15 no-treatment	Author concluded that findings suggest that group play therapy is more

(*Continued*)

Table 2.2
(Continued)

Author/Year/Title	Participants, *Treatment groups, # Sessions	Findings
displaying negative externalizing behaviors associated with childhood depression: Efficacy of play therapy in the school.	control 16 sessions (2/wk, 30 min)	effective at reducing negative problem behaviors than the typical behavioral intervention used in school systems. Between-group differences were not statistically significant.

*For controlled studies, treatment groups are denoted by E = Experimental Group, C = Control or Comparison; E1, E2, etc., was used to identify multiple treatments being investigated. CCPT = child-centered play therapy

Table 2.3
School-Based Play Therapy Research 1990 to Present—Paraprofessional/Child Intervention Supervised by Professional

Author/Year/Title	Participants/*Treatment Groups/# Sessions	Findings
Baggerly, J., & Landreth, G. (2001). Training children to help children: A new dimension in play therapy.	n = 29 at-risk Kindergartners E = 15 received play mentoring from CPRT-trained 5th graders C = 14 no-treatment control Random drawing to groups 5th-grade mentors received 10 sessions of adapted CPRT (1/wk, 1 hr) Children: 7 play sessions w/mentors (1/wk, 20 min)	Experimental group children's parents reported a significant reduction in their kindergartners' internalizing behavior problems. Although not statistically significant, teachers and parents reported a reduction in the children's overall behavior problems and an increase in self-esteem following seven supervised play-mentoring sessions with their 5th-grade mentor.
Ceballos, P., & Bratton, S. (in review). School-based parent child relationship therapy (CPRT) with low-income immigrant Hispanic parents: Effects on child behavior and	n = 48 immigrant Hispanic parents of Head Start children identified w/ academic and behavioral problems E = 24 CPRT filial model C = 24 no-treatment control	Results from parent-report measurements showed statistically significant improvement, from pre- to post-testing, in children's externalized, internalized, and combined problem behaviors and reduction in

parent-child relationship stress.

Random drawing to groups
Parents: 11 sessions conducted in Spanish (1/wk, 2 hr)
Children received 7 play sessions from their parents.
(1/wk, 30 min)
CPRT materials were translated into Spanish.

parent-child relationship stress when compared to the control group. CPRT demonstrated large treatment effects on all dependent variables. 85% of children in the CPRT group moved from clinical or borderline levels of behavior problems to normal levels of concern, and 62% of parents reported a reduction from clinical levels of parenting stress to normative functioning. Findings were discussed in light of culturally relevant observations.

Collett, B. (2002). Addressing disruptive behaviors in the preschool classroom: An adaptation of parent-child interaction therapy.

n = 26 Head Start teachers
No control group

Results indicated a significant decrease in disruptive child behaviors and child problem behaviors as measured by the teacher-completed rating scale. Observational data reflected a decrease in children's pro-social and disruptive behaviors. There were minimal changes in observed teaching behavior and no significant changes in teacher's self-efficacy.

Draper, K., White, J., & O'Shaughnessy, T. E. (2001). Kinder training: Play-based consultation to improve the school adjustment of discouraged kindergarten and first grade students.

n = 14 K–1st-graders whose teachers received Kinder training (filial model)
No control group
Children received six (1/wk, 30 min) play sessions from Kinder-trained teachers, under supervision of professional.

From pre- to post-test, children showed a statistically significant decrease in problematic behaviors and a significant increase in adaptive behaviors. Though not statistically significant, children improved on Social Skills, Academic Competence, and Problem Behavior scales. Teachers increased in use of

(*Continued*)

Table 2.3

(Continued)

Author/Year/Title	Participants/*Treatment Groups/# Sessions	Findings
		encouragement and decreased in use of praise.
Fantuzzo, J., Manz, P., Atkins, M., & Meyers, R. (2005). Peer-mediated treatment of socially withdrawn maltreated preschool children: Cultivating natural community resources.	n = 82 withdrawn preschoolers E1 = 19 maltreated RPT E2 = 22 nonmaltreated RPT C1 = 18 maltreated AC C2 = 23 nonmaltreated AC Random assignment to groups Resilient Peer Treatment (RPT) group children played with a Play Buddy (peer with high social skills) coached by trained Play Supporters (parent volunteers). Active control (AC) group children received same amount of attention playing with a peer. 15 sessions (3/wk over 2-month period)	According to objective raters, prior to treatment, the maltreated group demonstrated statistically significantly lower levels of collaborative play than the nonmaltreated preschoolers. After participating in the experimental condition, both maltreated and nonmaltreated children evidenced statistically significant improvement in collaborative play and reduction in isolated play, while the control group children did not. While findings from neither objective raters nor teacher reports revealed any interaction effect between treatment groups from pre to post, both groups of children participating in RPT showed gains on the majority of measures compared to the AC group.
Filcheck, H., McNeil, C., Greco, L., & Bernard, R. (2004). Using whole-class token economy and coaching of teacher skills in a preschool classroom to manage disruptive behavior.	n = 17 preschool children in classroom described as "out of control" No control group Teacher/aid pairs were trained in PCIT and token economy.	Results provided preliminary support for the use of both PCIT and token economy to manage disruptive behavior in class. While not statistically significant, the amount of inappropriate behavior exhibited in the

classroom decreased with teacher implementation of the token system and PCIT.

Helker, W., & Ray, D. (in press, 2009). The impact of child-teacher relationship training on teachers' and aides' use of relationship-building skills and the effect on student classroom behavior.	n = 24 (12 teacher-aide pairs) E = 12 (6 pairs) CTRT model C = 12 (6 pairs) active control Random drawing to groups n = 32 Head Start children with academic and behavioral problems, assigned to treatment based on teacher assignment Exp. teachers received teacher-adapted 10-session CPRT protocol, followed by 8 weeks (3/wk, 15 min) in-class coaching.	A statistically significant relationship was found between CTRT-trained teachers' and aides' higher use of relationship-building skills in the classroom and students' decrease in externalizing behaviors as compared to the active control group. Experimental group children (n = 19) demonstrated a significant decrease in Externalizing Problems from pre to mid to post when compared to the children in the active control group (n = 13).
Hess, B., Post, P., & Flowers, C. (2005). A follow-up study of kinder training for preschool teachers of children deemed at-risk.	n = 16 teachers of at-risk preschoolers E = 8 filial model C = 8 no-treatment control 1 year follow-up study to Post et al. (2004)	One year after filial training, there was a statistically significant difference in filial trained teachers' use of play therapy skills and communication of empathy in individual play sessions, when compared to the no-treatment control. Classroom observations revealed no difference between groups on teachers' in-class use of skills. Filial trained teachers reported increased confidence.
Jones, L., Rhine, T., & Bratton, S. C. (2002). High school students as therapeutic agents with	n = 31 high school student mentors enrolled in 2 Peer Assistance and Leadership (PALS)	Compared to students receiving the PALS curriculum, high school mentors trained in the

(*Continued*)

Table 2.3

(Continued)

Author/Year/Title	Participants/*Treatment Groups/# Sessions	Findings
young children experiencing school adjustment difficulties: The effectiveness of a filial therapy training model.	classes; classes randomly drawn to treatment. Children randomly assigned. E = 16 mentors-CPRT/filial E = 16 at-risk preschoolers C = 15 mentors-PALS protocol C = 15 at-risk preschoolers Mentors: 24 weeks of 1/wk training for 1hr (both groups). Children in both groups received 20 one-on-one play sessions with their mentor (1/wk, 20 min)	adapted CPRT protocol (a filial therapy model) demonstrated a statistically significant increase in empathic interactions with children, as directly observed by objective raters. According to parent reports, children in the CPRT group demonstrated statistically significant reductions in internalizing and total behavior problems from pre- to post-testing, compared to children in the PALS group. CPRT children also demonstrated marked improvement in externalized behavior problems. CPRT-trained mentors received direct observation and supervision of their play sessions weekly from professionals trained in play therapy and CPRT.
Kale, A., & Landreth, G. (1999). Filial therapy with parents of children experiencing learning difficulties.	n = 22 parents of K–4th-graders with learning differences E = 11 CPRT/filial protocol C = 11 no-treatment control Random drawing to groups Parents received 10 sessions of CPRT training (1/wk, 2 hrs)	Results indicated statistically significant improvement in parental acceptance and reduction in parent-child relationship stress from pre- to post-testing for the CPRT-trained group compared to the no-treatment control. As part of CPRT training, parents completed 7 supervised, 1/wk 30-min. play sessions with their children, under direct

Morrison, M., & Bratton, S. (in review). An early mental health intervention for disadvantaged preschool children with behavior problems: The effectiveness of training Head Start teachers in child-teacher relationship training (CTRT).

n = 24 (12 teacher/aide pairs)
Random drawing to groups
E = 12 (6 pairs) CTRT model
C = 12 (6 pairs) Active control
n = 52 Head Start children, identified with academic and behavioral problems, assigned to treatment by teacher's group
E = 26 CTRT group
C = 26 Active control group
Exp. teachers received adapted CTRT 10-session protocol, followed by 8 weeks in-class coaching (3/wk, 15 min)

supervision of a CPRT professional.

According to teacher reports, CTRT treatment group children demonstrated statistically significant reductions in externalizing and total behavior problems compared to the active control group, across three points of measure. Treatment effects were determined to be large. CTRT also showed a moderate treatment effect on reducing children's internalizing problem behaviors over time, as compared to the active control group. 84% of the children receiving CTRT moved from clinical or borderline levels of behavioral concern to normal levels of functioning, demonstrating the clinical significance of findings.

Pears, K., Fisher, P., & Bronz, K. (2007). An intervention to promote social emotional school readiness in foster children: Preliminary outcomes from a pilot study.

n = 24 foster children enrolled in public school
E = 11 therapeutic play groups
C = 13 standard foster services
14 sessions (2/wk, 2 hrs)
Therapeutic play groups were conducted by trained teachers, supervised by clinical staff.

When compared to the control group receiving traditional foster care services, the Intervention group (IG) children receiving therapeutic play showed increased social competence over time, while the comparison group (CG) children showed slightly decreased social competence over time. Although there were no significant group differences on the other scales, the means for foster parent–reported lability indicated that IG
(Continued)

Table 2.3
(Continued)

Author/Year/Title	Participants/*Treatment Groups/# Sessions	Findings
		children showed a decrease in lability that was greater than three times that shown by CG children. 82% of IG children showed a greater, although nonsignificant, decrease over time in externalizing behavior, as reported by foster parents.
Pollock, K. L. (1996). The effectiveness of parent-child interaction therapy conducted in a Head Start workshop.	n = 23 parent-child dyads of at-risk children in Head Start Training delivered in workshop format	Children whose parents participated in PCIT demonstrated significant improvements in intensity of behavior problems four weeks after workshop, but showed no change in self-esteem. Parents demonstrated no observable change in parental attitudes toward their children.
Post, P., McAllister, M., Sheely, A., Hess, B., & Flowers, C. (2004). Child-centered kinder training for teachers of preschool children deemed at-risk.	n = 17 preschool teachers E = 9 Kinder training (filial) C = 8 no-treatment control Kinder-trained teachers conducted one-on-one play sessions with exp. group children, under direct supervision of play-therapy trained professional.	Results indicated three statistically significant group x time interactions. Children whose teachers received kinder training (n = 9) showed improvement, pre- to post-testing, in Internalizing problems, Behavioral Symptoms Index and Adaptive Skills as compared to the control group (n = 8). From pre to post, experimental group teachers demonstrated statistically significant increases in targeted therapeutic play skills as compared to the control group.

Quayle, R. L. (1991). The primary mental health project as a school-based approach for prevention of adjustment problems: An evaluation of play therapy as an early intervention.

n = 54 at-risk K–3rd-graders
E = 18 play intervention
C1 = 18 attention control
C2 = 18 no-attention control
26 sessions (1/wk, 30 min)

Significant within-group improvement was noted for 6 of 15 dependent measures for the experimental group. Children in the Individual Attention control also showed improvement. Teachers rated experimental group children as improving in learning skills, assertive social skills, task orientation, and peer social skills.

Robinson, J., Landreth, G., & Packman, J. (2007). Fifth-grade students as emotional helpers with kindergartners: Using play therapy procedures and skills.

n = 23 5th-grader mentors
E = 12 CPRT-adapted model
C = 11 no-treatment control
CPRT-trained mentors received 10 sessions of training (1/wk) and conducted 7 supervised 20-min play sessions with at-risk kindergarten children.

Fifth-grade students in the CPRT-trained group demonstrated a statistically significant increase in empathic interactions during observed one-on-one play sessions with their mentees as compared to the control group mentors. Specifically, they made statistically significant gains in their level of involvement and in facilitating children's self-direction. Communication of acceptance of the child's feelings also improved.

Sheely, A., & Bratton, S. (in review). School-based child-parent relationship therapy (CPRT) with low-income Black American parents: Effects on children's behaviors and child-parent relationship stress: A pilot study.

n = 27 low-income Black American parents of Head Start children identified with school and behavioral problems
E = 14 CPRT filial model
C = 14 no-treatment control
Random drawing to groups
CPRT: 11 sessions (1/wk, 2 hr)

Findings indicated that when compared to the no-treatment control group children and parents, the CPRT group children and parents demonstrated statistically significant improvements over time in: (a) children's Externalizing and Total Problem Behaviors, and (b) parent-child

(Continued)

Table 2.3
(Continued)

Author/Year/Title	Participants/*Treatment Groups/# Sessions	Findings
	Children received 7 play sessions from their parents (1/wk, 30 min) supervised by CPRT-trained professional.	relationship stress. Treatment effects were large. While not statistically significant, CPRT demonstrated a moderate treatment effect for children's internalizing behavior problems when compared to the control group. Cultural considerations for use of CPRT with this population were discussed.
Smith, D., & Landreth, G. (2004). Filial therapy with teachers of deaf and hard of hearing preschool children.	n = 24 preschool teachers E = 12 CPRT/filial model E = 12 preschoolers C = 12 no-treatment control E = 12 preschoolers CPRT: 10 sessions (1/wk, 2hr) Hearing-impaired children received 7 play sessions from their teachers (1/wk, 30 min)	Experimental group children and teachers made statistically significant gains on target behaviors as compared to the control group. Children receiving CPRT significantly improved overall behavior problems and social-emotional functioning. CPRT-trained teachers significantly increased their attitude of acceptance and observed communication of empathy with students.
Sosna, T. (1992). The impact of parent-child interaction therapy on the verbalizations and compliance of nonclinical preschool children.	n = 17 parent-preschooler dyads E = 9 PCIT model C = 8 no-treatment control	There was a significant decrease in problematic behavior on the parent report measure, dramatic changes in parental verbalizations, and less dramatic changes in preschool children's verbalizations.
Tiano, J., & McNeil, C. (2006). Training Head Start teachers in behavior	n = 7 Head Start teachers n = 25 children E = 4 teachers; 13 children	Based on measures of teacher observation, student behavior

management using parent-child interaction therapy: A preliminary investigation.	C = 3 teachers; 12 children Teachers randomly assigned	observations, and teacher reports, findings suggest child behavior and teacher behavior improved for both groups. No statistically significant between-group differences were reported. The PCIT-trained teachers gave more labeled praise following training.
Villarreal, C. E. (2008). School-based child-parent relationship therapy (CPRT) with Hispanic parents.	n = 14 Hispanic parents (English speaking) E = 7 CPRT/filial model C = 7 no-treatment control	Parents reported enhanced parent-child relationship, positive changes in themselves and their children, and decreases in externalizing child behaviors, although not at a statistically significant level.

[*]For controlled studies, treatment groups are denoted by E = Experimental Group, C = Control or Comparison; E1, E2, etc., was used to identify multiple treatments being investigated. CPRT = child-parent relationship therapy; PCIT = parent-child interaction therapy

A few studies focused on play therapy with preadolescents (n = 5) and early teens (n = 3), however the majority of studies examined the effects of play therapy with preschool through fifth grade. Specifically, the greatest number of studies (n = 17) were conducted with Head Start and similar at-risk public preschool populations. Studies targeting this population of children also represented the most noticeable change over pre-1990 studies—a change likely due to the significant increase in the inclusion of these programs in public schools to address the at-risk factors that can impede young children's ability to succeed academically. Nine studies specified kindergarten through third-graders as the participants, while 17 identified kindergarten to fifth-graders. Lack of specificity regarding mean ages and grades made it difficult to calculate an exact mean across studies, but a calculation based on available data revealed an approximate mean of 6.1 years, somewhat lower than the mean of 7.0 years reported by Bratton et al. (2005). Again, the increase in research on preschool populations since the late 1990s is a plausible explanation for the lower mean age in the present review.

Contemporary play therapy research in the schools has addressed many of the pressing needs of a rapidly changing population of school children, including increased numbers of preschool children attending public school due to at-risk factors, rapid growth in minority children and families in the United States, and an increase in children from impoverished families. Nineteen studies focused on the effects of play therapy on children specifically identified as low-income, impoverished, or homeless, primarily in Head Start/at-risk preschool settings. Several other studies identified the study setting as a Title I school, with many participants meeting criteria for free or reduced lunch. Minority populations in the U.S. were the focus of 7 studies (3 Hispanic, 1 Black American, 1 Japanese, and 2 with mixed minority populations). The majority of studies identified participants as *at-risk,* which in school settings generally means that children have been identified as at-risk for succeeding in school for one or more factors, including such things as poverty, limited English ability, low academic achievement, and emotional or behavioral problems sufficient enough to distract from their ability to learn in the classroom.

While children's externalizing, internalizing, and combined problem behaviors were the focus in the majority of studies, recent research has begun to focus on the effects of play therapy on more specific presenting behavioral issues and diagnoses. Diagnoses of attention deficit, aggressive behavior, conduct disorder, disruptive behavior disorders, learning disability, anxiety, and depression were among the presenting concerns of children in the included studies. Given the prevailing focus on behavior problems, it is not surprising that, for children, behavioral outcomes were the most frequently measured (n = 45), followed by self-esteem (n = 7), social skills/adjustment (n = 7), and academic/school achievement (n = 9). For parents and teachers, measures of stress in the parent-child or teacher-child relationship were used in 13 studies, followed by an assessment of teacher/parent skills (n = 12).

When theoretical approach was noted, child-centered play therapy (CCPT) or nondirective play therapy was the most frequent play therapy intervention used by professionals (n = 21), followed by humanistic approaches (n = 5), and cognitive-behavioral play therapy (n = 3). For the paraprofessional interventions, filial therapy models were most used, with a total of 13, followed by 5 studies using Parent-Child Interaction Therapy (PCIT). The filial models included Child-Parent Relationship Therapy (CPRT; Landreth & Bratton, 2006) and Kinder Training, originally named Kinder Therapy (White, Flynt, & Draper, 1997). The CPRT filial model was used in 10 studies; 7 studies focused on its use with parents, and 3 used a teacher-adapted CPRT model, also referred to as Child Teacher Relationship Therapy (CTRT). Kinder Training is a teacher adapted filial model, thus teachers were the focus of all 3 Kinder Training studies. PCIT was developed as a parent model but has also been adapted for use with teachers and referred to as Teacher-Child Interaction Therapy (TCIT). Two PCIT studies focused on its use in the schools with parents of preschool children and 3 targeted training teachers to deliver the intervention.

The number of play therapy sessions per study ranged from 4 to 32, with an overall mean across studies of 10.5 sessions. While this is higher than the mean number of sessions for schools reported by Bratton et al. (2005), it is considerably lower than the mean of 22.4 sessions that they reported for clinic settings and falls far below the 30 to 40 sessions that they found predictive of optimal treatment effects. As proposed by Bratton et al., it is probable that factors unique to the school environment prevent long-term therapy; hence, the length of treatment may be less a function of children's needs than school logistics. In the 51 studies reviewed, once-a-week, 30-minute play sessions were the norm, which is much shorter than the typical 40–50 minutes children are seen in community settings. Limited time to see children in schools is consistent with the author's experiences as a school counselor and is supported by surveys of school mental health professionals (Berkowitz, 2005; Ray et al., 2005). Intensive play therapy, in which children received twice-weekly play therapy, was reported in 8 studies. Preliminary findings support the notion that children may benefit more from condensed twice-per-week play therapy than the same number sessions extended over the traditional once per week format (Ray et al., 2008).

Outcome research summaries are presented in a convenient chart format organized by play therapy delivery by professional (see Table 2.2) and paraprofessional (see Table 2.3) to allow school mental health professionals to more readily access the information for the purpose of educating administrators, parents, teachers, legislators, funders, and so forth. Because of space limitations, only major findings were reported. In studies measuring multiple dependent variables, statistically significant beneficial change may have been found on one or more dependent variables, but not on others. Because it was impossible to report all results within the scope of this chapter, readers are urged to review the study in its entirety to glean a full understanding of findings.

CONCLUSION

Although more rigorous research is needed in order to meet the most stringent criteria for school-based play therapy to be considered evidenced-based (Society of Clinical Child and Adolescent Psychology & Network on Youth Mental Health, 2009), meta-analytic research supports its use for a variety of presenting issues and diverse populations across multiple settings, including schools (Bratton et al., 2005) and reveals an overall large treatment effect for play therapy interventions. Specific to school settings, Bratton et al. found that play therapy demonstrated a moderate treatment effect over comparison or no treatment groups. A review of individual studies provides further support for the efficacy of applying play therapy in schools. A major strength of play therapy research over other research in the field of child psychotherapy is its application to real-world settings, such as schools.

While certainly not true for all studies reviewed for this chapter, school-based play therapy research, in general, is hindered by lack of specificity in presenting problem, small sample sizes, lack of replication of studies by independent researchers, lack of well-described protocols or treatment manuals, and a tendency to rely on no-treatment controls rather than comparison treatment groups. Researchers in recent years have addressed these limitations and must continue to do so, in order for play therapy to be considered a well-established school-based intervention.

The good news is that play therapy is well on its way to establishing a solid base of empirical support. The body of existing experimental research on school-based play therapy equals or exceeds experimental research on other mental health interventions used in the school setting. Play therapy has been shown to decrease internalizing and externalizing behavior problems, increase self-concept, improve social skills and social adjustment, increase achievement and skills related to academic performance, and reduce ADHD symptoms, aggression, conduct problems, and disruptive behaviors. Further, studies have shown the significant benefits of training young children's caregivers, including parents and teachers, as well as mentors in play therapy skills. Benefits include reduction in children's behavioral problems, improvement in parent-child and teacher-child relationships, decrease in stress in caregiver-child relationships, and increase in caregivers' empathic behavior and level of acceptance.

Play therapy provides a unique and viable solution to responding to the crises in children's mental health in this country (New Freedom

Commission on Mental Health, 2003; U.S. Public Health Service, 2000). Consistent with the recommendations from these recent government reports, play therapy: 1) is responsive to the developmental needs of young children, 2) has been successfully applied with diverse and at-risk populations in school settings where all children have equal access to services, and 3) has been applied systemically and comprehensively by involving young children's caregivers (parents and teachers) in the delivery of school-based mental health services. For these reasons, it is up to school professionals to utilize the substantial empirical evidence presented here to advocate for increased use of play therapy in school settings to break the current cycle of neglect in our children's care and well-being.

REFERENCES

Ackerman, B., Brown, E., & Izard, C. (2003). Continuity and change in levels of externalizing behavior in school children from economically disadvantaged families. *Child Development, 74,* 694–709.

Allin, H., Wathan, C., & MacMillan, H. (2005). Treatment of child neglect: A systematic review. *Canadian Psychiatric Journal of Psychiatry, 50*(8), 497–504.

Axline, V. (1947). Nondirective therapy for poor readers. *Journal of Consulting Psychology, 11,* 61–69.

Axline, V. (1949). Mental defiency: Symptom or disease? *Journal of Consulting Psychology, 13,* 313–327.

*Baggerly, J., & Jenkins, W. (2009). The effectiveness of child-centered play therapy on developmental and diagnostic factors in children who are homeless. *International Journal of Play Therapy, 18*(1), 45–55.

*Baggerly, J., & Landreth, G. (2001). Training children to help children: A new dimension in play therapy. *Peer Facilitator Quarterly, 18*(1), 6–14.

Beelmann, A., & Schneider, N. (2003). The effects of psychotherapy with children and adolescents: A review and meta-analysis of German-language research. *Zeitschrift für klinische Psychologie und Psychotherapie, 32*(2), 129–143.

Berkowitz, D. (2005). Perceived efficacy of play therapy as a treatment model in schools (Doctoral dissertation, Fairleigh Dickinson University, 2005). *Dissertation Abstract International, 66,* 1161.

Bills, R. (1950a). Nondirective play therapy with retarded readers. *Journal of Consulting Psychology, 14,* 140–149.

Bills, R. (1950b). Play therapy with well-adjusted retarded readers. *Journal of Consulting Psychology, 14,* 246–249.

*Indicates school-based outcome research studies, 1990 to present, summarized in this chapter.

Bratton, S., Landreth, G. L., Kellam, T., & Blackard, S. R. (2006). *Child-parent relationship therapy (CPRT) treatment manual: A 10-session filial therapy model for training parents*. New York: Taylor & Francis Group.

Bratton, S., & Ray, D. (2000). What the research shows about play therapy. *International Journal of Play Therapy, 9*, 47–88.

Bratton, S., Ray, D., & Landreth, G. (2008). Play therapy. In M. Hersen & A. Gross (Ed.), *Handbook of clinical psychology, Vol II: Children and adolescents* (pp. 577–625). New York: John Wiley & Sons.

Bratton, S., Ray, D., Rhine, T., & Jones, L. (2005). The efficacy of play therapy with children: A meta-analytic review of treatment outcomes. *Professional Psychology: Research and Practice, 36*(4), 367–390.

Brestan, E., & Eyeberg, S. (1998). Effective psychosocial treatments of conduct-disordered children and adolescents: 29 years, 82 studies, and 5,272 kids. *Journal of Clinical Child Psychology, 27*, 180–189.

Casey, R., & Berman, J. (1985). The outcome of psychotherapy with children. *Psychological Bulletin, 98*(2), 388–400.

*Ceballos, P., & Bratton, S. (in review). School-based child-parent relationship therapy (CPRT) with low-income first-generation immigrant Hispanic parents: Effects on child behavior and parent-child relationship stress. *Psychology in the Schools*.

*Collett, B. (2002). Addressing disruptive behaviors in the preschool classroom: An adaptation of parent-child interaction therapy (PCIT) for Head Start teachers (Doctoral dissertation, Utah State University, 2002). *Dissertation Abstracts International, 63*, 518.

*Crow, J. (1990). Play therapy with low achievers in reading (Doctoral dissertation, University of North Texas, 1989). *Dissertation Abstracts International, 50*, 2789.

*Danger, S., & Landreth, G. (2005). Child-centered group play therapy with children with speech difficulties. *International Journal of Play Therapy, 14*(1), 81–102.

*Draper, K., White, J., & O'Shaughnessy, T. E. (2001). Kinder training: Play-based consultation to improve the school adjustment of discouraged kindergarten and first grade students. *International Journal of Play Therapy, 10*, 1–30.

Drewes, A., Carey, L., & Schaefer, C. (Eds.). (2001). *School-based play therapy*. New York: John Wiley & Sons.

Dulsky, S. (1942). Affect and intellect: An experimental study. *The Journal of General Psychology, 27*, 199–220.

Duncan, G., Brooks-Gunn, J., & Klebanov, P. (1994). Economic deprivation and early childhood development. *Child Development, 65*, 296–318.

Erikson, E. (1963). *Childhood and society*. New York: Norton.

Evans, G. W. (2004). The environment of childhood poverty. *American Psychologist, 59*, 77–92.

Eyberg, S., Boggs, R., & Algina, J. (1995). Parent-child interaction therapy: A psychosocial model for the treatment of young children with conduct problem behavior and their families. *Psychopharmacology Bulletin, 31*, 83–91.

Eyberg, S., Nelson, M., & Boggs, S. (2008). Evidence-based psychosocial treatments for children and adolescents with disruptive behavior. *Journal of Child and Adolescent Psychology, 37*(1), 215–237.

*Fall, M., Balvanz, J., Johnson, L., & Nelson, L. (1999). A play therapy intervention and its relationship to self-efficacy and learning behaviors. *Professional School Counseling, 2*(3), 194–204.

*Fall, M., Navelski, L., & Welch, K. (2002). Outcomes of a play intervention for children identified for special education services. *International Journal for Play Therapy, 11*(2), 91–106.

Fantuzzo, J., Manz, P., Atkins, M., & Meyers, R. (2005). Peer-mediated treatment of socially withdrawn maltreated preschool children: Cultivating natural community resources. *Journal of Clinical Child and Adolescent Psychology, 34*(2), 320–325.

Filcheck, H., McNeil, C., Greco, L., & Bernard, R. (2004). Using a whole-class token economy and coaching of teacher skills in a preschool classroom to manage disruptive behavior. *Psychology in the Schools, 41*(3), 351–361.

Flahive, M., & Ray, D. (2007). Effect of group sandtray therapy with preadolescents. *Journal for Specialists in Group Work, 32*(4), 362–382.

Galassi, J., Griffin, D., & Akos, P. (2008). Strengths-based school counseling and the ASCA National Model. *Professional School Counseling, 12*(2), 176–181.

Gallagher, N. (2003). Effects of parent-child interaction therapy on young children with disruptive behavior disorders. Bridges: Practice-based research syntheses. *Research and Training Center on Early Childhood Development, 1*(7), 1–17.

*Garza, Y., & Bratton, S. (2005). School-based child-centered play therapy with Hispanic children: Outcomes and cultural considerations. *International Journal of Play Therapy, 14*, 51–79.

Gil, E., & Drewes, A. (2005). *Cultural issues in play therapy.* New York: Guilford Press.

Guerney, B. (1964). Filial therapy: Description and rationale. *Journal of Counseling Psychology, 28*, 304–310.

Hamre, B., & Pianta, R. (2001). Early teacher-child relationships and the trajectory of children's school outcomes through eighth grade. *Child Development, 72*(2), 625–638.

*Helker, W., & Ray, D. (in press, 2009). The impact of child-teacher relationship training on teachers' and aides' use of relationship-building skills and the effect on student classroom behavior. *International Journal of Play Therapy.*

*Hess, B., Post, P., & Flowers, C. (2005). A follow-up study of kinder training for preschool teachers of children deemed at risk. *International Journal of Play Therapy, 14*, 103–115.

Hetzel-Riggin, M., Brausch, A., & Montgomery, B. (2007). A meta-analytic investigation of therapy modality outcomes for sexually abused children and adolescents: An exploratory study. *Child Abuse and Neglect, 31*(2), 125–141.

*Hull, S. D. (2008). The effects of weekly child-centered play therapy on the behavioral problems of elementary students (Master's thesis, University of Central Missouri, 2008). *Masters Abstracts International, 46.*

*Jones, L., Rhine, T., & Bratton, S. (2002). High school students as therapeutic agents with young children experiencing school adjustment difficulties: The effectiveness of filial therapy training model. *International Journal of Play Therapy, 11*(2), 43–62.

*Kale, A., & Landreth, G. (1999). Filial therapy with parents of children experiencing learning difficulties. *International Journal of Play Therapy, 8*(2), 35–56.

Kazdin, A., Bass, D., Ayers, W., & Rodgers, A. (1990). Empirical and clinical focus of child and adolescent psychotherapy research. *Journal of Consulting and Clinical Psychology, 58*, 729–740.

Keiley, M., Bates, J., Dodge, K., & Pettit, G. (2000). A cross-domain growth analysis: Externalizing and internalizing behaviors during 8 years of childhood. *Journal of Abnormal Child Psychology, 28*(2), 161–179.

Knitzer, J. (2000). Early childhood mental health services: A policy and systems development perspective. In J. Shonkoff & S. J. Meisels (Eds.), *Handbook of early childhood intervention* (2nd ed., pp. 416–438). Cambridge, MA: Cambridge University Press.

*Kostina, L. (2004). Adjustment of first-year school children to school by means of lowering their anxiety level. *Voprosy Psychologii, 1*, 137–143.

Kratochwill, T. (2004). Evidence-based practice: Promoting evidence-based interventions in school psychology. *School Psychology Review, 33*, 351–361.

Lambert, S., LeBlanc, M., Mullen, J., Ray, D., Baggerly, J., White, J., et al. (2005). Learning more about those who play in session: The national play therapy in counseling practice project (Phase I). *International Journal of Play Therapy, 14*(2), 7–23.

Landreth, G. (1987). Play therapy: Facilitative use of child's play in elementary school counseling. *Elementary School Guidance and Counseling, 21*(4), 253–261.

Landreth, G. L. (2002). *Play therapy: The art of relationship.* New York: Brunner-Routledge.

Landreth, G., & Bratton, S. (2006). *Child-parent relationship therapy (CPRT): A 10-session filial therapy model.* New York: Routledge.

LeBlanc, M., & Ritchie, M. (1999). Predictors of play therapy outcomes. *International Journal of Play Therapy, 8*(2), 19–34.

LeBlanc, M., & Ritchie, M. (2001). A meta-analysis of play therapy outcomes. *Counseling Psychology Quarterly, 14*(2), 149–163.

Mashburn, A., Pianta, R., Hamre, B., Downer, J., Barbarin, O., et al. (2008). Measures of classroom quality in prekindergarten and children's development of academic, language, and social skills. *Child Development, 79*(3), 732–749.

*McGuire, D. (2001). Child-centered group play therapy with children experiencing adjustment difficulties (Doctoral dissertation, University of North Texas, 2000). *Dissertation Abstracts International, 61,* 3908.

*Morrison, M., & Bratton, S. (in review). An early mental health intervention for disadvantaged preschool children with behavior problems: The effectiveness of training Head Start teachers in child-teacher relationship training (CTRT). *Psychology in the Schools.*

*Muro, J., Ray, D., Schottelkorb, A., Smith, M., & Blanco, P. (2006). Quantitative analysis of long-term child-centered play therapy. *International Journal of Play Therapy, 15*(2), 35–58.

New Freedom Commission on Mental Health. (2003). *Achieving the promise: Transforming mental health care in America. Final Report.* (DHHS Publication No. SMA-03-3832). Rockville, MD: Department of Health and Human Services.

Oaklander, V. (2003). Gestalt play therapy. In C. Schaefer (Ed.), *Foundations of play therapy* (pp. 143–155). Hoboken, NJ: John Wiley & Sons.

O'Connor, K. (2001). Ecosystemic play therapy. *International Journal of Play Therapy, 10*(2), 33–44.

*Ogawa, Y. (2007). Effectiveness of child-centered play therapy with Japanese children in the United States (Doctoral dissertation, University of North Texas, 2006). *Dissertation Abstracts International,* 68.

*Packman, J., & Bratton, S. (2003). A school-based group play/activity therapy intervention with learning disabled preadolescents exhibiting behavior problems. *International Journal of Play Therapy, 12,* 7–29.

*Paone, T., Packman, J., Maddux, C., & Rothman, T. (2008). A school-based group activity therapy intervention with at-risk high school students as it relates to their moral reasoning. *International Journal of Play Therapy, 17*(2), 122–137.

*Pears, K., Fisher, P., & Bronz, K. (2007). An intervention to promote social-emotional school readiness in foster children: Preliminary outcomes from a pilot study. *School Psychology Review, 36*(4), 665–673.

Piaget, J. (1962). *Play, dreams, and imitation in childhood.* New York: Routledge.

Pianta, R., & Stuhlman, M. (2004). Teacher-child relationships and children's success in the first years of school. *School Psychology Review, 33,* 444–458.

*Pollock, K. (1996). The effectiveness of parent-child interaction therapy conducted in a Head Start workshop (Doctoral dissertation, University of Alabama, 1996). *Dissertation Abstracts International, 57,* 4039.

*Post, P. (1999). Impact of child-centered play therapy on the self-esteem, locus of control, and anxiety of at-risk 4th, 5th, and 6th grade students. *International Journal of Play Therapy, 8*(2), 1–18.

*Post, P., McAllister, M., Sheely, A., Hess, B., & Flowers, C. (2004). Child-centered kinder training for teachers of preschool children deemed at risk. *International Journal of Play Therapy, 13*, 53–74.

*Quayle, R. (1991). The primary mental health project as a school-based approach for prevention of adjustment problems: An evaluation of play therapy as an early intervention (Doctoral dissertation, The Pennsylvania State University, 1991). *Dissertation Abstracts International, 52*, 1268.

Rains, C. (2004). Evidence-based practice in school social work: A process in perspective. *Children and Schools, 26*(2), 71–85.

*Ray, D. (2007). Two counseling interventions to reduce teacher-child relationship stress. *Professional School Counseling, 10*(4), 428–440.

Ray, D., Armstrong, S., Warren, E., & Balkin, R. (2005). Play therapy practices among elementary school counselors. *Professional School Counseling, 8*(4), 360–365.

*Ray, D., Blanco, P., Sullivan, J., & Holliman, R. (in press) An exploratory study of child-centered play therapy with aggressive children. *International Journal of Play Therapy.*

Ray, D., Bratton, S., Rhine, T., & Jones, L. (2001). The effectiveness of play therapy: Responding to the critics. *International Journal of Play Therapy, 10*(1), 85–108.

*Ray, D., Henson, R., Schottelkorb, A., Brown, A., & Muro, J. (2008). Effects of short- and long-term play therapy services on teacher-child relationship stress. *Psychology in Schools, 45*(10), 994–1009.

*Ray, D., Schottelkorb, A., & Tsai, M. (2007). Play therapy with children exhibiting symptoms of attention deficit hyperactivity disorder. *International Journal of Play Therapy, 16*, 95–111.

*Reams, R., & Fridrich, W. (1994). The efficacy of time-limited play therapy with maltreated preschoolers. *Journal of Clinical Psychology, 59*(6), 889–899.

Reddy, L., Files-Hall, T., & Schaefer, C. (2005). *Empirically based play intervention program.* Washington, DC: American Psychological Association.

*Rennie, R. (2003). A comparison study of the effectiveness of individual and group play therapy in treating kindergarten children with adjustment problems (Doctoral dissertation, University of North Texas, 2000). *Dissertation Abstracts International, 63*, 3117.

*Robinson, J., Landreth, G., & Packman, J. (2007). Fifth-grade students as emotional helpers with kindergartners: Using play therapy procedures and skills. *International Journal of Play Therapy, 16*(1), 20–35.

Satcher, D. (2000). Mental health: A report of the Surgeon General. *Professional Psychology: Research and Practice, 31*(1), 5–13.

Schaefer, C. (2001). Prescriptive play therapy. *International Journal of Play Therapy, 10*(2), 57–73.

*Schottelkorb, A. (2008). Effectiveness of child-centered play therapy and person-centered teacher consultation on ADHD behavioral problems of elementary school children: A single case design (Doctoral dissertation, University of North Texas, 2007). *Dissertation Abstracts International, 69.*

*Schumann, B. (2005). Effects of child-centered play therapy and curriculum-based small-group guidance on the behaviors of children referred for aggression in an elementary school setting (Doctoral dissertation, University of North Texas, 2004). *Dissertation Abstracts International, 65/12,* 4476.

Seeman, J. (1954). Child therapy in education: Some current trends. *Education, 74,* 493–500.

*Sheely, A., & Bratton, S. (in review). School-based child-parent relationship therapy (CPRT) with low-income Black American parents: Effects on children's behaviors and parent-child relationship stress, a pilot study. *Professional School Counselor.*

*Shen, Y. (2002). Short-term group play therapy with Chinese earthquake victims: Effects on anxiety, depression, and adjustment. *International Journal of Play Therapy, 11*(1), 43–63.

*Shen, Y. (2007). Developmental model using gestalt-play versus cognitive-verbal group with Chinese adolescents: Effects on strengths and adjustment enhancement. *Journal for Specialists in Group Work, 32*(3), 285–305.

*Shen, Y., & Armstrong, S. (2008). Impact of group sandtray therapy on the self-esteem of young adolescent girls. *Journal for Specialists in Group Work, 33* (2), 118–137.

*Smith, D., & Landreth, G. (2004). Filial therapy with teachers of deaf and hard of hearing preschool children. *International Journal of Play Therapy, 13*(1), 13–33.

Society of Clinical and Child and Adolescent Psychology and Network on Youth Mental Health. (2009). *Evidence-based treatments for children and adolescents.* Retrieved February 1, 2009, from http://sccap.tamu.edu/ EST.html.

*Sosna, T. (1992). The impact of parent-child interaction therapy on the verbalizations and compliance of nonclinical preschool children (Doctoral dissertation, Washington State University, 1991). *Dissertation Abstract International, 53,* 1617.

Subcommittee on Children and Family (2003). *Promoting, preserving and restoring children's mental health.* Retrieved January 5, 2009, from http:// www.mentalhealthcommission.gov/subcommittee/Sub_Chairs.html.

*Tiano, J., & McNeil, C. (2006). Training Head Start teachers in behavior management using parent-child interaction therapy: A preliminary investigation. *Journal of Early and Intensive Behavior Intervention, 3*(2), 220–233.

U.S. Public Health Service. (2000). *Report of the Surgeon General's conference on children's mental health: A national action agenda.* Washington, DC: Author.

*Utay, J. (1992). Effectiveness of a cognitive-behavioral group play therapy intervention on selected aspects of social skills of third through sixth grade students with learning disabilities (Doctoral dissertation, East Texas State University, 1991). *Dissertation Abstracts International, 52*, 2826.

VanFleet, R. (2005). *Filial Therapy: Strengthening parent-child relationships through play*. Boiling Springs, PA: Play Therapy Press.

*Villarreal, C. (2008). School-based child-parent relationship therapy (CPRT) with Hispanic parents (Doctoral dissertation, Regent University, 2008). *Dissertation Abstracts International, 69*.

Vygotsky, L. (1966). Play and its role in the mental development of the child. *Voprosy Psikhologii, 12*, 62–76.

*Watson, D. (2007). An early intervention approach for students displaying negative externalizing behaviors associated with childhood depression: A study of the efficacy of play therapy in the school (Doctoral dissertation, Capella University, 2007). *Dissertation Abstracts International, 68*, 1820.

Webster-Stratton, C., & Reid, M. (2003). The Incredible Years parents, teachers and children training series. In A. E. Kazdin & J. R. Weisz (Eds.), *Evidence-based psychotherapies for children and adolescents* (pp. 224–240). New York: Guilford Press.

Weisz, J., Weiss, B., Han, S., Granger, D., & Morton, T. (1995). Effects of psychotherapy with children and adolescents revisted: A meta-analysis of treatment outcome studies. *Psychological Bulletin, 117*, 450–468.

Wethington, H., Hahn, R., Fuqua-Whitley, D., Sipe, T., Crosby, A., Johnson, R., et al. (2008). The effectiveness of interventions to reduce psychological harm from traumatic events among children and adolescents: A systematic review. *American Journal of Preventive Medicine, 35*(3), 287–313.

White, J., Flynt, M., & Draper, K. (1997). Kinder therapy: Teachers as therapeutic agents. *International Journal of Play Therapy, 6*(2), 33–49.

PART II

IMPLEMENTING PLAY THERAPY IN THE SCHOOLS

CHAPTER 3

Guidelines for Incorporating Play Therapy in the Schools

KRISTI PERRYMAN and
JUDY DORAN

INTRODUCTION

RATIONALE FOR COUNSELING IN THE SCHOOL SETTING

Historically, the role of counseling in the school setting has been ambiguous. Counselors have been responsible for everything from vocational planning, class scheduling, testing coordination, and teaching guidance programs, to responsive services for at-risk and gifted populations as well as individual and group counseling. In addition to the school counselor, other mental health professionals providing counseling services in the school setting may be licensed clinical social workers, psychologists, or licensed counselors. School counselors play an important role in the school setting. This chapter will focus specifically on the school counselors' role, as they are primarily responsible for implementing counseling services in the school.

School counseling originated from a need for vocational counseling. It began in the United States around the turn of the twentieth century. This was the basis upon which legislation was created culminating in the National Defense Education Act (NDEA) of 1958, which established programs for school counselors (Austin, 1999). The focus of NDEA was on career guidance, with counselors using assessment instruments such as the Strong Vocational Interest Blank. Early counseling and guidance activities included a focus on "testing, registration, and placement of students in appropriate classes; [developing] a system for monitoring student records; and [being] available for individual student advising" (Amatea & Clark, 2005, p. 24).

During the 1980s and 1990s, the work of Norm Gysbers and others (Aubrey, 1982; Gysbers & Henderson, 1988) re-evaluated the mental health responsibilities of the counselor and included developmental awareness and recognition of the "student in context," as well as addressing a need for role clarification and accountability. There have been numerous studies documenting the benefits of fully implemented model guidance programs for K–12 students (Lapan, Gysbers, & Sun, 1997; Lapan, Gysbers, & Petroski, 2001; Sink & Stroh, 2003). Benefits include higher scores on standardized achievement tests for third- and fourth-graders and a sense of safety and greater satisfaction with the quality of their education for middle school students. High school students felt they had better access to the career and college information available to them, as well as feeling that they had been prepared for their life away from their school setting.

Today's schools face different challenges in meeting the needs of the growing number of issues that students possess as they enter their doors. School counselors must be better equipped than their predecessors to tackle the number of situations that present daily in a school setting. They must be equipped with a variety of ideas in their counseling toolbox to protect and advocate for their students. This is no small task. According to Children's Defense Fund (2005), there has been a significant increase in the number of children in poverty in the last five years. Zill and West (2000) cite four ECLS-K risk factors associated with general knowledge, lower reading, and lower math skills in students entering kindergarten. The factors include: having a mother with less than a high school education, living in a family that receives food stamps or cash welfare payments, living in a single-parent household, and having parents whose primary language is other than English.

It is essential that school counselors have an in-depth understanding of the school culture. The school setting is unique to any other counseling arena. It is very different from other counseling settings, such as an agency or in-patient hospitals. School counselors have to be able to work with many personalities and professionals from parents, teachers, staff, and administration. The school is a public domain and, often, the heartbeat of a community. It is unlike an agency or in-patient hospital where there are programs and numerous staff members to address physical and mental needs of their clients. The school setting goal is to teach academics and ensure students attend school to receive an education. Counseling services are in place to facilitate student success. The duties of the school counselor are oriented to help students achieve success.

Professional school counselors must also have an understanding of the governance or chain of command in the school setting. While they work amongst colleagues, they are often the only counseling professional in the setting. School counselors are not administrators nor are they teachers. Due to confidentiality, they often have access to information that only they can know. This can leave counselors feeling isolated. Counselors are advocates for students. It is crucial that they be able to use their voice to support the student, oftentimes placing them in an unpopular position with teachers and/or administrators. They may also serve as a confidant or sounding board for the principal and the teachers.

School counselors must remember that their referral sources are often their colleagues and should work to maintain good working relationships with them. The school nurse may refer students who often have physical complaints. The art teacher may refer students who create disturbing artwork. A classroom teacher may refer students for alarming writing. The physical education teacher may refer the student who repeatedly refuses to dress out, to assess for physical abuse. The cafeteria staff may refer students who consistently overeat or dispose of their food. The custodian may refer a student who has unusual bathroom habits or who throws up often.

Professional school counselors must know when to tackle the problem or refer out, remembering their scope of practice and limitations. Skills such as being well-versed in public speaking, multi-tasking, classroom management, leadership, marketing and public relations, conflict resolution, grief counseling, crisis counseling, assessment, and identifying mental illness are necessary. Knowledge in the areas of parenting skills, family constellations and dynamics, advocating for children, interventions and strategies, ethics counseling theories, and play therapy are also crucial. School counselors' expertise cannot be limited to one population because they have to use their skills to address these tasks with teachers, administrators, parents, school nurses, social workers, volunteers, and other school staff. The professional school counselors' time is distributed in many areas rather than just concentrated on individual and group counseling. In addition to actual counseling, school counselors also teach classroom model guidance lessons to each grade in their school. They frequently assist with special education and gifted program duties, such as IQ testing, and serving as members for team meetings in these areas. Depending on the school district, it is likely that they will have numerous nonguidance activities such as lunchroom, recess or bus duty, test coordination, scheduling, and various administrative tasks.

AMERICAN SCHOOL COUNSELOR ASSOCIATION NATIONAL STANDARDS

The National Model for School Counseling Programs was published in 2003 by the American School Counselors Association (ASCA). Its intent was to promote its existence in public schools throughout the United States. The model is targeted at student achievement and activities that will increase student performance. Today's schools focus on closing the gap between classroom performance and student achievement scores. Counselors in today's school settings are asked to prepare action plans, write mission and vision statements, and set goals and objectives toward their school's improvement plan. They participate in Whole Faculty Study Groups, target the dropout rate, and assist the teachers in raising standards to meet annual yearly progress as defined in No Child Left Behind legislation (2002). The ASCA National Model encourages the school counselor to address its counseling services in a way that promotes student achievement through its program management mechanisms. The ASCA National Model also suggests that counselors provide direct and indirect services for their students in their school settings.

Ray, Armstrong, Warren, and Balkin (2005) recognized play therapy as being helpful in implementing the ASCA standards. Play therapy is an ideal way to provide these services to students. School counselors can use these techniques in small groups, with individuals, and even in their classroom guidance lessons to provide services to students. Play therapy is frequently mentioned in the counseling field as the most developmentally appropriate way to meet the counseling needs of children in the school setting (Landreth, 1993; Drewes, Carey, & Schaefer, 2001; Ray, Armstrong, Warren, & Balkin, 2005).

Play is a culturally sensitive approach because play is universal and the natural language of children. According to Wynne (2008),"Because schools are a microcosm of society, school-based mental health practitioners regularly work with children who experience interpersonal, emotional, and behavioral difficulties that interfere with learning as a result of stressors in their lives. (e.g., [sic] trauma, natural disasters, abuse, illness/death, disabilities, divorce, addiction, etc.)" (p. 1). Leaders in the field of school counseling believe play therapy is a viable counseling modality to meet the diverse needs of the school-age population (Drewes, Carey, & Schaefer; 2001; Fall, 1994; Landreth, 1993; Wynne, 2008).

One program incorporating play therapy in the school setting is the Primary Project model. It began in 1957 and has measurable data that proves its success with children. It is a school-based early intervention and prevention program that helps reduce difficulties in children in kindergarten through third grade (Peabody, 2008). The child works with a trained child associate in a playroom equipped with material that has been selected, matching the project's criteria. This early intervention supports the academic needs and focuses on helping children adjust to school more quickly and begin the necessary steps to learning (Peabody, 2008).

PLAY THERAPY IN THE SCHOOL SETTING

Play therapy is defined by Landreth (1991) as "a dynamic interpersonal relationship between a child and a therapist trained in play therapy procedures who provides selected play materials and facilitates the development of a safe relationship for the child to fully express and explore self (feelings, thoughts, experiences, and behaviors) through the child's natural medium of communication, play" (p. 14). Developmentally, play therapy is the most logical choice for counseling children in a school setting. According to Piaget's theory, elementary age children fall into the following chronological age stages: preoperational (2–7 years) and concrete operations stage (8–11 years). It is not until approximately age 11 that children become able to engage in abstract thinking and reasoning. Miller (2002) noted that Piaget's theory denies earlier views that representational thought comes from the ability to use words but rather, "thought is both prior to language and broader than language" (p. 47). The main purpose of language is to express thoughts. In these stages, children are able to express their cognitions and feelings through play that they are not developmentally capable of expressing verbally. O'Conner (1991) asserted that play therapy is also developmentally appropriate for children through high school ages. Perhaps Landreth (2002) best described the role of play in the life of children by saying that play is their language and toys are their words.

Landreth (2002) explains that the purpose of play therapy in schools is to prepare children for learning. Ray, Armstrong, Warren, and Balkin (2005) state that, "Play therapy is an approach that may help school counselors to effectively assist children in their developmental growth" (p. 361). Ray, Bratton, Rhine, and Jones (2001) conducted a meta-analysis of play therapy outcome research and found that play therapy was an effective treatment for helping children deal with their problems. This groundbreaking research included 94 studies, 36 of which were conducted in school settings, and spanned a 60-year period.

Many children today are at-risk because of situations they live in or are exposed to in the home environment. Schools have become an ideal setting to implement interventions and proactive measures to help them. Drewes (2001) suggests the school can become a bridge to link services to those children coming from special education preschool or therapeutic nurseries. The school setting allows more children and families to receive services than through private agencies because there are usually more staff members to serve children and more areas of expertise available. Input can be offered from not only the counselor but the nurse, speech therapist, title services, and other specialists that visit or are housed in the school building. Also, children are in school longer periods of the day and come daily. The nature of a school day lends itself to opportunities to access services without the parent having to transport the child to another location to be treated. It also relieves the financial burdens that parents face. Children can build relationships with the school personnel that build trust. Children play in the school setting and it is well documented that play is a natural way for children to express themselves. All of this adds up to success for parents, teachers, counselors, and students.

According to Wynne (2008), "The potential for effective practice of play therapy in schools depends on several factors, including resources, beliefs, and training" (p. 2). A study by Ray, Armstrong, Warren, and Balkin (2005) reported that 67 percent of counselors surveyed had no university-level courses in play therapy, even though 97 percent of them strongly agreed that play is a child's natural first language. According to VanFleet (2005), the school counselor uses play-based interventions to:

1. Communicate with students.
2. Help students build a wide range of skills.
3. Improve students' adjustment to classroom and other school environments.
4. Improve peer relationships.
5. Prevent bullying, school violence, and other serious problems.
6. Address the needs of at-risk students.
7. Remove emotional and behavioral obstacles to learning (p. 1).

THEORIES MOST FREQUENTLY PRACTICED
IN THE SCHOOL SETTING

Developing a theoretical approach is crucial for play therapists in any setting. In the school setting, there are four theoretical approaches that are frequently mentioned. These include Child-centered, Adlerian, Cognitive Behavioral, and Eclectic Prescriptive. The school counselors' chosen theoretical perspective depends greatly upon the training they received in their master's program, post-master's continuing education, and where they are on the continuum of their own counselor development. The types of play therapy techniques may also vary depending on the age of the students (i.e., elementary, middle, or high school). For example, elementary counselors may have a playroom or play area in their office for the children to better express themselves according to their own theoretical perspective. Middle and high school counselors are more likely to have art supplies or games available as they deem necessary to incorporate with expressive arts or play therapy techniques. The theoretical approaches and their applicability to the school setting will be further explored in the next section.

CHILD-CENTERED PLAY THERAPY

Child-centered play therapy has long been successfully incorporated into elementary counseling programs (Landreth, 1993). Landreth stated that it is likely the most developmentally appropriate approach since the therapist doesn't try and make the child change but follows the child's lead. Landreth (2002) explains that the purpose of play therapy in schools is to better prepare children for learning. Landreth, Baggerly, and Tyndall-Lind (1999) further attribute the developmental nature of child-centered play therapy and describe the therapist's role in the process:

> The child-centered play therapist believes in and trusts the child's intrinsic motivation toward adjustment, mental health, independence, autonomy, and self-actualization and therefore allows the child to move at a pace of growth determined by the child's unique, forward-moving, inner directedness. As the child reacts to his or her changing world of experience, the child does so as an organized whole so that a change in any one part results in changes in other parts. (p. 278)

The core conditions established by Carl Rogers (1961) are the premise for child-centered play therapy. These include empathy, genuineness, and unconditional positive regard. The goal of the therapist is to see the world through the eyes of the child. They therefore take a nondirective approach. "Child-centered play therapy is both a basic philosophy of the innate human capacity of the child to strive toward growth and maturity and an attitude of deep and abiding belief in the child's ability to be constructively self-directing" (Landreth, 1991, p. 60).

Landreth (1993) explains that, "The elementary school counselor uses play therapy with children because play is the child's symbolic language of self-expression and for children to play out their experiences and feelings is the most naturally, dynamic, and self-healing process in which children can engage" (p. 17). He also explains that children's cognitive development supersedes their verbal development, thus allowing them to naturally communicate their perception of their world through play.

Child-centered play therapy is especially ideal for the elementary setting as it engages the child at a developmental level and in his or her own language. One drawback to using this theoretical perspective in the school setting is time constraints. It is rare that counselors have time to see a child on a regular basis, for an extended period of time, in a school setting.

ADLERIAN PLAY THERAPY

Adlerian play therapy is based on the works of Alfred Adler, developed early in the twentieth century (Kottman, 2003). "Adlerians believe that people who come to counseling because they are experiencing difficulties dealing with life's problems are discouraged" (Kottman, 2003, p. 139). The therapist's role is therefore to be active and directive and encourage the child. Terry Kottman adapted Adler's theory for its application to children and play therapy and is widely accepted as the expert in Adlerian play therapy. According to Kottman and Warlick (1990), Adlerian play therapy is most appropriate for children between the ages of 4 and 9 years old, "who are young enough to prefer using the language of play to communicate but are old enough to understand some standard English words" (p. 127). This type of play therapy is holistic in its approach, including significant others from the child's social world. Adlerian play therapy focused on establishing and maintaining an egalitarian relationship, with the therapist and child viewed as partners in the process, which is the first phase of this theory. Other phases include: exploring the child's lifestyle, helping the child gain insight, and finally, reorienting/reeducating the child (Kottman, 2003).

One positive aspect of using this approach in the school setting is the opportunity it offers to work with the child in their own social setting, including teachers and parents in the process. It is also somewhat more of a direct approach to dealing with maladaptive behaviors and offers specific suggestions for parents and teachers depending on what the goal of the misbehavior is. The idea of encouragement is also well suited to the school setting. Possible challenges to this approach in the school are the difficulty involved in getting parents in and engaged in the process and the time it requires in assessing and working with them and the teachers.

Cognitive Behavioral Play Therapy (CBPT)

This theoretical perspective is derived from the work of behavioralists like Ellis (1971), Beck (1976), and Bandura (1977). Gleaning from their theories, Knell (1998) further developed this approach for work with children into cognitive-behavioral play therapy. Knell used structure, being directive and goal-oriented to teach children to think of a new way to play, solve their problems, build relationships, and think about the person they are becoming. The application of CBPT includes assessment and introducing an individually tailored intervention to "increase behavioral competence" (p. 30). The therapist sets up scenes from the child's life and uses modeling, role playing, desensitization, and other techniques to aid the child in changing his or her behavior (Knell, 1998). Homework is assigned after therapy sessions, positive reinforcers are used, shaping, self-monitoring, confronting irrational thoughts, and involving the child in setting goals for his or her behavior. Play therapy skills are used to treat the child, and techniques such as bibliotherapy, games, puzzles, drawing, storytelling, and puppets are utilized to help the child manage his or her behavior. This approach has specific treatment goals that are based on the assessment and incorporate research-based techniques to eliminate the undesired behaviors.

A positive aspect of this approach in the school setting is that it is narrowly focused on the presenting problem and finding empirical data to change the behavior. It is a time-efficient approach, which is very important in this setting. The supplies needed for incorporating the techniques are usually readily available in a school setting, such as art supplies, games, books, etc. A possible challenge to using this approach in the school can be the time it requires to conduct the assessment and develop research-based treatment goals.

ECLECTIC PRESCRIPTIVE PLAY THERAPY

The third approach often used in the school setting is Eclectic Prescriptive. This theory is based on the idea that there are certain types of play therapy interventions that work best for certain diagnoses and that the more tools counselors have, the better equipped they are to help more children. The Eclectic Prescriptive therapist seeks to fit the intervention specifically to the need of the student or client. Research-based treatments are used for the student's intended disorder. The basic tenets according to Schaefer (2001) include: differential therapeutics, eclecticism, prescriptive matching, change mechanisms, treatment specificity, realistic expectations, multi-component intervention, and practice guidelines.

Frequently more seasoned counselors, who have been in the school counseling field for a number of years, describe themselves as more eclectic. A positive aspect of using this approach in the school setting is that it offers evidenced-based techniques for specific problems in a setting with a multitude of children with various issues. It offers a more direct and time-sensitive approach to dealing with maladaptive behaviors. A possible negative aspect is the extensive knowledge that is needed in various play therapy techniques. Another downfall is the time it can take to research the best possible methods for specific problems.

In summary, while these four theoretical approaches are the most reportedly used by professional school counselors, it is unlikely that they are strictly adhering to them in the purest sense, due to the overwhelming demands placed on their time. For example, while many school counselors would report that they are eclectic in their approach, what they are more likely describing is haphazardly choosing techniques without considering the underlying theories. It is highly recommended that professional school counselors equip themselves early on with a theoretical approach that they can build into their own philosophy and beliefs about human nature. It is essential that they have a foundational base from which to draw on as a resource for their therapeutic work with children. Otherwise they render themselves ineffective and possibly unethical.

EDUCATING ADMINISTRATORS, TEACHERS, AND PARENTS ABOUT PLAY THERAPY

The school counselor serves as a liaison between administration, parents, teachers, and students. This is an important role, as counselors are the common denominator in an effective school counseling program. The key to any successful counseling program begins with the buying in of the stakeholders. In this case, they are the parents, teachers, administration, the community, the school board, and the students. It is important to note that administrators are not required to receive training in the area of counseling; therefore, their knowledge is limited to what was modeled for them by their own (K–12) school counselors or what the professional school counselors in their school teach them by advocating for their role and their programs. This begins in the interview process. It is essential that counselors be aware of the ASCA model, as well as their state comprehensive guidance program and the pertinent questions to ask. Counselors also have the responsibility of educating their administrators and faculty about the benefits of play therapy. This section outlines specific suggestions for buying in these stakeholders, thus, creating advocates for your school counseling program and your students. The Association for Play Therapy has "Why Play Therapy?" brochures and a short informational video available at www.a4pt.org, which would be extremely beneficial for educating all the stakeholders.

CONDUCT A PRESENTATION FOR THE SCHOOL BOARD

Educate your district school board. There are several important points that should be covered in presenting information to them. An important point to remember is to speak their language. A critical part of this language is dollars and cents. It is equally important that you discuss play therapy and model guidance in laymen's terms. The educational levels of the board will vary, as will their experiences and expertise. We suggest the following outline for presenting to the school board:

Define *play therapy* and explain why this is the most developmentally suited and empirically based method of counseling students.

1. Explain this to them by saying that children develop cognitive abilities prior to their verbal abilities and that therefore play is their language and toys are their words (Landreth, 2002).

2. Highlight the advantages to using play therapy or "counseling with toys" in the school setting.
3. Describe the function of play therapy in the School Improvement Plan of the district and specifically to individual schools within the district (when applicable).
4. Conduct a professional presentation using research data regarding your counseling program and the benefits of it to the district. An example would be selecting a group of students who have poor attendance and conducting a six-week play therapy group intervention. The students' attendance could be compared from the quarters prior to and after the group. Since school districts receive funding based on each student's attendance, the amount of money the district has earned should be highlighted as a benefit to this intervention. The same could easily be accomplished with behavior referrals and grade point averages to show academic benefits.

PROFESSIONAL DEVELOPMENT FOR TEACHERS AND PRINCIPALS

The teachers and principals can become your advocates in promoting play therapy. This can be accomplished by presenting the information previously used with the school board. It is important that they are knowledgeable about the financial benefits, as they are also likely members of the community and will spread the word. Since they work directly with the students, they also need more detailed information about play therapy and its impact. Two added suggestions for accomplishing this are to conduct an experiential activity with your colleagues and to present case studies. Using your professional judgment, choose a simple experiential play therapy activity and invite participants to join in the play. Remember that the purpose of this is not therapy, but awareness of the power of play. Presenting a case study, preserving the identity of the student, can also allow the participants a glimpse into the world of play therapy and its impact on an individual. Leave teachers and principals with a handout of an inspirational quote or poem about play as a reminder of what they have experienced and learned.

CORRESPONDENCE WITH PARENTS

Parents are important stakeholders in this process as they send their children to school for an education. A successful school counseling program is one where the counselor communicates with the parents on a regular basis and in a variety of ways. Educating the parents about play therapy is the best way to include them as advocates. The following suggestions are useful in this process:

A. Monthly Newsletter
   The counseling newsletter can include any of the following:
   1. A monthly schedule outlining guidance lesson topics
   2. Featured parenting books and topic-specific books for children (divorce, grief, starting a new school, anxiety, etc.)
   3. School-year-specific suggestions (i.e., back to school, test-taking strategies during assessment time, holiday stress, etc.)
   4. Referral forms for both group and individual counseling
   5. Advertisements for upcoming parenting classes, open house, upcoming groups (friendship, divorce, grief, social skills, etc.)
   6. Parent-child activities involving play
   7. A list of items needed for the playroom
B. Open House
   It is important that the school counselors are available and visible during Open House and that there is an effort made to direct and invite parents to visit the counselors' rooms. Counselors may wish to provide snacks and/or door prizes. The visit will allow parents to see the atmosphere and gain a better understanding of the counseling environment. This may provide an opportunity to discuss play therapy and its usefulness. Often times, parents have more than one teacher to visit. This limits the time they have to spend at Open House. The counselor's office is often in a remote part of the building and often hard to find, which also limits access to parents. Signs with directions to the counseling office are helpful, with contact paper in the shape of footsteps marking the path. Offering snacks in the counselor's office or door prizes, such as inexpensive toys (stress balls, bubbles, etc.), can guide parents and students to the counseling office. Once there, the parents will see the tools of the counselor's trade and experience the inviting nature of the room. This is valuable as their perceptions of school counselors may be very different, depending upon their own experiences. This will provide an opportunity for the counselors to talk about play therapy and its usefulness in helping children.
C. Parenting Programs
   School counselors are often responsible for offering parenting programs in their school setting. Topics for these programs vary

from discipline techniques to improving self-esteem, family game nights, and/or enhancing family relationships. Counselors are generally the coordinators for these programs but they can also partner with community programs, such as mental health agencies, universities, churches, hospitals, and businesses. There are generally a plethora of resources available for programs; therefore, it can be very difficult to get parents to participate in them. One way to remedy this problem is to have door prizes, childcare, and food available. This can offer parents an evening together without the expense and stress of finding childcare and feeding the family. One research-based program that incorporates play therapy is Child-Parent Relationship Therapy training.

Child-Parent Relationship Therapy (CPRT) teaches parents play therapy skills to incorporate with their children. The goal of CPRT is to "enhance and strengthen the parent-child relationship" through improving problem-solving skills and interactions within the family and through "increased feelings of familial affection, warmth, and trust" (Landreth & Bratton, 2006, p. 11). CPRT is a 10-week session model, based on filial therapy. In this model, Landreth and Bratton (2006) define *Filial Therapy* as:

> A unique approach used by professionals trained in play therapy to train parents to be therapeutic agents with their own children through a format of didactic instruction, demonstration play sessions, required at-home laboratory play sessions, and supervision in a supportive atmosphere. Parents are taught basic child-centered play therapy principles and skills including reflective listening, recognizing and responding to children's feelings, therapeutic limit setting, building children's self-esteem, and structuring required weekly play sessions with their children using a special kit of selected toys. Parents learn how to create a nonjudgmental, understanding, and accepting environment that enhances the parent-child relationship, thus facilitating personal growth and change for child and parent. (p. 11)

Landreth and Bratton (2006) summarized 33 studies with over 800 subjects and stated, "The evidence for the efficacy of this treatment methodology is impressive, supporting its usefulness with a variety of presenting issues and with diverse populations" (p. 457). Studies in the school setting have investigated the use of teachers and mentors with deaf and hard-of-hearing preschool children, juniors and seniors in high school as helpers with fourth- and fifth- grade students, and even fifth-graders for peer-based mentoring (pp. 466–468), all with positive results. This would be an ideal parenting program to incorporate into a school counseling setting. It is beneficial to families and promotes an understanding for, and in support of, play therapy.

SETTING UP A PLAYROOM IN THE SCHOOL

The environment and toys in the playroom are important as they are the first impression that children, parents, and teachers receive. As Landreth (1991) states, it "conveys warmth and a clear message 'This is a place for children'" (p. 109). Students and parents are more likely to feel comfortable and welcomed in such a space. The school counselor's playroom can vary from a classroom-size space with a marvelous array of toys, to a remodeled closet, or even to a tote bag. For most counselors, their playroom and office are the same; therefore, they must be creative in finding ways to equip it as both and still maintain the warmth needed to make it inviting. Other counselors have no permanent space and must use borrowed space in the corner of a library, nurse's office, or empty classroom. Confidentiality must be considered foremost in all situations and will be discussed in detail later in this chapter. Since the majority of school counselors do have their office and playroom as one and the same, it will be approached from that standpoint in this section. While it is important that the school counselor's office be accessible to all students, privacy for the purposes of confidentiality is also a concern. For this reason, the school counselor's office should never be next door to the principal's office or too near an all-purpose room (lunchroom or gym). This proximity could damage the relationship between the students and the counselor, as well as threaten confidentiality or even the appearance thereof. Well-meaning teachers or staff may question students as to why they were visiting the counselor's office, which places students in an uncomfortable situation. One of the problems with being too close to these areas is that they are in full view of the student body, teachers, principal, staff, and visitors. Being close to the principal's office can create anxiety for the students, as they may associate the counselor with discipline.

Phone calls and conferences with students and parents, teachers and staff must be protected so that nothing can be overheard. Any notes or files must be in locked file cabinets. This responsibility is on the shoulders of the counselor, and this is not the time to be timid with an administrator about asking for a private, low or no noise level, confidential location.

Landreth (1991) describes the ideal playroom size as about 150 to 200 square feet, with soundproof walls. This is large enough for the child to be near the counselor without being too large. He also suggests that the room be durable and easy to clean, with tile floors and walls that are washable. With adequate funding, child-sized furniture and running water can also be very conducive to the play environment. Again, assuming the counselor's playroom is in his or her office, the counselor may use a cabinet, a desk, a curtain, or even a portable dry erase board to divide the area, creating a play space.

The toys for the playroom serve as the counselor's tools. Landreth (1991) stresses that toys for the playroom or play space, "should be selected, not collected" (p. 117). Landreth also describes in rich detail the categories and specific kinds of toys to include in the playroom. The categories include: real-life toys, such as dolls, puppets, cars, etc.; acting-out aggressive-release toys, such as guns, knives, alligators, bop bag, toy soldiers, etc.; and toys for creative expression and emotional release, such as blocks, clay, markers, and other art supplies (Landreth, 1991). According to Lomas and Morrison (2008), counselors also consider functionality, durability, versatility, cultural responsiveness, and how the toy facilitates the therapeutic process, in selecting toys for the playroom. In the school setting, the choice of toys may be somewhat limited due to the heightened awareness of school violence in recent years. It is therefore recommended that toys such as guns and knives be excluded from the playroom but the school counselor may accommodate for this with other aggressive toys such as puppets, toy soldiers, blocks that can be kicked or thrown, a bop bag, or even a log that they may hit with a hammer. However, children will be creative in their own way to meet this need. They may use their pointing finger or devise a weapon out of blocks, sticks, clay, etc.

Counselors have a tendency to be very creative when it comes to finding a place to work with children in their schools. One counselor shared a renovated janitor's closet with the school nurse, keeping her totebag and sandbox under the bed and a fold-up easel behind the door. Another alternated between the library and the lunchroom, where she used her totebag in a corner area. While these situations are not ideal, according to Landreth (1991) "children can communicate a wide range of messages and feelings with a limited number of toys and materials" (p. 124). Tote bag playrooms are a viable alternative to having a playroom. Landreth (1991) suggests a list of toys that he considers to be "the minimal requirements" for play therapy with children (p. 125).

Funding is a never-ending problem with school districts and, thus, with counselors. There are, however, many ways in which to create your own effective play space. Parent-Teacher Associations are often happy to assist with fundraising for the counselor to purchase toys and materials. Civic organizations that lend themselves to aiding children and churches will often donate money or needed items, with a simple request or presentation from the counselor. Garage sales and resale shops are also good resources for finding play therapy–appropriate toys at a reasonable price.

ETHICAL CONSIDERATIONS IN THE SCHOOL SETTING

School counselors are professionals. As such, they are required to know and understand the ethical standards and codes they are to follow. Counselors must adhere to their ethical codes and use sound professional judgment. Confidentiality, consulting other professionals, knowing when to keep or destroy records, and making it clear when confidentiality cannot be kept is most critical.

Ethics for school counselors present in a precarious way because of the nature of the profession. They work with children who are minors and are challenged daily to accept responsibilities that require thinking in legal and ethical ways. In every decision they must consider the student, parent, teacher, and the rights of the community. School counselors must be aware of their own professional behavior, using ethical codes as a measuring stick to make the best decision for all those involved. The American Counseling Association Code of Ethics and Standards of Practice (American Counseling Association, 2005) and, more specifically, the American School Counselor Association (American School Counselor Association, 2004) are available to consult and follow. It is prudent of counselors in a school setting to familiarize themselves with both of these models.

In her book, *School Counseling Principles Ethics and Law,* Stone (2005) has adapted the ACA practitioner's guide to ethical decision making. She uses the acronym STEPS, which stands for "Solutions to Ethical Problems in Schools" (p. 16). She lists nine sequential steps in this model to which counselors can refer.

1. Define the problem emotionally and intellectually.
2. Apply the ASCA and ACA codes and the law.
3. Consider the students' chronological and developmental levels.
4. Consider the setting, parental rights, and minors' rights.

5. Apply the moral principles.
6. Determine your potential courses of action and their consequences.
7. Evaluate the selected action.
8. Consult.
9. Implement the course of action.

School counselors are advised to educate themselves with this model. According to Stone (2005), STEPS can assist counselors as they "negotiate the nuances of ethical dilemmas arising within an environment significantly different from those found in agency, community, private, or hospital counseling settings." (pp. 16–19).

Getting permission from parents and guardians for group and individual counseling, how many times a student is seen before making a referral, federal and state laws that apply to the school setting, school board policies, reporting abuse, dealing with suicide threats or threats toward another person, negligence, and the counselors' role in a court of law are all things that counselors must have an understanding of and a plan to follow when needed. The counseling code of ethics is the guide for decision making. Familiarity of one's ethical code is not enough to count on; counselors need to be familiar with several codes of ethics. On a daily basis, numerous ethical issues arise in a school setting and must be dealt with case by case. It is of vital importance that school counselors also have sound professional judgment and are skilled in working within their scope of practice. In regards to play therapy, it is important that counselors receive training specific to this area in order to work within their ethical bounds. This training can take place in a graduate program or through continuing education credits at various locations. Unless they have been specifically hired to do so, such as a school-based clinician, it is important that they realize they are providing counseling and not therapy. The majority of certified school counselors are not licensed counselors and even if they are, administrators discourage the use of the word *therapy*, due to perceived liability issues. School counselors therefore, refer to play therapy as "counseling with toys" or "play counseling."

Another misconception regarding school counseling is that there is a specific rule to the number of times students may be seen by school counselors. Unless the school board has a specific policy (and few if any do), there is no such rule. It is therefore up to counselors to decide when it is time to refer out for more long-term or intensive counseling than they are able to provide in the school setting. In rural settings, this may not be an option. Many times school counselors are the only mental health professionals that students and their families have access to. There are many instances of dual relationships in small communities that cannot be avoided. In this case school counselors have to be vigilant in recognizing dual relationships and must have a keen sensitivity to the confidential nature of their counseling relationships.

School counselors are mandated reporters, and as such, they are required by law to report any suspected abuse or neglect to the proper authorities. School counselors must be aware of the mandated reporter laws in their state. It is crucial that school counselors educate themselves specifically about play therapy and any ethical considerations that may arise during play sessions. They must have the training to interpret their students' play and knowledge of how to convey this information as a way to advocate for their students.

RESEARCH POSSIBILITIES

EVALUATING YOUR PLAY THERAPY PROGRAM

Stone and Clark (2001) described school reform as "the business of every member of the school team" (pp. 46–53). In today's data-driven world, it is important for school counselors to provide information from research conducted in evaluating their program and its effectiveness. School counselors are expected to be accountable for their counseling program. By gathering and researching data, professional school counselors can use the results to increase awareness of their stakeholders and strengthen their program. The benefits of ongoing data-driven school counseling to the play therapy program are numerous. First of all, it informs counselors of the effectiveness of their efforts, allowing them to make changes as necessary. Secondly, this information arms school counselors with proof that their programs, and specifically play therapy, are beneficial to students. Lapan and Stanley (2006) from The Missouri Department of Elementary and Secondary Education have developed a program for counselors to use to identify a problem, collect data, and show how to make changes using a specific technique or intervention. It is called PRBE, or Partnership for Results-Based Evaluation. The steps through which PRBE is implemented are: Identify, Describe, Existing date, Analyze, Summarize (IDEAS) (Lapan & Stanley, 2006).

Identify

A topic of importance and a way to work on it should be identified. Common problems in schools are absences, behavior referrals, tardiness, and low grade point averages. The example used earlier in this chapter was absences.

Describe

Use SIMS—students, interventions, measurements, and settings—to describe the situation or problem you are tackling.

For this example, three play therapy groups will be comprised of six students per group. The school counselor will facilitate these groups for eight weeks.

Existing Data

This is data that is readily available in schools through the administrative assistant.

Students for this example will be sixth-graders whose attendance falls below 95 percent from the first quarter of school.

Analyze

Data can be easily analyzed through the use of Excel, computing percentages, means, and standard deviations. Results should be displayed in easy-to-comprehend graphs and charts to present to the principal, counseling coordinator, superintendant, Board of Education, and parents.

The group's attendance from the second quarter will be compared to that of the first quarter, most likely seeing positive results. A follow-up comparison could be made after the third quarter, to see if the benefits are long lasting.

Summarize

Results should be presented in a report or a PowerPoint, demonstrating to your audience the proof of your findings. Be sure to include:

1. Problem Statement—What you did in response to the problem (i.e., used play therapy).
2. Findings—How you plan to use the information to help students and improve your program based on your findings.

Finally, from the example above, compare the amount of money the school district lost in the first quarter—due to absences—to the money saved during the second (and third) quarters. This is just one example of the way PRBE can be used to promote play therapy in schools. Other examples include conducting individual play therapy sessions, or CPRT groups, and measuring behavior referrals before and after.

WORKING WITH SPECIAL POPULATIONS

Cultural competence is crucial for school counselors because the schools are a melting pot of diversity. The use of play in the school setting is an essential tool in connecting with all children. Play exists in every culture and in every population and is a place of connection for all living beings, without any words at all. "Play is the universal expression of children; it can transcend differences in ethnicity, language, or other aspects of culture," thus making it "an extremely effective therapeutic intervention to help heal and resolve children's emotional conflicts and issues" (Drewes, 2005b, p. 72).

DIVERSITY

School counselors must accommodate the increasing number of culturally diverse students by acquiring the knowledge and skills needed to relate to them. Counselors as people approach the world initially from their own paradigm or world view. The awareness of one's beliefs and biases is essential to building a therapeutic relationship with those of other ethnicities or cultures. The diversity of others cannot be understood by the color of their skin or their language alone. The historical and contemporary meanings of their culture and the racism associated with it are equally relevant (Sweeney & Homeyer, 1999).

Diversity in the school setting may include cultural, ethnic, sexual, and socioeconomic diversity, as well as working with students with special needs. Gil (2005) suggested the following principles for becoming a cross-culturally competent and responsible play therapist: building sensitivity, obtaining knowledge responsibly, and developing active competence (pp. 7–10). In the playroom or play space, it is important "that our collection contain as many representations as possible of the world and its diverse and plentiful cultures" (Gil, 2005, p. 21). Often, students from other cultures will experience others using language that is insulting to them or be expected to do a better job because they are from a particular cultural or linguistic group. School counselors must educate themselves and be sensitive to the culture of their students. An example of this includes interpreting the meaning of various symbols according to that student's culture. Drewes (2005a) states, "Cultural differences can also play out in language, social interactions, and methods of child rearing, all of which can easily be misunderstood and cause problems" (p. 63). "As professionals, we need to be alert for whatever we might say that conveys a value judgment" (p. 63). It is our ethical and legal responsibility to gain an understanding of the student's ethnic and cultural background to understand the specific cultural meaning of their play (Drewes, 2005a, pp. 63–64). As play therapists and school counselors, it is highly recommended that school counselors acquire a thorough book on counseling culturally diverse clients to which they can refer to help understand specific cultures, and so on.

SPECIAL EDUCATION

In working with students with special needs, the playroom and materials may also need to be adapted. For children with medical issues, toys representing medical equipment and staff are helpful. One counselor incorporated the use of clay with visually impaired students during an expressive arts guidance activity instead of painting or drawing. Another purchased a TV tray for a student in the playroom who was in a wheelchair and couldn't reach the table as she played with the clay. The school counselor may need to educate the classmates of a student with special needs. Including students in this presentation whenever possible is recommended to empower them and assist with their own grieving or healing process. Classmates have the opportunity to explore their own attitudes and beliefs about disabilities. This can be accomplished through puppet play, bibilotherapy, use of videos and the Internet, metaphoric story telling, and psychodrama. When appropriate, the students may also answer questions that their classmates may ask.

Lomas and Morrison (2008) suggest that counselors, "make minor alterations to their toys to be more inclusive of children with disabilities or even children who have someone in their lives who has a disability." They also suggest that large bandages that can be wrapped around them or toys, eyeglasses, dolls with hearing aids, wheelchairs, walkers, and braces. The room should also be arranged in a way that toys are accessible for children in wheelchairs and with wide spaces for them to move around as necessary. The important part is to plan ahead for the children and then talk with them and their parent about what their specific needs are (p. 7). Counselors have a legal and ethical responsibility "to acquire and to maintain skills and knowledge to work appropriately with clients who have disabilities" (p. 8).

Today's schools, more than ever before, present an array of cultural backgrounds and experiences, resulting in the need for the professional school counselor to be culturally competent. Play is universal and offers a natural avenue to begin working with a culturally diverse child. It is the responsibility of school counselors to be equipped to do so. This includes adapting the playroom and materials as needed as well as having a working knowledge of diverse cultures and any special needs they may encounter. Counselors must also educate themselves about any disabilities that the children they encounter may have and make the needed accommodations for these children. This will allow the children to get the most from their play therapy experience.

SUPERVISION

Finding a supervisor with the necessary expertise can be very difficult in the school setting. The majority of school counselors have not had the training needed to supervise, and many have not had positive experiences while being supervised. Most school counselors are not licensed professional counselors and are therefore not eligible to become Registered Play Therapists (RPT). While being an RPT is not a requirement for supervising play therapy, it is preferred. Allen, Folger, and Pehrsson (2007) state, "It is apparent that traditional supervision models will not consistently meet the needs of supervisors for effective supervision of interns learning to use Play Therapy." They also stress that the traditional models used for supervision, "do not easily cross the barriers of nonverbal clients, projective manipulation of objects, and the adult–child client power differential."

It is equally important, and required in some states, that the supervisor be a certified school counselor. Although generally not required by state licensure law, ethically they need supervision specific to the population they are working with. As previously discussed in this chapter, the culture of the school setting is unique and it is therefore vital that the supervisor have this awareness. The school counselor working toward licensure and RPT certification should seek out someone with both areas of expertise. Even if the school counselor is not seeking licensure, ethically they still need to seek supervision from someone with expertise in working with children and in the school setting. This may be accomplished by employing the expertise of two supervisors. Finding two individuals, one with school counseling certification and another who is an RPT and who are willing to work together, could be more practical. Ultimately, finding a qualified supervisor will be up to the supervisee, and therefore, it will be their responsibility to seek out the best possible supervision.

CONCLUSION

This chapter discussed the varied role of school counselors and how it encompasses many tasks and duties. School counselors' education does not end with a degree or certification but is an ongoing learning process. They are obligated to stay abreast of the current literature and training regarding play therapy techniques and school counseling as well as diversity and ethics. In summary, the following guidelines are suggested for incorporating play therapy into the school setting:

1. Be aware of the unique culture of the school setting.
2. Be the advocate for your school counseling program by educating administrators, teachers, and parents about play therapy.
3. Set up a working playroom, play space, or tote bag playroom.
4. Be ethically aware and competent.
5. Evaluate your play therapy program.
6. Be culturally competent.
7. Seek out supervision.

REFERENCES

Allen, V. B., Folder, W. A., & Pehrsson, D.C. (2007). Reflective process in play therapy: A practical model for supervising counseling students. *Education, 127*(4), 472–479.

Amatea, E. S., & Clark, M. (2005). Changing schools, changing counselors: A qualitative study of school administrators' conceptions of the school counselor role. *Professional School Counseling, 9*(1), 16–27.

American Counseling Association. (2005). *ACA code of ethics.* Alexandria, VA: Author.

American School Counselor Association. (2005). *National standards.* Retrieved October 2008, from the ASCA Web site, http://www.schoolcounselor.org.

Aubrey, R. F. (1982). A house divided: Guidance and counseling in 20th century America. *Personnel and Guidance Journal, 61,* 198–204.

Austin, L. E. (1999). *The counseling primer.* Philadelphia, PA: Accelerated Development Taylor & Francis Group.

Bandura, A. (1977). *Social learning theory.* Englewood Cliffs, NJ: Prentice Hall.

Beck, A. T. (1976). *Cognitive therapy and the emotional disorders.* New York: International Universities Press.

Children's Defense Fund (2005). *The state of Americans' children.* Retrieved November 10, 2008, from http://www.childrensdefense.org.

Drewes, A. A. (2001). Implementing play therapy in the schools. In A. A. Drewes, L. J. Carey, & C. E. Schaefer (Eds.), *School-based play therapy* (pp. 41–81). New York: John Wiley & Sons.

Drewes, A. A. (2005a). Play in selected cultures: Diversity and universality. In E. Gil & A. A. Drewes (Eds.), *Cultural issues in play therapy* (pp. 26–71). New York: Guilford Press.

Drewes, A. A. (2005b). Suggestions and research on multicultural play therapy. In E. Gil & A. A. Drewes (Eds.), *Cultural issues in play therapy* (pp. 72–95). New York: Guilford Press.

Drewes, A. A., Carey, L. J., & Schaefer, C. E. (Eds.). (2001). *School-based play therapy*. New York: John Wiley & Sons.

Ellis, A. E. (1971). *Growth through reason: Verbatim cases in rational-emotive therapy*. Palo Alto, CA: Science and Behavior Books.

Fall, M. (1994). Physical and emotional expression: A combination approach for working with children in the small areas of a school counselor's office. *School Counselor, 42*(1), 73–77.

Gil, E. (2005). *Cultural issues in play therapy*. New York: Guilford Press.

Gysbers, N. C., & Henderson, P. (1988). *Developing and managing your school guidance program*. Alexandria, VA: American Association for Counseling and Development.

Knell, S. (1998). Cognitive-behavioral play therapy. *Journal of Clinical Child Psychology, 27*(1), 25–30.

Kottman, T. (2003). *Partners in play* (2nd ed.). Alexandria, VA: American Counseling Association.

Kottman, T., & Warlick, J. (1990). Adlerian play therapy. *Journal of Humanistic Education and Development, 28*, 125–131.

Landreth, G. (1991). *Play therapy: The art of the relationship*. Bristol, PA: Accelerated Development.

Landreth, G. (1993). Child-centered play therapy. *Elementary School Guidance & Counseling, 28*, 1–17.

Landreth, G. (2002). *Play therapy: The art of the relationship* (2nd ed.). New York: Brunner-Routledge.

Landreth, G., Baggerly, J., & Tyndall-Lind, A. (1999). Beyond adapting adult counseling skills for use with children: The paradigm shift to child-centered play therapy. *The Journal of Individual Psychology, 55*(3), 272–287.

Landreth, G., & Bratton, S. C. (2006). *Child-parent relationship therapy (CPRT): A 10-session filial therapy model*. New York: Routledge Taylor & Francis Group.

Lapan, R., Gysbers, N., & Petroski, G. (2001). Helping seventh graders be safe and successful: A statewide study of the impact of comprehensive guidance and counseling programs. *Journal of Counseling and Development, 79*(3), 320.

Lapan, R., Gysbers, N., & Sun, Y. (1997). The impact of more fully implemented guidance programs on the school experiences of high school students: A statewide evaluation study. *Journal of Counseling & Development, 75*(4), 292–302.

Lapan, R., & Stanley, B. (2006). *Partnership for results-based evaluation*. Presentation for Missouri School Counselors at Jefferson City, MO.

Lomas, G. I., & Morrison, M. O. (2008). Encountering clients with disabilities. *Play Therapy*, 3(4), 6–8.

Miller, P. (2002). *Theories of developmental psychology*. New York: Worth Publishers.

No Child Left Behind. (2002). *Florida department of education*. Retrieved November 11, 2008, from http://www.fldoe.org/nclb/.

O'Conner, K. J. (1991). *The play therapy primer: An Adlerian approach to play therapy* (2nd ed.). Alexandria, VA: American Counseling Association.

Peabody, M. A. (2008). Facts for teachers. *Primary Project Handout from Association for Play Therapy Annual Conference*.

Ray, D., Armstrong, S., Warren, E., & Balkin, R., (2005). Play therapy practices among elementary school counselors. *Professional School Counseling*, 13(1), 79–100.

Ray, D., Bratton, S., Rhine, T., & Jones, L. (2001). The effectiveness of play therapy: Responding to the critics. *International Journal of Play Therapy*, 10, 85–108.

Rogers, C. R. (1961). *On becoming a person: A therapist's view of psychotherapy*. New York: Houghton Mifflin.

Schaefer, C. (2001). Prescriptive play therapy. *International Journal of Play Therapy*, 10(2), 57–73.

Sink, C. A., & Stroh, H. R. (2003). Raising achievement test scores of early elementary school students through comprehensive school counseling programs. *Professional School Counseling*, 6(5), 350–364.

Stone, C. (2005). *School counseling principles: Ethics and law*. Alexandria, VA: American School Counseling Association.

Stone, C. B., & Clark, M. A. (2001). Schools counselors and principals: Partners in support of academic achievement. *National Association of Secondary School Principals Bulletin*, 85(624), 46–53.

Sweeney, D. S., & Homeyer, L. E. (1999). *Group play therapy*. San Francisco: Jossey-Bass.

VanFleet, R. (2005). *Play therapy ideas: Play counseling in schools*. Retrieved October 3, 2008, from http://www.play-therapy.com/ideas-1.4htm.

Wynne, L. S. (September, 2008 mining report). Play therapy in school settings. *September 2008 Mining Report*: Retrieved September 2008, from the Association for Play Therapy web site: http://www.a4pt.org/ps.index.cfm.

Zill, N., & West, J. (2000). Entering kindergarten: A portrait of American children when they begin school. *National Center for Educational Statistics*. Retrieved November 2008 from the U.S. Department of Education: http://nces.ed.gov/pubs2001/2001035.pdb.

CHAPTER 4

Challenges and Barriers to Implementing Play Therapy in Schools

DEE C. RAY

THROUGHOUT THIS BOOK, authors offer the reader rationale for using play therapy in the schools, methods of conducting play therapy, and multiple examples of how play therapy is enacted in the school environment. There is a strong foundation to conclude that play therapy is an effective way of working with students. It would be reasonable to assume that school counselors, social workers, psychologists, and other school-based therapeutic personnel would and could be successful with the implementation of play therapy. And yet, this is not the case. Ray, Armstrong, Warren, and Balkin (2005) reported that among a national sample of school counselors, 62 percent of the participants used play therapy for less than three hours per week. In a statewide study with Texas school counselors, Shen (2008) reported that among the participants, only 36 percent facilitated play therapy in the schools even though close to 73 percent of the sample reported having taken play therapy courses or workshops. Play therapy is not being utilized in the schools to the full extent of its possibilities. This chapter will explore the possible obstacles to implementing play therapy in school settings and will offer suggestions on overcoming some of these barriers.

RESEARCH REGARDING BARRIERS TO PLAY THERAPY

As an instructor of play therapy classes and workshops for over 10 years, I have been honored to teach the principles and practice of play to excited and skillful students. Because I served as a school counselor, I also tried to offer students practical advice on how to implement play therapy in schools. After my first few years of teaching, I began to notice a pattern among several graduate students who completed play therapy training, exhibited enthusiasm for the modality, and demonstrated effective skills in facilitating play therapy. In making contact with them following their training, they would confess that they were not facilitating play therapy in their schools. In order to improve my own teaching, I began to informally survey these former students on reasons for their nonuse of play therapy. Several answers were provided including, "I don't have enough time with students," "My principal won't allow me," "My office is too small," "I need a quicker method of solving problems," and many others. These justifications were usually delivered with a wistful tone indicating sadness that they were not using play therapy. This informal experience led to the more formal investigation of barriers to play therapy conducted by Ray et al. (2005).

Among a sample of 381 elementary school counselors representing every state in the United States, except Alaska, participants reported barriers to their use of play therapy in schools. Results of this survey indicated that more than 73 percent of respondents believed that play therapy is an effective or highly effective tool for elementary school counselors even though most participants had not been trained in play therapy. When asked to identify specific barriers, only 1.6 percent (6 respondents out of 381) identified that the belief that play therapy is not effective was the rationale for not using play therapy in schools. Overall, participants demonstrated a strong support for using play therapy in elementary schools.

Specific barriers to facilitating play therapy in schools were reported as lack of time available with students, lack of training in play therapy, lack of facilities, lack of supplies, time consumed with noncounseling duties, lack of administrative support, and belief that play therapy is not effective (see Table 4.1). Other pertinent findings from this study addressed relationships between the use of play therapy and intervening variables. Counselors who reported counseling students in general more hours per week were significantly more likely to be facilitating play therapy with students. Hence, counselors who facilitate more counseling in schools are more likely to be using play therapy.

Table 4.1
Factors That Limit Play Therapy in Schools

Factor	Percent*
Lack of time available to students	70%
Lack of training in play therapy	63%
Lack of facilities	43%
Lack of supplies	42%
Time consumed with noncounseling duties	40%
Lack of administrative support	17%
Don't believe that play therapy is effective	1.6%

*Percentage of respondents who marked that this factor was a barrier to play therapy

Participants who were formally trained in play therapy (a course in play therapy) were significantly more likely to use play therapy in their schools. And counselors with more years of experience in play therapy were significantly more likely to engage in more hours of play therapy per week. In summary, counselors who are trained in play therapy and have conducted play therapy over a longer period of time are more likely to be using this modality in their schools.

In Shen's (2008) study of school counselors, she surveyed school counselors only in Texas, due to the state's distinction as having the largest number of school counselors and play therapy training programs in the United States. Unlike Ray et al. (2005), Shen extended her survey to both elementary and secondary school counselors, citing literature supporting the use of play therapy with adolescents. For further discussion on the use of play therapy by secondary counselors, see Shen (2008). Shen's findings supported earlier results that elementary school counselors are idealistically supportive of play therapy but do not facilitate play therapy due to lack of training or confidence in their abilities and lack of resources. She also concluded that administrative and teacher support did not appear to be a deciding factor in their use or nonuse of play therapy. Interestingly, Shen found that positive counseling outcomes and convincing empirical data showing the effectiveness of play therapy were deciding factors in the use of play therapy. However, these same factors presented in a negative sense (negative counseling outcomes and lack of empirical data supporting play therapy) were not considerations among counselors who did not use play therapy. Both Ray et al. and Shen presented a picture of characteristics that hinder the use of play therapy in schools.

BARRIERS AND SOLUTIONS

LIMITED TIME WITH CHILDREN

School counselors are consistent in identifying a lack of time spent with children as the primary barrier to facilitating play therapy. School-based mental health professionals cite various duties that prohibit them from offering direct services to children. This specific barrier is cited by both school psychologists and school counselors and serves as a barrier to all direct services, not just play therapy. Curtis, Grier, and Hunley (2004) indicated that school psychologists are restricted by high case-loads. Although the profession of school psychology is moving toward an expansion of services to include direct intervention, specifically individual and group counseling, high ratios of students to psychologists coerce psychologists to continue in an assessment role. In a study of actual practice to preferred practice among school counselors, Scarborough and Culbreth (2008) reported that school counselors spend less time providing intervention to students than engaged in other nonguidance activities. School psychologists are limited by assessment needs and report writing for excessive numbers of students. School counselors cite activities such as hall and bus duty, testing administration, substituting, administrative duties, and clerical tasks as limitations to their time spent with children. This particular barrier to play therapy is systemic in nature and speaks to a much larger problem among school mental health professionals. In its simplest terms, mental health professionals have a difficult time finding time to meet with children and facilitate any kind of counseling.

However, there are some encouraging findings and possible solutions to finding a way to provide counseling services to children. Among school counselors, those who are more experienced are more likely to structure their schedules to provide intervention to students (Scarborough & Culbreth, 2008). This finding indicates that as school counselors gain experience and confidence, they find ways to structure their school counseling programs to provide direct services to students. This conclusion is consistent with play therapy survey results (Ray et al., 2005) reporting school counselors who had engaged in play therapy for a longer number of years were likely to be facilitating more play therapy than those less experienced. There is no clear explanation for the finding that more experienced counselors are doing more counseling. Possible reasons might include that as counselors become more familiar with the school system, they become creative at finding ways to implement counseling within environmental restrictions.

Another possibility is that as counselors gain years of experience, a sense of professional security emerges, allowing greater assertion of principles in their job duties. An alternate hypothesis might be that as counselors become more experienced in facilitating counseling, they develop a sense of self-efficacy manifested in outcome expectancy whereby experience has taught them that they will experience more success with children if they provide counseling interventions. A higher sense of this type of self-efficacy is significantly correlated with the ability to facilitate more preferred duties among school counselors (Scarborough & Culbreth, 2008).

In addition to counselor-related variables, there are external pressures that influence a counselor's ability to provide counseling in the schools. The influence of high-stakes testing has negatively affected the ability of school mental health professionals to provide counseling services to students (Brown, Galassi, & Akos, 2004; Dollarhide & Lemberger, 2006). Teachers are more reluctant to give school mental health professionals access to students during classroom instructional time for counseling (Dollarhide & Lemberger, 2006). Access to counseling can be negatively affected by the time of year. Research has reported that scheduling counseling was more difficult during a standardized testing semester than during the alternate semester (Ray, Henson, Schottelkorb, Brown, & Muro, 2008). Negotiating with teachers to find time that does not interfere with instruction has become an art among some mental health professionals.

Literature has offered some ideas on how to address scheduling issues. Drewes (2001) recommended limiting session lengths to 30 minutes instead of the traditional 50-minute session utilized in clinic and private practice settings. Additionally, practitioners may wish to consider meeting with students on a more intensive basis, such as multiple sessions per week for a shorter session length and for a reduced number of weeks in the school year. Ray et al. (2008) found that 16 sessions held over 8 weeks demonstrated strong positive results, possibly stronger than 16 sessions held over 16 weeks. Landreth (2002) suggested children might receive more benefits in counseling when opting to use an intensive format of more than one session per week due to their developmental level. Intensive short-term counseling allows the play therapist freedom to focus on a smaller number of students at one time, thereby increasing consistency of services and hopefully gaining teacher support. Consistency is improved by the counselor's ability to determine definitive scheduling more accurately for a short time rather than over an entire semester or year. Teacher support is increased due to the defined parameters of the schedule. When teachers realize that this relationship will occur for a defined period of time, they may feel that they are less restricted by frequently having to make academic adjustments for one child.

A final suggestion to address the barrier of available time with students is the use of a prioritizing system in working with children. When faced with an unreasonable counseling caseload, Ray and Schottelkorb (2009) proposed a system of considering certain factors in prioritizing intervention. Factors include severity of problem, appropriateness for group counseling, level of confidentiality that can be assured, and developmental level. In this system, a counselor would meet with high-priority students on an individual basis for a predetermined number of weeks and then assess outcome. If academic/behavioral concerns are ameliorated, play therapy would terminate, and the counselor would move on to the next priority student. The benefit of using such a system in school settings is that if the counselor has terminated prematurely as indicated by a deterioration in the child's behavior, the counselor can resume the play therapy relationship. Clearly, prioritizing children from a triage perspective is not an ideal way to provide play therapy. However, constraints in the school setting might create the need to find ways to provide play therapy that go beyond traditional ways of working.

TRAINING AND CONFIDENCE

Shen (2008) and Ray et al. (2005) both reported that a lack of training was a significant contributor to the lack of play therapy being conducted in schools. Shen further defined lack of training to include a counselor's feeling of incompetence in facilitating play therapy even among counselors who had some training in play therapy. The issue of play therapy education has been discussed widely in the literature, concluding that training is limited and often play therapists operate without adequate training (Cerio, Taggart, & Costa, 1999; Drewes, 2001; Ryan, Gomory, & Lacasse, 2002). Play therapy trainers report that schools are settings in which play therapy would be useful but that school counselors are not adequately prepared to utilize the approach (Cerio et al., 1999).

Although it is commendable that school-based mental health professionals do not engage in a practice for which they are not trained, lack of training must no longer be used as an excuse to limit children's access to an effective developmental approach. Universities across the

United States are increasingly offering play therapy courses. Because research has revealed that more play therapy training leads to the facilitation of more play therapy, a full course in play therapy is recommended. However, with technological advances, school mental health professionals are able to find training in play therapy from many different sources. The Association for Play Therapy (APT; www.a4pt .org) has rapidly increased its membership and is committed to providing training resources for play therapy. On APT's web site, mental health professionals will find a list of universities that offer play therapy programs and courses, a calendar of workshops being held throughout the United States, and online workshops that provide training from basic skills to more advanced topics in play therapy.

FACILITIES AND SUPPLIES

Unlike many talk therapies, play therapy requires certain physical resources that must be available to school-based counselors in order to effectively utilize the modality. Because play is the developmental language of the child, a playroom is designed and filled with materials that help the child speak with clarity. The size of the playroom allows enough space for a child to move freely without becoming overwhelmed with too much space. Landreth (2002) suggests that an ideal playroom be 12 feet by 15 feet. Although this is an ideal size for playrooms, most school-based therapists are restricted in their settings and compromise space for utility. Play therapy can be effective in different sizes of rooms. Essential features of a playroom include shelves for placing toys above the floor and allowing more room for movement and at least some space for free movement. Optimal features include access to water through a sink, noncarpeted floors, and durable wall paint. Again, these are ideal conditions. School-based play therapists can successfully facilitate play in a conference room, bookroom, behind a cafeteria stage, or in a storage portable. School counselors typically are assigned offices, some small and some large. In small spaces, school counselors should be creative with room placement. Shelves can be used to place toys within reach of children and still provide floor space. Desk room might be minimized to create more free space in the office. A conference table might double as a craft table. If a school counselor is one of the fortunate few who is assigned a classroom, dividers/shelves can be used to divide parts of the room. One example is to use bookshelves to divide a classroom into four equal spaces. One space is for a desk area, one space is a play therapy area, one space is a guidance area, and one space is a conference area.

However, many school-based mental health professionals are relegated to moving around a school with no stable base from which to work with children. As mentioned, this lack of permanent space does not need to be a barrier to providing play therapy. A portable playroom can be developed to allow a play therapist to operate out of most spaces. Toys can be stored in large tote bags or large plastic bins, preferably on wheels. For sessions, play therapists lay out toys in an organized way prior to the child's entry. If a play therapist is mobile, there are some key considerations for effective play therapy. The first is the attempt to provide some consistency to the child regarding setting. Even if play therapy is conducted in a borrowed classroom only free for a 30-minute session, the play therapist should aim to provide play therapy for that child in that same classroom for each session. Providing this type of setting consistency to the child will help send a message of safety, thereby improving the effectiveness of play therapy. Yet, if mobility cannot be structured in any way, play therapists are still encouraged to provide play therapy. The child's relationship with the therapist will soon develop a sense of safety that will override the sporadic mobility. Another key, and vital, consideration for the mobile school-based play therapist is confidentiality. The play therapist should ensure the confidentiality of the child by insisting that whatever space is being used only belongs to that child and therapist at that time. If a play therapist is providing play therapy behind a cafeteria stage curtain, the play therapist works with the administrators and custodians to make sure the space is not being used and that other children or staff cannot hear what is going on in session. Both consistency and confidentiality can be achieved in the school environment if the play therapist is persistent and clear about what is needed. In my experience, I have moved from classroom to empty classroom throughout the day to conduct sessions while teachers were at lunch or planning periods. It can be done.

Of course, facilitating play therapy requires play materials. When setting up a playroom for the first time, a play therapist might become overwhelmed by the vast number of different toys and materials, especially if space is limited. Kottman (2003) provides categorization of materials in five general areas, including family/nurturing, scary toys, aggressive toys, expressive toys, and pretend/fantasy toys. This more global approach to selecting materials might be helpful to a new play therapist. Although it is helpful to conceptualize toys categorically in order to design a playroom, it should be noted that effective expressive toys in the playroom are used by children in a multiplicity of different ways. Knives can be used to cut a therapist free for safety while baby bottles can be used to choke a baby doll. A cuddly stuffed bear can be used to suffocate a small cub while a bop bag can be used to hug for an entire session. The successful selection of a toy is confirmed when a play therapist sees that children are using it for varying purposes of expression.

The acquisition of toys might serve as a barrier to some school-based mental health professionals. Shen (2008) reported that over half of the school counselors facilitating play therapy in her study reported paying for play materials personally. This might be a desired approach by some mental health professionals because they can then take materials with them when they leave their positions. Ideally, schools will provide a budget for toys. School counselors are encouraged to request monies for play materials as part of school budgeting, even if another school-based professional will be conducting play therapy. The school's willingness to provide monetary support for a play therapy program demonstrates its commitment to its use. If school budget is not an option, a counselor has other possibilities. A formal request to the school's parent organization (such as the PTA) might be openly supported. Other ideas include asking parents and teachers to donate toys. If a counselor uses this approach, it is advised that a list of specific toys be provided to parents and teachers so there is not an abundance of unneeded toys. If all of these options fail, the play therapist might consider approaching a local business that would be willing to donate funding. Although the amount needed to get a playroom started varies, it can be done quite inexpensively. My first playroom was supplied for approximately $100 with a need for additional resources costing around $50 once per semester.

Administrative and Teacher Support

Surprisingly, research has not demonstrated that administrative or teacher support plays a significant role in the use or nonuse of play therapy. Counselors have even indicated that they do not require the support of teachers for play therapy, only the lack of objection from teachers (Shen, 2008). Yet, anecdotally, school-based professionals will often cite specific incidents wherein administrators or other school staff prohibited the use of play therapy. For this reason, I will address this issue as a barrier to play therapy.

There are several specific steps that can be taken to gain administrative and teacher support for a play therapy program. Most of them involve a play therapist's intentional approach to educating school personnel on the practice of play therapy. But there is an initial step that will pave the way for setting up a play therapy program in a school. The first step in overcoming administrative resistance is carefully choosing a school that will be open to play therapy. Although not true in all areas, there are many states citing a shortage of school counselors and school psychologists, or school districts that are specifically searching for mental health professionals to conduct counseling with children. In such an environment, the play therapist is wise to bring up the use of play therapy at the interview stage of choosing a job. Often, in desperation to be chosen, school-based mental health professionals do not adequately interview the interviewer. The interview period is the time to find out how open an administrator is to supporting a play therapy program. If the administrator is not knowledgeable of play therapy, the interviewee can use this time to briefly educate the administrator or at least to find out the administrator's attitude toward counseling children in general. The interview is the beginning of a fairly important relationship for school-based mental health professionals. Most schools are the kingdoms of the principals. There is a need to choose wisely. The following are additional recommendations to gain support from administrators, teachers, and parents.

Develop a Brief Brochure Explaining Play Therapy.   School counselors have become more knowledgeable regarding the importance of marketing a school counseling program. Marketing play therapy is essential to its acceptance in schools. A brochure should be a brief introduction defining *play therapy* and how it is helpful to students in schools. The brochure should highlight the relationship between play therapy and its effects on academic success for children. The APT web site might be helpful in providing wording to use in such a brochure.

Formally Present the Play Therapy Program.   On the most basic level, the facilitation of play therapy by the school mental health professional requires the cooperation of teachers in scheduling play sessions. Landreth, Ray, and Bratton (2009) proposed that teachers may exhibit resistance to the idea of a child leaving class to "play" if a child is not progressing well academically or if a child has exhibited behavioral problems in the classroom. Starting the academic year with a brief staff development training explaining play therapy, listing its emotional and behavioral benefits, and sharing how the program will be implemented helps to initiate teacher support of the program.

Participate in Every Staff Development Opportunity and Meeting. Just as play therapy is predicated on relationship, the support for play therapy is also built on a positive relationship with staff. A play therapist should request at least five minutes of every staff meeting and preferably a larger amount of time for staff development trainings. During these times, the use of playful activities to help staff develop an appreciation of how play is used will support the use of play therapy with students. Helpful resources for activities are Kottman, Ashby, and Degraaf's (2001) *Adventures in Guidance: How to Integrate Fun into Your Guidance Program* and Ashby, Kottman, and Degraaf's (2008) *Active Interventions for Kids and Teens: Adding Adventures and Fun to Counseling.*

Update Teachers and Administrators with General Progress Reports. To ensure and grow support, play therapists conduct consistent consultations on a monthly basis (approximately every 3 to 5 sessions) with teachers of children in play therapy. Consultations consist of listening to the teacher's concerns, checking in on changes in the child's behavior or emotions, and sharing updated general progress, such as, "In the last few play therapy sessions, Michael has exhibited the same types of anger concerns that you have described in your classroom. He appears to be working toward expressing these feelings positively. Hopefully, this will translate to the classroom within time." Such consultations build the relationship between play therapist and teacher, yet maintain confidentiality. Consultations help the teacher understand the play therapy process and thereby create support for the play therapy program.

Hold Open House for Teachers/Parents in the Playroom. School-based mental health professionals can help garner support by opening up the process of play to teachers, parents, and administrators. One way to start the process is to offer an open house in the playroom. During the open house, toys will be marked and organized by category. There will be a card to explain the need for each category and its purpose in the playroom. Teachers and parents can peruse the toys and pick them up to play. And, of course, free food is essential to all open houses.

SUPPORTING EVIDENCE

On several levels a lack of evidence supporting play therapy in schools can work against its implementation. Extending upon ways to gain administrative support, providing evidence of effectiveness and impact of play therapy is critical to the continuation of a program being approved by the principal. Evidence-based practice is not just a concern in the world of mental health; it is also an approach advocated in the field of education. Principals are often required to provide data justification for programs taking place in their schools. In order for a play therapist to expect support for a play program, collection of data must become a priority as part of delivering the intervention.

The purpose of all mental health professionals in schools is to work toward the academic success of students. The role of school counselors is tied to providing services that will enhance academic achievement. Mental health professionals clearly see the link between mental health services and academic success and progress. Yet, educational specialists often need to be informed about this link in a clear way. Data collection can involve formal procedures of distributing standardized measures to teachers or parents to mark changes in children's attitudes or behaviors. In this case, the use of assessment-gathering instruments provides great opportunity for school counselors and school psychologists to work together. However, the use of such formal procedures might be daunting to the school mental health professional who is overloaded with many other duties. Less formal ways of evaluation can also provide needed and meaningful data to administrators. For example, a play therapist might track discipline referrals to the office for children who are participating in play therapy. A percentage decrease in referrals indicates a percentage increase in instructional time. A play therapist might develop a 5–10 objective question assessment for the teacher to fill out on the child's progress, administering it three to four times throughout the play therapy relationship. Although it is not a standardized instrument, the play therapist can use this assessment to evaluate progress at that particular school and report findings to the principal.

In working in the schools as a consultant-based play therapist, I have incorporated the use of a yearly evaluation report to school administrators and teachers. Typically, I use behavioral instruments completed by teachers on each child prior to and after completion of play therapy. At the end of the year, I provide visual graphs to teachers at each school charting the progress of the students as a group, ensuring individual confidentiality. When teachers see graphic representation of the benefits of play therapy as reported by them, they grow in their belief system about the program.

Beyond local data collection, it is also helpful to keep up with research findings in the field of play therapy. Scholarly findings lend broader credence to the use of play therapy. Again, APT (www.a4pt.org) is a resource for discovering the most current findings in research. Several resources provide data regarding research supporting play therapy such as Bratton, Ray, Rhine, and Jones (2005), who statistically summarize research findings in play therapy, or Landreth, Sweeney, Ray, Homeyer, and Glover (2005), who present a detailed explanation of research to date.

FURTHER CHALLENGES TO PLAY THERAPY IN SCHOOLS

Up to this point, this chapter addressed issues that appear to limit the use of play therapy in school settings. The aforementioned barriers can possibly serve as impasses that stop the use of play therapy altogether. But there are other smaller challenges to the use of play therapy in schools. These challenges may not prohibit play therapy, but they do provide obstacles to providing play therapy in the most effective manner.

CONSISTENCY

Children in play therapy thrive on consistency. Initially, children sporadically explore the playroom and the relationship with the therapist. As they learn they can trust the environment and the therapist, they quickly begin to use the playroom to work toward resolution for their struggles. The school environment can be very chaotic for many children. They are often not treated respectfully in decision-making processes, and many events happen to them, not with them. For example, a child's teacher may be absent, recess is taken away because of forgotten homework, a teacher decides to give an unexpected quiz, or a fire drill takes the place of music class. Although these events are not to be blamed on any one person, they contribute to a feeling of lacking control or mastery over the environment. In my observations of school counselors over many years, I have concluded that school counselors sometimes fall prey to the inconsistencies of school scheduling and focus on crisis. This is exhibited through such behaviors as a school counselor changing the time for seeing a child but not telling the child beforehand, a school counselor leaving for a district meeting called at the last minute and not informing the child that the session would not take place that day, or a school counselor calling in sick but no one tells the children who expected to be seen.

To drive this point home to school counselors in training, I point out the acceptability of these types of behaviors in private practice. If a private practice counselor was sick and decided not to go into work one day, what would happen if she didn't notify her clients and they all showed up? If a private practice counselor decided to switch sessions between clients, what if he did not tell one of them? How much respect is the counselor showing to clients with these types of behaviors? And how long would they stay in business? School practice should not be treated with any less respect to clients simply because it is in a school or because children are "lesser than" compared to clients. If children are to succeed in play therapy, the play therapist needs to provide as much consistency, or at least respect, as possible. Children should be notified when they will not be attending their session. A simple note will suffice, but personal communication is optimal.

Consistency can also be enhanced by a structured, organized system of providing play therapy to children. As previously addressed, a prioritization system in which children are seen for six to eight weeks at a time and then evaluated for the need for further sessions allows the play therapist to conduct a limited number of sessions on a consistent basis. Sporadically providing play therapy on an "as needed" basis is questionable at best and will probably not yield the changes that can be enacted from consistent facilitation of play therapy.

SESSION DISTURBANCE

Just as consistency can be threatened through school culture, so can session privacy. Throughout schools, it is common to interrupt whatever process is taking place. In fact, the only process that appears to receive reverence is mandated standardized testing. Teachers are interrupted in the middle of lessons by the loudspeaker, phone, or children leaving and entering the classroom. This is the common accepted culture in schools, and it extends to play therapy sessions. At the risk of being repetitive, consistency in play therapy is vitally important whether that involves providing expected sessions or ensuring that sessions are not interrupted. When children are interrupted in play sessions, it will often take several minutes for them to recover and refocus. Sometimes they are simply so disrupted by the interruption that they are unable to return to their therapeutic expression. Interruptions interfere with safety. And safety is integral to progress in play therapy.

School-based mental health professionals can limit interruptions with a few simple steps. The first step is to be aware of the environment of the session. Is there an intercom system? Is there a phone? Will a school staff member need the room during the next 30 minutes? Attempting to limit these interferences proactively is the best approach. Second, in developing relationships with teachers, administrators, and clerical staff, play therapists should educate them on the importance of uninterrupted sessions, providing anecdotal stories on how disruptive an interruption is to a child. Third, play therapists can use door signs to indicate when they are in sessions. And finally, school-based play therapists can expect that even if they follow the above steps, they will still be interrupted. When this occurs, play therapists must assertively address the interruption with the interrupter after the session is over. Although this can be awkward, it is the only way to let school staff know that interruptions are serious violations to the children in play therapy.

DAILY SCHEDULING

Scheduling play therapy sessions can be a challenge to school-based play therapists. School mental health professionals enjoy the benefit of having access to a child five days a week for at least six hours each day. Yet, school activities actually limit the child's schedule as to when sessions can take place. Referring back to an earlier barrier to play therapy, scheduling problems can be exacerbated by teachers who are not supportive of the play therapy program. Hence, the first step in successful scheduling is educating teachers on the importance of play therapy and developing positive relationships with teachers to help grow their enthusiasm for play therapy. A common experience for many play therapists is to be told by a teacher that a child cannot come to play because he has been so "bad" today, that he doesn't deserve to play. This type of interaction is often a symptom of teacher frustration with the child and possibly with the play therapy program. One of the best responses I have developed to this situation is to ask to speak to the teacher in the hallway. I use reflection skills to let the teacher know I understand and accept her frustration, and then I assert the need for play therapy. I continue this type of response until the teacher can see the benefit or possibly until the teacher is worn down by my persistence. If this tactic does not work, I will attempt to talk to the teacher when she is calmer and I can be even more assertive about the needs of the child. And finally, if all else fails, I will discuss the teacher with my principal and gain her support for dealing with this teacher on this issue.

Other considerations in scheduling involve the desires and needs of the child. Teachers do not want children taken from instructional time, and children are conflicted when they are taken from activities they enjoy. One general rule of thumb is to not ask a child to choose between play therapy and recess. For many children, this conflict alone causes emotional turmoil. Fortunately, there are times throughout the week that are conducive to scheduling play therapy. Typically those times include specials, such as music, art, computer, and foreign language, when a child is not bothered by missing these areas. When a play therapist has a good relationship with a teacher, the teacher can usually help find an acceptable time that is not disruptive to the child's learning or needs.

TRANSITIONING THE CHILD

Play therapy is an expressive arts therapy whereby emotional expression can quickly escalate in intensity, and sometimes with no verbal warning. Transitioning children in and out of play therapy in schools is a particular concern that most community counselors do not have to consider. In schools, a child might be returning from play therapy to a spelling test, complicated math lesson, or an unhappy teacher. The child has to be ready to immediately focus on the academic world upon entrance into the classroom. When play therapy sessions are intense, this is sometimes difficult for children. The play therapist can provide strategies for the child to help with re-entering the classroom. If a child has experienced a particularly intense session, the play therapist will not allow the child to walk back to the classroom alone. The play therapist might make an excuse to run an errand to another teacher so that he can walk with the child. Or the play therapist might suggest taking the long way back to the child's classroom. When walking with the child, the play therapist will want to only talk about academic subjects, not initiating any conversation about the play session. Appropriate questions might include, "So, are you ready for your math test tomorrow?" "I heard the third-grade field trip to the zoo is tomorrow. Are you excited?" These questions help direct the child back to a school focus and also provide the play therapist with a verbal indication of whether the child is ready to return to the classroom.

CONCLUSION

As written in this chapter and most likely experienced by readers of this book, there are many barriers and challenges to play therapy in the schools. Some are essentially insurmountable to the play therapy process, such as a lack of training for a school mental health professional. But most barriers can be addressed in creative and assertive ways that will allow school-based play therapists to implement play therapy in their school settings. The lack of mental health as a priority in schools threatens professionals' access to students to provide direct services. According to research, this is the primary concern of both school counselors and school psychologists. Further barriers, such as facilities and resources, require the creativity of the play therapist in learning how to work within school restrictions to acquire space and materials. Additionally, securing support from administrators, teachers, and parents allows the school-based play therapist to have more options regarding resources and scheduling.

Overcoming the barriers and challenges to play therapy is daunting for the school-based mental health professional. The belief that play therapy is the most effective developmentally appropriate intervention for children is the driving force behind the call for school-based play therapists to be assertive, creative, organized, and playful. Play therapists in schools will need to define themselves as play therapists, school professionals, researchers, and mental health advocates. Clear definition of the role of play therapy and the role of the play therapists in schools will help gather support among other school professionals so that barriers can be eradicated.

REFERENCES

Ashby, J., Kottman, T., & Degraaf, D. (2008). Active interventions for kids and teens: Adding adventures and fun to counseling. Alexandria, VA: American Counseling Association.

Bratton, S., Ray, D., Rhine, T., & Jones, L. (2005). The efficacy of play therapy with children: A meta-analytic review of treatment outcomes. *Professional Psychology: Research and Practice, 36*, 376–390.

Brown, D., Galassi, J. P., & Akos, P. (2004). School counselors' perceptions of the impact of high-stakes testing. *Professional School Counseling, 8*(1), 31–39.

Cerio, J., Taggart, T., & Costa, L. (1999). Play therapy training practices for school counselors: Results of a national survey. *Journal for the Professional Counselor, 14*(1), 57–67.

Curtis, M., Grier, J., & Hunley, S. (2004). The changing face of school psychology: Trends in data and projections for the future. *School Psychology Review, 33*(1), 49–66.

Dollarhide, C. T., & Lemberger, M. E. (2006). "No child left behind": Implications for school counselors. *Professional School Counseling, 9*(4), 295–304.

Drewes, A. (2001). The possibilities and challenges in using play therapy in schools. In A. Drewes, L. Carey, & C. Schaefer (Eds.), *School-based play therapy* (pp. 41–61). New York: John Wiley & Sons.

Kottman, T. (2003). *Partners in play: An Adlerian approach to play therapy.* Alexandria, VA: American Counseling Association.

Kottman, T., Ashby, J., & Degraaf, D. (2001). *Adventures in guidance: How to integrate fun into your guidance program.* Alexandria, VA: American Counseling Association.

Landreth, G. (2002). *Play therapy: The art of the relationship* (2nd ed.). New York: Brunner-Routledge.

Landreth, G., Ray, D., & Bratton, S. (2009). Play therapy in elementary schools. *Psychology in the Schools, 46*(3), 281–289.

Landreth, G., Sweeney, D., Ray, D., Homeyer, L., & Glover, G. (2005). *Play therapy interventions with children's problems.* Lanham, MD: Jason Aronson.

Ray, D., Armstrong, S., Warren, S., & Balkin, R. (2005). Play therapy practices among elementary school counselors. *Professional School Counseling, 8*(4), 360–365.

Ray, D., Henson, R., Schottelkorb, A., Brown, A., & Muro, J. (2008). Effect of short- and long-term play therapy services on teacher-child relationship stress. *Psychology in the Schools, 45*(10), 994–1009.

Ray, D., & Schottelkorb, A. (2009). Practical person-centered theory application in the schools. In A. Vernon & T. Kottman (Eds.), *Counseling theories: Practical applications with children and adolescents in school settings* (pp. 1–45). Denver, CO: Love.

Ryan, S., Gomory, T., & Lacasse, J. (2002). Who are we? Examining the results of the Association for Play Therapy membership survey. *International Journal of Play Therapy, 11*(2), 11–41.

Scarborough, J., & Culbreth, J. (2008). Examining discrepancies between actual and preferred practice of school counselors. *Journal of Counseling & Development, 86*(4), 446–459.

Shen, Y. (2008). Reasons for school counselors' use or nonuse of play therapy: An exploratory study. *Journal of Creativity in Mental Health, 3*(1), 30–43.

PART III

PLAY-BASED ASSESSMENTS

CHAPTER 5

Using Play Therapy Assessment in an Elementary and Intermediate School Setting

MARY MAY SCHMIDT

INTRODUCTION

Any school-based assessment, whether it is time limited for a specific purpose or ongoing, is an inescapable feature of education. Assessment occurs daily within the classroom as children work through the curricula. Teachers monitor growth using multidimensional curriculum tools such as Rubrics to measure acquisition of readiness skills and then the academic skills themselves. When learning is not occurring at the hoped-for rate, staff teams, often called Child Study Teams, meet to suggest and design individualized remediation models. Sometimes, the interference with learning is related to social-emotional-behavioral problems of the target child, the child in his or her classroom setting, and/or the child in his or her family. The tools of play therapy can be a more informative venue than that of typical social-emotional assessment tools. The principles and techniques of play assessment are widely applicable and developmentally appropriate to use to observe the target child across multiple settings in the elementary school, including the playground; to assist the Child Study Team in developing recommendations for remediation; for more formal processes such as developing a functional behavioral assessment and a Behavior Intervention Plan, a school intervention plan (now called Academic Intervention Services), a Section 504 Plan, or for developing a Committee on

Special Education Individualized Education Plan. The focus of this chapter will be on using a play assessment process for the Committee on Special Education (CSE) because these evaluations are the most comprehensive of the school-based assessments.

EVALUATIONS

An evaluation through the Committee on Special Education is multi-faceted. It includes ability measures, achievement measures, a review of the child's academic history, information about the child's health and physical development, and a social history interview with the parents. Other evaluations would be included as they relate to the referring question, or expanded evaluations when new hypotheses are raised by observations during testing, a classroom observation, and an assessment of the child's social and emotional functioning.

Play can be used as a primary source of information in several areas of the CSE evaluation: the classroom observation, the social-emotional assessment, and, borrowing from the filial play therapy model, a parent-child play-based interview. Play provides insight into how the child applies his native abilities from a developmental point of view.

The Committee on Special Education team approach is important from the play assessor's point of view (who may be a school counselor or school psychologist, by job title) because the play assessor can get feedback from, and make recommendations to, all involved staff as well as to the parents. Such collaboration puts these adults in the roles of co-therapists, an active rather than passive role. As a result, these adults feel supported and willing to try something new. For example, a simple system-level intervention might be to reconceptualize the behavior of a child who is "testing the waters." Rather than seeing the behavior as a challenge to the educator's or parent's authority, the behavior may actually be functioning for the child as a means of finding out what is constant from an object relation's point of view. Such a reconceptualization views the child's behavior as trying to connect with what is dependable rather than as trying to challenge and disconnect from what is antagonistic to the child's felt needs.

FORMAL ASSESSMENT

Schools are obligated to provide a free and appropriate education to all children. When parents and teachers have been steadily communicating about a child's strengths and weaknesses, there should be no surprise when the issue of assessment is raised. Sometimes there is resistance to assessment, particularly social-emotional assessment, which can make parents feel insecure in their parenting. Assessment, then, needs to be as comprehensive as possible, to avoid the blame trap of dichotomizing home and school, to be supportive of parents, to work to identify the presenting problem, the salient problem, the plan or method, and the measurement criteria. Assessment also needs to distinguish between the antecedent conditions/behaviors and the precipitating problem behavior using a methodology that measures developmental functioning for the setting. The setting has a powerful impact on behavior. Setting factors can influence the child's behavioral choices within his developmental repertoire.

Formal assessment implies a time-delimited task. Play therapy itself is process-oriented, and assessment within the therapy is ongoing. Both can dovetail nicely when the measures identify behaviors along a developmental grid.

OBSERVATIONS OF PLAY IN NATURALISTIC SETTINGS

Because school psychologists spend most of their time with at-risk children, it is a good practice to go into classrooms or go out to the playground with no particular agenda but to observe play. This refreshes observational skills in distinguishing between normal and at-risk children. In addition, the school psychologist becomes a familiar and approachable person in the school landscape. At a later time in the school year, the school psychologist may need to target a child in that classroom. If so, the school psychologist will want all the children to behave within typical patterns and not put on "party manners" for the unknown adult in the room.

I tend to use a combination of play observations in naturalistic settings (classroom and playground): formal schedules, informal multiple-observer type, and informal single-observer type. For formal observations, I sometimes refer to a comprehensive compilation of play diagnostics entitled *Play Diagnosis and Assessment* (Schaefer, Gitlin, & Sandgrund, 1991). When parents do not appreciate or value their child's social-emotional needs, a formal schedule can be used because of its research base and objectivity.

Also highly informative is the use of multiple observers who have documented behaviors over a relatively long period of time. Multiple observers might include the classroom teacher, a remedial teacher, a speech therapist, or any other professional staff member who works with the child. The gym teacher, the cafeteria aide, and the art teacher can have rich observations because there is less formality in these settings, and these settings can tax a child's ability to self-regulate. By way of contrast, the single observation, typical of many evaluations, is limited in its usefulness because it tends to be a "slice of life," which may not be representative of the total range of behavior salient to the assessment question.

Observations of play in naturalistic settings focus on how the child interacts with the environment and things in the environment, with other children (same age, younger, or older; same or different gender), with adults in the environment, and in environmental events such as predictable daily schedules and unpredictable events such as fire drills. (Special note: a comprehensive understanding of environment would encompass home, school, and community.) Broad-spectrum questions to keep in mind would include the following: How intense is the play? Is there repetition compulsion? Is play focused around a theme, or does play appear random or listless? Is there lack of engagement? How much confidence and mastery is exhibited? Is the child tentative and observing? Does the child seek eye contact with any particular person for acknowledgment, approval, or permission? What affect dominates the play? How interactive is the play? How sustained is the play?

DEVELOPMENTAL FACTORS

The developmental perspective cannot be ignored when observing a child, particularly for the purposes of assessment. The observation should be able to comment on five areas of development: cognitive, language, self-control/regulation, relationships, and self-concept/emotions.

DEVELOPMENTAL PERSPECTIVE ON COGNITIVE SKILLS

The cognitive skills of young school-age children (ages 4 to 6, kindergarten and first grade) lack the ability to distinguish between thoughts and actions. For instance, repetition of a thought may create a memory or an intention that has no truth but confuses, even terrifies, the child. To complicate the problem, the child may not be able to express or modulate his reactions. In addition, the child may not be able to distinguish that his needs (social, emotional, and physical) are separate from those of his family's or of the playgroup to which he temporarily belongs. For example, the observer might note that the child developed a game involving others but only partly explained his rules. As the game proceeds, a second child does something "wrong" and is criticized harshly. The child who invented the game did not distinguish between his thoughts and his action, the verbal explanation. He assumed that the other child thought as he thought and understood as he understood. His confusion and anger may end the game and negatively impact the potential or intention for future plays with the other child. These younger children think simplistically and concretely. They are not expected to be able to plan out a whole game, but only to get it started. Rules of play emerge as the children strive to balance their own needs for control and self-expression with their needs to build consensual agreement. A simple game of categorizing toys, such as parking toy cars together, is likely to be controlled by a single criterion such as size, color, or type. Similarly, linear thinking, hierarchical thinking, and cause and effect will also be simple and concrete. The other child/children in the play will likely have their own criterion for groupings, so although the play of a single child may be simple, the interplay between children as they try to negotiate which criterion rules may not be so simple.

Older children (ages 7–10, grades 2–5) will exhibit more complex schemata in their play, and their games are likely to be planned out to some degree of agreed-upon ending. They will use multiple criteria in their thinking and shift their organization consciously when the original game plan isn't working.

Developmental Perspective on Language Skills

The language skills of children ages 4–6 or 7–10 are closely tied to their cognitive development. Younger children use concrete vocabulary and simple sentence structures and are fascinated with pre-reading language skills such as rhyming words and rhythmic patterns. Pointing and touch counting can amplify their play intentions when vocabulary isn't developed enough to meet the play's need. *Candyland* is a popular game with small children because they can master the cognitive and language demands of this game. Older children are able to be more flexible in their use of language. They can understand the concept of multiple meanings, use some of the tools of supra-linguistics (inference, irony, and figurative language), and integrate language more fluidly. During play, older children might integrate many levels of play such as the physical rhythm of many children who are chanting rhymes or songs while playing an elimination competition of jump rope, hop scotch, Mother May I?, etc. The play observer should note the language content and structure of the child being observed. Is the language similar or different from the other children in this play group, or have these children gravitated toward each other because their ability to communicate and get along is equal but their ages or gender are different? If there are other playgroups of similar membership nearby, is the child in the observed group the same or different from the children in the second group?

There is a nonverbal activity called "Broken Squares," which is a group activity rich with opportunity to observe many kinds of behaviors. Children must work cooperatively to assemble five equal square puzzles. This exercise is successful when a classroom of children are arranged in groups of four or six to thwart the tendency to "own" one of the five puzzles being worked on. This creates an artificial setting where cooperation can emerge as the most effective means of completing the five puzzles. Communication in this exercise is entirely nonverbal. No pointing or taking puzzle pieces is allowed, only sharing or giving. For instance, if child A observes that he has a puzzle piece that would help child B, child A can offer the piece in such a way as to indicate the piece's position in relation to the other pieces in front of child B. The school psychologist can observe many dimensions of behavior between and among children as well as between groups. This particular exercise tends to equalize the high and low achievers in a classroom because individual achievement is not prized. I allow children to self-select group membership. Generally this results in competitive high achievers selecting each other. High achievers tend to not be socialized to cooperate, which puts these students at a disadvantage at this task, whereas other self-selected groups who may not enjoy as much academic success can emerge victorious. Ultimately, everyone wins.

Sometimes, a child's language seems to exceed the expectations based on age and on what is known about cognitive ability. Such a child may be parroting the prose of adults and appear to have advanced language skills but actually have only masked weaker skills. The observer should listen for quality of content, not quantity, and observe how content is strung together. Is the language cohesive? Some speech and language therapists call this phenomenon "cocktail chatter."

Broadly speaking, communication skills emerge on a developmental continuum: engagement play for infants; two-way communication and then shared meaning for toddlers; and beginning logic and emotional thinking for preschoolers. Even though a school-based assessment is concerned with school-age children, school-age children may have developmental delays or regressions to a younger set of play and communication skills. When communication skills lag behind cognitive skills, the child's frustrations to make his needs known often erupt into regressed and/or underdeveloped social skills. For example, a five-year-old boy with severely impaired expressive language is able to communicate a chaotic atmosphere at home by choosing an assortment of devils and vampires to play out family scenes in the sandtray. While in the sandtray, he is able to use his "big boy" voice and practice age-appropriate vocabulary. This same boy is not so willing to learn new games and reverts to his "baby" voice when challenged. What a difference the setting makes! I use a wide variety of sensory motor play activities that may underestimate a child's chronological development, but sensory motor tools are very good at teasing out language and social-emotional abilities by creating a milieu where the child has mastery.

DEVELOPMENTAL PERSPECTIVE ON SELF-CONTROL

Another area to be observed in the assessment process is the child's ability to exercise self-control. For younger children, self-control may be achieved by discovering the behaviors that please adults and performing those behaviors. Smiling and using good manners would receive adult approval and reinforce behaviors that conform to expectations for self-control. Self-control is not a given. Internalized self-control seen in older children requires patience for successive approximations, the ability to tolerate mistakes in oneself and in others, and the ability to detach and observe the self. These complex skills are lifelong learning skills that older children are developing but have not mastered. Children are aided in acquiring these skills by the structures of the environment: classroom routines, teacher intervention, limited resources in the environment that would require sharing and turn taking, and so on. The observer would look for ways in which the child demonstrates social problem-solving skills. Does he share, take turns, negotiate a win-win situation, set goals for himself, and assert himself when being bullied? Is he careful in choosing his words? Is he intrusive, tantruming, and egocentric? Is he fearful and insecure in his abilities to self-regulate? If so, he may be the bully, or he may retreat into solitude. Both roles, acting out or withdrawing, would protect him from having his felt deficiencies discovered.

DEVELOPMENTAL PERSPECTIVE ON RELATIONSHIPS

Related to issues of self-control are the issues of relationships. Children in both elementary and intermediate grades tend to gravitate toward children of the same gender. Children of the same gender are a mirror and a measuring stick for self-concept. Children form friendships and experiment with likes and dislikes. Their personalities expand with a growing sense of humor and wider interests. Younger children may identify a few friends, some absolute likes and dislikes, or a magnanimous love of all living things. Older children identify loyalties to best friends and begin to differentiate among friends based on common interests. Some friendships may be tied to settings or activities such as Little League or Cub Scouts. The observer will need to identify at least the important relationships that a child has. Are the relationships two-way and equally respectful relationships, or is there a greater need/dependency felt by one of the children in the relationship? If so, what is the role of the target child? Does the target child repeat a pattern in his other relationships? What if the child gravitates toward relationships with children of the opposite gender or of another age group, or of another qualifier? If these differences exclude other relationships, the observer would need to generate a hypothesis about the link. Perhaps the child is attracted to children of similar cognitive or language abilities, similar abilities to self-regulate or similar levels of self-concept. Precocious attractions to friends of the opposite gender may reflect a familial dynamic for which the friendship is intended to compensate.

During the Social History phase of the CSE evaluation, parents can provide information about the social functioning of the child within the family and within the community. If the child's social functioning has deteriorated in one or more of the three primary environments—home, school, or community—the interview needs to discern possible triggers and the ways parents have identified as successful interventions.

DEVELOPMENTAL PERSPECTIVE ON SELF-CONCEPT AND EMOTION

Finally, the observer must be concerned about issues of self-concept and of emotion. Self-concept and emotional development for younger and older children are intimately tied to self-control and self-regulation. Younger children depend more on externally imposed controls; older children are learning to internalize those controls and experiment with their own. When a child gains control over strong and frightening impulses, he gains self-esteem. A child with a healthy self-concept is able to risk, to initiate, to have considered opinions, to enjoy the company of others, to take in alternate points of view, to laugh at himself, to expect to be respected, to use appropriate means to express negative emotion, to freely access his imagination, and so on. Such a child is able to identify a self-regulated state as a happy one. Does the child being observed have these qualities?

Observations in naturalistic settings should address all five of these areas whether for young children or older children. Each of the five areas interacts dynamically with the other four; and to complicate the observation for evaluation, the naturalistic setting itself, whether it is the classroom or the playground, can change rapidly. How do setting changes affect the target child? Can the child adapt to fire drills or transition to different activities? Varying chunks of time across the setting and across the school day during the observation may involve a different constellation of actors within the observation, thus effecting dynamics but enriching the total observation.

USE OF RECORDS

Another source of observations coming out of naturalistic settings is discipline records. Discipline records presuppose that behaviors are negative. Most children do not behave so far from expectations that they have discipline records. But, for some, where such records exist, it is appropriate to include discipline reports as part of the multiple-observer method of gathering information. An analysis of these records would hope to quantify and qualify answers to these questions. What is the behavior? What are the triggers? Are triggers related to the time of day or to the degree of structure and adult supervision? Is behavior recent and time limited, or is behavior cyclical or over long periods of time? What function does the behavior serve for the child? The benefit of these records is that they broaden the scope of multiple observers and can help establish a longitudinal pattern if one exists.

The downside of discipline records is the problem of weighting them. The degree of objectivity in the discipline record is an unknown. Discipline records are often written in the heat of the moment, when the staff member or bus driver expects behavioral conformity now (a behavioral product) rather than teaching in a child-centered way to achieve internalized behaviors (a behavioral process).

FORMAL AND INFORMAL OBSERVATIONS OF PLAY IN THE PLAYROOM

Observations of play in the playroom are more controlled than in the classroom or on the playground. These sessions are individual as opposed to whole group and combine directive (formal) and nondirective (informal) play. In the playroom, the same developmental considerations apply as in naturalistic settings. When play is nondirective, the therapist can trust that the child will gravitate toward materials that are developmentally appropriate to express the needs of the child. When play is directive, the play therapist must choose developmentally appropriate materials; and the materials themselves may have structure, such as games.

Here, choices as to whether to use one or both directive and nondirective play or which to choose as a starting point depend upon what you already know or hypothesize about the child. Generally, I allow the child to explore the playroom first. There are games, toys, art supplies, puppets, and a sandtray with a generous supply of miniatures. The child's tentative and exploratory touch gives witness to the child's movement into sacred space. The child reacts with amazement that such a space is just for him and comes with a listening adult—amazingly—just for him. This is the starting point.

Some children can initiate their own play, while others are tentative and seek some direction. Some children invite the play therapist to join in, and some do not. When play is nondirective and the therapist is not invited to join the child, the therapist must be especially careful about arriving at any hypothesis too soon. The relationship between the child and the therapist is just beginning, and trust has not been established. Multiple observations over time increase the probability of accurate assessment because initial play may be guarded and stereotypical or may be testing the therapist and the setting. Drawing any hypothesis based upon one nondirective play observation risks too many confounds. But, for CSE evaluations, time is an important factor, as there are established time limits for the CSE process. It may not be possible to use a nondirective approach. Competing with assessment time constraints, it has also been my experience that children with deeper needs who are not willing or able to directly verbalize those needs are drawn to nondirective and nonverbal materials in the playroom, especially the sandtray.

Children do not need much introduction to sand play. They take to sand play quite naturally because of its familiarity, and this tool provides projective hypothesis material at least as rich as projective drawing techniques, which still requires the directive to draw. (The same child might be somewhat guarded if asked to draw a house, a tree, and a person. The context might seem artificial, and the elicited drawings may be very guarded and stereotypical.)

I recently used the sandtray technique with a 6-year-old girl who was caught between angry parents in a 4-year-long custody battle. Both her needs and her distrust were great. Her first attempt in the sand was a single line of animals, domesticated and wild, all facing her from the back of the sandtray. The animals were not perfectly divided by type, but the effort to do so was clear. Something about the lineup did not please her, so she scooped them all up and buried them in a common grave, brushed off her hands, and stomped out. Subsequent sandtrays also included burying and unburying with a general lack of organizing principles and a final common grave. As she became more trusting, she added subvocalizations that indicated her frustration and disgust and finally vocalizations of her confusion and distrust. During this period, to test my sincerity with her, she asked me to engage in a guessing game about which animal was buried or where. She always controlled the length of time she was willing to stay in my office, and I allowed her that control. Control was an important issue for her. The verbalizations came when she was satisfied with her audience: me.

Directive play in assessment often includes the use of games that have rules to follow or the use of projectives with gamelike attributes. A popular nontherapeutic game such as *Connect Four* is useful in assessing a child's ability to plan, anticipate, learn from experience, shift back and forth between two strategies (block the opponent and win), handle frustration, mediate social anxiety through the practice of game-controlled interaction, and so on. I sometimes end a testing session with a few rounds of *Connect Four*. The child feels rewarded for good effort, and I get to see how the child applies his abilities across the developmental schemata.

Play dovetails very nicely with formal social-emotional assessment tools, especially in poverty of expression versus richness of expression, themes, and developmentally appropriate tasks. *The Story Telling Card Game*, a game developed by Dr. Richard Gardner (1988), is similar to the Children's Thematic Apperception Test. The gamelike qualities include a spinner that lands on a space that asks the child to choose a setting card from a list of three, dice that indicate the number of people that can be chosen for the story, and chips that can be lost or accumulated.

Several years ago, I used this game to assess an 8-year-old boy whom I thought I knew quite well, but who often surprised me, too. By the time of his CSE evaluation, he had alienated every child in his class, had pressured speech with a great deal of interesting content, behaved impulsively and sometimes angrily, but who could have satisfying conversations with adults and who clearly sought that attention. Self-concept scales did not show at-risk or significant perceptions about himself. Ability and achievement testing showed him to be above average, but formal testing could not have tapped the creativity that I was about to observe. We had played several rounds of *The Story Telling Card Game* when he selected a setting card picturing a stage. He rolled a high number on the dice, but he negotiated the chance to use all the people in the game. He put all of the children on the stage and all of the adults in the audience. He said that "this was a National Geographic Special Performance at the famous Ford Theatre." Then, he spontaneously created and acted out a song-and-dance number. Not only had he integrated high levels of all the developmental issues, but he also intimated the seriousness of adults failing to pay attention to children—to him. "President Lincoln was shot at the Ford Theatre," he said at the end.

For the most part, play therapy observations dovetail very nicely with formal projective tools and self-concept rating scales used as part of the holistic evaluation for the Committee on Special Education. In the above example, play surpassed those instruments in getting to the heart of this child's need.

ONGOING ASSESSMENT

In 1993, I developed a checklist of desired behaviors (constructs) to help me track the themes that the children within a group were processing at any given time within the school year (see Figure 5.1). The checklist spanned cognitive, behavioral, and emotional constructs. I checked off constructs as they were incorporated into each session. For instance, did we focus on social problem solving? The accompanying notes would address who initiated the topic, what comments were made, and by whom? The checklist helped flesh out my notes enabling me to focus more on dynamics within the group and on individual development than on topics raised spontaneously by the children. At the end of the year, each child was given a blank checklist and asked to check off each topic/behavior that he recalls addressing in counseling during the year and check each one again if he tried to practice that behavior outside counseling. One year, a highly involved boy reviewed the list and said, "Mrs. Schmidt, you don't have anything about alcohol and drug abuse.

Check all that apply to *you*. Place a second check next to the skills you tried outside group.

This year, I learned about:

☐☐ Controlling stress
☐☐ Taking turns
☐☐ Finding someone to help me
☐☐ Apologizing
☐☐ Being responsible for my words and actions
☐☐ Making the best possible choices
☐☐ Helping friends do the right thing
☐☐ Listening
☐☐ Finding more than one way to look at and solve a problem
☐☐ Staying out of my parents' problems
☐☐ Cooperating
☐☐ Not giving up
☐☐ Saying comforting things to a sad friend
☐☐ Being loyal
☐☐ Trying something new
☐☐ Good sportsmanship
☐☐ Drug and alcohol education (Thor's contribution*)

This year, I feel:

☐☐ More trust
☐☐ Better about myself
☐☐ Less lonely
☐☐ Respected by my group members
☐☐ Less hurt by teasing
☐☐ More patient
☐☐ Capable
☐☐ Less afraid
☐☐ More tolerant of people I don't like

I can name _____ different feelings and emotions.
My group was (too big, too small, just right) for me.

*Written parent consent received to use this student's name.

Figure 5.1 Student evaluation of counseling

Source: Mrs. Schmidt's Smiling Through Playroom © all rights reserved by Mary May Schmidt.

We talked about that a lot." Children can be keen observers of the school psychologist, too.

I compiled the student data collected from this checklist for three consecutive years. Granted, a post-test-only design given to children struggling with a host of developmental issues has more confounds than can be counted but it is important to note that all constructs, measured in percentiles, grew consistently in years two and three as compared to the baseline year and the previous year. In other words, children reported greater and greater awareness of their own self-concept as measured by the cognitive, behavioral, and emotional constructs on the checklist, both in their self-concept in the group and in their efforts to generalize those constructs outside the group. If program success can be measured from the child's point of view, this technique has given me some important insights.

CRITERIA FOR DETERMINING INDIVIDUAL OR GROUP TREATMENT

Once the formal assessment is completed and goals are identified, how will treatment be expressed? Most children have social and emotional needs that are best served in a group setting. The group functions as a microcosm of family and social relationships. As group cohesion increases, children can safely experiment with social skills that they can take back with them into the settings where the problems had originated and into new settings, too.

Groups are organized around my philosophy that elementary-aged children need to develop friendships with others of the same age and gender. Age and gender are important aspects of self-concept. In addition, from a child's point of view, most problems "feel" about the same: lonely, sad, confusing, and so on. From a feeling perspective, empathy is learned, practiced, and valued as a means of understanding the self and others. Many diverse counseling goals across group members can be reached through such mutual understanding.

The difficult aspects of working with a group are the speed at which children interact and alter their relationships and their beliefs. For each child and for each dyad in the group, the multidimensional developmental model needs to be tracked. The checklist helps make tracking more efficient. For example, in a kindergarten boys group, I have used a game that emphasizes social problem-solving skills. I give the player one chip for each solution to a problem. When that player has exhausted his repertoire, I give other players a chance to make suggestions that have not yet been given and they, too, can earn chips. This particular group consisted of a boy with Attention Deficit with Hyperactivity Disorder (ADHD), at least average ability, and many socio-economic advantages; a developmentally delayed boy; and an angry boy with probably average ability. The angry boy could generate a single and passive solution, "tell a grown-up." The ADHD boy could also only generate simple solutions to social problems. The developmentally delayed boy did an above average job generating solutions that he could initiate, sometimes generating five or six alternatives. This example illustrates the need to be sensitive to all the developmental factors because all aspects of development are not necessarily evenly developed within a given child. In this case, each boy became aware of a shift in each other's status. An equalizing effect in their relationships had taken place. Subsequent sessions with this group showed increased camaraderie and increased tolerance for frustration.

When individual counseling is appropriate, it may be a precursor to readying a child to join an established group or to support a child who has needs beyond the scope of the group. A multiply traumatized child would need individual counseling as an adjunct to group counseling or as a sole service. The special needs of the child always influence the mode of intervention: directive play, nondirective play, with or without talk therapy.

CORRECTIVE EMOTIONAL EXPERIENCES

Corrective emotional experiences are experiences that work to undo wounding and to build self-concept. They are immediately recognized by the child who flushes with pleasure. Because of the immediacy of the experience, the insight need not be overanalyzed, only acknowledged (perhaps by a shared smile) and referenced in the notes. Over the course of a school year, the experiences for that child may require repetition and/or stepwise growth.

Corrective emotional experiences can impact a wide variety of deficits such as moral development, which depends upon emotional development, and emotional competencies, like any other developmental competency, may be delayed due to intrusive and traumatic events or repeated events that distort a child's worldview. If a child's sense of security and attachment are disrupted, the child's ability to trust in himself will be effected, and thus, so will his ability to trust others, develop social relationships, and so on. Additionally, some behavior problems, such as Attention Deficit with Hyperactivity Disorder, interfere with emotional development because the child is unable to tune into the cues of communication, both verbal and nonverbal. The power of corrective emotional experiences can mediate some behavior problems because of the intense attention that the child gives to these experiences. More than all other aspects of a child's educational program, play therapy must be especially sensitive to the child's capacity to tune in. Assessment and programming for emotional development lay the foundation for moral development and a happy school experience.

CONCLUSION

Play is tightly tied to developmental theories for assessment and to the projective hypothesis for insight and is applied to the uniqueness of the child. It is a very effective modality for time delimited assessment and for ongoing, or process-oriented, assessment for individuals and for groups. It fits very naturally into the school setting. The corrective emotional experiences that are born of the process help children learn to accept and tolerate each other's differences, recognize the universality of their own experiences, develop friendships, manage stress, and prepare for life. These are experiences of guided hope expressed in laughter and made possible through breadth and depth assessment to feed the whole child.

REFERENCES

Developmental Screening. www.CDC.gov/actearly (also 1–800-CDC-INFO). Gardner, R. (1988). *The story telling card game*. Cresskill, NJ: Creative Therapeutics.

Schaefer, C., Gitlin, K., & Sandgrund, A. (1991). *Play diagnosis and assessment*. New York: John Wiley & Sons.

Shelov, S. P., & Hannemann, R. E. (1994). Developmental checklists—Birth to age five. Adapted by the First Look and the Early Direction Center. *The American Academy of Pediatrics: Caring for your baby and young child—Birth to age five: The complete and authoritative guide*. New York: Bantam Doubleday Dell. Call the ECDC at 315–443–444 or 1–800–962–5488 or email at Ecdc@-sued.syr.edu.

GAME SOURCES

Childswork Childsplay. 135 Dupont Street, P.O. Box 760, Plainview, NY 11803–0760. Call 800–962–141 or www.childswork.com.

WPS Creative Therapy Store. 12031 Wilshire Boulevard, Los Angeles, CA 90025–1251. Call 800–648–8857.

CHAPTER 6

Transdisciplinary Play-Based Assessment and Intervention in the Primary Years

TONI LINDER and
BRITTNEY BIXBY

PLAY ASSESSMENT IS traditionally thought of as an approach for examining the inner emotional world of a child. Emotional issues, however, are often interwoven with other developmental and/or environmental issues. This is particularly true in school situations, where positive social skills and successful learning require the ability to conceptualize, comprehend language and communicate effectively, regulate sensory input and emotions, plan and solve problems, and engage with others physically, mentally, and emotionally. Because biology, health, social history, and development are all intertwined, the arenas of medicine, psychology, mental health, and education need to be integrated in order to obtain the best overall understanding of the child (Foley & Hochman, 2008). Examining "pieces" of the child can lead to fragmented rather than holistic understanding of the child's functioning.

Transdisciplinary Play-Based Assessment (TPBA-2) (Linder, 2000; 2008a; 2008b) is a play assessment that goes beyond looking at the child's social and emotional development to examine the relationships among all areas of development that are influencing the child's overall functioning. TPBA-2 is a strengths-based, holistic, functional approach to examining the developmental status of a child from one month to six years of age. It is also used with older children who are functioning within this age range. As a comprehensive examination of all areas of development, it is used for assessment of children with many different types of risk, including social, biological, developmental, and environmental (Linder, 2000; Linder, Linas, & Stokka, 2008). TPBA-2 is used for a variety of reasons in the schools, including: 1) determination of eligibility for special education or other services; 2) identification of the type of services the child and family need; 3) development of intervention plans, such as Individualized Family Service Plans (IFSPs) or Individualized Education Plans (IEPs); 4) evaluation of a child's progress within a program or as a result of intervention, and 5) determination of strategies to try in Response to Intervention (RTI) (Linder, 2008c). Using TPBA-2 for RTI will be discussed later in the chapter. Transdisciplinary Play-Based Intervention (TPBI-2) builds upon TPBA and provides alternative approaches for integrating interpersonal and environmental strategies into home, school, and/or individual therapy.

Transdisciplinary Play-Based Assessment-2 is a team process, with professionals from various disciplines along with family members examining the child's functioning across different environments, including home, school, and community. TPBA-2 is a multistep process that combines information about the child from multiple sources in order to determine the child's functioning levels, interaction patterns, developmental concerns and potential contributing factors, and appropriate approaches for interpersonal and environmental interventions. The steps of the process include:

1. obtaining preliminary information from parents and/or caregivers;
2. planning with the TPBA team for the assessment observations;
3. conducting the play session, while team members use TPBA developmental guidelines to observe and take notes;
4. analyzing the observation data using TPBA guidelines, age tables, and rating forms;
5. having a team discussion to integrate and interpret all information obtained;
6. sharing findings and recommendations with family members; and
7. planning treatment or services as appropriate.

OBTAINING PRELIMINARY INFORMATION

The first step in the TPBA-2 process is obtaining preliminary information from family members to help determine strengths and risk factors.

Family members, teachers, and other caregivers also provide information on how difficult various daily routines are for the child and/or caregivers, give input on how they perceive the child's overall functioning, provide information on favorite types of play and activities, and indicate what they see as next steps for the child. A comprehensive social and developmental Child and Family History Questionnaire (Petersen-Smith & Linder, 2008), the Routines Rating form, and the All About Me Scale (Linder, 2008a) are used to obtain this information. One team member then summarizes this information to share with the team in an assessment-planning meeting.

PLANNING

Prior to the actual assessment, professionals involved in the process meet to determine what the assessment should entail. Professionals on the team include representatives of the various domains to be addressed, including emotional and social, cognitive, communication (including hearing), and sensorimotor development (including vision). School district Child Find teams or other in-district assessment teams often comprise the TPBA team. Other medical, educational, or specialized professionals are included as needed to give a comprehensive picture of the child's functioning. Discussion is held regarding the referral questions and other concerns that may emanate from the preliminary information. Determination is made of what types of observations are needed in addition to a playroom observation to obtain the best picture of the child. In some cases additional academic, behavioral, or other measures may be desired, and planning for the administration of these is done during the planning session as well. In many cases, particularly when the referral comes from a classroom teacher, observations in the classroom will take place prior to the playroom session; and information from observing team member(s) will inform the TPBA planning. The TPBA planning process also involves assignment of roles within the team. In addition to observing and analyzing domain-specific skills and behaviors, one team member functions as the family facilitator and one team member functions as the play facilitator. The process is videotaped for future reference and discussion, which often involves another team member operating the camera.

THE PLAY SESSION

The actual play assessment session(s) takes place in a setting appropriate to the individual child and may involve multiple observations. For example, a school-aged child with behavioral and social issues at school and home may be observed in the classroom, on the playground, in the home environment, and in a playroom setting containing a variety of stimulating toys and materials. The sequence of these observations, as noted previously, will vary depending on the child, the reason for referral, and the need for comparison of behavior across contexts. For very young children or children in homebound education programs, play observation in the home may be all that is needed. The process is flexible to enable the team to obtain sufficient information, especially when the child functions differently across settings. Observation in natural environments is enhanced by observation in a playroom setting that enables the team to arrange materials and situations that elicit a range of responses and behaviors. The child is observed by the team in this setting behind a one-way window, on a closed-circuit television, or in a larger room, with all team members present but unobtrusive.

During the hour to hour-and-a-half play session, the child plays with the play facilitator, family members, siblings, peers, or other caregivers as needed to obtain the necessary information about all areas of development. The family facilitator watches the session with the family and both elicits additional information and provides information about what is happening. The family facilitator also listens and responds to feelings expressed by family members about the child, family relationships, and other relevant issues.

Play facilitation with the child involves a variety of different strategies, some of which differ from traditional play therapy (Linder, Linas, & Stokka, 2008). As in more traditional play assessments, the facilitator observes the child's spontaneous play behaviors, follows the child's lead, and responds to the child's actions and comments. In addition, in TPBA, the play facilitator experiments with interactional and environmental scaffolding to elicit higher levels of performance or a broader range of behaviors. During the play session, the play facilitator and the child engage in a wide range of play activities, depending on the developmental level of the child. These may include dramatic play, manipulative play, gross motor activities, academic and literacy activities, and sensory and functional play. Toys and materials used will vary for each child, depending on developmental abilities, interests, and concerns to be addressed.

ANALYZING THE DATA

Transdisciplinary Play-Based Assessment-2 (Linder, 2008b) contains detailed guidelines to direct observations for each of the four domains.

Within each of these domains, seven subcategories are outlined (see Table 6.1), with specific questions posed for the professionals to answer. Potential strengths also are suggested, along with areas that may be of concern for each subcategory. Each domain also contains detailed age tables that enable professionals to mark skills observed and determine gaps in development, as well as strengths and weaknesses. As many children with developmental challenges show scatter within and across domains, summary forms indicate the child's mode (or where the child's age level falls most frequently). Rating scales that look at functioning rather than age level are also available for each subcategory.

Use of the guidelines and age tables together enable the team to look at specific developmental processes as well as skills. For example, in the emotional and social area there is no age table for Adaptability/Emotional Style, which addresses the child's ability to adjust to new places, people, and activities, among other things. Ability to adapt is not a specifically age-related skill, but rather is a process that children need to be able to function easily in changing environments. Difficulty with such transitions can be a key indicator for regulatory issues and such diagnosis. Examination of key processes is as important as looking at developmental skills. Looking at both enables the team to make more accurate appraisals of what is contributing to the child's behavior, functioning, and abilities or disabilities.

TEAM DISCUSSION

The team discussion after the TPBA (and other observations) integrates information from all sources, including preliminary information; notes from observations in the home, school, or community; data from the TPBA playroom observation; and results of any other testing that was conducted. Comparison of behaviors and skills by various professionals across settings and people is important. If standardized or criterion testing was done, it is important to examine congruity or reasons for differences in varying assessment approaches if these occur. Preliminary ideas for services, therapies, intervention strategies, and other supports also may be part of the discussion.

SHARING FINDINGS

This discussion among the team members and the family is conducted by examining first the child's overall strengths and what the child is

Table 6.1
Domains and Subcategories within TPBA-2

Emotional and Social Domain

Emotional expression

Emotional style/Adaptability

Regulation of emotions and arousal states

Behavioral regulation

Sense of self

Emotional themes in play

Social interactions

Cognitive Development

Attention

Memory

Problem-solving

Social cognition

Complexity of play

Conceptual knowledge

Literacy

Communication Development

Language comprehension

Language production

Pragmatics

Articulation and phonology

Voice and fluency

Oral mechanism

Hearing

Sensorimotor Development

Functions underlying movement

Gross motor activity

Arm and hand use

Motor planning and coordination

Modulation of sensation and its relationship to emotion, activity level, and attention

Sensorimotor contributions to daily life and self-care

Vision

"ready for" next in relation to these strengths. Building on the child's strengths is less intimidating and stressful to parents than discussion of deficits or labels. Findings related to the referral questions also are addressed as the discussion proceeds, with all team members having input. Any additional assessment questions or information that emanated from the assessment process also is discussed as a team.

PLANNING INTERVENTION

In public schools planning for intervention usually takes place in an IEP meeting involving family members, the assessment team, teachers, and school administrators. The meeting has as its purpose: 1) to determine if the child is eligible for special education services; 2) if so, to determine what services will be provided and at what level; 3) to plan who will provide the services and how often; 4) to develop individual objectives for the child; 5) to plan how to monitor progress; and 6) to set a time for re-evaluation of the need for services. Planning for services for a child identified as being eligible for special education services is related specifically to what the school will provide. Outside services are not listed in any written report recommendations, as the school may then legally be required to pay for services. For this reason, school conferences may differ greatly from those held in private clinics or evaluation centers. Recommendations are specifically related to school placement and services to be provided within the school. Suggestions for outside therapies or treatment may be discussed, but recommendations for such do not come directly from the school personnel. This is a particularly "touchy" issue due to the financial constraints of the schools, with the unfortunate consequence that some needed outside services may never be obtained.

USE OF TPBA AND TPBI FOR RTI

Response to Intervention (RTI) is a new element of the Individuals with Disabilities Education Improvement Act (IDEA, 2004). The intent of this portion of the Act is to encourage teachers to try a variety of research-based supports within the classroom before referring a child for an assessment for special education related to a learning disability. A main issue in this process is how to determine what strategies to try. Some school districts send in psychologists or other professionals to observe and give recommendations. The structure of what to observe and how to interpret what is seen is left up to the individual service professionals. For RTI, teachers and other professionals can use the

TPBA-2 guidelines and rating forms in the classroom and in informal social situations to provide holistic information about what may be influencing the child's performance in the classroom.

Transdisciplinary Play-Based Assessment-2 is part of a system that includes Transdisciplinary Play-Based Intervention-2 as well. In the intervention guide, each of the TPBA domains and subcategories has corresponding chapters with research-based ideas for interpersonal and environmental intervention strategies associated with each of the guideline assessment questions. Depending on what is determined through observation of the child's functioning in the classroom, the teacher and school psychologist or other related services professionals may use the TPBI-2 manual as a resource for ideas. Summary Rating forms for each domain and skills lists on domain age tables are used to monitor progress and determine if further assessment is warranted after interventions have been tried for a stated period of time.

The following case study is presented to illustrate the use of the comprehensive TPBA/I process, when RTI strategies have not been successful or when the needs for special education services are probable. Observations in the classroom were combined with a more formal TPBA in order to arrive at a consistent plan for home and school.

CASE ILLUSTRATION

Background Information

John is a $5\frac{1}{2}$-year-old boy who was diagnosed with autism prior to the beginning of the school year and subsequently was placed in an inclusive kindergarten. His teacher referred him for a play assessment 2 months into the school year due to his difficult behaviors in the classroom. John is very disruptive in class, frequently screams, yells, or is physically aggressive toward his peers. John's teacher, Ms. Williams, wants to know if an alternative placement would be more appropriate. If not, she would like some recommendations on how to best help John be successful in her class. John's parents, Joe and Susan, also requested help to alleviate some of his negative behaviors at home.

John's developmental history revealed a typical pregnancy, birth at 39 weeks, and no complications. John was a fussy baby who did not enjoy cuddling, but his health was good and hearing and vision were tested to be within the normal range. Susan reported that John began walking at 14 months and he spoke his first word at 8 months. When

John was 26 months, he could speak in sentences, recite numbers, and say the alphabet; however, his functional communication, including both comprehension and production, has always appeared delayed. Susan reported a family history of allergies and asthma, but John does not appear to suffer from any of these ailments and is not currently taking any medications.

John's favorite activities include playing on the swings, watching TV, and walking his dog. He prefers to have a predictable schedule and can become upset when this schedule is not followed, screaming and hitting people or objects. He calms himself down by going to his room, getting hugs from his parents, or watching TV. John only recently became potty-trained and is still experiencing occasional accidents at night. John's activity level makes it difficult for Susan to take him to public places, such as the grocery store or restaurants, because he runs around and frequently leaves his mother's side. John is currently attending ABC Elementary School in Denver, CO, five days a week, where he receives services from a speech language pathologist and occupational therapist in the classroom. His negative behavior in the classroom escalated recently, leading to the desire for more information about what is contributing to his outbursts and strategies to help him cope more effectively.

Assessment Observations

The Child Find team, consisting of the speech/language pathologist, occupational therapist, school psychologist, and a special educator met to plan the assessment. Information collected from both John's parents and Ms. Williams using the Daily Routines Rating Form, All About Me Questionnaire, Child and Family Health Questionnaire, and informal interviews was reviewed. As several team members had previously observed John in the classroom, their information was included to complete the preliminary information. Observations in the classroom revealed that John frequently left a task in which he was engaged to wander around the room. When he heard loud noises coming from the hallway, John often looked up and walked to the door to investigate where the noise was coming from and what was producing it. He occasionally initiated interactions with his classmates but did not know how to sustain the interaction and quickly lost interest and walked away. John's communication attempts with peers were brief, and he did not appear to have any friends in his class. During transitions between activities, John followed the schedule when visual cues were used but had a difficult time adjusting to the new activity when visual cues were not present. Behavioral outbursts often happened in a group activity when he did not want to relinquish an object or when he was required to stop a preferred activity. At these times, John screamed or became physically aggressive toward his classmates.

During the play assessment, John had a friendly, but detached, demeanor. When he entered the playroom, John said, "Hello," to the professionals and smiled, but then quickly lost interest in the observers and began exploring the room. He separated easily from his mother, moving to investigate a toy telephone that made a variety of funny sounds. Although he appeared interested, it was often difficult to determine John's emotional state due to the monotone quality of his voice and lack of facial expression. At one point John went to the dramatic play area, where he placed food items into a basket. During this time, John was able to follow the play facilitator's directions by placing the fruits in one basket and the vegetables in another basket. John was resistant to transitioning to a new activity but when shown a noninterlocking car puzzle, he sat and matched many of the cars to their appropriate spaces. John was interested in looking at a book that he brought with him but had difficulty sustaining interest in a new book that was presented to him. He became very agitated when the play facilitator sat next to him and attempted to read him the new book. Motoric activities were of more interest. John became very interested in a toy rocket that launched when he stomped on a pad, jumping as hard as he could with both feet onto the toy. He also liked jumping on bubbles and using his right index finger to pop bubbles in the air. His mother reported that what was observed in the play session was typical of his overall play, communication, and behavior at home.

A summary of observations from the Emotional and Social Domain is illustrated in Table 6.2. This chart illustrates how the strengths-based approach is used in TPBA and how John's strengths are then used to develop strategies with a positive approach instead of a deficit model. The implications for areas in need of support are listed in the final column. What John is "ready for" serves as the foundation for planning intervention strategies that will be tried at home and school. Although only shown for one domain, each of the subcategories for the four domains of development are similarly summarized, though not necessarily in chart format. It is important to remember that though this chart summarizes information by domain, a great deal of overlap and cross-disciplinary influence exists.

Table 6.2
Summary of TPBA Observations

Developmental Area	Strengths	Ready for . . .
Emotional and Social		
Emotional expression	Showed happiness by laughing with his mother and anger by yelling "No!" when a favorite toy was taken away.	Expand emotional vocabulary and label own emotions.
Emotional style/ adaptability	Showed pleasure in silly games, gross motor activities, and showing his toys. Tolerated the presence of others.	Increase pleasure interacting with others and decrease difficulty with changes in his routine and transitions from one activity to another.
Regulation of emotions and arousal states	Self-calmed by separating himself from others. Sometimes verbally stated he was upset.	Increase regulation when transitioning from one emotional state to another.
Behavioral regulation	Understood rules and complied with his mother's requests when consistent with his expectations.	Use visual cues and verbal preparation with John's schedule. Expand understanding of socially acceptable behaviors in different situations.
Sense of self	Knew own and others' toys. Asked for help to complete a task.	Choose more novel toys. Accept adult direction.
Emotional themes in play	Enjoyed dramatic play related to familiar activities.	Expand play themes and range of emotions during play. Respond to others' emotions in play.
Social interactions	Aware of others' change of emotion. Knows routine social interactions in familiar play sequence.	Expand variety of interactions with others in play. Learn appropriate responses to others' emotions.

SUMMARY OF KEY FINDINGS

The TPBA-2 revealed that John has many strengths. He relates well to his mother, is aware of the presence of others, can be prompted to include others in his play, and is beginning to be aware of others' emotions. He has preferred play routines with toys and can be encouraged to expand these through modeling. He is able to recreate familiar daily routines in dramatic play and repeats the text of familiar simple books. John's sensory, communication, social, and play patterns are characteristic of a child with autism. In addition, low muscle tone contributes to awkward fine and gross movement patterns. John is easily overstimulated and distracted by noises, close proximity of peers, and visual movements in his periphery. Some of his negative behaviors in class appear to stem from his perceiving a variety of seemingly minor intrusions (someone sitting too close in circle) as threatening. John often responds to these perceived threats with screaming and hitting. Limited emotional and conceptual vocabulary also constrains effective communication about what is bothering him. He has difficulty moderating his anxiety and emotions, which often results in tantrums. John's distractibility also contributes to a lack of persistence in challenging tasks, as it is easier to refocus on something else when a task is difficult, and therefore not rewarding. John functions best in familiar routines, with familiar materials and people. His limited tolerance for novel situations, however, restricts his acquisition of new knowledge, ability to practice skills in novel situations, and opportunity to learn adaptive social skills. Although referred for emotional and behavioral concerns, it is important to recognize that all areas of development are influencing John's behavior and, thus, need to be included in an intervention plan.

RECOMMENDATIONS

The following recommendations evolved from the information gained about John from all sources and observations. Emotional and Social recommendations are listed first so that the reader can compare the findings documented in Table 6.2 with the recommendations. As noted previously, all domains are interrelated, so the recommended strategies influence more than just the domain specified. Recommendations following Emotional and Social reflect transdisciplinary strategies.

Intervention Strategies for John for the Classroom and Home

Emotional and Social

1. John demonstrates some emerging skills in regulating his emotional outbursts. To further help John better regulate emotions, provide him with a "special place" (e.g., bean bag chair, tent, or area of interest) where he can go when he is anxious or upset. Allow him to help create the area to provide opportunities for

soothing and enjoyable activities (e.g., reading books, singing songs, playing games, etc.) that make the area special and inviting. Invite him to spend time there when he is not upset, as this will encourage him to think of this as a safe place, rather than for punishment. Model how to go to and use that area appropriately. Talk about the feelings you think he is experiencing and comment on the actions that make you think so. For example, "I hear you screaming. I heard the siren, too. You can tell me, 'Too loud!' Let's go sit in your quiet spot and relax."

2. Currently, John demonstrates a limited range of emotional expressions, including happy and angry. He is ready to experiment with more types, levels, and forms of emotional expressions to communicate his needs. At home and school, continue labeling John's emotions and providing adult examples of a variety of feelings, like frustrated, happy, sad, and excited (e.g., When attempting a hard task, say, "It's hard! Whew! I'm frustrated!"). Practice making different emotional faces (surprise, disgust, sadness, etc.) in the mirror when you read a book where the characters are demonstrating these emotions.

3. Currently, John benefits from scripts and prompts to facilitate healthy social interactions and other adaptive skill-building techniques. "Social stories" that relate specifically to John's issues are a great way to teach him new skills. Write a short story with pictures of John that illustrate a specific common situation (e.g., someone sitting too close or touching him) and write the exact words that he can say in that situation ("I don't like touching. Please stop.") Read the social story with him several times during the day and/or prior to events that may cause a problem. Social stories can also help to explain different emotions and the appropriate responses to emotions and would be beneficial for both home and school.

4. In the classroom, John would benefit from more opportunities to interact socially with his classmates and teacher. Use activities that necessitate cooperation (e.g., painting on one big piece of paper), and provide scripts or social stories for usual interactions (e.g., table-top activities, book time, etc.) to help John learn how to interact appropriately with others.

5. John demonstrates some challenging behaviors in the classroom when trying to gain his peers' attention. Provide him with strategies he can use to appropriately gain attention, such as tapping a classmate on the shoulder and saying his or her name or using words like "excuse me" when he wants to talk to someone. Social

stories (mentioned above) also may be helpful for teaching these prosocial behaviors.

6. John responds well to familiar routines and situations. He might benefit from a visual schedule of the school day that he can refer to throughout the day. For example, have each part of the day (e.g., coming into class, reading a book, math activity, lunch, writing activity, go home, etc.) represented with a visual image that he can look at and anticipate what will be next. Also use a visual cue to prepare him for upcoming events that are not part of the traditional schedule. Talk positively about the new event and what he will see, hear, and so on. Additionally, position yourself at John's eye level and wait for him to give eye contact before you respond. Use heightened emotional responses to encourage John to recognize your reactions and continue to engage with you.

7. Help the peers in the class understand individual differences by talking about what "bothers" them or makes them mad. Help the peers to understand that loud sounds or being too close bothers John and sometimes makes him mad. Discuss how to handle the various situations the children bring up. Make this a class discussion, rather than singling out John's issues. Group problem-solving will also provide an opportunity for peers to generate suggestions for dealing with some of the problem behaviors.

Transdisciplinary Recommendations

1. John enjoys movement activities and shows increased positive affect when engaged in high-energy games. During recess, play games that involve John with his peers. For example, "Red Light, Green Light" involves all children moving and stopping on command. Such a game will encourage John to watch others and listen for and follow directions. An obstacle course on the playground will also encourage movement imitation and turn-taking, as well as transitioning from one activity to another.

2. John is in the process of learning many new vocabulary words and concepts. To continue and encourage this development in a functional manner, provide John with realistic, multisensory experiences and introduce the vocabulary/concepts across different environments to promote generalization. For example, for science concepts, have him help water the plants or trim the dead leaves. This way he is touching and feeling the plants so that he understands the concepts of soft, dry, or smooth. Have him

grow his own plant at home to expand use of the concepts. Play with pretend plants or jungle scenes in a dramatic play scenario, go on walks and talk about the different plants, and read about various plants in magazines or books. Different experiences with plants will help John develop functional concepts of plant life and the descriptors of plants (e.g., grow, plant, seeds). Apply this approach as widely as possible to his concept learning.

3. John often plays with familiar toys and uses limited play sequences. He is ready to increase the variety of actions he uses with one toy as well as the complexity of his play with a diverse range of toys. Encourage John to discover new ways to play with toys by modeling new interesting actions. After he imitates these actions, add another step or prompt a new use of the toy. Increasing play sequences also increase his attention span for these materials. Additionally, try removing some of John's favorite toys in favor of new materials that he has yet to explore.

4. To work on problem-solving skills and facilitate more language, provide opportunities for John to create solutions based on new circumstances (e.g., putting an object up higher than he can reach, hiding an object he wants or needs, omitting an object needed to complete a task, etc.). Create situations that require him to think, communicate, and use effort to solve the problem. Challenge is important to his continued learning.

5. Provide John with a wide range of themes for dramatic play. For instance, act out play sequences related to books of interest that have a beginning, middle, and end or everyday routines (e.g., cooking, going places like the store or school). This will help improve John's vocabulary, sequencing of actions, and social and conversational skills.

6. When John uses jargon with intelligible words inserted, give meaning and add vocabulary to his statements. For example, when John begins to use jargon, provide him with the words and sentence structure that he can hear and/or imitate.

7. John enjoys silly sensory games. Mouth and sound games are great for making and maintaining eye contact and engaging in reciprocal play. Take turns making sounds and then imitating each other (e.g., a car engine, an animal sound, a vacuum cleaner). This will also help him practice making specific sounds in an enjoyable way and is important for making his language more intelligible.

8. Build emerging literacy skills by reading a variety of books, particularly those with realistic pictures. Relate to real-life experiences and give John an opportunity to experience use of vocabulary whenever possible through home and classroom opportunities. For example, after reading about wild animals, visit the zoo and see and talk about the animals. Alternatively, look for web sites with video clips of the animals in real life (e.g., National Geographic has sites to observe animals in their natural habitats).

9. John seems to function best with defined parameters, both with his physical boundaries and with visual boundaries to help him focus his attention. For example, using colored paper as a background on which he can do specific tasks may help him highlight the tasks he is working on (e.g., constructing block patterns, letter sequences, etc.). Other types of parameters might include using highlighters to show what he needs to look at, drawing a defined mark around a picture, or separating visual tasks by defined colors, spaces, or marks.

Results of Intervention　After the meeting to discuss recommendations, a plan was developed to integrate the recommendations into home and the school. John's family, teacher, and support staff worked on developing and implementing the plan. The psychologist and the special education teacher on the team provided support to the classroom teacher and John's family around increasing the use of books, play materials, and real materials for learning. They also provided suggestions for use of individual and group visual schedules, increasing peer pairing and turn taking within the classroom, and helped train peers to support and reward John's positive social interactions. The special education teacher created a sample social story that could be used at home and at school and modeled its use in the classroom. The psychologist and the special educator worked with the teacher and John's mother to understand the importance of teaching John how to engage in dramatic play and how to use books to increase dramatic play themes. They emphasized that logical thinking skills, social problem solving, and application of concepts is enhanced through play. Play was previously not a large component of the kindergarten program and required the engagement of the whole team to demonstrate how adding this to the academic curriculum would benefit the learning and development of the whole class. The occupational therapist also provided suggestions on positioning John within the classroom in large and small groups, adapting materials, and modifying the classroom environment. The speech therapist provided ideas around language and literacy and demonstrated using appropriate interactive communication at John's developmental level. She observed and gave feedback to the teacher and parents about providing simple sentence structure, adding novel vocabulary, and generalizing the use of vocabulary throughout the day.

After two months of intervention, the team, including the family, met again to discuss John's progress and determine if modifications to the plan were needed. Table 6.3 documents the results corresponding to

Table 6.3
Progress Monitoring

Intervention Recommendation	Results/Progress Monitoring	Implications
Emotional and Social		
Provide a specific location for self-calming.	Able to use beanbag chair at school and home with verbal suggestion from adult 80% of the time.	Continue using self-calming site and encourage self-verbalization prior to going to site.
Expand range of emotional expressions through modeling and use of words.	Some facial expression with increased emotional vocabulary. Using "Stop that" and "I want."	Continue to discuss and model emotional range and add additional vocabulary, such as "That bothers me."
Use social stories to increase appropriate social behaviors.	Decreased aggression, increased positive social initiations. Now says, "Please stop touching."	Add new social stories as he learns new scripts or social conventions.
Use cooperative learning and eye contact to increase social interaction.	Will tolerate a joint project if turn taking is prompted by an adult or a peer.	Increase formal and informal opportunities for joint play and activities.
Teach appropriate social initiation with peers.	Taps shoulder to get peer's attention 50% of the time.	Continue strategy, but reduce request to say name, as may be too demanding.
Use visual schedule of the day to help with transitions.	Tolerates new situations when visual schedule is paired with verbal preparation 50% of the time.	Add a realistic object representing the next activity along with verbal preparation.
Help peers in class understand differences.	80% of class is able to identify what bothers John, themselves, and others.	Continue discussions of individual differences.

each recommendation in the Emotional and Social domain suggested in the case illustration presented previously and corresponding to findings in Table 6.2. In addition, the implications of the findings for the plan are indicated, revealing whether to continue with the same strategies, modify them, or change the desired outcome. As can be seen from Table 6.3, John made considerable progress during the 2 months of intervention. His attention is longer, negative behaviors decreased, social skills improved, vocabulary expanded, and his play sequences increased. He still needs adult and peer prompting and considerable environmental and interpersonal structuring, but he is beginning to initiate social interaction with peers and use more verbal means of interacting.

CONCLUSION

Although kindergarten and primary classes are increasingly diminishing the role of play (Zigler & Bishop-Josef, 2004), many opportunities exist to incorporate developmental observations and therapeutic interventions into functional classroom routines, play activities, and recess. Especially in kindergarten, children need opportunities for dramatic play, informal social problem solving, turn taking in games that apply new concepts, as well as structured social interactions. Dramatic play enables children to create their own story, apply concepts, develop a sequence of thoughts and corresponding actions, and establish the social patterns needed to perform actions and feelings. Kindergarten and primary classrooms also present many opportunities for social problem solving. With thoughtful planning and use of insightful observations, teachers can create and use spontaneous classroom situations as opportunities for teaching and practicing social skills and understanding others' thoughts and feelings. Physical games, board games, computer games, and simple social games involving turn taking provide the occasion for children to observe, imitate, initiate, wait, monitor, and regulate their own and others' actions. Transdisciplinary Play-Based Assessment-2 and Transdisciplinary Play-Based Intervention-2 are part of a system of observation and intervention useful in a variety of situations. As the case presented illustrates, with the support of a variety of professionals, teachers and parents can understand the multitude of influences on children's development and cultivate practical ideas to increase emotional and social skills and improve learning.

REFERENCES

Foley, G. M., & Hochman, J. D. (2008). *Mental health in early intervention: Achieving unity in principles and practice*. Baltimore, MD: Brookes Publishing.

Individuals with Disabilities Education Improvement Act of 2004, PL 108–446, 20 U.S.C. §§ 1400 et seq.

Linder, T. (2000). Transdisciplinary play-based assessment. In K. Gitlin-Weiner, S. Sandgrund, & C. Schaefer (Eds.), *Play diagnosis and assessment* (pp. 139–166). New York: John Wiley & Sons.

Linder, T. (2008a). *Administrative guide: Transdisciplinary play-based assessment and intervention 2*. Baltimore, MD: Brookes Publishing.

Linder, T. (2008b). *Transdisciplinary play-based assessment 2*. Baltimore, MD: Brookes Publishing.

Linder, T. (2008c). *Transdisciplinary play-based intervention 2*. Baltimore, MD: Brookes Publishing.

Linder, T., Holm, C., & Walsh, K. (1999). Play-based assessment. In E. Vasquez-Nuttall, I. Romero, & J. Kalesnik (Eds.), *Assessing and screening preschoolers: Psychological and educational dimensions* (2nd ed.; pp. 161–185). Needham Heights, MA: Allyn & Bacon.

Linder, T., Linas, K., & Stokka, K. (2008). Transdisciplinary play-based intervention with young children with disabilities. In C. Schaefer, S. Kelly-Zion, J. McCormick, & A. Ohnogi (Eds.), *Play therapy for very young children* (pp. 307–337). Lanham, MD: Rowman and Littlefield.

Petersen-Smith, A., & Linder, T. (2008). Obtaining preliminary information from families. In T. Linder (Ed.), *Administrative guide for TPBA-2 and TPBI-2* (pp. 95–136). Baltimore, MD: Brookes Publishing.

Zigler, E. F., & Bishop-Josef, S. J. (2004). Play under siege. Yale's Center in Child Development and Social Policy. In *21 Community News: A Newsletter for Schools of the 21st Century* (Winter, 2004), 1–4.

PART IV

PLAY-BASED PREVENTION PROGRAMS WITH PARAPROFESSIONALS AND TEACHERS

CHAPTER 7

Helping Preschool and Kindergarten Teachers Foster Play in the Classroom

KAREN STAGNITTI

P LAY MAKES AN important contribution to the literacy, language, and social development of children. Teachers who provide a rich environment and the scaffolding of ideas to extend children's development within a classroom that is play-based create a socio-cultural environment that is developmentally appropriate for children (Korat, Bahar, & Snapir, 2002/2003). This chapter focuses on how to work beside teachers to foster play in the classroom and covers a short discussion on play to refine this behavior more clearly. An explanation is given of the links between play, literacy, and language. Such an approach is taken because when the concept of play is raised within an educational setting, the reaction from many is one of scepticism as to what play could contribute to a child's learning. There are many assumptions that come with this reaction, including that children no longer need to play when they start school, that play is not related to learning, and that play has no value within an educational setting. It is important for teachers to understand how play contributes to a child's literacy foundation. The chapter also explores the role of the teacher within a play-based classroom, and practical suggestions are given for helping teachers foster play.

PLAY

Many authors agree that play is important for learning (Long, Bergeron, Leicht Doyle, & Gordon, 2005; Reilly, 1974) and that spontaneous play that is child-initiated is important for cognitive growth (Sutton-Smith, 1967). Long et al. (2005) examined the relationship between parental reports of their child's play activities and their child's school readiness as assessed on a therapist-directed assessment called the Screening Device for School readiness by Danzer, Gerber, Lyons, and Voress (1991). Long et al. (2005) defined play broadly as a concept that included voluntary participation, nonroutine and imagination, and choice. They found a moderately significant relationship between the frequency of participation in play activities and a child's performance on a school readiness therapist-directed assessment. When Long et al. (2005) clustered the play activities reported by parents into either fine or gross motor play, fine motor activities had a moderately significant relationship with overall school readiness scores. It is curious that when Long et al. divided play activities into fine and gross motor activities, they did not consider imaginative or pretend play activities as defined as play in their study.

Pretend play (also called imaginative play, symbolic play, representational play, and make-believe play), in particular, has been directly related to literacy and language development in children. According to Stagnitti and Jellie (2006, p. 4), pretend play has four distinct behaviors that can be observed, which make this type of play distinct from other forms of play. The distinct behaviors are:

1. The child uses symbolic thinking in play (for example, a stick becomes a bridge).
2. The child attributes a property to an object.
3. The child refers to an absent object during play.
4. The child logically and sequentially orders play actions to form a story.

As an addition to this list, the following is added in this chapter:

- Pretend play involves sustained symbolic thinking, that is, thinking in another reality or imposing meaning into a situation or set of objects.
- Pretend play involves the use of a story and story characters.
- Pretend play involves the use of an object outside of the self, such as a doll or teddy (called *decentration*).

Children engage in pretend play because it is nonthreatening and fun and it is the natural mode for them. The use of pretend play in the classroom can help to provide a classroom that is nonthreatening to children, especially to those who come to school lacking in skills and from disadvantaged families. The following section of this chapter outlines why fostering play in the classroom is important for the educational development of the child.

WHY PLAY IS IMPORTANT TO A CHILD'S EDUCATIONAL LEARNING

A growing body of literature is showing that play—in particular high-quality pretend play—is directly linked with children's abilities to think abstractly and to take the perspectives of others (Tepperman, 2007). Vygotsky (1967; 1962) believed that pretend play was an important activity for the development of higher level cognitive functions in children and that these cognitive functions could be influenced by the environment around them, particularly more capable peers and adults. A child's development and environment are important from birth. A child's natural development and environment work together in building emergent literacy skills before formal schooling begins, and when a child attends formal schooling, literacy is referred to as conventional literacy (Justice & Pullen, 2003).

EMERGENT LITERACY

When children begin school, it is assumed that they come ready to learn; however, many children come to school with no emergent literacy skills. Emergent literacy is a child's precursory knowledge about reading and writing, and it provides the foundation for higher level literacy skills (Justice & Pullen, 2003). Low levels of emergent literacy have been associated with children from lower socioeconomic areas and children from high-risk environments (Bronson, Tivnan, & Seppanen, 1995; Clark & Kragler, 2005). Through play, teachers can provide a classroom environment that meets a child's language and literacy needs as well as a classroom environment that enriches a child's literacy development (Saracho, 2002a; Justice & Pullen, 2003).

Children's emergent literacy knowledge arises from "adult-mediated interactions with oral and written language embedded within meaningful, contextualized early childhood experiences" (Justice & Pullen, 2003, p. 100). Particularly important to acquiring emergent literacy skills "are frequent, informal, and naturalistic interactions with written and oral language within the broader context of supportive, mediated opportunities with adult caregivers" (Justice & Pullen, 2003, p. 100). Highly contextualized, meaningful, and familiar environments are shared book reading between a child and adult and literacy-enriched play settings within the classroom or home (Justice & Pullen, 2003). Children from impoverished environments are at-risk for difficulties in developing literacy skills because their homes have not provided highly contextualized, meaningful contexts. Children who enter school with an inadequate emergent literacy foundation are at risk of failing in the school environment (Bronson et al., 1995; Justice & Pullen, 2003). Fostering play classrooms for children from lower socioeconomic and high-risk environments is particularly important in order to build the foundation skills for learning that are missing.

Children reproduce in their play what they observe around them. They act out stories from their life, and they do this before they can read. This reenactment of events from their lives builds a child's emotional understanding of a context and provides practice with the language associated with that context and experimentation with roles and behaviors associated with characters in that context. Life events can be reenacted in play in a logical, sequential manner from 24 months of age (Stagnitti, 1998). This ability to play out their stories in an organized way demonstrates that children have logical, sequential thought; for example, teddy has a cup of tea and then goes to bed. When children act out stories in play they are involved in pretend play action sequences because they act *as if* they really were having a cup of tea during a tea party with their dolls or teddies. As children approach 3 years of age, they begin to add fictional characters to their play, such as characters they have seen on TV or read about in a book (Stagnitti, 1998). Engel (2005) gives an explanation of children's understanding of the *what is* world and the *what if* world using Werner's theory of children's psychological thought processes, which were explained in forms of spheres. When 3-year-olds begin to play out fictional stories, Engel (2005) suggests that children begin to explore the fictional world of fantastic possibilities (*what if*) and the world of everyday life (*what is*). Older 3-year-olds preplan their play by thinking about what they want to play and then finding the play materials they need to carry out that idea (Stagnitti, 1998).

By 4 years of age children engage in role play with others or by themselves, preplan play ideas, use objects in play, and negotiate with others as well as problem solving dramatic events in their play story (for example, the car tire is flat, or the "baddies" come and rob the "house") (Stagnitti, 1998). By 5 years of age, children within a secure enriching family environment have engaged in playing out numerous scenarios with peers, begun to scribble on paper as if it is meaningful (such as a shopping list or doctors medicine), pretended objects are other things, used fictional and nonfictional characters in their play, and have used vocabulary to match the numerous play scenarios played out (Stagnitti, 2009). By 5 years of age, children have built up a foundation of emergent literacy skills because they understand role, associate vocabulary with different contexts (e.g., compare oceans and jungles), have an understanding of story, can predict how a character in the play may react and behave, and understand that scribbles on paper can be meaningful. Lynch and van den Broek (2007) examined 6- and 8-year-old children's ability to infer a character's goals from a story and confirmed that children at 6 years of age have the ability to infer a character's goals within a story.

When the play experience nurtures language and thinking, emergent literacy is acquired (Saracho, 2004). Emergent literacy also includes a child's understanding of context; and play can provide this through exploration of the environment, interaction with others, a safe place to express oneself, playing out past incidences, and using text such as shopping lists and doctors' prescriptions (Saracho, 2004).

When a child's pretend play skills are poor, they begin school at-risk for failure because poor pretend play also reflects a child's lack of ability to sequentially think through a logical sequence of thought, use symbols in play, create play scenarios, and understand character. Stagnitti, Unsworth, and Rodger (2000) found that children aged 4 to 5 years who were at-risk of failing at school could be accurately identified by the quality of their pretend play as assessed on the Child-Initiated Pretend Play Assessment. The Child-Initiated Pretend Play Assessment (Stagnitti, 2007) measures a child's ability to spontaneously initiate pretend play as well as the complexity and elaborateness of their play, including the ability to substitute objects. In Stagnitti et al.'s (2000) study, two groups of 41 children were matched by age and sex. One group was identified as typically developing, and one group was identified as at-risk for failure at school, in the absence of any major developmental delay. The two groups of children were discriminated between based on the elaborateness and complexity of their play as well as the ability to substitute objects in play (Stagnitti et al., 2000). Children's emergent literacy abilities are a foundation to conventional literacy skills. Conventional literacy skills are those that are most often considered in classroom settings, and the development of conventional literacy skills are the main reasons why children attend school.

CONVENTIONAL LITERACY

Literacy can be understood as "language in use—in speaking, listening, reading, viewing, writing, and drawing" (Department of Education and Children's Services [DECS], 1996). Literacy involves a child's understanding of language, both narrative and oral language. Each of these abilities and how they link with pretend play is explained below.

NARRATIVE

It has been recognized for some time that children's pretend play includes narrative features (Walker, 1999). Nicolopoulou (2005) crystallized this connection by arguing that pretend play and narrative are on a continuum, with play being the acting out of stories on one end and narrative being the discursive exposition on the other end. Indeed, Jellie (2007) found that children who had more elaborate pretend play as assessed on the Child-Initiated Pretend Play Assessment (Stagnitti, 2007) had longer narratives in their play and used more words and more different words. Children who had poorer narrative language had poorer pretend play and tended to imitate the play of others because they were poorer at self-initiated play (Jellie, 2007).

Feldman (2005) suggests that play (i.e., symbolic/pretend play) and narrative share mimesis. "Mimesis is an imitative representation of life" (Feldman, 2005, p. 503) where there is a shared resemblance between the imitated and the enactment. There are now many studies that provide evidence that children who act out the story in pretend play have a deeper understanding of the story or narrative. For example, Baumer, Ferholt, and Lecusay (2005) found that children who reenacted stories under the direction of adults improved their narrative skills more than children who just read and discussed the story. Pellegrini and Galda (1993) found that peer-directed pretend play and adult-directed pretend play centered on reenactment of a story facilitated the children's story comprehension and was more effective than discussion or drawing in younger children. Sook-Yi (1999) divided 32 children aged 4 to 5 years into four groups. Two groups were given toys to reenact a story told by the researcher. Two groups were shown pictures and asked to retell the story after the story was told. The children in the pretend play groups (with the toys) showed higher levels of narrative structure than those children in the storytelling-only groups. One week later, the children were asked to retell the story again, and children in the pretend play groups were significantly better at retelling the story than children in the picture groups. There were not significant differences between the groups when the children were tested a third time and no props (toys or pictures) were given. The children in the pretend play groups provided more complex narratives than the children in the storytelling only group, which suggests that pretend play decisively facilitates narrative recall (Sook-Yi, 2005). Christie (1994) used dramatic play to improve children's story comprehension by reenacting the story. This was effective for young children as well as for older children who were delayed in their reading comprehension.

Nicolopoulou (2005) put forward the suggestion that effectively integrating pretend play and narrative is a key developmental achievement that can accelerate further development. The developmental links between pretend play and narrative were expounded by Stagnitti and Jellie (2006), who outlined the developmental sequence of pretend play and narrative and showed that pretend play development parallels narrative development. For example, at 3 years of age children incorporate fantasy figures in their play from TV or books and also at the same age begin to tell fictional stories.

Pretend play, during the act of acting out stories, involves logically and sequentially organizing play actions into a coherent *narrative*. This also leads to the child's ability to think forward and predict what will happen (Stagnitti & Jellie, 2006; Westby, 1991). By predicting what will come next—or several options as to what may come next—children become nonliteral thinkers because they understand that there are many solutions and consequences depending on the characters goals, the context of the story, and the events leading up to the story so far.

In a longitudinal study, Stagnitti (2002) found that the quality of pretend play at the preschool level was moderately predictive of a child's narrative retell four years later when he or she was in early primary school. In particular, it was the child's ability to use symbols in play that was the key to pretend play behavior, that is, the ability to use an object as something else. The link is thought to be the child's ability to suspend reality, to problem solve, to use decontextualized language (that is, language that does not rely on context), that contributes to a child's ability to retell a story. Engel (2005) also found that understanding a character's goals contributed to a child's understanding of the narrative. A child's understanding of story is strongly correlated to later linguistic abilities because a child who is constructing coherent narratives is producing cohesive texts (i.e., language events that are inherently meaningful in their own right, without the support of gestures or context) (Pellegrini, 1985).

Language and Oral Language   When children pretend in play, they use both actions in the play and language to depict events (Sook-Yi, 1999). Object use and language are tools of thought, and they are used in advancing thought processes (Fishbein & Burklow, 1993). Many authors have argued that the ability to symbolize in play leads to the internalization of the mental image in thought (Fein, 1975; McCune Nicolich, 1981; Vygotsky, 1962).

The link between pretend play and language has been well established (Doswell, Lewis, Sylva, & Boucher, 1994) with the argument being that pretend play and language share a common cognitive base (Lewis, Boucher, & Astell, 1992; Westby, 1991). Westby (1980) explained that the ability to use language and to pretend requires representation; for example, a box represents a doll's bed and the word *bed* is the abstract symbol for an object that the child sleeps in. The key elements of symbolizing and representing are used in language (e.g., a child's ability to represent the concept *cat* with the sound and letter graphophonemes c-a-t) and pretend play. When children talk about pretend play, they do so with what is known as *decontextualized language*—that is, when meaning is conveyed independently of context (Pellegrini, 1985). For example, a child can tell a story about swimming in the ocean when in reality she is lying on her stomach on the floor moving her arms and legs. Pretend play and language-literacy are thought to share a common base because when children pretend play they use decontextualized language.

McCune (1995) and Lewis, Boucher, Lupton, and Watson (2000) found that pretend play developed before expressive language and young children's development in language has been linked closely with development in pretend play with one play action preceding one-word utterances and two play actions preceding two-word utterances (Lowe, 1975).

Neuman and Roskos (1990) found that literacy-enriched play environments in the classroom where low-income children go to school resulted in children increasing their written language awareness. Talking during play was also found to be a significant predictor of a child's knowledge of print. Talking about the pretend play as the child plays has been referred to as *metaplay* (Pellegrini & Galda, 1993). Children observed in pretend play situations, compared to other forms of play, have been noted to use more cohesive oral language and metaplay skills (Pellegrini & Galda, 1993).

Children who engage in quality pretend play use more language (Jellie, 2007). When children pretend in play with others, they need to talk to other children about what the play objects symbolize in order for other children to understand what is going on. Children also elaborate on the play scenes, the use of objects by attributing properties to objects (e.g., a doll may be sick), and reference to absent objects (such as an invisible wall that has to be avoided). As Lewis et al. (2000, p. 117) stated: "There is now considerable evidence supporting a relationship between play and language in normally developing children."

These findings suggest that oral language surrounding pretend play is extremely important to literacy skills.

THE ROLE OF THE TEACHER IN A PLAY-LITERACY CLASSROOM

A classroom that incorporates play requires different skills of the teacher compared to a classroom where the teacher is the "sage on the stage." Clark and Kragler (2005), when conducting a study with 34 children aged 4 to 5 years from low-income families, found that just providing materials related to literacy (such as providing writing materials and literacy opportunities in the classroom) did not lead to increased literacy skills in children. Rather, they concluded that the role of the teacher in promoting literacy concepts in a developmentally appropriate way was crucial and also missing in their study. Children who come to school with poor emergent literacy are at-risk in their ability to develop conventional literacy skills. For these children in particular (as well as all other children), the teacher's role is to create an environment that is highly contextualized, meaningful, and familiar to the child with interactions with a teacher who is "highly responsive to children's interests and activities" (Justice & Pullen, 2003, p. 101). A meaningful and highly contextualized environment for a child is a play environment. A play environment is the opposite of an environment that is "nonfunctional and contrived," where children are "passively engaged," and it is these environments that Justice and Pullen (2003) argue do not engage children in how they acquire literacy knowledge (p. 101). Korat et al. (2002/2003) gave examples of how play can extend literacy skills in the classroom by the teacher providing a rich environment, facilitating play scenes by giving information, following a child's lead, and posing new questions for the child to consider within the play scene.

Literacy-enriched play settings have centered on pretend play (called dramatic play in educational literature) where a naturalistic, hypothesis-generating scenario has been associated with frequent use of literacy events by children (Justice & Pullen, 2003). For example, Schrader (1990) recounted children playing roles of a mother and child where children used written symbols such as the making of shopping lists and reading of magazines. Korat et al. (2002/2003) described detailed interactions between the teacher and children involving language, problem solving, and suggestions to potential behavioral characteristics of play characters when the classroom was set up with play centers such as an office, a doctor's operating room, and a shop. This play reflected social and cultural contexts of the child's life—a rich and meaningful environment for the child.

Teachers influence student learning through their actions, their thought processes, and their beliefs (Saracho, 2002a). When children are engaged in spontaneous play, teachers can foster children's literacy learning through a variety of roles, such as storytellers, group discussion leaders, mediators of conflicts, and psychological diagnosticians (Saracho, 2002a, p. 24). To come to this conclusion, Saracho (2002a), in conjunction with three research students, analyzed videotapes of five teachers interacting with the children in their classrooms. The videotapes were analyzed using inductive content analysis for units of literacy-play behavior. The activities that were focused on were often tabletop activities using objects such as sponges, blocks, and shapes.

The roles that teachers assumed in the literacy-play environment were: discussion leader, storyteller, examiner, instructional guide, informer, learning center monitor and decision maker, transition director, supporter of learning, and instructional guide (Saracho, 2002a, p. 25; 2002b, p. 675). In essence, the role of discussion leader entailed the teacher encouraging children to think and solve a problem in relation to a concept they were learning at the time. In the storyteller role the teacher would interrupt her reading of the story by asking questions that encouraged the children to predict events, participate in the storytelling, clarify how they comprehended the story by asking questions, reread the story to verify the children's responses, used visual cues of the story from the storybook pictures, and brought to children's attention the range of emotions that the book characters might be feeling. By engaging in a game, the role of examiner enabled the teacher to review the children's understanding of concepts in a nonthreatening way. The role of instructional guide assisted learning by giving concrete instructions and facts, and the informer role provided children with specific information on the meaning of words by providing objects, defining the object, explaining, demonstrating, and questioning children on their understanding of following directions. While the children engaged in activities, the teacher monitored the activities by joining in conversations with the children to extend on what was discussed, refocused their attention when needed, and changed the materials to challenge the children. All these roles are carried out to ensure that effective learning takes place (Saracho, 2002a). In 2004, Saracho modified these roles to: constituent of children's learning, promoter and monitor of children's learning, storyteller, group discussion leader, and instructional guide. Overall, the teacher is reflective in practice; observant of the children's activities, language, and learning; and looks for opportunities to extend children's learning through scaffolding, modeling, and asking questions.

These behaviors have been found to be effective in storybook reading to encourage emergent literacy and oral language. Justice and Pullen (2003) discussed the intervention approach of dialogic reading with the role of the adult being to question the child's story knowledge using open-ended questions, following the child's answers with questions, repeating and expanding what the child said, encouraging the child and giving feedback, following the child's lead and interests, and having fun (Justice & Pullen, 2003). For literacy play, adult scaffolding, modeling, role playing, and conversation, behaviors of the adult have been shown to be effective (Justin & Pullen, 2003). This adult mediation is an important aspect of play-based classrooms (Justin & Pullen, 2003). Many of these adult behaviors are reflective of child-centered therapy—follow the child's lead and interests, repeat and expand on what the child says.

How to Set Up the Classroom

Play-literacy environments have been shown to influence positively emergent literacy development. Saracho (2004) outlined how teachers are able to encourage language and literacy through play-based literacy by referring to the National Research Council in the United States (National Research Council, 1998). In essence, within the classroom, the teacher needs to allow time and space for play, supply the material resources (that is, play props), discuss and talk with children so that they develop a background knowledge for the play context, scaffold dramatic retelling of the story, model and interact with the children in order to guide children's attention (Saracho, 2004).

Justice and Pullen (2003, p. 108) give specific examples of a play-literacy classroom with "deliberate integration of literacy props and materials" to be used in children's pretend play. These examples include: setting up a shop/store and including play materials such as wall signs, shelf labels, lists, and product containers; setting up an office with play props such as telephone message forms, stationary, and envelopes; and setting up a veterinarian office using appointment books, signs, patient charts, and prescription forms. Literacy props integrated into pretend/dramatic play settings in the classroom together with adult involvement have resulted in significant increases in children's literacy related play (Christie, 1994).

To create a rich play environment, Bodrova and Leong (2003) suggested the following: allow a long, uninterrupted block of time because children need time to plan their play; have a combination of play materials, both conventional toys and unstructured materials; supply pictures of activities the children have undertaken or visits they have been on; allow space across several centers in the classroom for the encouragement of pretend play; have similar play scripts (stories) over several centers; incorporate pretend play in all activities; and regularly change the play materials.

PRACTICAL CONSIDERATIONS

In this following list, practical suggestions are given on how to foster play in the classroom, taking into account the literature findings as well as my own clinical experience.

- It is essential that the teacher understands the link between pretend play and literacy, otherwise she/he will not be convinced that play is important and following through will be more difficult. As the role of the teacher is so crucial in a classroom with play as the base, the teacher's understanding of why play is used cannot be underestimated.
- Play props are important—both conventional toy props and unstructured objects. Unstructured objects allow for the use of symbols in play. Examples of unstructured objects are: boxes, sticks, material, paper, buttons, cotton balls, corks, and so on.
- Provide activities that systematically integrate pretend play with narrative; for example, storytelling, story-acting practice, and

journal writing activities can successfully engage children from lower socioeconomic areas and promote their learning and development (Nicolopoulou, McDowell, & Brockmeyer, 2006). For example, a story is told to the class, with the teacher interrupting the story and asking questions. After the story is read, the children are divided into groups (or the class is used as a whole), and the teacher leads the children in the reenactment of the story. Fein, Ardila-Rey, and Groth (2000) found that when a story is acted out by a group of children, the children focused on the story with emphasis on character and action.

- Run classroom activities where a child-authored story is read to the group and then discussed. Fein et al. (2000) found that children who engaged in this activity likened their work to a book and began to incorporate book features into their work.
- When reading a story or creating a play scene, use voice, body, and facial expressions so that the emotions of the characters and the feeling of the play scene are part of the teacher interaction. Moschovaki, Meadows, and Pellegrini (2007) found that the affective presentation of a story engaged children's interest and emotional engagement with the narrative. Emotional engagement heightens learning in a safe environment.
- When a child understands narrative, that child is able to forward think, or *predict*, what will happen next in the story. For example, when children are playing shop, they can tell you what will happen and answer such questions as: "What will people do when they come to your shop? What if you run out of shop items? What will you do if a customer wants to buy an object and you don't have it in the shop? Do you have a lunch break when you work in the shop?"
- Storytelling requires the ability to sequence events, creative cohesive text, use precise vocabulary, understand cause and effect, and structure the story using universal narrative forms such as stories with a beginning, middle, and end. Therefore, in classroom activities, set up play corners or areas of play where precise vocabulary is needed (such as an office or shop) (Korat et al., 2005). As the children play in these areas, use leading questions and extend children's ideas by presenting problems and encouraging them to think of sequences of events as suggested in the questions given above.
- Provide a play space that stimulates children's language and play by putting in unstructured objects, conventional toys, and space

for up to five children to move about. This creates a social play space where children will need to negotiate with each other and discuss the use of objects.

Stagnitti and Jellie (2006) provide many practical activities that can be used in the classroom to encourage a play-literacy environment. When a play situation is created by the teacher, the behaviors to note are: Do the children logically and sequentially play out a scenario? Are they able to use unstructured objects and pretend the object is something else? Can they attribute properties to objects, such as a *sick* doll? Can they refer to absent objects, such as a wall in a room, when nothing is visible? Do they use characters? What do the characters do, how do they behave? Are there problems created in the narrative? How do they solve the problems?

CONCLUSION

Integrating play in the classroom provides children with an enriching learning opportunity. This is particularly so for children from lower socioeconomic and high-risk families where an enriching environment has not been provided prior to the child coming to school. Pretend play is a powerful way to build a child's emergent literacy skills, which in turn are the foundation for a child's conventional literacy abilities.

REFERENCES

Baumer, S., Ferholt, B., & Lecusay, R. (2005). Promoting narrative competence through adult-child joint pretense: Lessons from the Scandinavian educational practice of playworld. *Cognitive Development, 20,* 576–590.

Bodrova, E., & Leong, D. (2003). Building language and literacy through PLAY. *Early Childhood Today, 18,* 34–43.

Bronson, M., Tivnan, T., & Seppanen, P. (1995). Relations between teacher and classroom activity variables and the classroom behaviors of pre-kindergarten children in Chapter 1 funded programs. *Journal of Applied Developmental Psychology, 16,* 253–282.

Christie, J. (1994). Academic play. In J. Hellendoorn, R. Van der Kooij, & B. Sutton-Smith (Eds.), *Play and intervention* (pp. 203–213). Albany: SUNY Press.

Clark, P., & Kragler, S. (2005). The impact of including writing materials in early childhood classrooms on the early literary development of children from low-income families. *Early Child Development and Care, 175*(4), 285–301.

Danzer, V., Gerber, M., Lyons, R., & Voress, J. (1991). *Daberon-2 screening for school readiness: Examiner's manual*. Austin, TX: Pro-ed.

Department of Education and Children's Services (1996). *Early years literacy profile*. Adelaide, Australia: Department for Education and Children's Services.

Doswell, G., Lewis, V., Sylva, K., & Boucher, J. (1994). Validation data on the Warwick Symbolic Play Test. *European Journal of Disorders of Communication, 29*, 289–298.

Engel, S. (2005). The narrative worlds of what is and what if. *Cognitive Development, 20*, 514–525.

Fein, G., Ardila-Rey, A., & Groth, L. (2000). The narrative connection: Stories and literacy. In K. Roskos & J. Christie (Eds.), *Play and literacy in early childhood: Research from multiple perspectives* (pp. 27–43). Mahwah, NJ: Lawrence Erlbaum.

Fein, G. G. (1975). A transformational analysis of pretending. *Developmental Psychology, 11*, 291–296.

Feldman, C. (2005). Mimesis: Where play and narrative meet. *Cognitive Development, 20*, 503–513.

Fishbein, H. D., & Burklow, K. (1993). Age related changes in object use and verbalization among pre-school children in a free play setting. *International Play Journal, 1*, 27–37.

Jellie, L. (2007). *The relationship between pretend play and narrative in preschool children*. Unpublished master's, thesis, Flinders University, Adelaide, Australia.

Justice, L., & Pullen, P. (2003). Promising interventions for promoting emergent literacy skills: Three evidence based approaches. *Topics in Early Childhood Special Education, 23*(3), 99–113.

Korat, O., Bahar, E., & Snapir, M. (2002/2003). Sociodramatic play as opportunity for literacy development: The teacher's role. *The Reading Teacher 56* (4), 386–393.

Lewis, V., Boucher, J., & Astell, A. (1992). The assessment of symbolic play in young children: A prototype test. *European Journal of Disorders of Communications, 27*, 231–245.

Lewis, V., Boucher, J., Lupton, L., & Watson, S. (2000). Notes and discussion. Relationships between symbolic play, functional play, verbal and nonverbal ability in young children. *International Journal of Language and Communication Disorders, 35*, 117–127.

Long, D., Bergeron, J., Leicht Doyle, S., & Gordon, C. (2005). The relationship between frequency of participation in play activities and kindergarten readiness. *Occupational Therapy in Health Care, 19*(4), 23–42.

Lowe, M. (1975). Trends in the development of representational play in infants from one to three years—an observational study. *Child Psychology Psychiatry, 16*, 33–47.

Lynch, J. S., & van den Broek, P. (2007). Understanding the glue of narrative structure: Children's on- and off-line inferences about characters' goals. *Cognitive Development, 22*, 323–340.

McCune, L. (1995). A normative study of representational play at the transition to language. *Child Development, 31*, 198–206.

McCune Nicolich, L. (1981). Toward symbolic functioning: Structure of early pretend games and potential parallels with language. *Child Development, 52*, 785–797.

Moschovaki, E., Meadows, S., & Pellegrini, A. (2007). Teachers' affective presentation of chldren's books and young children's display of affective engagement during classroom book reading. *European Journal of Psychology of Education, 22*, 405–420.

Neuman, S., & Roskos, K. (1990). Play, print, and purpose: Enriching play environments for literacy development. *The Reading Teacher, 44*, 214–221.

Nicolopoulou, A. (2005). Play and narrative in the process of development: Commonalities, differences, and interrelations. *Cognitive Development, 20*, 495–502.

Nicolopoulou, A., McDowell, J., & Brockmeyer, C. (2006). Narrative play and emergent literacy: Storytelling and story-acting meet journal writing. In D. G. Singer, R. Golinkoff, & K. Hirsh-Pasek (Eds.), *Play = learning. How play motivates and enhances children's cognitive and social-emotional growth* (pp. 124–144). New York: Oxford University Press.

Pellegrini, A., & Galda, L. (1993). Ten years after: A reexamination of symbolic play and literacy research. *Reading Research Quarterly, 28*, 162–175.

Pellegrini, A. D. (1985). The relations between symbolic play and literate behavior: A review and critique of the empirical literature. *Review of Educational Research, 55*, 107–121.

Reilly, M. (1974). *Play as exploratory learning. Studies of curiosity behaviour.* Beverly Hills, CA: Sage.

Saracho, O. N. (2002a). Teachers' roles in supporting children's literacy development through play. *Perceptual and Motor Skills, 94*, 675–676.

Saracho, O. N. (2002b). Teachers' roles in promoting literacy in the context of play. *Early Child Development and Care, 172*(1), 23–34.

Saracho, O. N. (2004). Supporting literacy-related play: Roles for teachers of young children. *Early Childhood Education Journal, 31*(3), 201–206.

Schrader, C. T. (1990). Symbolic play as a curricular tool for early literacy development. *Early Childhood Research Quarterly, 5*, 79–103.

Sook-Yi, K. (1999). The effects of storytelling and pretend play on cognitive processes, short-term and long-term narrative recall. *Child Study Journal, 29*, 175–192.

Stagnitti, K. (1998). *Learn to play: A program to develop the imaginative play skills of children.* Melbourne, Australia: Co-ordinates Publishing.

Stagnitti, K. (2002). *The development of a child-initiated pretend play assessment.* Unpublished doctoral thesis, LaTrobe University, Melbourne, Australia.

Stagnitti, K. (2007). *The child-initiated pretend play assessment. Manual and kit.* Melbourne, Australia: Co-ordinates Publications.

Stagnitti, K. (2009). Children and pretend play. In K. Stagnitti & R. Cooper (Eds.), *Play as therapy: Assessment and intervention* (pp. 59–69). London: Jessica Kingsley.

Stagnitti, K., & Jellie, L. (2006). *Play to learn: Building literacy in the early years.* Melbourne, Australia: Curriculum Corporation.

Stagnitti, K., Unsworth, C., & Rodger, S. (2000). Development of an assessment to identify play behaviors that discriminate between the play of typical preschoolers and preschoolers with pre-academic problems. *Canadian Journal of Occupational Therapy, 67,* 291–303.

Sutton-Smith, B. (1967, September). The role of play in cognitive development. *Young Children,* 361–369.

Tepperman, J. (2007). *Play in the early years: Key to school success. A policy brief.* San Francisco: Bay Area Early Childhood Funders.

Vygotsky, L. (1962). *Thought and language.* Cambridge, MA: MIT Press.

Vygotsky, L. (1967). Play and its role in the mental developmental of the child. *Soviet Psychology, 5,* 6–18. (Originally published in Russian in 1933.)

Walker, C. (1999). Playing a story: Narrative and writing-like features in scenes of dramatic play. *Reading Research and Instruction, 38*(4), 401–413.

Westby, C. (1980). Assessment of cognitive and language abilities through play. *Language, Speech, and Hearing Services in Schools, 11,* 154–168.

Westby, C. (1991). A scale for assessing children's pretend play. In C. Schaefer, K. Gitlin, & A. Sandrund (Eds.), *Play diagnosis and assessment* (pp. 131–161). New York: John Wiley & Sons.

CHAPTER 8

Primary Project

An Evidenced-Based Approach

MARY ANNE PEABODY, DEBORAH B. JOHNSON, and
A. DIRK HIGHTOWER

NATIONALLY, THE U.S. Surgeon General's report on children's mental health emphasized the critical need for early intervention and prevention-focused, empirically validated treatments designed to respond to the distinct needs of children (U.S. Public Health Service, 2000). In many states, plans to meet the growing needs of children are being developed. These plans are calling for a continuum of care and support that addresses the mental health needs of children ranging from prevention to treatment. Schools are an ideal setting for meeting these needs. Schools in particular can be the provider of first choice to offer early intervention and prevention programs that support and build children's emotional competence. In an era of cost-containment and accountability, the need to provide evidence of the effectiveness of interventions and programs is increasingly important to gain acceptance by school boards, school administrators, the legal community, funders, and consumers. Programs must show they are effective through strong research and evaluation. Increasingly, interventions that have undergone scientific evaluation are being strongly recommended to schools for implementation, so as to increase the likelihood of setting a strong foundation of early school success.

Primary Project (formerly known as Primary Mental Health Project [PMHP]) is one such early intervention program that is designed to help children become better adjusted to the school experience. Primary Project is targeted to enhance and maximize young children's school adjustment and other related competencies and to reduce social, emotional, and school adjustment difficulties from preschool through third grade. Primary Project uses the developmentally appropriate intervention of expressive, child-centered play.

Children today are living in a world with increased demands on performance, economic insecurity, changing international dynamics, and increased families living under stress. In the school environment, children face many challenges and stresses, including increased structure, adherence to schedules, the need to work cooperatively, and increased expectations for academic achievement. While most children adjust to these stresses and expectations, many do not. Some begin to worry or lose confidence, while others may have difficulty getting along, following rules, or staying on task. Left unattended, these children often become more disengaged, withdraw from the learning process, and may begin to develop behaviors that interrupt the flow of the classroom experience. Early intervention is critical, with a growing body of research suggesting the importance of providing early positive school experiences to young children.

Schools are important settings for implementing preventive interventions. First, it is estimated that 70 to 80 percent of mental health services received by children are provided in schools (Burns et al., 1995). Young children may be referred to mental health services because of the difficulty they are experiencing adjusting to the school environment including peer relationships and classroom expectations. Attending to difficulties early in young, modifiable children is better and more effective than waiting until problems are fully entrenched and the prognosis for change is the poorest.

Schools will be most successful in their educational mission when they integrate efforts to promote children's academic, social, and emotional learning (Elias et al., 1997). Patterns of school failure often begin in the first three years of school; research on potential dropouts indicates that characteristics associated with such outcomes can often be identified early (Rotheram, Armstrong, & Booraem, 1982). Primary Project can be implemented as part of a comprehensive continuum of services that schools can offer to meet the educational mission.

Primary Project began as a small, pilot demonstration project in a single school. It has been widely disseminated to over 2,100 elementary schools throughout the world. Primary Project is supported by decades of research demonstrating its effectiveness (Cowen et al., 1975, 1996;

Nafpaktitis & Perlmutter, 1998). Primary Project is currently listed as an evidenced-based intervention on the National Registry of Evidence-Based Programs and Practices (U.S. Department of Health and Human Services: Substance Abuse and Mental Health Services Administration, 2007). Reviewers have cited Primary Project as an exemplary prevention program (Dwyer & Bernstein, 1998; Elias et al., 1997; Natasi, 1998; Weissberg, Gulotta, Hampton, Ryan, & Adams, 1997). PMHP has received a number of awards as an outstanding prevention program. In 1984, the National Mental Health Association awarded Primary Project the Lela Rowland Prevention Award as the outstanding prevention program (Cowen & Hightower, 1989). In 1993, the Clinical and Child Psychology section 1 of the Clinical Psychology Division of Child Youth and Family Services of the American Psychological Association awarded Primary Project the "Model Program in Service Delivery in Child and Family Mental Health."

Primary Project has six core components that define the program. These core components have been in place since its early beginning in 1957, with the last component emerging in the last decade. The components are:

1. A focus on young children (prekindergarten through third grade).
2. Early detection and screening of children's social and emotional well-being.
3. The use of carefully selected and trained child associates as direct service providers.
4. A role change of the school-based mental health professional to that of supervisor, coordinator, trainer, and mentor.
5. Ongoing program evaluation.
6. Integration of the Project into the schools' continuum of services for children.

Once children are identified through a psychometrically sound screening instrument and selection process, parental permission is obtained. These children meet individually, once a week, with a carefully selected and trained paraprofessional called a child associate, who is supervised regularly by a school-based mental health professional. The child meets individually with the child associate in a specially created playroom in the school to develop a strong relationship. The intervention used is based on expressive play with the child associate using basic listening skills and creating a warm, caring, empathic relationship with the child through a child-centered play approach. This approach develops competencies and reduces less desirable behaviors.

Inherent in Primary Project is the belief that a child experiencing school adjustment problems can become more socially and emotionally competent when allowed to lead the child associate in a developmentally appropriate activity such as play (Cowen, Hightower, Pedro-Carroll, Work, Wyman, & Haffey, 1996).

A team approach geometrically increases the number of children who are helped and who might otherwise slip through the cracks in our educational system. Children's adjustment difficulties are identified early and support is given early instead of waiting for more significant issues to appear. The school-based mental health professional closely supervises the child associate's work with the children to monitor child progress and to transition to a more intensive type of service if needed. Ongoing training, program consultations, clinical consultations, and program evaluations help to support the school-based team's effectiveness and the program's integrity.

While the key components provide its basic framework, the mental health field has prompted all interventions to become clearer about program components and fidelity. To address this, Primary Project has developed national standards, supporting resource manuals, and DVD resources. Additionally, a process to address model fidelity has been developed that results in school programs receiving national certification. Programs that have been in existence for three years and adhere to the core components are visited by a national endorser. Interviews with team members, including parents, are conducted. These findings are then reviewed by a national board of professionals familiar with Primary Project program fidelity, and recommendations are made. If criteria are met, recognition as an exemplary Nationally Certified Primary Project site is awarded. In this age of accountability, programs that follow the model as it was originally developed will produce the strongest results for children.

Successful prevention program implementations must adapt to the realities of each setting, the resources available, the underpinning belief systems, and the prevailing practices (Hightower, Johnson, & Haffey, 1995). This is particularly true now, where evidenced-based programming is a clear expectation of schools. Dissemination of effective programs is also demanding that in order for effective programs to be replicated, clear definitions of program practices, interventions, theoretical underpinnings, training protocols, and supporting materials must also exist.

Every school should implement Primary Project with attention to the six core components. Where some flexibility and variation is found is in the following areas:

1. Specific measures used in the early detection and screening component.
2. Types of child associates (e.g., paid nonprofessionals, students, retired persons, educational levels, and gender).
3. Types of professional staffing patterns (community-based clinicians now collaborating with schools to implement the program with counselors, psychologists, social workers as key supervisors.
4. How child associates work with children (individually for the complete 12-to-15-week cycle only and then into play pair grouping).
5. The intensity of parent participation (from permission only, to observations, involvement in goal setting conferences, transition conferences, parent education groups).

Primary Project has a track record of demonstrated success in reducing school adjustment difficulties in a variety of settings (Cowen et al., 1983, 1996; Thomas, 1989; Weissberg, Cowen, Lotyczewski, & Gesten, 1983). It is a model that has worked effectively in the states of California, Connecticut, Florida, Hawaii, Louisiana, Maine, Massachusetts, Michigan, Minnesota, Missouri, New York, and Washington and in Canada and Brazil. Similarly, it has been effective in small rural schools as well as large urban settings. Significant improvement has been demonstrated for boys and girls, as well as for African American, Asian, American, Caucasian, Hispanic American, and Native American children (Cowen et al., 1996).

BASIC PROGRAM COMPONENTS

This section is intended to be a summary of Primary Project's basic components. It begins with a basic sequence of how to set up a Primary Project program and the playroom setting and materials. Next, it describes Primary Project's core defining components in more detail: the screening and referral processes, the types of children involved, and the typical team, including the school staff roles and responsibilities. Special emphasis is given to the characteristics of the child associate and the equally important role of the supervisor. Finally, the model's attention to fidelity is presented through a review of opportunities for technical assistance, training, and the national certification process.

Primary Project Start-Up: Planning and Preparation

School stakeholders, including school district administration, school boards, mental health professionals, teachers, and parents, all contribute to successful start-up. By participating in the planning and start-up steps, each group is given the opportunity to educate themselves about Primary Project and to offer input into where it will be integrated into the school system's continuum of support services that lead to student success. Such involvement increases participants' sense of program ownership, responsibility for the program, and success of implementation. Program start-up is successful when stakeholders 1) have identified and articulated a need for serving young children's mental health needs early; and 2) understand Primary Project's rationale, goals, and core components. Because schools differ in their readiness and acceptance of social and emotional programs, time between initial exposure and program start-up varies. Detailed descriptions of start-up processes are provided in Cowen et al. (1996), Hightower et al. (1995), and Johnson et al. (2006).

Additionally as more community mental health and behavioral care agencies work in schools, upfront and ongoing collaboration between community organizations and school systems is critical. Determining how Primary Project can best be integrated into the school system is important. This involves reviews of budgets, personnel, organizational charts, school schedules, screening and evaluation processes, available program options for young children at-risk, staff receptivity, existing mental health staff responsibilities, communication systems for staff and parents, and available space. In addition, careful planning as to how Primary Project will complement existing systems, processes, and programs is necessary. Without careful planning, the start-up process will be less than totally successful.

Presentations, site visits, research articles, and program materials are all available through Children's Institute in Rochester, New York, to help any interested school or community agency assess readiness for planning and future implementation.

The Playroom Space and Materials

In most elementary schools, space is a luxury. Typically the school principal designates what space is available for a Primary Project playroom. Ideally the space should be a warm, comfortable place that is welcoming and invites children to play. It is desirable for child associates and children to have individual spaces that become their own. A permanent space instead of a space that must deal with ongoing scheduling conflicts is best. However, if a space must be shared in a larger area, partitions have been successfully used to accommodate more than one child associate. Empty classrooms have creatively become inviting playrooms with the use of dividers, bookshelves, and storage bins. The goal, in any case, is to carve out an environment that is engaging to young children and gives the message that play is encouraged.

Playrooms are like personalities; no two are exactly alike. However, some materials that engage children in expressive, creative, or imaginative play are core in a Primary Project playroom; examples include: art materials, paints, crayons, a sandbox, a dollhouse, a school house, small animal figures, small family figures, action figures, dramatic play, puppets, building blocks or other manipulative toys, soft balls, clay, and drawing materials. Materials should be selected that allow children a wide range of expressive play opportunities, including toys that may invite expression of both comfortable and uncomfortable feelings.

Attention to different ethnic groups, diverse family configurations, culture, and gender should all be a part of the selection of materials. Materials should adhere to school policies; for example, if an elementary school has a "no weapons" policy in the classroom, including toy weapons, this should also be true in the playroom. This is different from the outside counselor or therapist who may be freer with their selection of expressive toys. We know that children who truly need more aggressive types of play will make the materials they need out of blocks or art, or simply act our dramatic stories by role playing themselves. A final guiding principle is that the supervisor and child associate must be comfortable with the materials and organization of the playroom.

SCREENING AND REFERRAL PROCESSES

Early detection, screening, and referral are focal in Primary Project; they form the basis on which the program's early preventive intervention steps rest. Conceptually, screening in Primary Project is an ongoing process. It extends over time, uses multiple methods and sources, and reflects informal as well as formal components.

School personnel witness children's behavior daily. Typically, when concerns about a child's behavior reach a certain threshold, which is often quite high, the child is referred to a building team or mental health professional. In Primary Project schools, a formal screening occurs at particular weeks of the school year. Simultaneously, a similar informal process occurs, but the acceptable threshold for staff to seek assistance and consultation is lowered significantly. There is ready access to the Primary Project team (e.g., principal, school-based mental health professional, teacher, and child associate) for raising concerns, discussing them, and getting immediate feedback about next possible steps. Hence, there is a continuous informal screening in Primary Project schools and a mechanism of team contact for addressing concerns that arise throughout the school year.

Screening   The formal Primary Project screening process attempts to develop an accurate representation of children's early school adjustment so that appropriate effective services can be provided as early as possible for those children who will benefit the most from Primary Project. Additionally, this program structure provides an efficient mechanism by which the school staff, including the Primary Project team, can review the early school adjustment of all children targeted (first grade, kindergarten to third grade, etc.). However, not all pertinent emotional and social dimensions can be assessed in an initial screening step. Metaphorically, a series of "snapshots" are taken over time, using various lenses and different angles, so that a composite description of each child's adjustment and needs becomes more vivid.

The screening process begins with the collection of information as soon as school starts. One way that "snapshots" over time and in various school settings occur is through the use of observation. Teachers and Primary Project team members observe children in classrooms, halls, lunchrooms, and on the playground. Supervisors may review school records and do more structured observations with standardized assessments as well as interview parents of selected students.

Many schools use rating scales developed and/or refined by Children's Institute. Universal screening ensures that all children will be looked at for possible inclusion. For example, the 12-item AML-R Behavior Rating Scale is often completed by the primary grade teacher for each child. This short instrument assesses the frequency of acting out, moodiness, and learning problem behaviors (Primary Mental Health Project, 1995). Other schools use the slightly longer Teacher-Child Rating Scale (TCR-S) that assesses both problem behavior and competencies (Perkins & Hightower, 2000).

The overall screening process for Primary Project strives to be systematic, multidimensional, and outreaching. Its prime goal is to identify by both informal and formal methods, existing problems and competencies in several relevant domains of school functioning for all children in their early school careers.

Referral   Although the formal screening process identifies most children who are referred to Primary Project, referrals are accepted throughout the school year. For some children, initial problems that did not meet threshold criteria could increase as the school year progresses, and the teacher might subsequently feel a referral is warranted. Many children with school adjustment difficulties transfer into a school throughout the year. Sometimes children who were doing well initially experience situations that adversely affect their school adjustment.

In summary, referrals to Primary Project can, and do, come from many sources. A child's functioning cannot accurately be assessed from only one moment in time or by one viewpoint. Both formal and informal screening should be part of the referral process, and program scheduling should remain flexible enough to accommodate new referrals throughout the school year. It is ultimately a team decision, guided by the mental health professional's knowledge and judgment, to decide whether a referred child is most appropriate for Primary Project or whether another service would best meet his or her needs.

CONFERENCES

After initial screening steps are complete, relevant information is brought together at a selection conference. The Primary Project team reviews both formal and informal screening results, creates profiles of children's school adjustment, identifies children who are most appropriate for Primary Project services and which children may need more intensive services, and then seeks written parental permission.

Children Served by Primary Project   Primary Project's preventive approach is to intervene effectively with children as soon as problems are identified to optimize children's school functioning. In reaching this goal, Primary Project targets young children with school adjustment problems in the mild to moderate range—not children who need professional help. Children most appropriate for Primary Project include those who 1) are shyr, withdrawing from engagement, nervous, sad, hesitant to speak up in class; 2) become easily frustrated, act out mildly, lose their tempers, seek attention aggressively, or do not always follow school rules; 3) have few friends, do not get along with their peers, are socially isolated; 4) fail to complete their schoolwork, have limited attention spans, are frequently off-task and need adult attention; 5) are experiencing something in either their school or home environment that is effecting their learning.

In summary, Primary Project targets and works most effectively with those children who are just beginning to show a few of the aforementioned problems, rather than those with numerous and deeply entrenched difficulties. These children may not need outside therapy or school-based counseling, but they often need a connection with an adult in the school.

THE PRIMARY PROJECT TEAM

Central to the Primary Project team are school-based mental health professionals, such as school psychologists, school social worker, school counselors, child associates, and teachers and administrators. Increasingly, over the past few years, schools have partnered with community behavioral health care agencies to expand the array of services that are offered on a school campus. These community behavioral health agencies employ mental health professionals to work directly in the schools and collaborate with all school-based professionals. Many community behavioral health care agencies are successfully partnering with elementary schools to implement Primary Project into the school setting. This partnership allows for integration into the community and helps expand the role and services available to children.

A principal's positive involvement in Primary Project sets a tone for staff and parents as to the important linkage between the social and emotional needs for all children and their success with academic learning. Primary grade teachers are also central to Primary Project as they are the key referral source and complete many of the outcome measures. In some schools, the team includes other key players (e.g., school nurse, occupational therapist, physical therapist, English as second language educators). The team understands the core components and which children will best benefit. In that context, teams hold meetings throughout the school year to assess program progress, evaluate group data, and plan for the future.

PROFESSIONAL ROLES AND ACTIVITIES

School-based mental health professionals are intimately involved in the entire program and are responsible for overseeing the day-to-day operations. They manage the early detection and screening process; coordinate communication with parents and the public; help select, train, and provide clinical supervision to the child associates; consult with teachers and other school staff; facilitate or conduct the evaluation; assist in preparing project reports; and participate in ongoing staff development. As part of their involvement in Primary Project, a role shift occurs. Rather than doing in-depth diagnostic and therapeutic activities with a few of the school's most troubled children, the professionals involve themselves in effective early detection and prevention interventions for many more children than traditional approaches can reach. Balancing both prevention efforts with more intensive services allows a wider approach to school mental health services.

The Child Associate

Over the long history of Primary Project, using paraprofessionals to address the shortage of mental health professionals and to apply direct services to children has proven to be a successful model (Cowen et al., 1996; Durlak, 1979; Hattie, Sharpley, & Rogers, 1984). Key to the success however has been the recruitment and selection of persons with "natural talents" who can learn new ways of being with young children.

Child associates possess many special qualities that include, but are not limited to, maturity, a history of successful experiences with young children, flexibility, good communication skills, intellectual interest in learning about child development and mental health, responsiveness to supervision and feedback, good personal adjustment, a sense of humor, and nurturing and intuitive capabilities.

The process of identifying appropriate child associates takes priority over all other considerations, for no training program can compensate for a poor selection at the outset. Insofar as the selection process is critical to the ultimate success of the program, it is strongly recommended that the individuals who will be actively involved in supervision of the child associates be involved in their selection. A rule of thumb is that if any member of the team is uncomfortable with a candidate, the individual should be referred elsewhere for employment.

Training for Child Associates and Supervisors   Training is a key component in the delivery of Primary Project services. Training for both child associates and mental health supervisors is critical. Training is generally divided into two broad categories: introductory and continuing. Introductory training covers a variety of topics to ensure successful start-up and will be discussed in further detail below, while continuing training is designed to deepen and refine the skills of child associates and supervisors and to address more challenging areas.

The introductory training is typically a two-day training, which supervisors and child associates are required to attend. Additional team members are always encouraged to attend, enabling buy-in from the beginning and a foundational knowledge base that is consistent and thorough. It begins with an overview of Primary Project, its history and core components, and a discussion about barriers to children's learning. An orientation to the various screening and pre/post measures is undertaken, with a review of the options available for schools in terms of scoring and identifying the most appropriate children for the project. Discussion about school-based procedures regarding confidentiality, child abuse reporting guidelines, selection conferences, gaining parental permission, and successful scheduling of children are all touched upon. Roles and responsibilities of each team member are explained. Care is given to help team members know how to explain the linkages between relationships, resiliency, school adjustment, and the importance of play to children's overall learning. The role of both clinical and administrative supervision is explored, and the dual responsibility of successful supervision from both the supervisor and the child associate is explained.

Time is spent on the intervention of child-centered play and the playroom environment and materials. A significant amount of time is spent on relationship-building skills and language, including reflective listening, verbal and nonverbal attending behaviors that enhance trust building, and unconditional positive regard. Structuring the beginning and ending of playroom sessions, empathic listening and responding, and limit setting under the nondirective stance of a child-centered play approach are all emphasized. Other skills introduced and practiced are giving encouragement statements, returning responsibility back to the child to increase competence and decision making, and imaginative role playing with children. This introduction to child-centered play and ways of building relationships with young children is demonstrated. Participants then engage in several different role playing opportunities themselves with guidance from the trainers. Many participants have commented that while the practice is initially difficult and unfamiliar, it is the best way to become more natural and proficient at the skills. Our experience is that with time and supervision, child associates become quite natural and skilled at this intervention. Having experienced child associates participate with new associates in introductory sessions can be extremely helpful.

Another topic covered in the introductory component deals with ending of Primary Project sessions. Termination regularly arouses powerful feelings for both the children and the child associates, so dealing with transference and counter transference issues are commonly addressed in supervision. Examples of various strategies to prepare for the final sessions and even celebrate with specific termination activities are shared. Some programs include parents in a positive, uplifting termination event that also serves to underline the legitimacy of the program in the school setting and helps establish support for the program.

Final training components include a timeline of monthly deadlines and tasks that help organize a new program and help ensure smooth implementation. Additionally, sharing of successful public relations efforts and ways to elicit buy-in from educators are discussed. Before ending, a review on how play is linked to healthy development is summarized. Finally, an emphasis on early commitment to program fidelity is stressed, and ongoing training and consultation is offered.

Continuing training should serve to expose both supervisors and child associates to a variety of supporting topics. Working with both shy and active children, refining limit setting, parent involvement, child development topics, communication with parents and teachers, marketing, and advocating for play and Primary Project are some examples of topics that are offered. A rule of thumb is that continuing training supports the consistent message that nondirective, expressive play and prevention are the core ingredients of Primary Project. If the team feels a more directive approach is needed, then the team, guided by the mental health supervisor, has the responsibility of determining what other services and interventions in the school would better meet the needs of the child than Primary Project.

While there are nationally certified trainers that offer Primary Project training throughout the country, it should be noted that the supervisor will be responsible for most ongoing training. Hence, it becomes imperative for supervisors to undertake their own course of study in play, play therapy, and supervision. Many school mental health professionals have found this to be a huge professional and personal bonus of becoming involved in Primary Project.

Supervision of Child Associates   In addition to training, child associates are provided with regular, typically weekly, supervision to ensure their growth and development. Supervisors assume clinical responsibility for child associates' work, which means ongoing supervision, is necessary.

Supervision will vary from program to program, depending on the team's resources, and supervision style. Many programs use a combination of individual and group supervision if more than one child associate is part of the program. While weekly scheduled time is critical, "as needed" supervision must be anticipated and accommodated. Child associates should always feel that their supervisor is reachable and should be taught what is immediate and what can wait for the weekly set aside time.

School mental health professionals vary in their clinical supervision experience, lack of training, and/or experience in supervising. Added to the formula is that the supervision of a child associate as a paraprofessional is different than supervising someone who is studying to become a mental health professional, like an intern or someone who shares the same educational background. In contrast, child associates are chosen for their ability to relate to children, not for their professional training. Some professionals may express concerns about the ability of paraprofessionals to be effective or may lead them to expect and perform beyond their training. It is important for supervisors to take advantage of new supervisory materials available through Primary Project training centers (Primary Project, 2007).

Clinical supervision in Primary Project provides child associates with skill feedback about their time with children and guidance about what to do in times of confusion or need. A supervisor needs to understand and respect the modality of play for young children (Primary Project, 2007). Topics of future training for supervisors include understanding the process and content of play sessions; possible play themes that may emerge and how to share those with child associates, teachers, and parents; note taking; understanding supervisee developmental levels; and finding a supervision model that matches the supervisor.

One way of conceptualizing the supervisory role in Primary Project is by a framework developed by Bernard and Goodyear (2004). The roles of teacher, consultant, and counselor are explored and Primary Project supervisors challenge themselves to find ways to use all three roles.

Additionally, assessment of the supervisee's skill level is part of supervision. The child associate's ability to form a helping relationship, verbal and nonverbal behaviors, willingness to share, and willingness to work through challenging situations are all considered in the supervision process. Supervisors will also need to evaluate the child associates' knowledge level regarding their feelings in relation to the child and their ability to conceptualize. These areas will develop over time, and we often find that experienced child associates become extremely competent in child-centered play, due to the consistent practice of practicing one intervention with numerous and varied children.

As a program, and particularly in the last few years, Primary Project has placed great emphasis on the supervisory process. Workshops and two-day academies now exist for supervisors to receive specific training. With effective supervision, Primary Project is a robust and effective program; without effective supervision, Primary Project will falter.

TECHNICAL ASSISTANCE AND TRAINING

Developing, implementing, and maintaining school-based prevention programs require technical assistance and ongoing support (Hightower et al., 1995). Primary Project provides technical assistance, consultation, and training from its home base in Rochester, New York, as well as nationally and internationally. In areas where Primary Project–initiated programs are more densely located, such as New York and California, a system of technical assistance centers or Regional Centers has been developed. Services and materials available worldwide include assistance with all aspects of initial program setup; program development manuals, DVDs, resource books; consultation with potential funders; support and customization of ongoing trainings to meet the needs of programs; selection and evaluation of technical assistance; and a full of array of evaluation services, including evaluation design, measures, analyses, and reports.

CONCLUSION

Few programs of any type can trace their history back five decades. Primary Project's success exemplifies how prevention programs can start, evolve, accommodate, adapt, and grow. The first reason Primary Project has enjoyed success is that its foundation is built on research and continuously evaluated program effectiveness. Second, although the key structural elements of the program have remained surprisingly consistent, as the mental health field has called for clearer definitions of interventions, standards of program fidelity measures and best practices, Primary Project has refined its trainings and dissemination materials. Third, Primary Project is cost-effective. Children receive excellent services from truly exceptional adults in an efficient and timely manner. Parents, teachers, administrators, and elected officials all enjoy benefits of the program that range from changes in children's behavior to a decreased tax burden. Therefore, Primary Project, implemented with program fidelity, not only can survive, but can flourish in times of wealth as well as in times of scarcity.

Professionals with long-term vision and plans based on solid research and forward thinking create services that people want and need. We believe that Primary Project is a school-based service that can be implemented successfully and become an integral program in the array of school-based mental health services that are part of a comprehensive and coordinated approach in an elementary school. Because social-emotional competence and academic achievement are highly interwoven, school mental health providers must continue to integrate and coordinate efforts to maximize the potential of young children.

SOURCE FOR PRIMARY PROJECT MATERIALS, TRAINING, TECHNICAL ASSISTANCE

Primary Project: Children's Institute
274 N. Goodman Street, Suite D103
Rochester, New York 14607
Toll free 1–877–888–7647
www.childrensinstitute.net

REFERENCES

Bernard, J. M., & Goodyear, R. K. (2004). *Fundamentals of clinical supervision* (3rd ed.). Boston: Allyn & Bacon.

Burns, B. J., Costello, E. J., Angold, A., Tweed, D., Dalene Stangl, E., Farmer, M. Z., & Erkanli, A. (1995). Children's mental health service use across service sectors. *Health Affairs, 14*, 147–159.

Cowen, E. L. & Hightower, A. D (1989). The Primary Mental Health Project: Thirty years after. In R. E. Hess & J. DeLeon (Eds.), *The National Mental Health Association: Eighty years of involvement in the field of prevention* (pp. 225–257). New York: Haworth Press.

Cowen, E. L., Hightower, A. D., Pedro-Carroll, J., Work, W. C., Wyman, P. A., & Haffey, W. C. (1996). *School-based prevention for children at-risk: The Primary Mental Health Project*. Washington, DC: American Psychological Association.

Cowen, E. L., Trost, M. A., Lorion, R. P., Dorr, D., Izzo, L. D., & Isaacson, R. V. (1975). *New ways in school mental health: Early detection and prevention of school maladaptation.* New York: Human Sciences Press.

Cowen, E. L., Weissberg, R. P., Lotyczewski, B. S., Bromley, M. L., Gilliland-Mallo, G., DeMeis, J. L., Fargo, J. P., Grassi, R. J., Haffey, W. G., Weiner, M. J., & Woods, A. (1983). Validity generalization of a school-based preventive mental health program. *Professional Psychology, 14,* 613–623.

Durlak, J. A. (1979). Comparative effectiveness of paraprofessionals and professional helpers. *Psychological Bulletin, 86,* 80–92.

Dwyer, K. P., & Bernstein, R. (1998). Mental Health in schools: Linking islands of hope in a sea of despair. *School Psychology Review, 27,* 277–286.

Elias, M. J., Zins, J. E., Weissberg, R. P., Frey, K. S., Greenberg, M. T., Haynes, N. M., Kessler, R., Schwab-Stone, M. E., & Shriver, T. P. (1997). *Promoting social and emotional learning: Guidelines for educators.* Alexandria, VA: Association for Supervision and Curriculum Development.

Hattie, J. A., Sharpley, C. F., & Rogers, H. J. (1984). Comparative effectiveness of professional and paraprofessional helpers. *Psychological Bulletin, 95,* 534–541.

Hightower, A. D., Johnson, D. B., & Haffey, W. G. (1995). Best practices in adopting a prevention program. In A. Thomas & J. Grimes (Eds.), *Best practices in school psychology: III* (pp. 311–323). Washington, DC: National Association of School Psychologists.

Johnson, D. B., Demanchick, S. P., & Peabody, M. A. (2006). *Primary project program development manual.* Rochester, NY: Children's Institute.

Nafpaktitis, M., & Perlmutter, B. F. (1998). School-based early mental health intervention with at-risk students. *School Psychology Review, 27,* 420–432.

Natasi, B. (1998). *Exemplary mental health program: School psychologists as mental health providers.* Bethesda, MD: National Association of School Psychologists.

Perkins, P. E., & Hightower, A. D. (2000). *Teacher-Child Rating Scale, V21: Technical manual.* Rochester, NY: Children's Institute.

Primary Mental Health Project. (1995). *PMHP screening and evaluation measures.* Rochester, NY: Author.

Primary Project (2007). *Supervision Resource Guide.* Rochester, NY: Children's Institute.

Rotheram, M. J., Armstrong, M., & Booraem, C. (1982). Assertiveness training in fourth and fifth grade children. *American Journal of Community Psychology, 10,* 567–582.

Thomas, C. F. (1989). *An evaluation of the effectiveness of the Primary Intervention Program in improving the school and social adjustment of primary grade children: Final report.* Los Alamitos, CA: Southwest Regional Education Laboratory.

U.S. Department of Health and Human Services: Substance Abuse and Mental Health Services Administration (2007). *National registry of evidenced-based programs and practices.* Rockville, MD: Author.

U.S. Public Health Service. (2000). *Report of the Surgeon General's conference on children's mental health: A national action agenda.* Washington, DC: Author.

Weissberg, R. P., Cowen, E. L., Lotyczewski, B. S., & Gesten, E. L. (1983). Primary Mental Health Project: Seven consecutive years of program outcome research. *Journal of Consulting and Clinical Psychology, 51,* 100–107.

Weissberg, R. P., Gulotta, T. P., Hampton, R. L., Ryan, B. A., & Adams, G. R. (1997). *Establishing preventive services* (Vol. 9). Thousand Oaks, CA: Sage.

CHAPTER 9

Child–Teacher Relationship Training

Using the Power of the Child–Teacher Relationship as a School-Based Mental Health Intervention

MARY O. MORRISON and
WENDY PRETZ HELKER

C HILD–TEACHER RELATIONSHIP TRAINING (CTRT) is a play-based counseling intervention adapted from Landreth and Bratton's (2006) 10-week Child–Parent Relationship Therapy (CPRT) model intended for use in the schools to enhance child–teacher relationships as well as to be a useful intervention for children experiencing mental health difficulties in early childhood. Teachers and paraprofessionals are trained in the basic principles of Child-Centered Play Therapy (CCPT) as well as specific relationship-building skills consistent with the CPRT model for use with an individual child in a special playroom. Participants are then trained in how to adapt these skills for use with groups of children in the general classroom. Throughout their sessions with individual children as well as throughout their work with groups of children, teachers and paraprofessionals are provided weekly supervision in order to assist them in gaining a better understanding of children, answering questions regarding skill use, offering support with challenges that may occur in their experiences using CCPT and relationship-building skills, and providing continued learning experiences and training opportunities. The basic components of

181

CTRT include a focus on enhancing the child–teacher relationship through the training and supervision of teachers and paraprofessionals by mental health professionals knowledgeable in the areas of Child-Centered Play Therapy and Child–Parent Relationship Therapy, as well as an early intervention for children who are at-risk.

CTRT originated as a research study seeking to investigate whether or not training teachers and paraprofessionals in CCPT and relationship-building skills may have an impact on student behavior. The investigation was prompted by two factors. First, according to the U.S. Surgeon General's report on mental health, there are a growing number of children suffering with emotional, behavioral, and developmental challenges. In fact the Surgeon General described the mental health situation for young children as a national "crisis." Children's needs in these areas are not being met due to a shortage of mental health professionals specially trained to work with children, a lack of accessible services, and perhaps most salient, the need for early intervention, specifically involving caregivers in the delivery of services (United States Public Health Service, 2000, p. 164). The President's New Freedom Commission on Mental Health (2003) reiterated the need for early intervention and emphasized a need for mental health services to be offered in accessible, low-stigma settings such as schools. The lack of services provided to children directly impacts teachers. Teachers work with children with a wide variety of emotional and behavioral difficulties on a daily basis. However, teachers often lack the training, knowledge, and skills necessary to respond to students' emotional and behavioral needs in addition to children's academic needs (Yokshikawa & Knitzer, 1997). This lack of training may increase teachers' stress and cause difficulty in relating to a child experiencing emotional or behavioral difficulties. Teachers who are more stressed tend to respond to students in ways that perpetuate rather than prevent problematic behaviors (Yost & Mosca, 2002), and children who experience relationships with teachers that are characterized by conflict are less engaged in school (Birch & Ladd, 1997; Pianta & Stuhlman, 2004). Therefore, teachers and students may become caught in a cycle in which both perceive the school environment as negative.

The additional component that is the second catalyst to the development of the CTRT program is how the student–teacher relationship connects to students' social/emotional, behavioral, and mental health as well as to students' ability to adjust to, and become successful in, school. Research indicates that the quality of the student–teacher relationship impacts students' social/emotional development, academic achievement, and classroom functioning (Helker, Schottelkorb, & Ray, 2007; Hamre & Pianta, 2001). Positive student–teacher relationships are of primary importance in promoting children's successful adjustment to school, whereas negative student–teacher relationships may exacerbate children's difficulty in adjusting successfully to school. In a comprehensive study of teacher–child relationship effect, Baker (2006) concluded that a positive teacher–child relationship correlated significantly with behavioral and academic indicators of school success across all elementary grade levels and gender. Children who demonstrated social and behavioral problems were especially positively impacted by an encouraging teacher–child relationship. Birch and Ladd (1998) indicated that teacher-reported closeness in the teacher–child relationship is positively related to students' academic growth in school as demonstrated by increased student independence and higher visual and language scores on standardized achievement tests. A longitudinal study conducted by Peisner-Feinberg, Culkin, Howes, and Kagan (1999) concluded that children who experienced warm student–teacher relationships performed better on thinking, language ability, and math skills when compared to children who did not experience such a warm relationship. Pianta and Stuhlman (2004) investigated different aspects of the teacher–child relationship and found that the interpersonal aspects (relationships with teachers and peers) make a difference in the children's ability to develop competencies in the early years of school. Characteristics of the teacher–child relationship may contribute to the child's ability to build peer relationships as well. Based on results from their study, Howes, Hamilton, and Matheson (1994) suggested that a child's emotional security with his/her first teacher provides a child-positive orientation to peer relationships, and socialization experiences help shape the child's particular behavior with peers.

It is evident that positive student–teacher relationships are important, but it is also important to note that negative teacher–child relationships may impact a child's social/emotional, academic, and classroom functioning as well. Studies indicate that children who experience relationships with teachers that are characterized by conflict and dependency (from the teacher's perception) tend to like school less, avoid school more, and are less engaged in class when compared to children whose teachers perceive a close, more positive student–teacher relationship (Birch & Ladd, 1997; Pianta & Stuhlman, 2004). Further, teacher–child relationships characterized by conflict were associated with a decline in the children's appropriate behavior and academic performance (Ladd & Burgess, 2001).

The development of CTRT was a natural response to the need for high-quality student–teacher relationships to attend to the mental health needs of young children.

ROOTS OF CHILD–TEACHER RELATIONSHIP TRAINING

The foundation of CTRT lies in the basic principles and tenets of Child Centered Play Therapy (CCPT) and filial therapy. In CCPT, Landreth (2002) proposes that children have the inner capacity to grow and develop in a positive, healthy direction and can access inner resources to cope with challenging experiences. It is through a caring relationship with a significant person who communicates to the child unconditional acceptance, genuineness, and prizing that the child can begin to accept himself or herself. The play therapist works to communicate understanding of the child, while the child communicates thoughts, feelings, and experiences through the child's natural means of expression, which is play (Landreth, 2002). Guerney (1964) expanded the ideas of CCPT to include parents as therapeutic agents and titled this new concept *filial therapy*. Bernard and Louise Guerney trained parents in foundational CCPT skills to use in play sessions with their children each week with the underlying rationale being that the parent–child relationship is more emotionally significant to the child than a relationship with a play therapist and consequently meets the child's emotional needs in a more meaningful way (Guerney, 1964; Guerney, 2000). Parents participated in a group format that included didactic instruction, demonstrations, role-playing, at-home play sessions, and supervision (Guerney, 1964). Early research by the Guerneys and their protégées demonstrated that parents/caregivers were capable of learning essential CCPT skills and were effective therapeutic agents with their children (Guerney & Stover, 1971; Guerney, 2000; Stover & Guerney, 1967; Oxman, 1972).

CHILD–PARENT RELATIONSHIP THERAPY (CPRT)

Building on the Guerneys' work, Landreth (2002) developed a more time-sensitive model of filial therapy. Landreth and Bratton (2006) formalized this 10-session model as *Child–Parent Relationship Therapy: A 10-Session Filial Therapy Model*. Grounded in the same philosophy as the Guerney model, Child–Parent Relationship Therapy (CPRT) uses a balanced approach of didactic and experiential supervision experiences in a small-group training model that requires parents to conduct weekly videotaped play sessions with their child under the supervision of a specially trained mental health provider. The CPRT protocol was manualized by Bratton, Landreth, Kellam, and Blackard (2006), allowing for replication of the model.

Extensive research has been conducted with a wide variety of populations using the CPRT model through 35 studies, including 28 controlled-outcome studies involving more than 1,000 subjects. Bratton, Ray, Rhine, and Jones (2005) report in their meta-analytic research of play therapy that 26 of the 93 studies included used filial therapy methodology and demonstrated a treatment effect size of ES = 1.05. Landreth and Bratton (2006) further analyzed only those studies using the CPRT protocol (unpublished at that time) often referred to in the literature as the Landreth 10-session filial therapy model. In order to ensure treatment protocol, the authors only included studies conducted by researchers directly trained and supervised by either Landreth or Bratton in the analysis. Statistical analysis revealed a large treatment effect size of 1.25 for CPRT conducted by parents/caregivers, teachers, and mentors, thus demonstrating the effectiveness of this treatment approach. Landreth and Bratton (2006) provide a thorough review of the aforementioned CPRT outcome research studies. The substantial body of CPRT/filial therapy outcome research provides support for the efficacy of this approach and its applicability with a broad array of issues with varied and diverse populations.

ADAPTATION OF FILIAL THERAPY WITH TEACHERS

Andronico and Guerney (1969) first recommended using teachers as therapeutic agents, relying on the idea that the child–teacher relationship is valuable and that teachers are identified as significant people in children's lives. Guerney and Flumen (1970) researched this premise and found that teachers were capable of learning CCPT skills and implementing them in play sessions with their students. Several CPRT studies have also shown the effectiveness of the CPRT model with teachers in the school setting (Helker, 2007; Morrison, 2007; Smith & Landreth, 2004) and pre-service teachers (Brown, 2003; Crane & Brown, 2003).

Smith and Landreth (2004) examined the effectiveness of the 10-session CPRT model with teachers of hard of hearing and deaf preschool children. Compared to a no-treatment control group, the teachers in the experimental group significantly improved their empathic interactions with students. CPRT demonstrated a large treatment effect on reducing total problems and internalizing behavior problems for children in the experimental group. In similar studies, Brown (2003) and Crane and Brown (2003) investigated the effects of CPRT with undergraduate students who were preparing to become teachers/human service providers for children. Both studies revealed that students receiving the CPRT intervention demonstrated statistically significant gains in empathic interactions with children.

Kinder Therapy

Using an approach based on principles and procedures similar to CPRT titled Kinder Therapy, White, Flynt, and Draper (1997); White, Flynt, and Jones (1999); Draper, White, O'Shaughnessy, Flynt, and Jones (2001); and Post, McAllister, Sheely, Hess, and Flowers (2004) researched the effects of training teachers in filial therapy methodology and also demonstrated promising outcomes. While the strength of these studies is limited by the absence of random assignment and control groups, the results are encouraging, revealing increases in teachers' empathic interactions with students, decreases in child behavior problems, and improvement in early literacy skills.

The idea to adapt Landreth and Bratton's (2006) Child–Parent Relationship Therapy model for teachers was based on the successful outcomes of the previously mentioned research. Specific changes were made to the Child–Parent Relationship Therapy Treatment Manual (Bratton et al., 2006) to accommodate the differences in the child–teacher relationship as compared to the child–parent relationship and to provide training examples that would encompass the school climate rather than the home climate and experiences unique to the classroom setting and school schedule.

STRUCTURING CHILD–TEACHER RELATIONSHIP TRAINING

Planning

Gathering members of the school community who have identified the need for addressing young children's social, emotional, and mental health needs early on is an essential first step in putting CTRT into place. These members may include school board members; school administrators; school mental health professionals, such as the school counselor, social worker, or school psychologist; teachers; and other invested parties. For successful implementation of this intervention, team members should have an understanding of the premise, goals, and methods of the CTRT program and support how CTRT will blend with the school's mission. One primary goal of this team is to review discipline policies, school schedules, staff receptivity, current staff responsibilities, and communication with parents and staff to determine how CTRT may complement the existing programs and resources available at the school. In addition, space availability for play sessions, supervision sessions, and meeting space will need to be determined.

SPACE AND MATERIALS

Ideally, a space in the school building will be allocated for a CTRT playroom. The perfect playroom would be a dedicated space that is warm and inviting, allows for privacy, mess, noise, and no interruptions. For supervision purposes, the room should allow for the capability of video and audio recording of sessions; a small eyeball security camera mounted in a corner connected to a VHS or DVD recorder works well. This equipment is inexpensive and can be purchased at any electronics store. It is important that the electronic equipment be simple so the teachers can easily put in their tape or DVD, push Record, and then focus on their session.

Because space is highly valuable and often difficult to obtain, creativity in choosing a space is helpful. Playroom space can be found in a variety of unexpected places. A large unused closet or storage space, the corner of an office, an old classroom, or a section of the stage are all possible spaces for a playroom. Larger spaces can be converted by using dividers and shelves to create smaller space if necessary. A small storage drawer to hold extra toys and a map of the arrangement of toys is recommended and will allow for consistency in the playroom. Categories of toys necessary to furnish a playroom include real-life toys (dolls, dollhouse, puppets, car, truck, boat, cash register), acting out or aggressive toys (toy soldiers, rubber knife, something that can be destroyed such as an egg carton, a variety of animals including alligators, dinosaurs, sharks, etc.), and creative release toys (sand, water, blocks, paints). For a complete list and further information on playroom toy selection, see Landreth (2002). If space is limited, then a traditional filial kit will work as well (Landreth & Bratton, 2006).

CHILD–TEACHER RELATIONSHIP TRAINING

SUPERVISOR QUALIFICATIONS AND RESPONSIBILITIES

The CTRT supervisor is the school-based mental health professional with advanced knowledge and skills in Child Centered Play Therapy, filial therapy, and the CPRT model (Landreth & Bratton, 2006) and is responsible for teaching and supervising the participants in CTRT skills. This model is possible to execute with one school-based mental health professional; however, if there are additional qualified professionals available, dividing up the responsibilities of training, supervision, and general logistics might be helpful.

PARTICIPANT TRAINING

Phase I   During Phase I, teachers are taught core CTRT principles and skills, including allowing the child to lead, reflective listening, reflecting content, recognizing and responding to children's feelings, therapeutic limit setting, building children's self-esteem, facilitating creativity/spontaneity, facilitating decision making, returning responsibility, and structuring. Phase I training content is equivalent to the curriculum covered in the CPRT 10-session model outlined in the *CPRT Treatment Manual* (Bratton et al., 2006). It may be helpful to structure the training in a way that utilizes the teachers' time most efficiently. Providing intensive training during teacher inservice days at the beginning of the school year and holding the weekly one-hour supervision meetings during teachers' planning period effectively uses teachers' time. According to the CTRT model, 2.5 days of intensive didactic instruction covers the equivalent of the content of the first four sessions in the *CPRT Manual*. Following this intensive training, teachers select one child of focus to practice their CTRT skills in seven weekly 30-minute play sessions. An important component to this step is ensuring that teachers choose a specific 30-minute time block and a specific day that they can commit to on a weekly basis in order to ensure the consistency of the seven play sessions. Keeping in mind that several teachers will be using the playroom for play sessions, it is essential for a playroom schedule to be created during this phase. Sessions are videotaped in Phase I so that videotapes can be viewed during the weekly one-hour supervision time. During supervision in Phase I, supervisors provide didactic and experimental practice of skills that are presented in sessions 4 to 10 in the *CPRT Manual* (Bratton et al., 2006) and adapted for the school setting. It is critical that supervisors provide specific feedback regarding teachers' use of skills demonstrated in their re-corded play sessions, as well as encouragement and support, and help teachers understand children's expression of experiences and feelings during the play session. Consistent with the CPRT model (Landreth & Bratton, 2006), the weekly child–teacher play sessions and weekly supervision provide a controlled setting for teachers to focus and practice their skills before attempting to generalize their skills to everyday use. In fact, teachers are specifically instructed not to practice CTRT skills in the classroom during this phase in order to ensure successful integration prior to using their newly acquired skills in the more difficult setting of their classroom (Helker, 2007; Morrison, 2007).

Phase II The focus of Phase II is to assist teachers in generalizing their use of relationship-building skills with an individual child in the playroom to use with small groups of children in the natural classroom setting. To facilitate this transition, individual play sessions are dis-continued and replaced with Child–Teacher Relationship-Time (CTR-Time) in the classroom. Supervisors work with teachers to establish a daily time in the classroom in which children are allowed to direct their own play at centers such as dramatic play, blocks, manipulatives, and home center. During a 15-minute portion of this time, teachers with modeling/coaching from the supervisor are asked to practice using relationship-building skills with small groups of children. During this time the other teaching partner focuses on general classroom manage-ment, and then teachers switch roles to allow both teaching partners the opportunity to have CTR-Time with students. It is essential that teachers use this specifically structured time to practice utilizing skills to avoid overwhelming teachers and to encourage successful imple-mentation of the new skills. As part of the supervision process, the CTRT supervisor spends several weeks modeling/coaching how to transition the use of relationship-building skills with a small group of children in the classroom while the teacher watches and participates as needed (Helker, 2007; Morrison, 2007).

As CTR-Time continues over the course of 10 weeks, modeling decreases as teachers become more proficient in using CTRT skills, eventually using the skills independently of the supervisor. Addition-ally during Phase II, teachers and supervisors continue to meet for one-hour weekly supervision sessions and focus on more advanced skills, such as group reflection skills, advanced limit setting, and choice giving (Bratton et al., 2006). The supervisor continues to support the teachers and address the challenges, questions, and difficulties associated with transitioning from individual play sessions to the classroom setting. At the completion of the 10-week Phase II of training, the supervisor's role shifts. Weekly supervision sessions and in-classroom modeling are discontinued but may be offered to teachers on an as-needed basis. It is at this point that program evaluation can be conducted (Helker, 2007; Morrison, 2007).

Evaluation of Child–Teacher Relationship Training

CTRT can be evaluated using both formal and informal assessment measures. In the pilot study, the Child Behavior Checklist-Caregiver-Teacher Report Form (C-TRF; Achenbach & Rescorla, 2000) was used as a primary assessment tool. This particular instrument is widely utilized in the mental health community to measure problematic child behaviors as identified by teachers/caregivers. For the purpose of this study, the C-TRF was used to qualify children for this study (pretest), and then given again at midpoint (after Phase I), posttest (after Phase II), and a final time at follow-up (10 weeks after the conclusion of Phase II) to examine treatment effects. The C-TRF is comprised of eight syndrome and six *DSM*-oriented scales, as well as three domain scores: Internalizing Problems, Externalizing Problems, and Total Problems. To screen children for the study, teachers completed a C-TRF on all children whose parents gave consent to participate. Children who qualified for the study scored in the borderline or clinical range on at least one scale of the C-TRF. This rigorous schedule of measurement is not required; evaluation can be a simplified pre- and posttest model to evaluate treatment effects of CTRT on children's behavior.

To determine whether teachers are able to learn the skills and utilize them in the classroom setting, an additional assessment tool, The Child–Teacher Relationship Training Skills Checklist (CTRT-SC; Helker, 2007) can be used. The CTRT-SC (Helker et al., 2007, as cited in Helker, 2007) was created using the Play Therapy Skills Checklist, originally developed by the Center for Play Therapy (Ray, 2004), as a guide. The CTRT-SC (Helker, 2007) is an observation form designed to identify whether responses teachers make to children in the classroom can be classified as being consistent with skills taught in CTRT or are responses that are not designated as CTRT relationship-building skills.

More informal means of data collection may also be used to evaluate the effectiveness of CTRT. Determining the number of office referrals from participating teachers before training compared to after training may provide valuable information as well. A reduced number of office referrals could indicate that teachers felt more equipped to handle classroom difficulties or that the severity of behavioral problems had decreased. Teacher interviews at pretest, midpoint, posttest, and follow-up could also be conducted to determine the teachers' perceptions of CTRT and its impact on student classroom behavior. Parent data could also be collected to determine if parents saw behavioral changes at home.

RESULTS OF PILOT STUDY

As previously mentioned, CTRT originated as a pilot study conducted in a Head Start Center in the Southwest region of the United States. For a detailed explanation of the research, please consult Morrison (2007) and Helker (2007). Morrison (2007) collected data regarding the behavior change in children at pre-, mid-, and posttesting, while Helker (2007) collected data regarding teachers' use of skills and then collected follow-up data regarding the behavior change in the children and correlated results to the teachers' use of skills. These research studies yielded some interesting results. Helker (2007) found that preschool teachers and aides who participated in the CTRT program were able to learn and utilize CTRT relationship-building skills in the general classroom. Preschool teachers and aides who participated in CTRT used relationship-building skills more frequently compared to teachers and aides who had not participated in the CTRT program. Also, CTRT participants were able to maintain the use of relationship-building skills ($p < .01$) in the general classroom 10 weeks following the completion of the CTRT program, demonstrating that the CTRT program is an effective means for teaching relationship-building skills to teachers and aides and that CTRT facilitates participants' abilities to generalize the use of relationship-building skills to the general classroom.

Helker (2007) also found that participants' demonstration of CTRT relationship-building skills impacted students' behavior. Students whose teachers and aides participated in the CTRT program demonstrated statistically significant ($p = .04$) improvement in externalizing problems compared to students whose teachers and aides did not participate in CTRT.

Morrison (2007) found that in three points of measure (pre-, mid-, posttest), CTRT was an effective treatment for externalizing behavioral problems. These findings reveal that CTRT demonstrated a large treatment effect (partial $\eta^2 = 0.22$) on children's externalizing behavior problems when compared to children whose teachers participated in the active control group. Furthermore, children in the CTRT group demonstrated a statistically significant ($p = .002$) reduction in target behavior over the three points of measure.

Results of the Internalizing Problems Scale revealed no statistically significant improvement in this area for children in the experimental group ($p = .092$). However, it is important to note that CTRT demonstrated a moderate treatment effect (partial $\eta^2 = 0.09$) for children's internalizing behavior problems when compared to children in the active control group (Morrison, 2007).

Results of the Total Problems Scale indicate that CTRT was an effective treatment for these behavioral problems. These findings indicate that compared to the active control group, children in the CTRT group demonstrated a statistically significant ($p = .01$) decrease in Total Problems, with the magnitude of the effect of the CTRT treatment considered large (partial $\eta^2 = 0.17$) (Morrison, 2007).

These findings demonstrate the effectiveness of this treatment modality in children with behavioral problems in the early childhood setting.

An additional noteworthy finding from Helker's (2007) study is that a statistically significant ($p < .05$) relationship was found between teachers' and aides' most frequent use of CTRT relationship-building skills, and a significant decrease in students' externalizing behavior was found.

In addition to quantitative results from the study, participants receiving the CTRT intervention were asked to include written information at follow-up testing on whether or not they believed behavioral changes had occurred in the children who qualified to participate in the study. Participants reported that students had improved in several areas including the ability to manage frustration and to control their own behavior, a willingness to try new things, an increase in self-confidence, and an improvement in academic performance. Participants also reported changes in their own perspectives in working with children. Several participants reported being more patient, having an increased ability to take in the child's point of view, being more willing to let children make their own choices, and re-evaluating some ideas about classroom relationships (Helker, 2007; Morrison, 2007).

CONCLUSION

Child–Teacher Relationship Training (CTRT) utilizes the power of the child–teacher relationship to impact children's lives. Results of the pilot study provide strong support for the use of this model to attend to the behavior problems of children. Results also indicate that teachers are capable of learning and implementing the relationship-building skills into the culture of their classroom. CTRT attends to children in a developmentally responsive manner and utilizes the resources available in the school setting. Utilizing school-based programs such as CTRT is especially helpful for disadvantaged children who most likely would not receive mental health services outside of the school setting. CTRT is a model that uses the school-based mental health professional's time and energy in an efficient manner, allowing the teachers to work with children with moderate problems and freeing up time for the mental health professional to work with the children with more severe difficulties. The power of the child–teacher relationship is limitless; it is critical we utilize it to change children's lives.

REFERENCES

Abel, M. H., & Sewell, J. (1999). Stress and burnout in rural and urban secondary school teachers. *The Journal of Educational Research, 92,* 287–293.

Achenbach, T. M., & Rescorla, L. A. (2000). *Manual for the ASEBA preschool forms & profiles.* Burlington: University of Vermont, Research Center for Children, Youth, & Families.

Andronico, M. P., & Guerney, B. G. (1969). The potential application of filial therapy to the school situation. In B. G. Guerney (Ed.), *Psychotherapeutic agents: New roles for non-professionals, parents and teachers* (pp. 371–377). New York: Holt, Rinehart & Winston.

Baker, J. (2006). Contributions of teacher–child relationships to positive school adjustment during elementary school. *Journal of School Psychology, 44,* 211–229.

Birch, S. H., & Ladd, G. W. (1997). The teacher-child relationship and children's early school adjustment. *Journal of School Psychology, 35,* 61–79.

Birch, S. H., & Ladd, G. W. (1998). Children's interpersonal behaviors and the teacher-child relationship. *Developmental Psychology, 34,* 934–946.

Borg, M. G., & Riding, R. J. (1991). Towards a model for the determinants of occupational stress among school teachers. *European Journal of Psychology of Education, 6,* 355–373.

Bratton, S., Ray, D., Rhine, T., & Jones, L. (2005) The efficacy of play therapy with children: A meta-analysis review of treatment outcomes. *Professional Psychology: Research and Practice, 36*(4), 376–390.

Bratton, S. C., Landreth, G. L., Kellam, T., & Blackard, S. R. (2006). *Child-parent relationship therapy (CPRT) treatment manual.* New York: Routledge.

Brown, C. (2003). Filial therapy training with undergraduate teacher trainees: Child-teacher relationship training (Doctoral dissertation, University of North Texas, 2000). *Dissertation Abstracts International*, A 63(09), 3112.

Crane, J. M., & Brown, C. J. (2003). Effectiveness of teaching play therapy attitudes and skills to undergraduate human services majors. *International Journal of Play Therapy*, 12, 49–65.

Draper, K., White, J., O'Shaughnessy, T. E., Flynt, M., & Jones, N. (2001). Kinder training: Play-based consultation to improve the school adjustment of discouraged kindergarten and first grade students. *International Journal of Play Therapy*, 10, 1–30.

Guerney, B., & Stover, L. (1971). *Filial therapy final report (MH 18264-01)* University Park: Pennsylvania State University.

Guerney, B. G. (1964). Filial therapy: Description and rationale. *Journal of Consulting Psychology*, 28, 303–310.

Guerney, B. G., & Flumen, A. B. (1970). Teachers as psychotherapeutic agents for withdrawn children. *Journal of School Psychology*, 8, 107–113.

Guerney, L. (2000). Filial therapy into the 21st century. *International Journal of Play Therapy*, 9, 1–17.

Hamre, B. K., & Pianta, R. C. (2001). Early teacher–child relationships and the trajectory of children's school outcomes through eighth grade. *Child Development*, 72, 625–638.

Helker, W. P. (2007). The impact of child–teacher relationship training on teachers' and aides' use of relationship-building skills and the effect on student classroom behavior. *Digital Dissertations*, DAI-A 68/02, August 2007.

Helker, W. P., Bratton, S., Morrison, M., & Ray, D., as cited in Helker, 2007. The Child–Teacher Relationship Training Skills Checklist (CTRT-SC). Unpublished instrument.

Helker, W. P., Schottelkorb, A. A., & Ray, D. (2007). Helping students and teachers CONNECT: An intervention model for school counselors. *Journal of Professional Counseling: Practice, Theory, and Research*, 35(2), 31–45.

Howes, C., Hamilton, C. E., & Matheson, C. C. (1994). Children's relationship with peers: Differential associations with aspects of the teacher-child relationship. *Child Development*, 65, 253–263.

Ladd, G., & Burgess, K. (2001). Do relational risks and protective factors moderate the linkages between childhood aggression and early psychological and school adjustment? *Child Development*, 72, 1579–1601.

Landreth, G. L. (2002). *Play therapy: The art of the relationship*. New York: Brunner-Routledge.

Landreth, G. L., & Bratton, S. (2006). *Child–parent relationship therapy: A 10-session filial therapy model*. New York: Brunner-Routledge.

Morrison, M. (2007). An early mental health intervention for disadvantaged preschool children with behavior problems: The effects of training Head

Start teachers in child–teacher relationship training (CTRT). *Digital Dissertations*, DAI-A 67/08, February 2007.

New Freedom Commission on Mental Health. (2003). *Achieving the promise: Transforming mental health care in America.* Final report (DHHS Publication No. SMA-03-3832). Rockville, MD: U.S. Department of Health and Human Services.

Oxman, L. K. (1972). The effectiveness of filial therapy: A controlled study (Doctoral dissertation, Rutgers University, 1972). *Dissertation Abstracts International B 32*(11).

Peisner-Feinberg, E. S., Culkin, M. L., Howes, C., & Kagan, S. L. (1999). The children of the cost, quality, and outcomes study go to school (Executive Summary). Retrieved May 15, 2008, from http://www.fpg.unc.edu/~ncedl/PDFs/CQO-es.pdf.

Pianta, R. C., & Stuhlman, M. W. (2004). Teacher-child relationships and children's success in the first years of school. *School Psychology Review, 33,* 444–459.

Post, P., McAllister, M., Sheely, A., Hess, K., & Flowers, C. (2004). Child-centered kinder training for teachers of preschool children deemed at-risk. *International Journal of Play Therapy, 13,* 53–74.

Ray, D. (2004). Supervision of basic and advanced skills in play therapy. *Journal of Professional Counseling: Practice, Theory, & Research, 32,* 29–40.

Smith, D. M., & Landreth, G. L. (2004). Filial therapy with teachers of deaf and hard of hearing preschool children. *International Journal of Play Therapy, 13,* 13–33.

Stover, L., & Guerney, B. G. (1967). The efficacy of training procedures for mothers in filial therapy. *Psychotherapy: Theory, Research and Practice, 4*(3), 110–115.

United States Public Health Service. (2000). *Report of the Surgeon General's conference on children's mental health: A national agenda.* Washington, DC: Author.

White, J., Flynt, M., & Draper, K. (1997). Kinder therapy: Teachers as therapeutic agents. *International Journal of Play Therapy, 6,* 33–49.

White, J., Flynt, M., & Jones, N. P. (1999). Kinder therapy: An Adlerian approach for training teachers to be therapeutic agents through play. *Journal of Individual Psychology, 55,* 365–382.

Yoshikawa, H., & Knitzer, J. (1997). *Lessons from the field: Head Start mental health strategies to meet challenging needs.* New York: National Center for Children in Poverty, Columbia University School of Public Health and American Orthopsychiatric Association.

Yost, D. S. & Mosca, F. J. (2002). Beyond behavior strategies: Using reflection to manage youth in crisis. ERIC Clearinghouse, 20020501, 75, 264–268.

CHAPTER 10

Treating Disruptive Classroom Behaviors of Preschoolers Through Teacher–Child Interaction Therapy

DAVID McINTOSH

INTRODUCTION

This chapter provides an overview of Teacher–Child Interaction Therapy (TCIT), which is an adaptation of Parent–Child Interaction Therapy (PCIT; Eyberg, 1988; Hembree-Kigin & McNeil, 1995). The theoretical framework of TCIT is discussed, as well as a brief overview of the TCIT program. Special considerations when implementing TCIT within day care and preschool settings are reviewed. Lastly, a case study is presented demonstrating the effectiveness of TCIT.

THEORETICAL FOUNDATION OF TEACHER–CHILD INTERACTION THERAPY

TCIT has been found to effectively decrease the disruptive behaviors (e.g., yelling, hyperactivity, talking back, fighting, hitting, throwing things) among preschool children by working closely with teachers within preschool settings (Cronch et al., 2006; McIntosh, Rizza, & Bliss, 2000; Tavkar et al., 2007). The aforementioned studies also suggested TCIT has the potential to improve the teacher–child relationship while enhancing teachers' skills in addressing current and future disruptive behaviors in their classroom. In general, TCIT can be implemented as part of a preschool's mental health services.

TCIT is an evidence-based program that uses the same theoretical framework as Parent-Child Interaction Therapy (Eyberg, 1988; Hembree-Kigin & McNeil, 1995). PCIT, developed by Dr. Sheila Eyberg in the 1970s, is a well-established treatment for children between the ages of 2 and 7. A significant amount of research has been conducted demonstrating the efficacy of PCIT with children with disruptive behaviors (Eisenstadt, Eyberg, McNeil, Newcomb, & Funderburk, 1993; Eyberg & Boggs, 1989; Newcomb, Eyberg, Funderburk, Eisenstadt, & McNeil, 1990; Schuhman, Foote, Eyberg, Boggs, & Algina, 1998). The effects of PCIT also have been found to generalize to the home and school settings (Boggs, 1990; McNeil, Eyberg, Eisenstadt, Newcomb, & Funderburk, 1991), suggesting that TCIT can have similar effects when implemented within the preschool setting. As with PCIT, TCIT incorporates elements of applied behavioral analysis, developmental theory, and traditional play therapy. With PCIT, the parent and child are worked with simultaneously, whereas with TCIT the teacher and a specific child can be worked with simultaneously and/or the teacher and multiple children can be worked with simultaneously. While it is not uncommon to see generalization of skills learned by the parent during PCIT to other children in the family, with TCIT, it is often one of the primary objectives to see generalization of skills learned by the teacher with all children in the classroom. When working with a specific teacher, Cronch et al. (2006) found TCIT resulted in an overall improvement in the teacher's use of Child-Directed Interaction (CDI) skills both within the training sessions and in the classroom.

Gershenson, Lyon, Farahmand, Behling, and Budd (2007) identified several other adaptation and implementation differences between PCIT and TCIT. PCIT is primarily utilized with a single parent or family, while training can be conducted as a group with teachers. Training typically occurs within a clinical setting with PCIT, while a natural setting (e.g., classroom) is often used with TCIT. PCIT is a data-driven treatment where progression through Child-Directed Interaction (CDI) to Parent-Directed Interaction (PDI) and from CDI to PDI is dependent upon the skill acquisition of the parent(s). With TCIT, there is often a predetermined time frame for training, observations, data collection, and follow-up. Direct coaching or in-room coaching is often utilized with TCIT, while most clinical settings where PCIT is implemented use a wireless system and the clinician coaches the parent from another room while watching the parent-child interaction through a one-way mirror. During PCIT, parents wear a small wireless receiver in their ear when being coached by the clinician. Compared to TCIT, PCIT follows a fairly prescribed protocol as the parent and child progress through CDI, PDI, and from CDI to PDI. More flexibility is needed with TCIT, where trainings, coaching sessions, and homework may need to be adaptive to reflect the strengths and weaknesses of the teacher, the classroom, or daily classroom schedules. Flexibility also is needed when adapting the standardized discipline procedures used with PCIT to TCIT. Many preschools and Head Start classrooms often implement specific discipline procedures consistent with their philosophy of child development and learning. Therefore, collaboration and flexibility with teachers when implementing the discipline portion of TCIT is often required.

Since TCIT was first adapted (McIntosh, Rizza, & Bliss, 2000) using the same methods and principles as PCIT (Eyberg, 1988; Hembree-Kigin & McNeil, 1995), only a few studies have been conducted demonstrating the efficacy of TCIT within the preschool setting (Filcheck, McNeil, Greco, & Bernard, 2004; McIntosh, Rizza, & Bliss, 2000). However, it is apparent that researchers and clinicians alike are beginning to study and implement TCIT. The number of conference presentations, publications, workshops, and web sites focused on TCIT has increased since 2000 (Budd, 2009; Budd et al., 2007; Gershenson, Lyon, Farahmand, Behling, & Budd, 2007). This is not surprising, given the similarities between TCIT and PCIT, the demonstrated efficacy of PCIT, and the need for effective evidenced-based treatments that can be implemented within preschools.

REFERRAL PROCESS AND POPULATION BEING TREATED

TCIT is most likely to be implemented within the preschool or day care setting with children from ages 2 to 5. The use of TCIT within the traditional school setting most likely would be difficult given the structured nature of the curriculum, time constraints of the teacher, and classroom discipline procedures that are inconsistent with the discipline procedures used with TCIT. It also is not likely that TCIT would be implemented in the school setting because, as with PCIT, TCIT is not recommended for children over the age of 7.

Teachers interested in enhancing the psychosocial functioning, in decreasing the disruptive behaviors, and in preventing future behavior problems of preschoolers should be considered for TCIT. TCIT can assist preschool teachers in developing a classroom discipline program that is based upon a positive teacher–child relationship. Therefore, preschools and day cares may decide to have all teachers and aides trained to implement many of the techniques taught during TCIT. Teachers who are not overly ridged in their approach to discipline but who are willing to work collaboratively with the psychologist will most likely respond favorably during training, when being coached, when being observed, and when given homework. In addition, teachers who have an understanding of child development and behaviors of typically developing children most likely will learn and implement TCIT more readily compared to teachers who lack knowledge in these areas. However, it might be essential to spend time developing trust and rapport with some teachers with the goal of developing a collaborative relationship. It also might be necessary to help some teachers gain understanding of developmentally appropriate child behaviors (Cronch et al., 2006). Teachers who tend to be overly critical, overuse questions, or underutilize praise within their classrooms may benefit from participating in TCIT. While resistance may be an issue with these teachers because they will need to rethink their current methods of interaction, developing teachers' trust, using a collaborative model of consultation, and respecting these teachers' experience working with difficult children will enhance the psychologist's ability to modify these teachers' interactions with children.

While there is a strong emphasis with TCIT on restructuring the teacher–child interaction patterns, emphasis also is placed on modifying targeted behaviors of children within the classroom. Children who display oppositional and aggressive behaviors within the classroom would be considered good referrals to participate in TCIT. In addition, children with low self-esteem can benefit from the labeled praise, descriptive statements, and positive attention received from the teacher.

As with PCIT, children older than 7 years of age should not be referred for TCIT. At this age, children often become too big to utilize the discipline techniques used during the TDI phase of the program. In addition, children beyond age 7 often find the play therapy portion of TCIT to be too immature. Hembree-Kigin and McNeil (1995) indicated that unmedicated children diagnosed with attention-deficit hyperactivity disorder, children with severe thought disorders, low-functioning children, and young children with speech/language disorders most likely would not respond well to PCIT. In all likelihood, these children will not respond to TCIT as well, given the similarity between the two treatments.

VALUE OF PLAY THERAPY AND BEHAVIORAL THERAPY WITH CHILDREN WITH DISRUPTIVE BEHAVIORS

Treatment of disruptive behaviors is an important area of research, as they are among the most common reasons children are referred for psychotherapeutic interventions (Kazdin, Siegal, & Bass, 1990). Furthermore, several longitudinal studies have demonstrated that preschool children who manifest significant levels of externalizing behaviors are "at-risk for future social and emotional problems" (Olson, Bates, Sandy, & Lanthier, 2000; Patterson, DeBaryshe, & Ramsey, 1989). Addressing such behaviors presents a unique and pressing challenge to therapists when working with preschool children.

Because the cognitive development of preschoolers outpaces their language development, children at that age have great difficulty with verbal expression of emotions (Landreth, 1993). By allowing play to be their language and toys to represent words (Landreth, 2002), child-centered play therapy is "uniquely responsive to children's developmental needs" (Bratton, Ray, Rhine, & Jones, 2005).

A number of recent studies confirm the efficacy of play therapy in addressing disruptive behavior in children. Among these studies is a 2005 meta-analysis conducted by Bratton, Ray, Rhine, and Jones, which examined 94 studies on play therapy conducted from 1942 through 2000. The authors found children who received play therapy performed .80 standard deviations above children who did not receive such services. This effect size was seen across a variety of outcome measures, including behavioral outcomes. Furthermore, Schumann (2005) found play therapy to be equally effective in reducing students' observable aggressive behaviors when compared to research-based guidance curriculum. A study examining the effects of short- and long-term play therapy on student–teacher relationship stress due to problematic behaviors in students found substantial improvement in stress levels from pre- to posttest for both groups (Ray, Henson, Schottelkorb, Brown, & Muro, 2008).

In addition, several studies examining the use of play therapy include children of preschool age. Beers (1985) found that participation in play therapy groups significantly lowered nonacceptance behavior in parent-child interactions in families with at least one child diagnosed as oppositionally defiant. Hannah (1986) found significant positive change in targeted behavior of children receiving play therapy. Kaczmarek (1983) found that participation in play therapy significantly reduced occurrences of targeted behavioral excesses.

The efficacy of play therapy in reducing the disruptive behaviors of preschoolers is highly supported. This may be especially true for children who are in preschool and likely do not have fully developed verbal abilities.

DESCRIPTION OF TCIT PROGRAM

TCIT follows a very similar treatment program as PCIT. To date, no treatment manual has been published outlining the TCIT program. Therefore, it is recommended that clinicians use the treatment manual, *Parent-Child Interaction Therapy*, published by Hembree-Kigin and McNeil (1995) and make the necessary adaptations for the preschool setting. The following sections provide a brief overview of the TCIT program (Phase I: Child-Directed Interaction and Phase II: Teacher-Directed Interaction) and discuss several issues that are considered essential to effectively implementing TCIT within the day care or preschool settings.

Conceptual Understanding of Preschool Environment

Prior to be starting TCIT, it is essential to spend time developing an understanding of the social framework of the preschool where TCIT will be implemented (Gershenson, Lyon, Farahmand, Behling, & Budd, 2007). This can be done in a variety of ways. Meeting with teachers, observing classroom activities, observing transitions, observing discipline, reading procedure manuals, reading parent handbooks, and providing workshops can help you better understand the culture and social framework of a preschool. Many preschools' curricula and approaches to discipline are based on a certain philosophical perspective, and it is essential to gain an understanding of this philosophy. For example, many preschools use a center-based approach when designing and implementing a curriculum, and many will not use time-out as a form of discipline. However, many preschools will have some form of discipline in place. Others, often use some form of time-out but avoid using the term *time-out*, for example, the term *quiet-time* might be used instead. Understanding the curriculum and discipline procedures can assist in future communication with teachers and help recognize how TCIT will need to be adapted to conform to the culture and daily schedule of the preschool.

Consent

Whether TCIT will be conducted on an individual basis with a specific teacher and child or teachers are trained as a group and implemented with a number of children, it is essential to gain informed consent from teachers, parents, and children.

Prior to beginning TCIT, consent will be needed from the children's parents. A consent form describing TCIT needs to be developed in language parents can understand and reviewed with the parents. The consent form should include the following: a short description of TCIT, the time frame for implementing TCIT, potential benefits, potential risks, confidentiality, limits on confidentiality, and who will be involved in implementing TCIT with their child. When providing a description of TCIT, all phases of TCIT should be discussed. For example, Phase I: Child-Directed Interaction (CDI) and Phase II: Teacher-Directed Interaction (TDI) should be described. If time-out and a holding chair will be used as part of TDI, then parents need to be informed regarding these procedures and the time line for implementing TDI with their children. It is important to inform parents of the exact discipline procedures that will be used by the teacher with their children because this will avoid confusion and frustration on the part of parents when the children come home and inform them they were in time-out.

It also is essential that teachers consent to participating in TCIT. Essentially, teachers should gain the understanding that TCIT is a collaborative, voluntary process, with the teacher and psychologist working together with mutually agreed upon goals and objectives. The consent form should be used to describe the program and to discuss any adaptations that might be needed during TCIT. Reviewing the consent form also clarifies the responsibilities and expectations of the teacher, child, and psychologist; the time frame of the program; potential benefits; and risks involved in participating in TCIT. It should be noted that some teachers might initially elect, or later decide, to only participate in the first phase of TCIT, CDI, and not participate in the discipline portion, TDI. This decision should be supported. It also is not uncommon for teachers to initially only elect to participate in the CDI and then later request to continue in the second phase, PDI.

Finally, children also should consent to participate in TCIT. A brief review of the program should be provided to children at their level of development so they are aware of why they are participating in TCIT sessions outside and inside the classroom. An explanation (e.g., "Special Time" instructions) for each session should be included in the TCIT manual, just as it is in the PCIT manual.

RAPPORT BUILDING

Developing rapport and establishing trust with teachers are likely the two most important ingredients as to whether TCIT will be successfully implemented within the preschool setting. Teachers who are forced to participate by administration and/or who are unmotivated will likely be resistant during training and coaching sessions and likely will not follow through with homework. Therefore, it is crucial to gain both organizational support and teacher support for a successful TCIT program (Gershenson, Lyon, Farahmand, Behling, & Budd, 2007). Gershenson et al. (2007) also noted that meeting with preschool teachers and staff outside of conducting TCIT, providing opportunities for teachers to discuss experiences, providing teachers the opportunity to gain new skills, and providing continuing education credits are ways to help get teachers invested in TCIT. At the organizational level, administrators will be more likely to support a TCIT program if they can see the potential for more positive interactions between the teachers and children, if the parents see the generalization of decreased disruptive behaviors within the home, and if teachers report fewer disruptive behaviors in the classroom. By emphasizing the shared ownership of implementing a service-oriented program and stressing the collaborative focus of TCIT (Gershenson, Lyon, Farahmand, Behling, & Budd, 2007), both administrators and teachers will be more likely to participate in developing and implementing TCIT.

CONSULTATIVE INTERVIEW

After a referral has been made and it has been determined that TCIT should be considered as a viable treatment, a consultative interview with the classroom teacher should be conducted. The primary goal of this consultative interview should be to identify and operationally define the problem behaviors of the preschooler. The interview should also focus on gaining a history of the problem behaviors. How long have they occurred? When do they occur? Why do you think they occur? What has been successful or unsuccessful in addressing the problem behaviors? What do you think needs to be done to address the problems? What have been barriers to implementing prior behavioral programs? These are some of the questions that could be asked to help facilitate a better understanding of problem behaviors and better understand the teacher's attempts to address them. The consultative interview also is an opportunity to discuss the teacher's classroom management plan and philosophy on discipline. Time during the consultative interview should be spent on developing rapport and increasing the level of trust between the psychologist and teacher. The teacher needs to gain the sense that it is okay to take risks, that the psychologist is not going to be judgmental, and that both teacher and psychologist will take equal ownership when implementing TCIT, whether TCIT is ultimately successful or unsuccessful.

ASSESSMENT OF PRESENTING PROBLEMS

Prior to implementing TCIT, time should be spent conducting initial assessments and refining the definitions of the identified problem behaviors. These assessments can be focused on the individual child, a group of children, or an entire classroom. After conducting the consultative interview, several (three to four) classroom observations should be conducted to collect baseline data on the targeted behaviors. In addition, it is helpful to observe the teacher to determine how many commands, questions, unlabeled and labeled praises, and descriptive statements are being used in the classroom. This baseline data will be used for comparison with the post-TCIT observations that are conducted in the classroom.

More formal assessments also might be warranted. Some psychologists may elect to have formal rating scales completed by the teacher and parents prior to beginning TCIT. These structured behavioral scales often assess broad areas of behavior (e.g., hyperactivity, aggression, withdrawal, inattention) and emotions (e.g., depression, anxiety). The rationale for using a broad measure of behavior and emotions is to screen for underlying emotional issues that may be contributing to a child's disruptive behaviors. While TCIT will address many of the disruptive behaviors, additional mental health services many be needed to address a child's emotional issues. For a child with elevated ratings in the area of hyperactivity, further evaluation or a referral to a physician may be warranted to determine whether medication is needed to address the hyperactivity.

OVERVIEW OF CHILD-DIRECTED INTERACTION

Prior to conducting teacher training and the first session of CDI, baseline data is collected using the Dyadic Teacher–Child Interaction Coding System (DTICS), which was adapted from the Dyadic Parent–Child Interaction Coding System (Eyberg & Robinson, 1983). The teacher and child are observed during three 5-minute intervals. During the first 5-minute session, the teacher is asked to allow the child to lead the play (CDI), and the teacher is asked to follow the child's rules when playing. During the second 5-minute session, the teacher is asked to direct the child's play (TDI) and to have the child follow the teacher's rules when playing. During the last 5 minutes, the teacher is asked to have the child pick up the toys and put them away without the teacher's assistance. The DTICS also is used to record the teacher–child interactions during the first 5 minutes of every therapy session. These three 5-minute sessions serve as a baseline and comparison data for later CDI and PDI sessions.

Prior to the first CDI session, the teacher is taught specific skills that will be used during the CDI sessions. The teacher is taught how to Describe appropriate behaviors, Reflect appropriate talk, Imitate appropriate play, and Praise appropriate behaviors during the play therapy session with the child (DRIP skills). During the training, the teacher is given specific examples of these skills, and the psychologist demonstrates and role-plays these skills with the teacher. The teacher also is taught what *not* to do during CDI. Teachers are taught not to give commands, ask questions, or criticize. The goal during CDI is to have a positive interaction with the child. If the teacher gives commands, asks questions, or criticizes, then the interaction can become unpleasant and a power struggle may develop between the teacher and the child. The teacher also is taught to ignore inappropriate behaviors (except for dangerous or destructive behaviors). The teacher is also given homework to be completed and returned between the CDI sessions. For example, the teacher might be given homework and asked to identify examples of labeled praise or descriptive statements. The homework is then reviewed prior to beginning the next CDI coaching session.

After the first CDI coaching session, the teacher and the child begin having *Special Time* each day for 5 minutes. Special Time is designed as an opportunity for the teacher to practice using DRIP skills and to continue to work on enhancing the positive interactions between the teacher and the child outside of the CDI sessions. The teacher and the child work together in the classroom while the other children are engaged in other activities. Ideally, the teacher should work Special Time into the daily schedule and have it at the same time and in the same location and kept within a 5-minute time frame. Typically, five to six CDI instructional sessions are conducted with the teacher prior to starting TDI. The teacher should demonstrate mastery of the DRIP skills and use few if any commands, questions, and criticisms during CDI before starting the training for PDI.

Overview of Teacher-Directed Interaction

Prior to the first PDI session, the teacher is taught specific skills that will be used during the PDI sessions. The teacher is taught how to give instructions to children with oppositional behaviors (e.g., direct not indirect, specific not vague, developmentally appropriate, positively stated, given in neutral tone of voice, etc.). Specifically, the use of commands, choices, and discipline is the primary focus of PDI. There also is an emphasis on making clear requests (commands) and consistency in the enforcement of discipline procedures on the part of the teacher. The following description of TDI, discipline procedures, and the use of the *holding chair* should be considered a brief overview. For a more detailed description on how to implement these procedures, it is recommended that the reader refer to the treatment manual, *Parent-Child Interaction Therapy* (Hembree-Kigin & McNeil, 1995).

During the first session of PDI, the child is informed that Special Time will be different and that the focus will now be on "practicing minding and listening." The child is informed that certain requests will be made by the teacher and the specific consequences for noncompliance. Specifically, all levels of noncompliance are reviewed with the child. The first level of response to noncompliance involves asking the child to perform a behavior (e.g., Please place the yellow block in my hand. I would like to add it to my tower) or accept a logical consequence. Time-out is the next level of discipline for noncompliance. For example, a teacher asks a child to put a red car in the big toy box during cleanup or go to time-out. The teacher counts to three and the child still has not complied with the command, so the child has to sit in the time-out chair for 3 minutes. After 3 minutes (with the child sitting quietly), the teacher repeats the original command, and the child indicates readiness to comply with the request; then the child puts the car in the big toy box.

The third level of discipline is implemented if the child gets out of the time-out chair. If this occurs, a warning is given and the child is informed that the next time she/he gets out of the time-out chair, she/he will go to the holding chair and will still have to sit in the time-out chair. The teacher will hold the child in the holding chair for a specified period of time before having the child sit in the time-out chair. After the child is back in the time-out chair and has sat quietly for a specified amount of time, the teacher will give the child the original command. If the child affirms that she/he is ready to comply with the command, then the teacher indicates that the child may get out of time-out and do what was asked. After the child complies with the command, the teacher starts playing with the child and using the DRIP skills learned during CDI.

After the first TDI coaching session, the teacher and the child continue having Special Time each day the length of the session now increases to 10 to 15 minutes. The teacher now gives two or three commands, with the goal of increasing the child's level of compliance. The teacher implements the procedures taught and coached during TDI but uses them without the assistance of the psychologist. Typically, the psychologist conducts five or six TDI sessions with the teacher and the child. Also, the last two TDI coaching sessions are conducted in the classroom. The child should demonstrate a high level of compliance during TDI before stopping the coaching sessions.

SPECIAL CONSIDERATIONS

Conducting TCIT in the natural setting creates challenges compared to providing PCIT within a structured clinical setting. Finding space outside of the classroom where TCIT sessions can be conducted is often difficult in most preschools. It also is important to find a quiet, confidential, and safe location for TCIT. However, there are some creative options. Using the speech pathologist's or nurse's office during lunch or late in the afternoon is one alternative. Using an empty lunchroom or even an administrator's office can be arranged. With many preschools located in churches, some of the rooms used for Sunday services might be available. When going to another area of the preschool for TCIT, the child may need some reassurance and time to adjust to the different location. If there is a lack of space, it might be possible to use some of the other classrooms early in the morning or late in the afternoon. For many preschools, there are fewer children prior to 9 A.M. and after 4 P.M. and as a result the preschools combine classrooms so they can avoid paying staff. Also, in the afternoon, after naps, many preschools will go outside to play or move to a larger recreation area for large group play. If none of these alternatives work, it is always possible to conduct the TCIT sessions later in the evening after most of the children have gone home for the day. Coordination with preschool staff and parents will be needed to arrange for the child to be picked up at a later time.

Another option would be to conduct all of the CDI and PDI sessions within the classroom setting when all the children are present. This can be difficult unless other staff is available to work with the other children in the classroom while the teacher is being coached with a specific child. Also, it can be difficult to implement the first sessions of PDI within the classroom setting when other childrean are present and the teacher is starting to learn PDI skills. Therefore, it is not recommended to implement PDI within the classroom until the child has learned to respond to commands and there is limited need for the use of time-out or other discipline procedures. Typically, the last two PDI sessions are conducted in the classroom with the teacher and the child to increase the likelihood of generalization.

If the teacher is going to participate in TCIT sessions during the day, arrangements will need to be made for coverage in the classroom. In most day care and preschools, there are two teachers in every classroom. Also, most day cares and preschools have back-up coverage already designed into the day's activities. It is important to note that some state regulations require a certain number of teachers to be present in the classroom based upon the number of children present.

Some reorganization of rooms, toys, and materials may need to be done to ensure that the room is safe and that the child maintains a high interest in the toys that are being used during the TCIT sessions. Rooms that are being used for other activities (e.g., music, speech, lunch) may need to be rearranged prior to TCIT and put back in their original condition when the session is completed. In lunchrooms where there are several tables, it might be helpful to move the extra chairs and tables to one side of the room. When rearranging rooms, it is important to consider the safety of the child and the teacher, especially during TDI. If the child is too distracted, overly noncompliant, or physically aggressive, a room with only a small table and chairs will need to be utilized.

Toys of high interest to the child, in addition to paper and markers or crayons, should be available for use during the TCIT sessions. It is helpful to use toys that the child does not typically get to play with while in the classroom. Therefore, having extra toys that are only used during TCIT is helpful in maintaining the child's interest. The psychologist may need to bring toys for each session or ask for space to store the toys between sessions.

CASE STUDY—JASON

The preschool teacher referred Jason, a 4-year-old boy, for possible participation in TCIT. Jason was highly disruptive—hitting, kicking, and arguing with other children in the classroom. Jason's teacher was concerned that he might not be able to continue to attend preschool if his disruptive behaviors did not decrease. Several of the other preschool teachers had participated in prior TCIT training programs, and Jason's teacher felt it would be helpful as she developed a classroom discipline program. She also had several other children in her classroom who were hitting and kicking as well as ignoring her when she told them to do something. She felt that by learning the skills needed to implement TCIT in the classroom with Jason, many of her newly acquired skills could be generalized to other children in the classroom.

A school psychologist, who had been trained to implement PCIT, was asked to work with the teacher and implement a TCIT program with the goal of decreasing Jason's disruptive behaviors. Written permission was gained from Jason's mother, the teacher, and Jason prior to the consultative interview. During the consultative interview, the school psychologist provided an overview of TCIT, discussed, identified, and operationally defined Jason's disruptive behaviors with the teacher. The parent also asked to participate in the consultative interview. It was agreed that the school psychologist would conduct four 20-minute classroom observations with the goal of collecting baseline data on the targeted behaviors. Figure 10.1 shows the number of aggressive behaviors displayed by Jason during each observation. Data also was collected on the number of questions, commands, unlabeled praises, labeled praises, and descriptive statements the

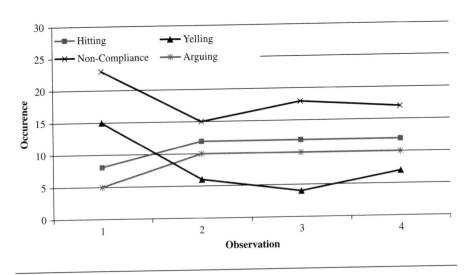

Figure 10.1 Classroom observations of Jason's targeted behaviors prior to implementing TCIT

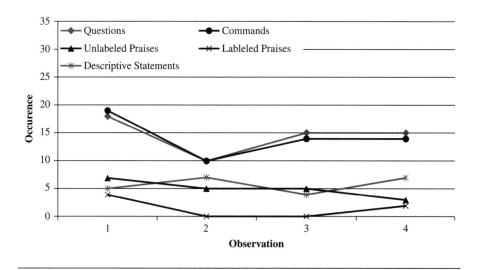

Figure 10.2 Classroom teachers use questions, commands, praise, and descriptive statements prior to implementing TCIT

teacher used during the four 20-minute classroom observations (see Figure 10.2). Figures 10.1 and 10.2 show that Jason was displaying high levels of noncompliance, while the teacher was using a large number of commands during 20 minutes of observation. Developmentally, Jason displayed higher levels of aggression (hitting and yelling) compared to other children his age. The teacher did use praise, but it was often unlabeled praise and the number of praises was significantly lower in proportion to the number of commands the teacher was using. It is important to note that the number of questions and commands used by the teacher was fairly consistent with the levels of noncompliant behaviors displayed by Jason. Jason's noncompliance appears to be a reaction to the number of questions and commands the teacher uses with him in a short period of time.

Prior to beginning TCIT, baseline data was collected using the Dyadic Teacher–Child Interaction Coding System (DTICS). The teacher and Jason were observed outside the classroom in a small room setup for play therapy for three 5-minute sessions (McNeil et al., 1991). During the first 5-minute session, the teacher was asked to allow Jason to lead the play (CDI), and the teacher was to follow Jason's rules when playing. During the second 5-minute session, the teacher was asked to direct Jason's play (TDI) and have Jason follow her rules when playing. During the last 5 minutes, the teacher was asked to have Jason pick up the toys and put them away without her assistance. The DTICS also was used to record the teacher–child interactions during the first 5 minutes of every therapy session. These three 5-minute sessions served as a baseline for later CDI and PDI sessions.

The school psychologist conducted teaching/training sessions prior to the implementation of each phase of TCIT—Phase I: CDI and Phase II: TDI. During CDI, the focus was on enhancing the teacher–child relationship by playing with Jason only in a positive manner. Prior to the first CDI session, the teacher was taught to Describe Jason's activities, to Reflect what Jason was saying, to Imitate Jason's actions, and to Praise Jason (DRIP skills). By learning to use DRIP skills, the teacher was able to reinforce Jason's positive interactions and increase his self-confidence. In addition, the school psychologist taught Jason's teacher how to avoid using questions or giving commands during the CDI play therapy sessions. She also was taught how to effectively ignore Jason's inappropriate behaviors (unless dangerous or destructive) and to not criticize. By not making negative or punitive comments, the interaction between Jason and his teacher remained positive, avoiding power struggles and he was allowed to lead, increasing his autonomy and control. The DTICS was used to record the teacher's DRIP skills and number of questions, commands, and critical statements during the first 5 minutes of each session. After the 5-minute recording session, the school psychologist would coach the teacher for the remainder of the session and focus on areas (e.g., descriptive statements, labeled praises) identified as needing improvement based upon the 5-minute recording session. The school psychologist coached the teacher directly by sitting behind the teacher during TCIT. A total of six 20-minute CDI sessions were conducted. The teacher also conducted Special Time four days a week. Special Time was conducted in the classroom during the morning when the other children were playing in Centers. Figure 10.3 shows the number of Descriptive statements, Reflective statements, Imitations, and Praises during each of the six CDI sessions. Compared to baseline, the teacher demonstrated a significant increase in her use of descriptive, reflective, and labeled praises over the twelve sessions (six CDI and six TDI). She also demonstrated a dramatic decrease in the use of questions to the point where she was not using questions during most of the coaching sessions. At one point in Session 8, the teacher's use of descriptive statements decreased dramatically. As a result, Session 8 focused on increasing descriptive statements, and homework was assigned focused on

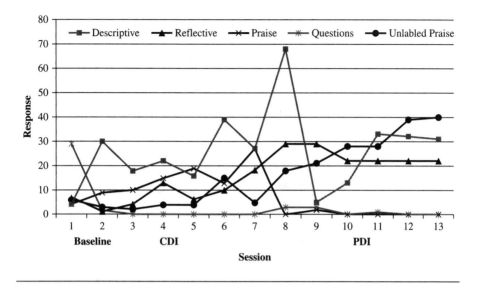

Figure 10.3 Teacher's Child-Directed Interaction skills for the 12 TCIT sessions using the 5-minute time sampling procedure

increasing descriptive statements. During the next session, Session 9, the teacher displayed an increase in descriptive statements.

During TDI, the teacher was taught how to give commands, follow-up on noncompliance, and increase consistency when responding to Jason's positive and negative behaviors. The primary objective of TDI was to decrease Jason's disruptive behaviors during the sessions and within the classroom while increasing the positive interactions between Jason and his teacher and between Jason and his classmates. A total of six TDI sessions were conducted. The last two TDI sessions were conducted in the classroom while the other children were playing in the Centers. Figure 10.4 shows the number of commands given by the teacher and Jason's response (compliance and noncompliance) to teacher commands. During baseline, the teacher used a larger number of commands by the last two TDI sessions, the number of commands decreased and Jason's compliance was consistent with the number of commands given by the teacher.

Four 20-minute observations were conducted over a 2-week period after the last TDI session (see Figures 10.5 and 10.6). Jason's level of aggression decreased dramatically compared to his levels of aggression prior to TCIT. He no longer was hitting, and his level of disruptive

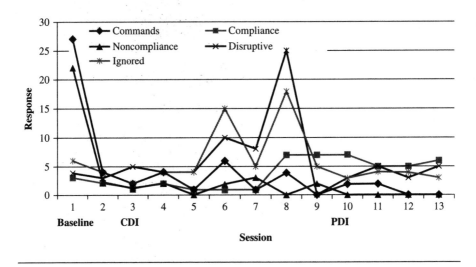

Figure 10.4 Teacher-Directed Interaction skills and child's responses for the 12 TCIT sessions using a 5-minute time sampling procedure

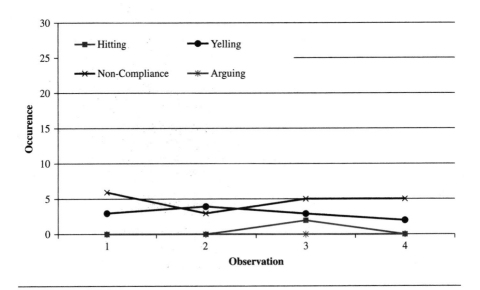

Figure 10.5 Classroom observations of Jason's targeted behaviors after implementing TCIT

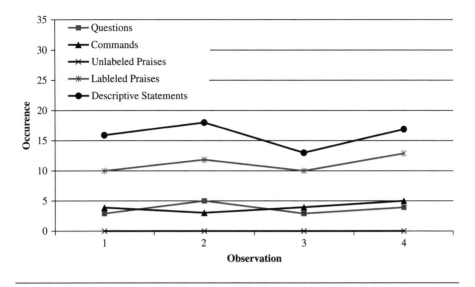

Figure 10.6 Classroom teachers use of questions, commands, praises, and descriptive statements after implementing TCIT

behaviors (yelling and arguing) was more consistent with children his age. The teacher also displayed an increase in labeled praise and descriptive statements. Jason also complied with requests by his teacher. During a follow-up three months later, Jason was still attending the preschool and was no longer displaying elevated levels of disruptive behaviors. The teachers also reported that the level of aggression among all children in the classroom had declined and that their level of compliance to teacher requests also had improved.

CONCLUSION AND RECOMMENDATION

Although TCIT is a relatively new concept, it is based upon the principles and methods of PCIT. PCIT is an empirically supported treatment that is well researched and has been implemented by clinicians all over the United States. While there are specific challenges to implementing TCIT within the day care or preschool settings, initial research has demonstrated the efficacy of TCIT within these settings. Additional research is needed to further validate TCIT and its use with teachers and children in nonclinical settings. There is also a need to formally develop a treatment manual for TCIT to allow consistency in implementation and duplication across clinicians (Kratochwill & Stoiber, 2000).

REFERENCES

Beers, P. A. (1985). Focused videotape feedback psychotherapy as compared with traditional play therapy in treatment of the oppositional disorder of childhood (Doctoral dissertation, University of Illinois). *Dissertation Abstracts International, 46* (4-B), 1330.

Boggs, S. R. (1990, August). *Generalization of treatment to the home setting: Direct observation analysis.* Paper presented at the annual meeting of the American Psychological Association, Washington, DC.

Bratton, S., Ray, D., Rhine, T., & Jones, L. (2005). The efficacy of play therapy with children: A meta-analytic review of treatment outcomes. *Professional Psychology: Research and Practice, 36*(4), 376–390.

Budd, K. S. (2009). *Research interests.* Retrieved March 12, 2009, from http://condor.depaul.edu/~kbudd/research%20interests.html#PCIT1

Budd, K. S., Gershenson, R., Lyon, A., Farahmand, F. K., Behling, S., Thaxter, P., & Montgomery, M. (2007, September). *Effectiveness of group TCIT: Multiple baseline evaluation in an urban day care for ethnic minority children.* Session presented at the 7th National Parent Child Interaction Therapy (PCIT) Conference, Oklahoma City, OK.

Cronch, L. E., Tavkar, P., Jordan, J., Huenink, M., Flood, M. F., & Hansen, D. J. (2006, November). *Effectiveness of a four-phase teacher–child interaction training protocol for reducing behavior problems in a preschool classroom.* Poster presented at the Association for Behavioral and Cognitive Therapies' 40th Annual Convention, Chicago.

Eisenstadt, T. H., Eyberg, S. M., McNeil, C. B., Newcomb, K., & Funderburk, B. (1993). Parent-child interaction therapy with behavior problem children: Relative effectiveness of two stages and overall treatment outcome. *Journal of Clinical Child Psychology, 22*(1), 42–51.

Eyberg, S. M. (1988). Parent-child interaction therapy: Integration of traditional and behavioral concerns. *Child & Family Behavior Therapy, 10*(1), 33–46.

Eyberg, S. M., & Boggs, S. R. (1989). Parent training for oppositional-defiant preschoolers. In C. E. Schaefer & J. M. Briesmeister (Eds.), *Handbook of parent training: Parents as co-therapists for children's behavior problems.* New York: John Wiley & Sons.

Eyberg, S. M., & Robinson, E. A. (1983). Dyadic Parent-Child Interaction Coding System: A manual. *Psychological Documents, 13*, Ms. No. 2582 (Available from Social and Behavior Sciences Documents, Select Press, P.O. Box 9828, San Rafael, CA 94912).

Filcheck, H. A., McNeil, C. B., Greco, L. A., & Bernard, R. S. (2004). Using a whole-class token economy and coaching of teacher skills in a preschool classroom to manage disruptive behavior. *Psychology in the Schools, 41*(3), 351–361.

Gershenson, R., Lyon, A., Farahmand, F. K., Behling, S., & Budd, K. S. (2007, September). *Establishing a Teacher–Child Interaction Training (TCIT) program: A community psychology conceptualization and adaptation of PCIT*. Session presented at the 7th National Parent Child Interaction Therapy (PCIT) Conference, Oklahoma City, OK.

Hannah, G. (1986). An investigation of play therapy: Process and outcome using interrupted time-series analysis (Doctoral dissertation, University of Northern Colorado, 1986). *Dissertation Abstracts International, 47*, 2615.

Hembree-Kigin, T. L., & McNeil, C. B. (1995). *Parent-Child Interaction Therapy*. New York: Plenum Press.

Kaczmarek, M. (1983). A comparison of individual play therapy and play technology in modifying targeted inappropriate behavioral excesses of children (Doctoral dissertation, New Mexico State University). *Dissertation Abstracts International, 44*, 914.

Kazdin, A. E., Siegal, T. C., & Bass, D. (1990). Drawing on clinical practice to inform research on child and adolescent psychotherapy: Survey of practitioners. *Professional Psychology: Research and Practice, 21*, 189–198.

Kratochwill, T. R., & Stoiber, K. C. (2000). Empirically supported interventions: Announcing a new standing section of *School Psychology Quarterly*. *School Psychology Quarterly, 15*(1), 69–74.

Landreth, G. L. (1993). Child-centered play therapy. *Elementary School Guidance and Counseling, 28*(1), 17–30.

Landreth, G. L. (2002). *Play therapy: The art of the relationship* (2nd ed.). New York: Brunner-Routledge.

McIntosh, D. E., Rizza, M. G., & Bliss, L. (2000). Implementing empirically supported interventions: Teacher–Child Interaction Therapy. *Psychology in the Schools, 37*(5), 453–462.

McNeil, C. B., Eyberg, S. M., Eisenstadt, T. H., Newcomb, K., & Funderbunk, B. W. (1991). Parent-child interaction therapy with behavior problem children: Generalization of treatment effects to the school setting. *Journal of Clinical Child Psychology, 20*, 140–151.

Newcomb, K., Eyberg, S. M., Funderburk, B. W., Eisenstadt, T. H., & McNeil, C. B. (August, 1990). *Parent-child interaction therapy: Maintenance of treatment gains at 8 months and 1 and ½ years*. Presented at the Annual Meeting of the American Psychological Association, San Francisco.

Olson, S. L., Bates, J. E., Sandy, J. M., & Lanthier, R. (2000). Early developmental precursors of externalizing behavior in middle childhood and adolescence. *Journal of Abnormal Child Psychology, 28*, 119–133.

Patterson, G. R., DeBaryshe, B. D., & Ramsey, E. (1989). A developmental perspective on antisocial behavior. *American Psychologist, 44*, 329–335.

Ray, D. C., Henson, R. K., Schottelkorb, A. A., Brown, A. G., & Muro, J. (2008). Effect of short- and long-term play therapy services on teacher–child relationship stress. *Psychology in the Schools, 45*(10), 994–1009.

Schumann, B. (2005). Effects of child-centered play therapy and curriculum-based small group guidance on the behaviors of children referred for aggression in an elementary school setting (Doctoral dissertation, University of North Texas, 2004). *Dissertation Abstracts International, 65/12,* 4476.

Schuhman, E. M., Foote, R. C., Eyberg, S. M., Boggs, S. R., & Algina, J. (1998). Efficacy of parent-child interaction therapy: Interim report of a randomized trial with short-term maintenance. *Journal of Clinical Child Psychology, 27*(1), 34–45.

Tavkar, P., Trask, E., Cronch, L. E., Huenink, M., Hill, M., Flood, M. F., & Hansen, D. J. (2007, November). *Evaluation of a four-phase teacher–child interaction training protocol for reducing behavior problems in preschool classrooms.* Poster presented at the Association for Behavioral and Cognitive Therapies, Philadelphia.

PART V

INDIVIDUAL AND GROUP PLAY THERAPY APPROACHES

CHAPTER 11

LEGO®-Based Play Therapy for Autistic Spectrum Children

DANIEL B. LEGOFF, G. W. KRAUSS, and
SARAH ALLEN LEVIN

THEORETICAL BASIS OF APPROACH

THE DEVELOPMENT OF LEGO THERAPY

The LEGO Therapy approach evolved as a clinical intervention, based on the observed joint interactions between school-aged children diagnosed with autistic disorders. Their positive interactions were somewhat unexpected, but certainly welcome. Although the initial participants had had little experience of successful interaction with peers, their coincidental mutual interest brought them together and established a framework for social interaction, communication, and relationship. The impetus for attempting a group-based social development therapy using LEGO materials arose from a single pair of children with a shared interest.

Each of the children had brought LEGO creations to their individual therapy sessions one day, and each showed great interest in the other's creation. These two children would eventually play and interact with each other using LEGO in a structured therapeutic way that emphasized and built upon the social aspects of their relationship. As a result of the fact that they were inherently motivated to construct with LEGO materials, it was relatively easy to establish a structure that required appropriate social interaction and communication as a condition for access to LEGO materials. The nature of the materials themselves increased the opportunities for close joint attention, communication, shared enjoyment, nonverbal communication, and joint accomplishment, all of which was quickly evident, although at a subjective level at that point.

When other children were eventually invited to join the first two, the first LEGO Therapy group was established. The resulting group activity was introduced to participants as "LEGO Club" and was enthusiastically received by both participants and parents. Soon the accumulation of LEGO creations, both sets and "freestyle creations," became an attraction for a growing cohort of devotees, as well as novices, who were intrigued and inspired by the evident ingenuity and creativity. The playroom—previously a mish-mash of expressive and remedial materials—was soon a dedicated LEGO room, with posters, creations, magazines, and catalogs. The impact of a LEGO room as a dedicated physical space representing a joint interest and joint activity has continued to contribute to our ability to motivate children to participate.

As membership increased, so did the need for establishing some guidelines and structure regarding the group activities. Rules were introduced that focused on collaborative engagement, division of labor, shared creativity, joint task focus, shared enjoyment and accomplishment, detailed and accurate verbal and nonverbal communication, and taking advantage of natural opportunities for practicing social and emotional support of peers (tearful meltdowns were a common occurrence), social problem solving, and conflict resolution. Even with addition of adult structure and rules, the children ultimately made the decisions together about how they would spend their time in any given session.

Currently, there are nine weekly LEGO Club groups running continuously through the year with children ranging in age from preschool to high school. This model of group therapy is also being implemented in both private and public school settings and is being introduced in the public school system in England (Owens, private communication).

Once involved, participants tend to stay involved. Some participants graduate but then volunteer to come back for years afterward as peer mentors. It seems evident that part of this commitment is due the nature of the activities themselves—they are fun—but also to the commitment to the group and the collateral support from families. Parents and siblings often establish informal support groups and social units outside of the group sessions themselves.

THE THEORY BEHIND LEGO THERAPY

LEGO Therapy is a child-led and peer-based intervention that utilizes the natural interest in construction play on the part of children with autistic disorders to elicit a willingness to collaborate and interact while engaging in this activity. This approach enables frequent, diverse, and naturally occurring interactions among the participants, allowing for many opportunities for practice, corrective feedback, and encouragement. Although this is a functional and outcome-oriented approach, generally consistent with many current evidence-based strategies—including the use of inherently rewarding materials (Koegel & Koegel, 1995), the utilization of peer models and mentors (Laushey & Heflin, 2000), and the combination of both of these (Kohler et al., 1997)—it was from the outset a methodology based on clinical observation and clinical outcome, not a particular theory or methodology.

The choice of LEGO as a therapy medium was influenced by the idea of "constructive application" (Attwood, 1998, p. 96), that is, using the child's natural interests to motivate learning and behavior change. Attwood described children with Asperger Syndrome as deficient in the need to please their teachers and parents (and therapists), ignoring the usual social pressures to conform to peer groups, imitate peers, cooperate with them, or compete with them. Consequently, many of the techniques recommended for social-skill building, which utilized peer instruction and peer modeling, have had little impact, or worse, result in robotic attempts at imitation.

Even on a one-to-one basis it is often difficult to sustain motivation to persist with learning tasks that they do not find inherently interesting. Although use of external rewards can improve compliance, these gains are usually short-lived, and intrinsic motivation for learning is rarely achieved (Greenspan & Wieder, 1998; Koegel, Koegel, Frea, & Smith, 1995). At the same time, these children often develop singular, obsessive interests and habits and appear to have limitless reserves of focused energy and drive when engaged in these activities. It has therefore been recommended that children's stereotyped interests and/or behaviors be used to promote the learning of social, communication, and play skills (Attwood, 1998; Greenspan & Wieder, 1998). This can be done by shaping activities and behaviors to promote interaction (Greenspan & Wieder, 1998) and by using a child's choice of stimulus to improve their motivation to participate in social interactions or as natural reinforcers for positive social interactions (Koegel & Koegel, 1995). Most published studies of social-skill interventions have also emphasized the importance of peer modeling, peer interaction, and opportunities to practice social competence with peers (cf. Harris & Handleman, 1997; Koegel, 1995).

REFERRAL PROCESS AND POPULATION BEING TREATED

Referral

Most LEGO Club participants are typically referred by one of three sources: about 50 percent are referred by word-of-mouth, usually from other parents or teaching staff; another 25 percent are referred by school district staff, including teachers or remedial specialists; and finally, the remaining 25 percent are referred by other health care providers, both primary care (e.g., pediatricians) and specialists, including agencies that are involved in providing case management.

Population

LEGO Therapy originally came about as a program for children with autism spectrum disorders. As it has continued to evolve, we have found that many other children with social development and communication difficulties have benefited from this approach. Our current groups include children with anxiety disorders (especially social anxiety and selective mutism), depression, and adjustment difficulties manifesting as depression or anxiety. These children are especially good candidates for LEGO Therapy when their symptoms appear to be exacerbated by problems with social development or communication or when their nonsocial symptoms have resulted in a decrease in overall experience or opportunity in the social realm.

Although the broadly defined target population for LEGO Therapy is children with delays or deficits in social and/or communication skills, there are some children in this category who we do not recommend for inclusion. Children with externalizing behavior problems, such as ODD or conduct disorder, who also have social problems often require a degree of supervision and behavioral intervention from adult leaders, which limits the progress of the group as a whole.

DESCRIPTION OF PLAY THERAPY MODALITY

General Overview

An effective LEGO Therapy session differs from children's typical experience of engaging with LEGO materials on their own because it involves collaboration and interaction with peers. LEGO therapy requires joint task focus, shared attention, and mutual goals, depending on one another and communicating effectively. The building tasks are typically divided among members in a way that creates interdependence among small teams of two or three. Typically, one member is initially in the role of *Engineer* who, using directions or some other plan or blueprint, directs others who fill the roles of *Builder*, who does the actual assembly of pieces, and *Parts Supplier*, who sorts and selects the pieces to be given to the Builder for assembly, based on the directions from the Engineer. Later, the roles are switched so that each member has a turn in each role during the project.

In the case of freestyle building, where pre-established sets with instructions are not used, there is also collaboration and conflict resolution associated with planning a project before assembly begins. While we sometimes work with children and LEGO in individual therapy sessions, this does not seem to be a necessary component of successful groups. Our focus here will be on the LEGO Therapy groups, since they are especially well suited to the school-based play therapy environment.

LEGO THERAPISTS OR FACILITATORS

The therapists or facilitators of the groups have had various levels of training and experience. Training and experience in the areas of education and mental health, especially involving children with autistic or other social development disabilities, are important. The willingness to be engaging and interactive, playful and energetic is important; however, therapists must also have the objective and clinical background to be able to provide corrective feedback and prompting. Given the frequent opportunities for conflict and close interaction among members, therapists should have some training and experience with verbal de-escalation techniques.

Most of the therapists involved currently have at least a bachelor's degree in education, psychology, or related fields, and many have master's degrees or doctoral degrees in these areas (e.g., speech-language pathology, occupational therapy, behavior analysis). All of the therapists have had previous experience working with children with autistic disorders in either clinical or educational settings. It should be noted, however, that some uses of this approach have been successfully implemented using inexperienced volunteers, without graduate education (Owens et al., 2008).

It should be apparent that therapists who intend to lead these groups should master at least the basics of the LEGO system. On one level children are being offered the opportunity to reap the rewards of LEGO play in return for their efforts in the direction of social competence. If the adults in the room are only involved at the social level and are unable to offer help or advice in the construction methods associated with the LEGO system, the children will not consider them a particularly useful resource. LEGO therapists should take the time to familiarize themselves with the pieces, sets, and instructions that will be used in sessions.

SESSION STRUCTURE

In the course of a session, there is typically a gradual shift from higher to lower structure. At the beginning, leaders guide the group and its agenda but then allow the children more freedom to choose their own activities by the end of the one-hour session. This early structure is critical since the opposite, free play, is very difficult to reverse. Once the children are settled, usually seated at a large table, the goal is group participation in a productive organized activity.

Initial Greeting   Many of the participants initially do not spontaneously greet each other upon entering the room, so this is usually the first order of business. Leaders coach the children to acknowledge each other with age-appropriate greetings and using names and eye contact. In some cases, we develop this time further by asking the children to share news since the previous week or to discuss projects of other topics. This is also a good time to address any issues related to transitioning into the room. Unrelated materials, including personal LEGO or other toys, food, or reading materials, should be left with parents in the waiting room.

Group Review and Discussion   The next step is to introduce a structured activity. In some cases, the activity is the obvious continuation of last week's unfinished projects. Other times, the leaders may provide several choices of activities like building new sets, restoring old ones, or spending some time organizing materials. When groups are involved in stop-animation movies, we use round-table discussions and voting to determine the characters and establish the story before building any of the items to be used in the movie. This more collaborative and open-ended style of decision making can be difficult for children who are especially fixated on ritual during the session. It is best to address the whole group about this issue, and occasionally to negotiate. Leaders should try to ensure that the chosen tasks are of appropriate number and complexity that they can be finished in the allotted time. Estimating this successfully takes some trial and error.

Role and Task Assignment   Once the group has established goals for the day, planning is required to divide time and labor. Working with the children to compromise in terms of who does what and for how long contributes to sharing, turn taking, and collaboration. It also establishes a structure, which helps to prevent chaotic individual free play later in the session.

Main Group Activities   During this core part of the session, each member should be actively engaged in his or her assigned task. Participation from leaders may focus on helping with actual building skills, but an experienced group at a relatively high developmental level is likely to engage in the LEGO construction activities fairly automatically and easily. In this ideal situation, leaders can direct most of their efforts into coaching social and communication skills. It also depends on the novelty of the task.

Free-Play   If there is time left over in a session after completion of the main activities, structure is relaxed in order to allow the members to interact and work on individual, often spontaneous, creative interests and projects naturally. Leaders still focus on interaction, encouraging members to work or play in pairs or small groups with shared themes or interests.

Cleanup   LEGO materials are very specialized. They are often very small and in the case of our LEGO Clubs, they are very numerous. Organization of the collection is both important and challenging. We are always working to instill in our members a sense of pride in the collection. Always give at least a 5-minute warning that cleanup time is approaching. With complex and messy projects, 10 minutes before cleanup makes sense. Repeat the warnings as cleanup approaches. In this brief pre-cleanup period, no new projects should be started, and no new play themes or LEGO sets are taken down from the shelf. "You have three minutes to finish up what you're doing." Expect actual cleanup to take about 15 minutes.

Finishing Up   After cleanup, have the children say goodbye appropriately, using each other's names. To minimize the possibility of stragglers who might want to stay behind hoping to extend their LEGO time, we have all of the children line up at the door before leaving the room. If parents or teachers will want feedback about the session, it is best to jot down some notes as soon as possible after the session ends.

THE LEGO CLUB LEVEL SYSTEM

We employ a level system to reward and motivate children. Once the skills for a particular level are demonstrated, a special LEGO Club certificate signed by all group members and leaders is awarded to that child. Peers rather than adult leaders decide when a child's project meets the specific criteria for a given level. Level progression seems to naturally come with "bragging rights," and this often leads to improved motivation, task persistence, and willingness to undertake more difficult tasks when a new level certificate is a possibility.

LEGO LEVELS

1. LEGO Helper   Members enter at the Helper level. At this level, they are encouraged to "help out" the group activities by presorting pieces when set building (e.g., all the grey pieces together), sorting freestyle pieces, checking sets for integrity against directions when completed, ordering, and cleaning the LEGO room. This level serves different functions for children depending on their skills: For children who are not yet proficient at set building or do not have the ability to sustain attention on a task long enough, this allows for participation and provides the context for peer approval and appreciation of input. For children with higher skills, these activities motivate them to demonstrate their proficiency at higher level skills in order to move up, including gaining peer approval and building peer alliances.

2. LEGO Builder   Once a LEGO Helper has demonstrated that he or she can construct LEGO sets of a moderate size (100 pieces and above) and can take the role of Builder in a group set-building activity, the group members will be asked if the participant warrants graduating up to LEGO Builder status. If the group agrees, the participant is then awarded a diploma, which is signed by the leader(s) and all other group members.

3. LEGO Creator   The challenge for a LEGO Builder who wants to move up to being a LEGO Creator is to construct a freestyle creation. This has to be an original idea, with a certain degree of complexity and gestalt integrity that makes it appealing to the other members. The other group members again make a group decision regarding the creation, and if they are agreed, the participant is given a Creator Certificate.

4. EGO Master   The challenge at this level is to lead a group project. The participant must have either initiated the purchase of a large LEGO set (over 300 pieces) for which they then coordinate the construction or the presentation to the group of a desirable group freestyle project (e.g., build a complex building, a small town, an airport, or a zoo, or construct a series of creations, such as a set of vehicles, robots, or other craft). The important point here is that the group members are assigned tasks and roles by the leader and that he or she effectively directs the project, enlisting support and input from other members, resulting in a project that all group members are agreed was challenging and worthwhile.

5. LEGO Genius This level was actually created to appease a few LEGO Masters who requested a new challenge against which to pitch their LEGO leadership skills. A criterion for achievement at this level is writing a movie script or story that they present to the group (they can choose a reader for this). The script must be critiqued by other members and edited as necessary. The final script is then analyzed in terms of how the project can be translated into a LEGO-based stop-action animated short film. The LEGO Master must lead the group in the project, including assigning building tasks for the set and characters; assigning action, voice, and sound-effects roles; controlling or assigning control of the camera and computer (a digital video camera and laptop with editing software are used); and then directing the film itself. The project can take numerous sessions to complete and requires considerable leadership skill in order to get all members to sustain focus on the task for the required length of time. The resulting animated short film is then edited by the producing member, is shown to the group and other groups, and the group members and participant discuss whether the work qualifies as worthy of the LEGO Genius diploma.

6. LEGO Legend This is not an official level but rather a term that has spontaneously developed at our center. A Legend is any club member who has participated long enough to rise through the other levels and has achieved the LEGO Genius level but wishes to continue participating. Typically, these participants have established relationships with their group members and although their social development goals have usually been met by this point, they and their parents wish to continue attending. These senior group members are offered the opportunity to attend without cost as peer mentors and are identified to their peers as LEGO Legends, although this is normally not necessary. Most participants who achieve Legend status are usually well-known to both their own group and other groups by their creations and film projects.

LEGO CLUB RULES

Rules for LEGO Club were officially developed by group consensus, with input from participants solicited by the group facilitators. Individuals interested in running their own groups based on this model are encouraged to develop their own participant-initiated rules. Different groups over time have come up with different rule sets, but they are often surprisingly similar to each other. The current set of proscriptive rules is as follows:

1. If you break it, you have to fix it.
2. If you can't fix it, ask for help.
3. If someone else is using it, don't take it; ask first.
4. No yelling. Use indoor voices.
5. No climbing or jumping on furniture.
6. No teasing, name-calling, or bad words.
7. No hitting or wrestling—keeps hands and feet to yourself.
8. Clean up—put things back where they came from.

The rules are printed in large print so they can be easily read and are posted on a poster board in the LEGO Therapy room. Whenever a new member is introduced to a group, one or more of the group members are asked to review the rules with the new member, and we often then have a group discussion about how each of the members has occasionally needed to be corrected about a rule violation.

An important aspect of having the rules is implementing them consistently and without negativity. The therapist should typically not offer direct feedback regarding inappropriate behavior. Instead, whenever possible, the therapist will request the other children in the group to remind each other about the rules. Using indirect and ambiguous terms enhances the participants' abilities to identify inappropriate behaviors in others and in themselves. For example, when a child climbs onto a chair to retrieve something from a high shelf:

DR. DAN: "Hey, guys, is someone in here breaking a rule?"

DAVID: "Uh, yeah, Peter is hogging the big truck wheels."

DR. DAN: "Anything else?"

PETER: "Yes! Sam is climbing on furniture. Get down Sam, that's rule number 5."

DR. DAN: "Good point, Peter. Sam?"

SAM: "Sorry, Dr. Dan, I just wanted to get R2D2 for my X-wing."

Dr. Dan: "Well, what should you do?"
Sam: "I couldn't reach it without getting up . . ."
Dr. Dan: "LEGO Club, what should Sam do?"
Group (together): "He should ask for help!"

SPECIAL CONSIDERATIONS OR CRITICAL ISSUES IN WORKING WITH POPULATION/PROGRAM

Behavior Management and Rewards

LEGO Club Approach to Behavior Parents, as well as teachers and other therapists who are not familiar with this treatment approach, often ask about discipline or behavior control procedures. It turns out that problem behavior is quite rare using this approach, especially when the participants are highly motivated and have been properly prepared during the initial interview.

A key to LEGO Therapy is establishing self-regulation and using peer-mediated corrective feedback. These skills are aided by the use of posted rules, the LEGO Club rules. During the initial interview, potential participants are told, "If you want to come to the LEGO Club, you have to be able to follow the rules." For nonverbal or pre-verbal children, this message is usually conveyed by correcting their behavior during individual therapy sessions. Children without verbal communication skills are not included in groups until they are proficient at the required skill set, which includes behavioral compliance. The LEGO Rules were developed by the original participants in the first LEGO-based social skills groups, and reflect the consensus regarding a necessary and sufficient set of rules for peer-mediated regulation of the group process.

LEGO Points A formal "LEGO Points" system can be used, in which points are awarded for behavioral, social, and LEGO-related achievements (e.g., complying with rules, building models with another child). These points can be collected and traded in for LEGO prizes (small sets, LEGO people, etc.). Prizes can be useful initially, but after a while, points tend to become inherently valuable and not associated with any tangible reward. Instead, children seek the social approval of earning points. For this reason, points are an option for LEGO Therapy.

Rules of Cool Unlike the proscriptive LEGO Club rules, the Rules of Cool are implicit, prescriptive rules that are not overtly written or otherwise indicated. These implicit rules are actually defined by the group members as part of an ongoing discussion that takes place during sessions informally. The topic is introduced to members in situations in which there may be socially inappropriate or stigmatizing behaviors evident that do not necessarily violate one of the LEGO Club rules. Positive or prosocial behaviors exhibited by group members should be noted and pointed out by the therapists or instructors. For example, "Hey, Matt, thanks for sharing with Nick. That was cool. Wasn't that cool, guys?" Also encourage other group members to comment on each other's behaviors, both positive and negative (e.g., "Hey, John, did you see Sean just grab that out of David's hand? Was that cool? What should he have done—tell him").

OUTCOME STUDIES

To date, there have been three published outcome studies that have focused on the efficacy of the LEGO Therapy approach. The first study (LeGoff, 2004) utilized a waiting-list time line design, with participants serving as their own controls before and after participating in LEGO Therapy. The study included outcome data of participants at both three- (N = 47) and six-month intervals (N = 21) and compared direct observations and parent ratings of autistic and social behaviors for the waiting-list time period compared with post-treatment. The outcome measures included two direct observational measures—frequency of self-initiated social contact during free-play time at school and duration of social interactions during free-play time—and a parent rating of potentially stigmatizing behaviors (using the Gilliam Autism Rating Scale, Stereotyped Behaviors scale).

All three measures were significantly improved after 12 weeks, compared with the 12-week waiting-list baseline two of the measures—duration of interaction and the GARS Stereotyped Behavior scale—were again significantly improved at 24 weeks. The leveling off of the third measure, frequency of self-initiated contact, was considered to be a ceiling effect, which resulted from the limited amount of time and opportunities for increasing frequency of contact during the observational period (15-minute recess).

The second study (LeGoff & Sherman, 2006) compared outcomes on measures of social development and adjustment for LEGO Therapy participants (N = 60) with matched control participants (N = 57). The control group was chosen so that all participants had similar diagnoses and comparable backgrounds and had received similar amounts of individual and group therapy. The two groups were compared using the Vineland Socialization Domain and the GARS Social Interaction subscale. The study examined outcomes on these measures in a retrospective 3-year follow-up design, using data collected as part of standard evaluations by the public school system. Although all participants in the study, both LEGO and control groups, improved significantly at the 3-year follow-up, the LEGO Therapy participants had improved significantly more than the non–LEGO Therapy participants.

The third study (Owens et al., 2008) was conducted as an independent replication study by a group of researchers at Cambridge University Medical School. This study utilized a randomized control group design, assigning subjects to LEGO Therapy groups, to a matched comparison group that utilized an established social skills therapy, the Social Use of Language Program (SULP), or to a no-treatment control group. Again, similar to LeGoff (2004) and LeGoff and Sherman (2006), both treatment groups improved significantly more than the no-treatment control after 18 weeks of once-per-week therapy. The LEGO group participants, however, showed significantly greater improvement on two important measures: parent ratings of social interaction using the GARS Social Interaction subscale, and directly observed duration of social interaction with peers during free play at school.

CONCLUSION AND RECOMMENDATIONS

The LEGO Therapy approach is a clinically derived intervention, explicitly designed to help improve adaptive social functioning—social competence—in children with deficits in social development diagnosed with autistic disorders. Three outcome studies, two by the current authors and one by an independent group, have been published, establishing the efficacy and generalized social improvements using this methodology. The outcomes have been demonstrated to be meaningful within fairly brief periods of time (12 weeks in one study, 18 weeks in another) and sustained over a much longer time frame (3 years in one study).

The essential features of this approach are:

1. The utilization of creative play materials that have a somewhat unique appeal for many children in this population;
2. An emphasis on joint accomplishment, group identification, and collaborative achievement;

3. The spontaneous and natural occurrence of frequent opportunities for close social communication, problem solving, and conflict resolution with peers, that is, a high frequency of interaction and opportunities for practicing appropriate social coping.

Group participants willingly remain engaged in the activity throughout the therapy sessions and are often motivated to continue participation for years. The groups have had considerable success in encouraging collateral social supports through parent and sibling involvement, as well as with participants seeking out other members outside of the group sessions.

Needless to say, despite the encouraging outcome studies and the directly observed clinical benefits for group participants, there are still many issues to be addressed and questions to be answered. For instance, the extant outcome studies have focused exclusively on children with pervasive development (autistic) disorders, although we have found clinically that this approach can be just as effective with nonautistic children who also have difficulties with social adjustment (e.g., anxiety disorders, mood disorders). We have also not had the opportunity to explore the potential impact that this approach might have for improving social competence of unaffected children, that is, utilization of LEGO Therapy as an assertiveness and social competence enhancement for children without a mental health or developmental diagnosis.

The current focus for the LEGO Therapy approach is to make it more widely accessible and available in more educational settings, as opposed to clinical settings. There are now just a few educational sites—both private and public schools—offering this approach currently. Utilization of the methodology by more educators and clinicians in a broader range of contexts (e.g., community settings, public schools, inpatient settings) and with a broader range of population groups (e.g., adults, nonautistic individuals) is encouraged and should lead to gains regarding both play therapy interventions, as well as the nature of play and its relationship to social development in general.

REFERENCES

Attwood, A. J. (1998). *Asperger's syndrome: A guide for parents and professionals.* London: Jessica Kingsley.

Greenspan, S. I., & Wieder, S. (1998). *The child with special needs: Encouraging intellectual and emotional growth.* Reading, MA: Perseus Books.

Harris, S. L., & Handleman, J. S. (1997). Helping children with autism enter the mainstream. In D. J. Cohen & F. R. Volkmar (Eds.), *Handbook of autism and pervasive developmental disorders* (2nd ed., pp. 665—675). New York: John Wiley & Sons.

Koegel, L. K. (1995). Communication and language intervention. In R. L. Koegel & L. K. Koegel (Eds.), *Teaching children with autism: Strategies for initiating positive interactions and improving learning opportunities* (pp. 17–32). Baltimore, MD: Brookes Publishing.

Koegel, R. L., & Koegel, L. (1995). *Teaching children with autism.* New York: Brookes Publishing.

Koegel, R. L., Koegel, L. K., Frea, W. D., & Smith, A. E. (1995). Emerging interventions for children with autism: Longitudinal and lifestyle implications. In R. L. Koegel & L. K. Koegel (Eds.), *Teaching children with autism: Strategies for initiating positive interactions and improving learning opportunities* (pp. 1–16). Baltimore, MD: Brookes Publishing.

Kohler, F. W., Strain, P. S., Hoyson, M., & Jamieson, B. (1997). Merging naturalistic teaching and peer-based strategies to address the IEP objectives of preschoolers with autism: An examination of structural and child behavior outcomes. *Focus on Autism and other Developmental Disabilities,* 12(4), 196–206.

Laushey, K. M., & Heflin, L. J. (2000). Enhancing social skills of Kindergarten children with autism through the training of multiple peers as tutors. *Journal of Autism and Developmental Disorders,* 30(3), 183–193.

LeGoff, D. B. (2004). Use of LEGO as a therapeutic medium for improving social competence. *Journal of Autism & Developmental Disorders,* 34(5), 557–571.

LeGoff, D. B., & Sherman, M. (2006). Long-term outcome of social skills intervention based on interactive LEGO play. *Autism,* 10(4), 1–31.

Owens, G., Granader, Y., Humphrey, A., & Baron Cohen, S. (2008). LEGO therapy and the Social Use of Language Programme: An evaluation of two social skills interventions for children with high functioning autism and Asperger syndrome. *Journal of Autism and Developmental Disorders,* 38(10), 1944–1957.

CHAPTER 12

Trauma-Focused Group Play Therapy in the Schools

YIH-JIUN SHEN

S CHOOL PERSONNEL WHO work with children developmentally wrestle with the consequences of children's trauma daily (Johnson, 1998). Observations of children may alert school personnel that a trauma could have happened (Johnson, 1998). These children typically manifest their symptoms or troubled behaviors in their daily living situations and learning environments. Oftentimes, children are unaware of their distress, and it may not be recognized until adults experience difficulties interacting with the child (Shen & Sink, 2002). Thus, it is critical that sensitive mental health providers take initiative in facilitating the referral process and effective treatments. Mingling play with verbalization as a means of catharsis, the process of group play therapy allows children to work through their trauma without being confronted by the typical ways of adult communication (Tyndall-Lind, Landreth, & Giordano, 2001). This chapter intends to equip school-based mental health professionals to effectively work with traumatized children. Specifically, the following areas will be addressed: what constitutes trauma, children's reactions to trauma, the screening and referral processes, the value of play therapy with traumatized children, theory-based group play therapy modalities, special considerations in working with traumatized children, and case examples.

WHAT CONSTITUTES TRAUMA

Trauma is a psychobiological reaction of a victim who overwhelmingly experiences or witnesses a disastrous event that threatens the person's life or integrity (American Psychiatric Association, 2000; Rothschild, 1998). The psychobiological reaction involves hyperarousal of the autonomic nervous system entailing an emotional discomfort and stress due to the shattering of the individual's invulnerability to harm (Rothschild, 1998). Instead of *medical trauma*, which refers to a serious bodily injury, this article focuses on *psychological trauma*, which refers to emotionally intense distress, horror, shock, and a sense of helplessness that often result in lasting physical and mental effects (House, Gillies, & London, 2006; MedicineNet. com, 2005). Notably, even secondhand exposure to a frightening event can be traumatic (MedicineNet.com, 2002).

The stressors, which are stored deep in the brain and hard to forget, may include a *social trauma* or a *cultural trauma* (a historic process that affects an entire population), a community disaster, a violent crime, or a single episode exclusively affecting an individual (Hutchison, 2005; Kaduson, 2006; Kreisler, 2005). Social or cultural trauma includes warfare (e.g., civil wars, World War II), massacres (e.g., the Holocaust), and terrorist attacks (American Psychiatric Publishing Inc. [AAPI], 2005; Hutchison, 2005; Kreisler, 2005). Community disasters include natural disasters (e.g., earthquakes, hurricanes, forest fires, floods, mud slides, tornadoes, tsunamis) and humanmade or technological disasters (e.g., sniper fire, bombings) (Hutchison, 2005; Ranawaka & Dewaraja, 2006; Shen & Sink, 2002). Violent crimes that victimize children include rape, sexual abuse, commercial sexual exploitation, physical or psychological abuse, homicide, school shooting, and kidnap (Hutchison, 2005; Miller, 1998; Webb, 2006). Other incidents include airplane crashes, car accidents, school bus accidents, ferry boat accidents, severe burns, domestic violence, and suicide or death of family or close friends (AAPI, 2005; Hutchison, 2005; Johnson, 1998; Miller, 1998; Webb, 2006). Among the aforementioned stressors, the most often recognized events that traumatized children are sexual abuse, domestic violence, natural disasters, and warfare (Miller, 1998).

Although noticeable incidents can traumatize children, they may also be affected by some hidden events that occur in children's daily living and are hardly noticed by adults. The cause could be a frightening image of "the onslaught of a ten-meter-high tidal wave" or "a rash of gunfire and the sight of blood splattering on the ground," the dehumanization due to sexual assault, brutality from caregivers, peer teasing or bullying, or the sense of abandonment caused by parental divorce (Hutchison, 2005, p. 8). Compared with other age groups, children are among the most susceptible to the harmful effects of trauma (Hutchison, 2005).

CHILDREN'S REACTIONS TO TRAUMA

Some children experiencing traumatic events may simply shut them out; nonetheless, many children do manifest salient reactions when confronted by acute stress (Johnson, 1998; Shen & Sink, 2002). Research shows that situational trauma sharply affects children in four major areas: cognitive (e.g., confusion, time distortions), emotional (e.g., anger, irritability, anxiety, depression), physical (e.g., pounding heart, nausea, cramps, headaches, nightmares), and behavioral (e.g., slowness, hysteria, hyperactivity) (Johnson, 1998; Shen & Sink, 2002). Delayed responses that appear after weeks, months, or even years continually affect these four areas in different forms, such as 1) preoccupation with the incident, orientation toward the past; 2) depression, grief, guilt, resentment; 3) fatigue, increased illness; and 4) flashbacks, avoidance of incident locations, or the need to talk compulsively about the events (Johnson, 1998). More severely affected children may suffer from trauma-related mental disorders, such as Posttraumatic Stress Disorder (PTSD) and Acute Stress Disorder (ASD) (Johnson, 1998; Shelby, 2000; Webb, 2006).

From a developmental perspective, the effects of traumatic incidents may cause certain abnormal behavioral patterns in different stages of development (Drewes, 2001; Johnson, 1998; Shelby, 2000). Specifically, lacking the ability to comprehend subjective distress, preschoolers and kindergarteners frequently respond with anxious attachment, denial, distrust, regression, specific fears, withdrawal, and thematic play (i.e., reenactments or ritualistic play of either the trauma itself or life upsets associated with the trauma) (Johnson, 1998). Elementary-age children may show a decline in school performance, compensatory behavior (for undoing the damage or making up for resulting loss), obsessive expression (of detailed facts), mood discrepancies, sudden behavior changes (troubled or nonproblematic), elaborate reenactments (progressively more sophisticated play of traumatic occurrences), and psychosomatic complaints (Johnson, 1998). Adolescents may demonstrate self-destructive behavior (e.g., delinquency, drug and alcohol abuse, isolation, sexual activity, suicidal attempts, violence, running away), low self-esteem, self-criticism, prematurely assuming heavy life responsibilities (e.g., planned pregnancy), displaced anger (often toward teachers or school personnel as undeserving recipients), and preoccupation with self (Johnson, 1998).

Although some have suggested that early traumatic experience has few lasting effects due to infantile amnesia or memory block in children, the lasting impact of traumatic events beyond recall has never been discounted (Archer, 2003; Johnson, 1998). Along with the aforementioned symptoms, these children may develop severe school attendance problems together with other self-destructive behavior even years after the event (Johnson, 1998). For instance, being severely affected by the terrorist attacks of September 11, 2001, in New York, many school-aged students near the World Trade Center had difficulty returning to their schools and progressing to the next grade levels (APPI, 2005). Particularly for teenagers, who face increased developmental pressure, trauma that might be distant in time may still surface when its associated underlying issues remain unresolved (Johnson, 1998). For example, the enduring psychopathology caused by early traumatic experience may become apparent during adolescence (or even adulthood), manifested in depressive, dissociative, eating, identity, and personality disorders (Archer, 2003; Johnson, 1998; Schore, 2001). Generally, unresolved trauma can disturb the continuity of an individual's positive sense of self (APPI, 2005; Young, 2008). Yet more seriously, unresolved issues that occur during a particular developmental stage may not only result in long-term dysfunctional patterns but also increase the likelihood of impeding the individual's ability to resolve future issues (Drewes, 2001; Johnson, 1998; Shen & Sink, 2002). Regardless of when the trauma occurred, referral for remedial interventions is needed and should take place in a timely manner (Ranawaka & Dewaraja, 2006).

SCREENING AND REFERRAL PROCESSES

Referrals could be initiated by children; however, parents, family members, caregivers, teachers, and school personnel are the typical gatekeepers who notice the need. These adults' detection is fundamental, but mental health providers should not completely rely on it. Ironically, the needs for interventional care are often underestimated especially when the adults are also victimized (Lamberg, 2005). With less energy and time for children, the affected adults may become less observant in the post-trauma chaos (Shen, 2002). Because child trauma may not catch adults' attention, instrumental screening should also take place. For children traumatized by hidden events, informal screening should occur via adults' daily observations. Troubled behavior, social problems, and dropped school performance are common cues.

In addition to informal screening, formal screening is imperative in the aftermath of major disasters, community tragedies, or substantial accidents. For instance, after the terrorist attacks of September 11, 2001, the Columbia Teen Screen, a program screening for depression and anxiety, partnered with the Mental Health Association to screen entire classes or schools surrounding the World Trade Center for identifying children and adolescents needing psychological interventions (AAPI, 2005; Lamberg, 2005). To efficiently identify large numbers of children, school-based mental health personnel should consider measures that are well designed. The following ones with properly established psychometric properties and good administration time (5 to 30 minutes) are highly recommended (AAPI, 2005; Shen, 2002).

THE UNIVERSITY OF CALIFORNIA AT LOS ANGELES POST-TRAUMATIC STRESS DISORDER (PTSD) REACTION INDEX

The UCLA PTSD-RI (Steinberg, Brymer, Decker, & Pynoos, 2004) revised from the *Child PTSD Reaction Index* is one of the most broadly applied instruments in childhood PTSD studies across a variety of ages (childhood and adolescence), cultures, nationalities, and trauma types, including major disasters and calamitous violence (AAPI, 2005; Fletcher, n.d.; Steinberg, Brymer, Decker, & Pynoos, 2004). The 20-item UCLA PTSD-RI, which covers all *DSM-IV* symptoms in child friendly statements, provides more scientific basis than the original version for screening and diagnosis purposes (Fletcher, n.d.).

CHILDREN'S DEPRESSION INVENTORY (CDI)

The 27-item self-report CDI (Kovacs, 1992) assesses the cognitive, affective, and behavioral signs of depression in children and adolescents between 6 and 17 years old. This commonly applied scale assesses the follow areas: negative mood, interpersonal difficulties, negative self-esteem, ineffectiveness, and anhedonia. A shorter 10-item form is available to provide a quick assessment of depressive symptoms. Additional perspectives on childhood depression can be acquired via CDI Parent and CDI Teacher Forms.

REVISED CHILDREN'S MANIFEST ANXIETY SCALE: SECOND EDITION (RCMAS-2)

The RCMAS-2 (Reynolds & Richmond, 2008) was revised from the first edition, which was often used in major catastrophic events (Shen, 2002). The second edition, a 49-item self-report inventory, measures children's anxiety, including physiological anxiety (anxiety manifested physiologically), worry, social anxiety, defensiveness, and an inconsistent responding index. A Short Form, composed of the first 10 items, is available to quickly assess the children's anxiety level. The scale is for ages of 6 to 19 and requires a second-grade reading level, but an audio CD is available for younger children and those with reading or attention problems.

Unsurprisingly, children who do not meet the thresholds—the cutoff scores of these instruments—initially may later develop interventional needs due to the addition of developmental challenges or life crises (Wohl & Hightower, 2001). Parents, teachers, or even children who detect the interventional needs may still refer the children afterward. Therefore, referrals should be accepted throughout an academic year.

VALUE OF PLAY THERAPY WITH TRAUMATIZED CHILDREN

Why play therapy with this population? From the perspective of neurobiology, traumatized children's connections between the left and right cerebral hemispheres are not healthy (Archer, 2003). The high arousal disrupts their cognitive processing of sensory information (Adler-Nevo & Manassis, 2005). The disorganized internal road maps distort the child's perceptual and cognitive systems, somatic sensory, emotional, and linguistic connections, as well as coherent self-integration (Archer, 2003; Parnell, 1999). With damaged ability to strive for healthy patterns of attachment, these children often build their interpersonal relationships upon mistrust, insecurity, and a sense of unpredictability (Archer, 2003). The children's ability for survival responses becomes selective, and their ability for cognitive re-structuring is also limited due to distorted cognitive and verbal approaches (Archer, 2003). Physically and psychologically, these areas remain disconnected unless therapeutic interventions occur (Archer, 2003). The lack of vital linguistic connections, however, creates more difficulties for these children in engaging in a meaningful language-based intervention process, which is primarily left-hemisphere communication (Archer, 2003; Parnell, 1999). Because the hippocampus of the child is "short-circuited," instead of producing a helpful influence, interventions primarily using verbal exchanges may further disadvantage the traumatized youngsters (Archer, 2003).

In order to restore good connections between the right and left brains and further lead to healthy right-and-left-brain communications, Schore (2001) stresses the importance of engaging the traumatized child initially via "right brain to right brain" interactions. To avoid serious formation of personality disorders, it is hence critical that before these traits are fixed and while the child's neural networks are most elastic, developmentally appropriate somatic-sensory and emotional interventions be provided (Archer, 1999a, 1999b, 2003). In addition, it is important to help these children restore a sense of safety and normalcy; correct any misconceptions; grieve over their losses; express trauma-related anger, guilt, and irritability; work through lingering issues; rejuvenate healthy attachments; enhance personal resilience; and achieve closure about the trauma to move forward (AAPI, 2005; Chemtob, Nakashima, & Hamada, 2002). For those who encountered social or community trauma, it is also important to cultivate a sense of community renewal (AAPI, 2005).

Among various mental health intervention strategies, play therapy whose features match with these children's needs has been recommended as a feasible tool (Adler-Nevo & Manassis, 2005; Kaduson, 2006). Play allows children to revisit traumatic events and to restructure the experience at various levels of functioning involving somatic sensation, affection, and cognition (Adler-Nevo & Manassis, 2005). Several empirical studies have evidenced the effectiveness of play therapy with this population. For instance, after a devastating earthquake took more than 2,300 lives in Taiwan, Shen's (2002) pre- and post-test, experimental-control group design significantly reduced child survivors' anxiety and suicidal ideation. Experimental studies using play therapy with child witnesses of domestic violence also suggest significant reductions of behavior problems, aggression, anxiety, and depression as well as significant increases in self-concept and self-esteem (e.g., Tyndall-Lind, Landreth, & Giordano, 2001). Additionally, the use of play therapy with traumatized children has been reported across different cases. They include war refugees (Bevin, Montgomery, & Takoma, 1999) and witnesses of terrorist attacks (AAPI, 2005; Webb, 2007). Other cases include survivors of car accidents (de Rios, 1997), hurricanes (Green, 2007), tsunamis (Baggerly, 2007), school fires (Satapathy & Walia, 2006), and sexual abuse (Hill, 2006). Many of these reports discussed the applications of play therapy with individuals or in group settings.

THEORY-BASED GROUP PLAY THERAPY MODALITIES

Despite the findings that both individual and group treatments are effective with traumatized children (Taylor & Chemtob, 2004; Tyndall-Lind, Landreth, & Giordano, 2001; Trowell et al., 2002), group counseling tends to be more effective in benefiting more children. In an after-hurricane intervention with elementary school children with disaster-related PTSD in Hawaii, Chemtob, Nakashima, and Hamada (2002) found that both individual and small-group treatments that incorporated play methods and cooperative play significantly reduced children's PTSD symptoms. However, group counseling resulted in better participant completion rates. Ideally children should be seen individually first and then gradually eased into group settings; nevertheless, group interventions may take place immediately, due to resource and schedule constraints in schools and mass needs reacting to unexpected crisis (Sweeney & Homeyer, 1999; Oaklander, 1999; Ray, Armstrong, Warren, & Balkin, 2005; Shen, 2007b, 2008). This situation is especially true after traumatic events victimized large numbers of children.

Combining the features of small-group counseling and individual play therapy, group play therapy generates an intervention process that is much more dynamic (Sweeney & Homeyer, 1999; Tyndall-Lind, Landreth, & Giordano, 2001). During group play therapy, children experience what Yalom termed a "social microcosm," in which new behavior can be tested out while receiving support or corrections by peers and group leaders (Sweeney & Homeyer, 1999; Yalom & Leszcz, 2005). Through children's own language—play—group members jointly apply play media to express troubling situations and to further grow out of the sense of loss, anger, and guilt (Sweeney & Homeyer, 1999). The modality makes it possible for the revitalization of healthy attachments and the achievement of closure in relation to the trauma. These changes ultimately empower the children to move forward.

In terms of major approaches to group play therapy, many have been recommended for use with traumatized children (Sweeney & Homeyer, 1999). The following paragraphs introduce child-centered and Gestalt approaches that can be applied effectively in school settings. Typically, the child-centered approach works better with children under ages 10 to 12; the Gestalt approach can be effective with teenagers as well (Landreth, 2002; Oaklander, 1978).

CHILD-CENTERED GROUP PLAY THERAPY

In a successfully implemented child-centered play therapy group, children search within themselves for the healing resources to solve problems and heal emotional wounds (Landreth & Sweeney, 1999). Based on the theory of Carl Rogers, Virginia Axline (1947) developed eight principles for child-centered approach, a nondirective model of play therapy. A group leader must 1) develop a warm and friendly relationship with members, 2) accept children as they are, 3) establish a sense of permissiveness, 4) recognize and reflect back children's feelings, 5) maintain a deep respect for children's ability to solve their problems, 6) follow the way children lead, 7) appreciate the gradual change of the healing process rather than attempt to hurry it along, and 8) only set up limits to therapeutically help children accept responsibility in the relationship.

Honoring individuals' intrinsic growing power and self-directive capacity, the approach attempts to help children grow as healthy persons through positive relationships between the group leader and members and among the members themselves (Landreth & Sweeney, 1999). Instead of being a director of group activities, a child-centered group leader should be a facilitator of safe relationships within which children's natural way of communication—play—is permitted. The therapeutic relationship is focused upon the following elements: person rather than problem, present rather than past, feelings rather than thoughts or acts, understanding rather than explaining, accepting rather than correcting, child's direction rather than therapist's instruction, child's wisdom rather than therapist's knowledge (Landreth & Sweeney, 1999).

In proposing child-centered play therapy groups, group leaders must keep in mind that the group process should evolve from the voluntary needs or issues of group members rather than from a previously planned specific agenda (Landreth & Sweeney, 1999). The structure of the group does not rely on prescribed techniques or activities. Due to communication problems resulting from developmental differences, the age range of group members generally should be within one year; the younger the children, the smaller the group size (Landreth & Sweeney, 1999; Tyndall-Lind, Landreth, & Giordano, 2001). It is not uncommon to have only two or three children in a group; however, it is not recommended to have more than five. Toys and materials should be selected based on their wide functions facilitating creative, emotional, exploratory, and expressive plays (Landreth, 2002). By taking the focus off the group leader, the environment should warmly cultivate the members to safely experience self-exploration, self-discovery, and self-realization (Landreth & Sweeney, 1999).

GESTALT GROUP PLAY THERAPY

For children who are placed in Gestalt play therapy group, the healthy functioning of their total organism, including their senses, bodies, emotions, and intellect, is the major concerns of the group leader (Oaklander, 1999). In this phenomenological, process-oriented therapy group, children will obtain better self-awareness via experiencing "who they are," "how they feel," and "what they want" (Oaklander, 1978). These elements are particularly important for traumatized children because they often block their feelings or otherwise express them in an unhealthy manner. The disconnection is the root of the sense of self-depreciation. Providing children with experiential activities for "seeing, hearing, touching, tasting, and smelling" can facilitate these children in growing out of their faulty sense of self and inability to make good contacts with others (Oaklander, 1978; Oaklander, 1999).

In facilitating the healing process of children, a group leader lays the cornerstone on the "I-Thou" relationship—the client-therapist relationship (Oaklander, 1999). It allows the group leader and members to take mutual leads. Respecting children's broad life experiences and resistance, if any, the group leader views the relationship as a privilege for both sides (Oaklander, 1999). To bring the self of the child into the present situation, the leader must maintain contact with the members. Projective techniques (e.g., body movement, clay sculpturing, drawing, fantasy, games, metaphors, photography, puppet, storytelling) are used (Oaklander, 1978). They may interest children, facilitate the contact, and further help them explore negative self-image, increase self-acceptance, establish self-worth, and move toward self-nurturing (Oaklander, 1978).

With regard to the group structure, leaders should set up goals and projective activities ahead of each session (Oaklander, 1999). As for the group size, for children above 8 years of age, six to eight members are recommended; under 8 years of age, three to six members (Oaklander, 1999). Although group protocols can be modified and paced according to the dynamics developed in each session, the session typically starts with rounds—each member takes turns to share anything or any concerns since previous session—and ends with a closure activity (Oaklander, 1978). Themes (e.g., loneliness, loss, anger, fears) relevant to children's trauma often emerge either from the rounds or the following projective activities. Children may share their efforts with each other, or the leader may at times focus on the product of one particular child while facilitating connections with other children (Oaklander, 1999). The emphasis of these interactions is not the products per se but children's concerns or feelings being respected and safely processed.

SPECIAL CONSIDERATIONS IN WORKING WITH TRAUMATIZED CHILDREN

When working with traumatized children, a few precautions should be considered. First, the selection of theoretical approaches should be treated with caution. With a shorter response period children who experience acute trauma may still be in strong denial and anger (Ivey & Ivey, 2007). Due to the lack of ability to accept the traumatic reality, they tend to mask their sadness and fears. Interventions provided to this type of population could be perceived overly intrusive by these children and thus provoke strong defensive reactions from them (Shen, 2007a). Hence, a theoretical approach that is nondirective or less invasive (i.e., child-centered approach) may produce smoother therapeutic relationships and better effects. Children with hidden trauma tend to have a stronger ability to accept the reality, and their tolerance level is often higher. The selection of theoretical approaches thus is more flexible for these children.

Second, it is very important to provide items and an environment that are relevant to the traumatic conditions children experienced. Although the selection of play materials may be pretty flexible when symbolic play is the children's major activity, it should be noted that toys used by children can be highly correlated with the play themes that emerge (Wu, 2001). As catharsis and reenactment of trauma are critical to the healing process of traumatized children, a physical environment that will facilitate children's association of thoughts and expression of feelings is a must. Added to typical play materials and cross-culturally sensitive objects (Ji, Ramirez, & Kranz, 2008; Kranz, Ramirez, Flores-Torres, Steele, & Lund, 2005; Landreth, 2002) are these specific items:

- Human figures that depict people similar to the client's helpers or perpetrators
- Animal figures that depict children's pets or key animals during traumatic moments

- Rescuer transportation vehicles such as police cars, fire trucks, ambulances, and helicopters
- Specific transportation items during airplane crash, car accidents, school bus accidents, ferry boat accidents
- A dollhouse, sandbox, or puppet theater that may be used to reenact the situations of earthquakes, tsunamis, hurricanes, and domestic violence
- Specially designed dolls that may be used to reenact the situations of sexual abuse or exploitation
- Items as anger expression or nurturing targets (e.g., punching bags, plush animals, clay)

Keep in mind that the aforementioned materials may provoke some children's negative feelings during play sessions, especially for those who have not attained the developmental level of accepting the traumatic reality. Nonetheless, these items may also serve as a key to empowerment as children gradually become more used to the existence of these items in a playroom where negative feelings or thoughts can be accepted safely all the time.

Third, although group play therapy has many advantages, a child whose individual needs demand more intense and undivided attention of the play therapist is not recommended for group settings (Ginott, 1994). Children with the following conditions often fall under this category: intense sibling rivalries, accelerated sexual drives, persistent stealing, and extreme aggressiveness (Ginott, 1994). Individual settings would be more appropriate for these children because their behavior may be destructive to other children in the group (Landreth & Sweeney, 1999).

CASE EXAMPLES

The following selective case examples illustrate the use of 1) a child-centered play group with child survivors from a devastating earthquake in an elementary school and 2) a Gestalt play therapy group with a middle school student with a hidden trauma.

SYNOPSIS OF CHILD-CENTERED GROUP PLAY THERAPY

Session 1   Emma, Kathy, and Linda, all fifth-graders, were referred to a school counselor after schoolwide instrumental screenings. They entered a playroom with the counselor. The playroom was set up in a school building, which was not damaged by the earthquake.

COUNSELOR: All of you can play with the toys in this room in any way you like.

KATHY: [Following Linda and walking around.] There are a lot of toys!

COUNSELOR: You are surprised, Kathy!

[While Kathy and Linda continued to touch several toys but were not serious with any of them, Emma moved much more slowly and did not say any words throughout this session.]

COUNSELOR: Feel free to play with them if you want.

The counselor fostered a permissive climate to help them reduce anxiety as they explored the environment.

Session 3

LINDA: [Looked at a puppet theater in the room and asked Kathy.] Do you want to play with puppets?

KATHY: [Looked around and answered a few seconds later.] I do not see any puppets.

COUNSELOR: Linda and Kathy want to play with puppets but cannot find any.

KATHY: [Asked the counselor.] Do you know where they are?

COUNSELOR: [Reflected her wants but allow her the opportunity to find them out.] You wonder if I know the answer.

EMMA: [Walked and looked around the room.] They must be somewhere.

COUNSELOR: Emma wants to join Linda and Kathy as well.

By mentioning every child's name, the counselor raised their awareness of the existence of every group member. Instead of doing the work for them, the counselor returned the responsibility to them and reminded Linda and Kathy that their partner Emma could be a helper.

Session 5

The children entered the playroom with smiling faces.

KATHY: Let's play a puppet show today. [She seemed to have it in mind prior to entering the room.]

LINDA: [Looked at the counselor.] What would you like to see?

COUNSELOR: Linda, you wonder what I want to see. You guys can decide what to show. [The counselor trusted that they might have their own agenda and allowed them to take the lead.]

EMMA: I got an idea. [She whispered to Kathy and Linda for a while.]

They used the puppets to play out the happening of the scary earth-quake, which killed some of their family members and relatives. In the following three consecutive sessions, the children played the same puppet show. Although the puppets they chose varied from time to time, the stories played out were similar from one play to another. In the following sessions, the themes of their play no longer adhered to the disaster. Apparently, the children's collective needs for reenacting the tragedy had been met.

SYNOPSIS OF GESTALT GROUP PLAY THERAPY

A group of six girls, ages 13 and 14, had met together four times. It was becoming clear that the 13-year-old Ling-Ling lacked a sense of belonging in her family, often felt unwanted, and wanted to transfer to another school with no school performance problems. As the oldest child, she played more of a caregiver's role—always helped her parents take care of her 6-year-old brother and 4-year-old sister. Although her father and stepmother, the mother of the two younger children, frequently assured her of their love, it seemed that she had been traumatized by parental divorce early in life. The school counselor decided to focus on self-nurturing as a central theme during the fifth session. Every group member was given a piece of clay to play with for a few minutes and then made an animal that could represent herself. Ling-Ling made a Chinese dragon. After taking their turns to introduce their animals, the counselor focused on Ling-Ling.

COUNSELOR: Ling-Ling, I want you to tell your dragon why you love her.
LING-LING: [Stared at the dragon for about 15 seconds.] I love you because you are a good daughter at home. You are a good helper. You take care of your younger brother and sister.
COUNSELOR: Can you tell her you are willing to give your love to people but you feel unwanted?
LING-LING: I am willing to give, but I always feel unwanted.
COUNSELOR: Can you tell her why you feel that way?
LING-LING: My [biological] mother did not want me. She left me alone. I don't know why.
COUNSELOR: Can you tell your dragon "I love you although your mother left you without giving you a good reason"?
LING-LING: [Looked at the dragon.] I love you although your mother left you without a good reason.

COUNSELOR: Can you tell your dragon "I will always protect you no matter how other people treat you"?
LING-LING: [In tears.] I will always protect you no matter how other people treat you.
COUNSELOR: No matter what happened, you are always in my heart.
LING-LING: [Tears were streaming down her face.] No matter what happened, you are always my baby.

The 14-year-old Mei-Ling gave her rabbit to Ling-Ling and said, "I want to give you my rabbit so that you have good company all the time." The other girls said, "We are with you, Ling-Ling." She wiped her tears off and smiled. Although she was the one who primarily benefited from the self-nurturing process, children in the group supported each other. With the use of clay, this session rejuvenated healthy contacts between each group member and herself and among group members.

CONCLUSION

Trauma in children can happen anywhere and at any moment. Although some are hard to detect by adults, there are signs that can alert adults who care and methods they can use. Although the impact of trauma on the life and development of children and adolescents can be enormous, it can be prevented and reduced via appropriate interventions. Thus, it is hoped that the trauma-focused group play therapy modalities presented in this chapter, along with many other existing programs, will help school-based mental health personnel work more effectively with this population to revive their development.

REFERENCES

Adler-Nevo, G., & Manassis, K. (2005). Psychosocial treatment of pediatric posttraumatic stress disorder: The neglected field of single-incident trauma. *Depression and Anxiety, 22*, 177–189.

American Psychiatric Association. (2000). *Diagnostic and statistical manual of mental disorders* (4th ed., text rev.). Washington, DC: Author.

American Psychiatric Publishing, Inc. (2005, October). Silver award: The child and adolescent services program of the World Trade Center Healing Services, Saint Vincent Catholic Medical Centers, New York—Providing trauma-related treatment to students after the terrorist attacks of September 11, 2001, and other traumatic events. *Psychiatric Services, 56*, 1309–1311.

Retrieved September 6, 2008, from http://ps.psychiatryonline.org/cgi/reprint/56/10/1309.pdf.

Archer, C. (1999a). First steps in parenting the child who hurts: Tiddlers and toddlers. London: Jessica Kingsley.

Archer, C. (1999b). Next steps in parenting the child who hurts: Tiddlers and toddlers. London: Jessica Kingsley.

Archer, C. (2003). Weft and warp: Developmental impact of trauma and implications for healing. In C. Archer & A. Burnell (Eds.), *Trauma, attachment and family permanence: Fear can stop you loving* (pp. 78–96). London: Jessica Kingsley.

Axline, V. (1947). *Play therapy: The inner dynamics of childhood.* Boston: Houghton Mifflin.

Baggerly, J. (2007). International interventions and challenges following the crisis of natural disasters. In N. B. Webb (Ed.), *Play therapy with children in crisis: Individual, group, and family treatment* (3rd ed., pp. 345–367). New York: Guilford Press.

Bevin, T., Montgomery, C., & Takoma, P. (1999). Multiple traumas of refugees—near drowning and witnessing of maternal rape: Case of Sergio, age 9, and follow-up at age 16. In N. B. Webb (Ed.), *Play therapy with children in crisis: Individual, group, and family treatment* (2nd ed., pp. 164–182). New York: Guilford Press.

Chemtob, C. M., Nakashima, J. P., & Hamada, R. S. (2002). Psychosocial intervention for postdisaster trauma symptoms in elementary school children: A controlled community field study. *Archives of Pediatrics and Adolescent Medicine, 156,* 211–216.

de Rios, M. D. (1997). Magical realism: A cultural intervention for traumatized Hispanic children. *Cultural Diversity and Mental Health, 3,* 159–170.

Drewes, A. A. (2001). Developmental considerations in play and play therapy with traumatized children. In A. A. Drewes, L. J. Carey, & C. E. Schaefer (Eds.), *School-based play therapy* (pp. 297–314). New York: John Wiley & Sons.

Fletcher, K. E. (n.d.). Scales for assessing posttraumatic responses of children. *The child survivors of traumatic stress: A newsletter for professionals.* Retrieved November 3, 2008, from http://users.umassmed.edu/Kenneth.Fletcher/scales.html.

Ginott, H. G. (1994). *Group psychotherapy with children: The theory and practice of play-therapy.* Northvale, NJ: Jason Aronson.

Green, E. J. (2007). The crisis of family separation following traumatic mass destruction: Jungian analytical play therapy in the aftermath of Hurricane Katrina. In N. B. Webb (Ed.), *Play therapy with children in crisis: Individual, group, and family treatment* (3rd ed., pp. 368–388). New York: Guilford Press.

Hill, A. (2006). Play therapy with sexually abused children: Including parents in therapeutic play. *Child and Family Social Work, 11,* 316–324.

House, A. S., Gillies, R. A., & London, J. P., Jr. (2006). *Trauma and women's health: From a biopsychosocial perspective.* Retrieved September 26, 2008 from http://fammed.mcg.edu/residency/modules/trauma/Web%20Trauma%20Homepage.htm.

Hutchison, S. B. (2005). *Effects of and interventions for childhood trauma from infancy through adolescence: Pain unspeakable.* New York: Haworth Maltreatment and Trauma Press.

Ivey, A. E., & Ivey, M. B. (2007). *Intentional interviewing and counseling: Facilitating client development in a multicultural society* (6th ed.). Belmont, CA: Thomson Brooks/Cole.

Ji, Y., Ramirez, S. Z., & Kranz, P. L. (2008). Physical settings and materials recommended for play therapy with Japanese children. *Journal of Instructional Psychology, 35*(1), 53–61.

Johnson, K. (1998). *Trauma in the lives of children: Crisis and stress management techniques for counselors, teachers, and other professionals.* Alameda, CA: Hunter House.

Kaduson, H. G. (2006). *Release play therapy for children with posttraumatic stress disorder.* In H. G. Kaduson & C. E. Schaefer (Eds.), *Short-term play therapy for children* (2nd ed., pp. 3–21). New York: Guilford Press.

Kovacs, M. (1992). *Children's depression inventory.* North Tonawanda, NY: Multi-Health Systems.

Kranz, P. L., Ramirez, S. Z., Flores-Torres, L. L., Steele, R., & Lund, N. L. (2005). Physical settings, materials, and related Spanish terminology recommended for play therapy with Mexican-American children. *Education, 126*(1), 93–99.

Kreisler, H. (2005). Neil Smelser Interview: Conversations with history. Retrieved September 27, 2008, from http://globetrotter.berkeley.edu/people5/Smelser/smelser-con5.html.

Lamberg, L. (2005, October 21). Young disaster evacuees may need MH screening. *Psychiatric News, 40*(20), 8. Retrieved November 2, 2008, from http://pn.psychiatryonline.org/cgi/content/full/psychnews;40/20/8.

Landreth, G. L. (2002). *Play therapy: The art of the relationship* (2nd ed.). New York: Brunner-Routledge.

Landreth, G. L., & Sweeney, D. S. (1999). The freedom to be: Child-centered group play therapy. In D. S. Sweeney & L. E. Homeyer (Eds.), *The handbook of group play therapy: How to do it, how it works, whom it's best for* (pp. 3–14). San Francisco: Jossey-Bass.

MedicineNet.com. (2002). *Definition of psychiatric trauma.* Retrieved September 26, 2008, from http://www.medterms.com/script/main/art.asp?articlekey=20130.

MedicineNet.com. (2005). *Definition of trauma.* Retrieved September 26, 2008, from http://www.medterms.com/script/main/art.asp?articlekey=8171#.

Miller, T. W. (1998). Introduction. In L. Goldberger (Ed.), *Children of trauma* (pp. xv–xx). Madison, CT: International Universities Press.

Oaklander, V. (1978). *Windows to our children: A Gestalt therapy approach to children and adolescents.* Highland, NY: Center for Gestalt Development.

Oaklander, V. (1999). Group play therapy from a Gestalt therapy perspective. In D. S. Sweeney & L. E. Homeyer (Eds.), *The handbook of group play therapy: How to do it, how it works, whom it's best for* (pp. 162–175). San Francisco: Jossey-Bass.

Parnell, L. (1999). *EMDR in the treatment of adults abused as children*. New York: Norton.

Ranawaka, D. S., & Dewaraja, R. (2006). Tsunami counselling project of the Sri Lanka National Institute of professional counsellors. *International Congress Series, 1287*, 79–81.

Ray, D. C., Armstrong, S. A., Warren, E. S., & Balkin, R. S. (2005). Play therapy practices among elementary school counselors. *Professional School Counseling, 8*, 360–365.

Reynolds, C. R., & Richmond, B. O. (2008). *Revised children's manifest anxiety scale: Second edition*. Los Angeles: Western Psychological Services.

Rothschild, B. (1998). *A trauma glossary*. Retrieved September 26, 2008, from http://home.webuniverse.net/babette/Trauma.html.

Satapathy, S., & Walia, A. (2006). Intervening with the process of recovery from a traumatic life event: Case study of a child victim of a school fire disaster in India. *Australian e-Journal for the Advancement of Mental Health, 5* (3), 1–7.

Schore, A. N. (2001). Effects of a secure attachment relationship on right brain development, affect regulation, and infant mental health. *Infant Mental Health Journal, 22*, 7–66.

Shelby, J. S. (2000). Brief therapy with traumatized children: A developmental perspective. In H. G. Kaduson & C. E. Schaefer (Eds.), *Short-term play therapy for children* (pp. 69–104). New York: Guilford Press.

Shen, Y.-J. (2002). Short-term play therapy with Chinese earthquake victims: Effects on anxiety, depression, and adjustment. *International Journal of Play Therapy, 11*(1), 43–63.

Shen, Y.-J. (2007a). Applying client-centered play therapy in Taiwan: Drying posttraumatic tears through the power of play. *Play Therapy, 2*(4), 18–19.

Shen, Y.-J. (2007b). Play therapy in Texas schools. *Journal of Counselling and Guidance, 21*, 230–235.

Shen, Y.-J. (2008). Reasons for school counselors' use or nonuse of play therapy: An exploratory study. *Journal of Creativity in Mental Health, 3*(1), 30–43.

Shen, Y.-J., & Sink, C. A. (2002). Helping elementary-age children cope with disasters. *Professional School Counseling, 5*, 322–330.

Steinberg, A. M., Brymer, M. J., Decker, K. B., & Pynoos, R. S. (2004). The University of California at Los Angeles Post-Traumatic Stress Disorder Reaction Index. *Current Psychiatry Reports, 6*, 96–100.

Sweeney, D. S., & Homeyer, L. E. (1999). Group play therapy. In D. S. Sweeney & L. E. Homeyer (Eds.), *The handbook of group play therapy: How to do it, how it works, whom it's best for* (pp. 3–14). San Francisco: Jossey-Bass.

Taylor, T. L., & Chemtob, C. M. (2004). Efficacy of treatment for child and adolescent traumatic stress. *Archives of Pediatrics and Adolescent Medicine, 158*, 786–791.

Trowell, J., Kolvin, I., Weeramanthri, T., Sadowski, H., Berelowitz, M., Glasser, D., et al. (2002). Psychotherapy for sexually abused girls: Psychopathological outcome findings and patterns of change. *British Journal of Psychiatry, 180*, 234–247.

Tyndall-Lind, A., Landreth, G. L., & Giordano, M. A. (2001). Intensive group play therapy with child witnesses of domestic violence. *International Journal of Play Therapy, 10*(1), 53–83.

Webb, N. B. (2006). Crisis intervention play therapy to help traumatized children. In C. Lois (Ed.), *Expressive and creative arts methods for trauma survivors* (pp. 39–56). London: Jessica Kingsley.

Webb, N. B. (2007). Sudden death of a parent in a terrorist attack: Crisis intervention conjoint play therapy with a preschool boy and his mother. In N. B. Webb (Ed.), *Play therapy with children in crisis: Individual, group, and family treatment* (3rd ed., pp. 389–407). New York: Guilford Press.

Wohl, N., & Hightower, A. D. (2001). Primary mental health project: A school-based prevention program. In A. A. Drewes, L. J. Carey, & C. E. Schaefer (Eds.), *School-based play therapy* (pp. 277–296). New York: John Wiley & Sons.

Wu, S. C. (2001). *The influence of scaffolding play group to high-functioning autism in symbolic play: A case study.* Unpublished master's thesis, National Taipei Normal College, Taipei, Taiwan, R.O.C.

Yalom, I. D., & Leszcz, M. (2005). *The theory and practice of group psychotherapy* (5th ed.). New York: Basic Books.

Young, M. E. (2008). Play therapy and the traumatized self. *Psychology and Education, 45*(1), 19–23.

CHAPTER 13

Group Sandplay in Elementary Schools

THERESA KESTLY

INTRODUCTION

"You mean you're just going to let us play?" asks a fifth-grade boy who is just beginning his first session in a sand tray friendship group at school. He and five other boys are going to play together for an hour using small trays of sand and miniature figurines. They will meet for the next 12 weeks to create scenes in their sand trays and then tell stories about their worlds if they choose. It is hard for the boys to believe they are actually going to play during school time.

Unless it is recess time, the idea of play with other children during school hours is a surprise for many children and for adults as well. Even more surprising is the idea that fundamental behavior changes can occur in children in a relatively short period of time through playing together and telling stories to one another.

Several months after one sand tray friendship group ended, the school principal noticed that the boys from the group had not been referred to her office since they had participated in the group. She was surprised. This group of fifth-grade boys, referred primarily for fighting on the playground and disruptive behavior in the classroom, had been frequent visitors to her office before they started the sand tray group play. The principal was especially impressed by their ability to maintain their behavior changes several months after the group ended, and as a result, she requested a significant increase in the number of friendship groups for the following school year. Once again, the principal noted a dramatic decrease in referrals to her office among the children who participated in the expanded group sandplay program.

Although the structure of the friendship groups is simple in form and function, the underlying concepts are grounded in current neuroscience and theoretical principles. Why and how these sand tray friendship groups work is the focus of this chapter.

RESEARCH AND THEORY

Two research-based concepts help to explain the positive outcomes of the sandplay group intervention. One concept comes from attachment theory, the other from the theory of consciousness. Storytelling, the brain's tendency to organize itself through narrative, may be the link between these two research areas, and it also seems to be a defining characteristic of group sandplay. Two conditions are necessary for storytelling to emerge from group members: 1) a sense of safety and belonging (attachment theory) and 2) freedom for exploratory play (consciousness theory). When these conditions are met, children have a natural tendency to play, to bond with each other, and to create and tell stories about their life experiences. In doing so, they generally project their personal life experiences onto the sand trays they create. This phenomenon allows each child to bring his or her growing edge into focus within the context of community where safety and belonging are paramount. The counselor, trained in group sandplay, maintains the conditions of safety and freedom for the group, and he or she provides contingent communication for the children's creative play and storytelling (the term *counselor* is used throughout the chapter to denote school counselor, school social worker, and other mental health workers).

As a unifying element, storytelling provides insight into an important aspect of sandplay groups. According to current neuroscientist Antonio Damasio (1999), storytelling begins as a nonlinguistic process embedded in the brain's innate tendency to sort, select, assemble, and integrate. The free, exploratory style of play that occurs in sandplay also involves these tasks, and it may be one of the ways children reflect and embody these natural brain tendencies. Another neuroscientist, Dan Siegel (Siegel & Hartzell, 2003), describes how stories help us make sense of our life experiences, and he notes that shared stories help to build community and a sense of belonging. We also have robust research data related to the Adult Attachment Interview (AAI) to support the notion that storytelling is a measure of one's mental health (Hesse, 1999). Researchers developed the AAI as a result of efforts to explain factors that contributed to secure attachment between parents and children. They discovered that a parent's ability to tell a coherent story seemed to be key. The researchers used the AAI to measure the strength of attachment relationships (secure, insecure, ambivalent, or disorganized attachment), and they found that it could even predict the attachment status of parents to their unborn child simply by analyzing how the parents told stories about their own early life circumstances. Surprisingly, it was "how" the parents told their stories more than the actual "facts" that made these predictions possible.

Based on this attachment research, Siegel (Siegel & Hartzell, 2003) noted that storytelling is one of the primary ways the brain organizes itself. This hypothesis is similar to the ideas of Damasio (1999), who says that consciousness arises on a continuum, from nonverbal storytelling to sophisticated autobiographical storytelling. Formulating his consciousness hypothesis from laboratory case studies, Damasio describes the brain's storytelling template as innate. He says that storytelling begins in the nonverbal proto-self and that we automatically tell wordless stories in response to every object we encounter (including other human beings and objects stored in memory). This storytelling begins in infancy, and it continues throughout the life span. Furthermore, Damasio suggests that we think in images; he notes that although it appears that we think with words, the images are still core. The trick, he says, is that language arises so rapidly in the adult mind when we respond to objects that we assume we are thinking with words, rather than with these sensory-based images. Damasio's consciousness hypothesis is relevant to the dynamic play activities of the sand tray modality because children can immerse themselves physically in the manipulation of hundreds of small objects (miniature figurines). They select and sort as they assemble what they need for their sand trays. According to Damasio, each time a child encounters an object, there is an automatic nonverbal storytelling response in the brain. In addition to the hundreds of external objects that are available in the sandplay activities, there are also countless objects that have been stored in the memory system. Children have all of these at their disposal. Each response to these objects serves as a building block for a further, more complicated, and integrated story.

Several decades before Damasio published his writings, Lowenfeld (1979/1993), originator of sandplay therapy, wrote and lectured about this nonverbal sensory-based thinking process, and she was the first to recognize that infants could think. (Incidentally, there is some contention in the field about ownership of the term *sandplay*. Followers of Dora

Kalff claim that Kalff coined the term sandplay after Lowenfeld introduced the modality.) Although Lowenfeld did not have the benefit of our current neuroscience knowledge, she understood that the infant's ability to think rested on nonverbal images, not language. Because of her highly developed skills of observation of infants and children, Lowenfeld came to understand the nonverbal aspect of the thinking process, and she questioned the conventional wisdom of her times—that infants could not think because they had no language.

Although she herself spoke seven languages fluently, Lowenfeld rejected the idea that language alone could heal trauma. She understood that trauma originated as a multifaceted sensory experience, and she believed it was necessary to connect at the sensory nonverbal level if she were to make a difference. It was this line of reasoning that led her to the discovery, with the help of the children in her clinic, of the nonverbal sand tray method.

When we first introduced group sandplay in 1997 in a large public school district in the southwestern United States, we believed it was necessary to create a structure for group intervention that integrated attachment theory, consciousness theory, and the concepts of storytelling emerging from brain science. In addition to the ideas of Lowenfeld (1979/1993), those of Dora Kalff (1980/2003), originator of a Jungian-based version of sandplay in Switzerland, were also beneficial. We drew from the rich legacy of both of these women to create a group structure that would give children the sense of safety and belonging necessary for exploratory play and the development of attachment bonds. Kalff's idea of a "free and protected space" was not only a core principle of our original design for the groups, it also became an ongoing principle that we used to deal with clinical issues that came up as we implemented the group program (Kalff, 1980/2003).

From the beginning of the project, we decided to do as much research as we could in a public school setting to help us refine our intervention protocol. At the outset, we received numerous anecdotal reports from principals, teachers, parents, and even children that the group experience was meaningful in terms of improvements in social, emotional, and academic behaviors. Teachers often reported calm behavior when children returned to class after participating in sand tray group counseling. One teacher said that her students could do academic group work better after participating in a sand tray group; she felt their group play spilled over into the classroom, helping them to cooperate more effectively in group academic tasks. One special education boy observed his own improved behavior. Without any solicitation from the counselor, he volunteered, "Since I have been in this group, I haven't been in any more trouble." Not long after he made this comment, his teacher reported that he had caught up on all his academic work. And finally, the principal simply wanted to expand the group sandplay program because of the dramatic decrease in office referrals for behavior problems.

Although we were encouraged by and grateful for the anecdotal reports, we were not satisfied until we found a way to collect data in a systematic manner to help us with assessment. With the help of the school district and the cooperation of teachers, we were able to implement basic data collection and analysis using a simple pre- and posttest design. We used a teacher rating scale, the Behavior Assessment System for Children (BASC), as our research instrument to assess the effectiveness of group sandplay in addressing emotional and behavioral concerns of elementary school children (Reynolds & Kamphaus, 1998). On average, students improved statistically significantly on three of the four composite scales of the BASC (externalizing, school, and adaptive scales); they remained about the same on internalizing problems. Unfortunately, we were not able to do an experimental design in the school setting because we were not permitted to randomly select and assign students to experimental groups (Kestly, 2001). Because our data did support the favorable anecdotal reports of school personnel and mental health workers, we believed we had good reason to pursue a more rigorous research study should the opportunity arise. Flahive (2005–2008), a doctoral student at the University of North Texas, did just that when she designed her dissertation to study preadolescents identified with behavioral problems. She used an experimental design with a wait-list control group to examine the overall effectiveness of sand tray group therapy. She used the BASC, along with several other instruments, to collect data. Flahive's results corroborated our initial research. She was able to present empirical support for the effectiveness of group sand tray therapy as a treatment intervention for preadolescents identified with behavioral problems. Her results are encouraging, and her research has moved us forward in developing the evidence base that is needed to support the utilization of this modality in elementary schools. Further research is needed to replicate the above findings and to extend the use of this modality to other clinical populations in school settings.

DESCRIPTION OF SAND TRAY FRIENDSHIP GROUP

Group sandplay is an intervention designed specifically to utilize both parallel and joint play in a therapeutic environment that encourages safety, a sense of belonging, and exploration of self in relationship to others. In schools where opportunities for sand tray group counseling occur, children meet regularly, usually every week, for group sand tray sessions. Calling these *sand tray friendship groups* gives children a natural frame and a focus for the group process, and it helps to reduce the stigma often associated with a trip to the school counselor's office.

The school counselor acts as a witness and a facilitator for the group process. Drawing from the ideas of Margaret Lowenfeld (1979/1993) and Dora Kalff (1980/2003), the counselor creates a protected space where children are free to play and create stories relevant to their lives. The protected play space provides children with the safety and freedom they need to play at the growing edges of their development. The counselor acts as a psychological container for the play and for the peer interactions that arise from it.

To begin, each child has an individual sand tray; if the budget permits, a large group tray for joint play is available when the desire and need for community play arises. From a collection of hundreds of miniature figurines, children may select the things they need to build their worldviews in the sand. The amount of time for the play and the storytelling depends on the age of the children; and usually, the groups meet weekly for 10 to 20 sessions. Although children may tell stories about the worlds they create, they are free to participate in the process without using any words. For nonverbal children or children with limited language proficiency, this choice is very freeing. Through symbolic thinking processes, these children sometimes learn how to establish communication, enabling them to use words more effectively.

RATIONALE FOR GROUP SANDPLAY IN THE SCHOOL SETTING

Sand tray group play seems to be a good fit for elementary school children. There is growing evidence that it influences behavior changes in a positive direction, is developmentally appropriate for the age group, and is efficient in terms of the counselor's limited time for in-depth work with children. In addition, it capitalizes on children's needs for friendship through playing with peers, and it offers a unique format for addressing social-emotional needs by engaging both right-brain and left-brain thinking processes.

From a developmental perspective, group sand tray counseling is a natural context in which children can work on issues relevant to their age group. The development of friendships is paramount for elementary school children. A great deal of social and emotional development occurs between the ages of 6 and 12, and much of it occurs within peer groups. Rules of social behavior, ideas about caring for others, and a sense of justice and self-esteem are some of the things children learn from peers firsthand. Whereas families and other significant adults are essential for teaching social and moral values, it is with peers that children learn how to negotiate and practice these skills. The equality children feel with their peers, unlike the inherently unequal relationships they have with adults, allows them freedom to try out social behaviors. The word *peer* means "equal standing." This equality gives children a level playing field where they may explore how to live in the world without the fear of negative consequences if their attempts do not succeed the first time around. They have opportunities to learn about fair play, to regulate aggression, to practice reciprocity and equality, and to develop empathy for others.

Because children have implicit understanding of their *equality among peers* and because they understand that *play is just for fun*, play serves another very important developmental function: It allows children to work on developmental tasks in whatever stage they are in without fear of ridicule from others. For instance, a fifth-grade girl pretending that a baby is throwing a temper tantrum in a sand tray world finds acceptance from her peers because it is *just play*, and yet it can satisfy and be very relevant to her if she has unresolved early developmental tasks around this issue.

According to Erikson (1963, 1968), children between the ages of 6 and 12 typically are dealing with developmental tasks related to industry versus inferiority (social interaction with peers and academic performance). Children referred for counseling services, however, often are dealing with earlier stages: basic trust versus mistrust, autonomy versus shame and doubt, and initiative versus guilt. These earlier developmental tasks may be worked on at any age in group sandplay. The fifth-grade girl cited above may still be working on very early issues around autonomy, but because it is *just play*, her peers accept her playing out the early tantrum behavior. Children play at their own growing edges, and so facilitators have many opportunities to support children exactly where they are.

One impetus for the development of the group sandplay process in schools is the need to see many children in a short time. Although sand tray play requires cleanup time, it is still more efficient in terms of doing in-depth work with a number of children. For example, Table 13.1 shows how much time it takes to work with individuals versus with groups of children. Seeing six children individually in counseling takes

Table 13.1
Group Efficiency and Effectiveness for 4 or 6 Children

	Time Needed			Quality Enhancement
	Session Hours	Cleanup Hours	**TOTAL**	1. Peer Motivation for Change
4 Individual Children	4 Hours	1 Hour	5 Hours	2. Positive Adult Attention by Trained Counselors
4 Children in Group	1 Hour	1 Hour	2 Hours	3. Prevention through Containment
6 Individual Children	6 Hours	1.5 Hours	7.5 Hours	4. Enhancement of Brain Functioning
6 Children in Group	1 Hour	1.5 Hours	2.5 Hours	5. Simultaneous Participant-Observer Capacity

7.5 hours (including 15 minutes for cleanup for each individual session). Seeing those same six children in a group takes 2.5 hours.

In addition to saving time, in many instances the group process is more productive because it 1) involves peer motivation for change, 2) provides positive adult attention that is nonintrusive, 3) serves to prevent later, more chronic problem behaviors, 4) enhances brain functioning, and 5) allows the child to be participant and observer simultaneously. In the sand tray friendship groups, specially trained counselors capitalize on the intrinsic motivation of peers to develop relationships through play. They help children apply and consolidate school and family values by setting kind but firm limits around negative interpersonal communications while simultaneously containing the potential of the group for positive and productive interpersonal relationships. Specific training enables the counselor to contain the group members in this protected social-emotional space without intruding on the peer play. The counselor refrains from either positive or negative reinforcement of children or from solving problems for the group. Once children know how to obtain what they need in socially appropriate ways, they are very willing to do so. The development of effective social skills early in life helps to prevent many chronic problems that can emerge in later life due to unmet social-emotional needs.

Although brain processing involves a complicated integration of the left and right hemispheres, in most people the right brain specializes in certain tasks such as spatial thinking, artistic and nonverbal processing, and emotional awareness. It sees the world in an all-at-once fashion. When children use the sand tray modality, they engage the right brain through symbolic thinking, often bypassing cognitive awareness when they first begin to play. They choose miniature figurines and play activities, however, that are central to the developmental tasks they need to accomplish. Because their abstract reasoning and language proficiency are not yet fully developed, they rely more heavily than adults on their symbolic, right-brain thinking processes, and they use experiential learning to deal with issues that are important to them. For example, children with posttraumatic stress play out the trauma event repeatedly to gain mastery over the situation. They replay so they can reexperience it until the pieces fit together in some satisfactory way.

Because experience is multidimensional in nature, it is necessary, as Lowenfeld (1979/1993) postulated, to provide children with an apparatus that is conducive to expressing simultaneously the various dimensions of experience, including color, form, movement, relationships among things and activities, and so on. Language, due to its linear nature, is inadequate for children who need to communicate their complicated inner experiences. Because of its miniaturization, the sand tray is an expansive language providing children with a large vocabulary of miniature images for expressing their elaborate inner worlds.

The participant-observer phenomenon is another unique and important aspect of the sand tray modality. With the sand tray, children are both participants and observers. They are the directors of their "plays" and the actors as well. Unlike conventional play therapy where the child is immersed in the play, the miniature sand tray allows the child to be *in* the play and *apart* from the play at the same time. This dual role allows children simultaneously to observe in concrete form their own inner worlds and to re-create them before their own eyes. Children project their worldviews into a miniature container, where it is held physically by the boundaries of the tray and psychologically by the trained counselor. Within this container, children see and feel and play their experiences in objective form. Words alone are not adequate for accomplishing this task, especially while children are still in the process of developing their capacities for verbal abstract reasoning.

ORGANIZING FOR GROUP SANDPLAY IN THE SCHOOL SETTING

The success of sand tray friendship groups is greatly improved with good preparation and organization. Adequate space, the collection of miniatures, composition of groups, and preparing children for group play are important for success.

CREATING AN APPROPRIATE SPACE

Available space for counseling services in schools varies widely, from large, attractive rooms to small, closetlike spaces that are dimly lit with no windows. It is difficult to work with sand tray groups in cramped quarters or in public spaces where children do not have a sense of privacy and safety. A sand tray group is at least two children and may be six or more, depending on the number of facilitators and the type of children in the group. At a minimum, there needs to be enough space for at least one miniature sand tray for each child, a small shelf or table for a collection of miniatures, and space for the counselor to sit nearby. In a space the size of a classroom, it is possible to accommodate two groups at the same time if there are two counselors and if there is some kind of physical divider to create a sense of a protected space for each group. If funds are available, it is helpful to have enough floor space for a large group tray (about 4 to 5 feet in diameter, or 5 feet square).

In addition to adequate physical space, it is important to create an attractive display that invites children to use their imaginations and creativity for building miniature worlds. Even in a small room with no windows, it is possible to arrange the miniatures and the sand trays in a way that stimulates delight when entering the room. Even teachers and parents notice when the environment is inviting; the room simply has an atmosphere that communicates, *This is a good place to play.* Often, even adults say, "I want to build a world." An appropriate space is inviting, and it speaks for itself. It clearly is designed with children in mind, and most children know exactly what to do when they enter it.

PREPARING CHILDREN FOR GROUP EXPERIENCE

It is important to introduce the sand tray friendship group to children without stigmatizing them for being in it. It is sufficient to tell them that they will have a chance to be in a sand tray friendship group where they will play with others because that is the way most children make and develop friendships. Children usually do not know the reason for referral unless the parent or someone other than the counselor tells them. The counselor can avoid this problem by instructing the referring person about the nature of the sand tray process. Whatever the counselor does to decrease stigma for the children will increase the safety and protection that is so essential to sand tray play. If the child does need to know about the referral situation, the counselor can discuss it apart from the sand tray so the child does not confuse the nonjudgmental nature of the sand tray play with the referral problem, which is often perceived as negative. It is essential to communicate to the children the special safety and protection that surrounds the sand tray play.

Permission forms are sent to parents depending on school policy about group counseling. The permission form contains a description about the process and includes the goals and purposes of the friendship group.

Obtaining Sand Trays and a Miniature Collection for School Settings

The cost of sand trays varies from about $7 for a plastic storage container to $230 for a beautifully crafted, wooden, water-resistant tray. Therapists who follow the Kalffian tradition use sand trays with a standard inside dimension of 28.5 inches wide by 19.5 inches tall by 3 inches deep (Mitchell & Friedman, 1994). For very active children, more depth (4 or 5 inches) is desirable to contain the sand within the tray during active and dynamic play. Although the wooden trays are aesthetically pleasing, most schools cannot afford the number needed for group play. Children do appreciate aesthetically pleasing sand trays, but they are quite happy to play in the inexpensive plastic storage trays (approximately 15 by 21 by 6 inches). Although the storage trays are a little small in terms of surface area, having a chance to play in a plastic tray is far better than not being able to play at all. It is important, however, to provide trays with blue bottoms to simulate water.

Typically, miniature collections for schools contain a wide variety of small objects that children encounter in their daily lives. The cost of a collection for group use ranges from about $600 to $2,000. In general, it is important to collect miniatures and to organize them in ways that reduce the need for limit setting while children are creating their worlds. If the counselor does not have to worry about objects that might break or get ruined if they get wet, it is easier to relax and focus on the crucial task of witnessing the children's worlds. Although limit setting is necessary and appropriate in therapy sessions with children, the aim of sand tray play is to provide as much freedom as possible within the constraints of the container and the miniature collection. This freedom encourages children to use imagination and creativity to play out their difficult situations.

Building an appropriate collection for children is a topic in numerous sand tray books and articles. Many catalogues exist specifically with sandplay therapists in mind, and most teachers who provide sand tray training include these kinds of resource lists in their training sessions.

The appropriate size of a miniature collection is sometimes debated. Some therapists worry that a large collection will overwhelm children, yet others believe children can work comfortably and intelligently with large collections similar to ones used by adults. If the collection is too small, it will be difficult for children to express themselves. Lowenfeld (1979/1993), originator of the sand tray modality, used a cabinet with labeled drawers to prevent children from being overwhelmed. Baskets are useful for organizing miniatures by categories to help children stay focused and to help counselors with reshelving. A combination of open shelves and baskets is good for creating an attractive collection that is also well organized. If children become chaotic with a large collection, it is usually a therapeutic issue. (See the section on limit setting for further discussion of large collections and chaotic behavior.)

Composition of Groups

The effectiveness of group sandplay depends to a great extent on the composition of group members. For example, a group of three or four attention-deficit-type children is very difficult and often not very productive; having too many shy children in a group is equally unproductive. It helps to balance a shy child with an extroverted child, if possible; they will teach each other alternative behaviors when they play together, and sometimes they mirror each other in terms of the kinds of objects they use. For instance, after about four weeks in a sand tray group, a very shy child began selecting a large striped tiger that was a favorite of an extroverted child in the same group. Soon after, the classroom teacher described the shy child as much less intimidated with his peers, and for the first time he was willing to go out with the other children at recess time.

Ginott (1961) recommends the following strategies for composing groups: 1) combining dissimilar personality syndromes, 2) using mixed-gender groups for young children and same-gender groups for older children, 3) selecting children by age within a range of 12 months, 4) not having more than five children in a group, 5) not combining siblings and classmates in the same group, and 6) not allowing antisocial children to be dominant in a group. Ginott also says children should be in a group where they will not reexperience the devastating influences of their outside lives. For instance, a submissive boy may not do well in a group where others dominate, thus prolonging the circumstance that makes it difficult for him to assert himself. Ginott's chapter on group composition in *Group Psychotherapy with Children* offers detailed discussion of these and other important considerations for organizing playgroups (pp. 29–36). Most of his ideas apply to sand tray group counseling.

Preliminary screening for the group, including a play interview with the child and standard referral information from teachers, parents, and other involved adults, is worthwhile. Fortunately, in the school setting there is flexibility for moving children from one group to another or even into individual counseling if, despite preliminary screening, a situation arises in which the child clearly cannot function in a way that is beneficial to self and others. If the need arises to transfer a child out of a group, it is essential to communicate this move to the child in a way that supports continued growth and will not be seen as a punishment for not being able to function with a particular group of children.

MANAGING GROUP ACTIVITIES

Group counseling requires structure and a management style different from working with individual children. There is more planning and organization before the group begins, and it is necessary to balance limit setting with the permissiveness that is needed for creative imagination to develop among the children. The counselor's attitude is central for effective sandplay groups, and the practical elements of structuring the group time, cleaning up, and protecting confidentiality all make a difference in how well the group process works.

Counselor's Role versus Teacher's Role in the School Setting

It is sometimes difficult for school counselors to maintain a therapeutic stance when so often they have to serve in other roles, such as playground duty person, disciplinarian, guidance teacher, and sometimes even administrative assistant to the principal. If counselors cannot avoid these multiple roles, it is very important to communicate when and where the children may be in relationship to the counselor as a counselor. Children need to know that in a sand tray play group the counselor will not issue discipline slips, share confidential information with their teachers or parents, give them grades, direct their play, or judge them as good or bad for the things they create in their worlds. Children need to know they are free to create.

Limit Setting That Maximizes Group Creativity

As the number of children increases in a counseling situation, the need for structuring also increases. Even so, the structuring can be done in nonjudgmental ways. At the beginning of group sand tray play, it is important to eliminate as many rules as possible so that the children's creative energy has a chance to express itself early in the group. Subsequently, the counselor can create rules as needed. For instance, if a child spills sand outside the tray, the counselor can say, "In here, the sand has to stay in the tray." With some groups there is never a need for this rule. Some children play very well together with almost no explicit rules. Too many rules at the beginning may thwart creativity and imagination.

Helping Children Respect Boundaries   One rule that seems to support the creative process at the beginning is asking children not to touch the worlds of other children and not to allow others to touch their own worlds. In this way, children know they have a space, a physical container, of their very own. It provides them with concrete boundaries that often are lacking for children who come into counseling. Later, if children elect to play in a large group tray, these boundaries may be renegotiated, but it helps children at the beginning to see and feel and work within the bounds of their own protected space.

Flooding with Water and/or Figurines   Occasionally, children decide to use a lot of miniatures in a very chaotic and disorganized manner. They use their arms to sweep entire shelves into their baskets or shirts and then dump them into their trays until the tray is full. This event is usually distressing for the counselor because of cleanup. When this happens, although it rarely does, it is usually an important therapeutic issue. One way to handle this situation is to encourage children to use as many things as they want. The counselor can say things like, "Oh, you need all of the cars today," or "I see you need a lot of things," or "Do you need some more?" From these kinds of statements, the children know the counselor is "containing" their chaotic energy psychologically but without any judgment. It may be the first time they have not heard someone say, "Stop it. That's enough." Some children truly feel there is never enough of anything they need, so it surprises them when an adult asks them if they need more, and it helps them to shift their point of view. If there is time to allow children this kind of disorganized play, they will often learn, from their own inner core, how to organize things by their own volition. One second-grader who flooded his tray with figurines for four sessions in a row finally pulled out of the chaotic play by himself. Once he achieved organization in his tray, he never went back to chaotic play, and his classroom teacher reported that he improved greatly in his ability to organize his academic classroom activities. He learned "order" at the core of his being, where real behavioral changes occur.

If children have opportunities to use as much water as they want, they often will flood their trays with water. This kind of flooding is very therapeutic, but in schools where there are time pressures for seeing a lot of children, it is difficult to allow this process on a frequent basis. Children who really need to use a lot of water for therapeutic reasons will wash items over and over again with spray bottles, or they will ask repeatedly for more water even after they know they have exceeded the limit on how much they may have. For these children, it is usually beneficial to schedule one or two individual sessions when they may use as much water as they wish. Children love to pour water into the sand trays, but it is not necessary to allow this if there are time pressures. Although it is traditional to have both wet and dry sand available, it is better to use only dry sand than to offer no sand at all.

Breaking Miniatures on Purpose Most of the time, children break miniatures accidentally, but occasionally a child demonstrates clearly that he or she intended to break an object. This intentional breaking calls for a limit or a shift in activity. The counselor might say in a neutral voice without any blame or negativity, "The toys here are not for breaking." Children appreciate receiving these limits in clear, neutral tones because then they know where the boundaries are and they feel safe when they know where and how they are being held psychologically.

Supporting Collaboration and Community Building If there is a large community tray in the sand tray room, children will usually notice it somewhere between week four and week eight. They will begin to ask what it is for and whether they may use it. This curiosity is usually a good indication that they are ready for the pleasures and challenges of community play. It helps to have divider sticks available to mark off space in the large tray. If these are not available or if the children decide not to use them, the counselor simply asks, "How do you want to share this space?" The counselor helps the group negotiate rules for playing in the communal space, both explicitly and implicitly. This is a perfect place for children to see firsthand what it means to share space, to live in the world together, to wage war, to deal with conflict, to negotiate, to make peace—while exploring the values their families and school have taught. What does it all mean? From peer play, they get a chance to see it in action.

Community play is very powerful for children. Although it presents additional challenges for the counselor, it is an important avenue of actual experience for children to learn how to negotiate with one another. Teachers sometimes notice the increased ability of children to cooperate more effectively with academic tasks after they have had a chance to play together. De Domenico (1999) provides a discussion on other aspects of community sand tray play, and some of her suggestions are helpful for sand tray group counseling in the schools.

Stealing   In individual sand tray counseling, stealing is not usually an issue, but it often comes up in the group counseling situation where it is much easier to conceal miniatures when leaving the play area. Limits need to be set around this issue to protect the integrity and safety of the sand tray environment. Several factors to consider are the age of the child, the intention, and therapeutic issues. If children are very young, the counselor can simply ask, "You know the little red car you were using today? We are missing it and wonder if you could help us find it?" Most often, they will soon "find" it on the playground and return it. Children learn that the counselor values the integrity of the collection and that there are expectations for how they behave in relation to objects they desire that do not belong to them.

With older children who take things intentionally in a provocative manner, it is important to confront them. One group of fifth-grade boys left a sand tray room, pulling objects out of their pockets and claiming they brought them from home. After several special items disappeared from the collection, the counselor told the boys that things were missing from the collection and that it would not be possible to continue with the sand tray group until everything was returned. They expressed unhappiness and anger about not getting to come for their group time. The counselor gave them suggestions for how to return the figurines anonymously so they could maintain their privacy around the issue, but she held firm. After about three weeks and several meetings to discuss the problem, the boys finally returned everything. In a very open and honest conversation, they told the counselor they had been stealing all over their neighborhood and no one had even noticed. This group of boys had to problem solve together to figure out how to resume their sand tray group. It was an important step for them, and it helped them establish a very productive working relationship with the counselor for the remainder of the year.

Disrupting the Group Process   Some children try to be the center of attention in the group through negative behavior, and this usually creates disruption for the group process. If this happens even after careful screening and careful group composition planning, the counselor will need to set clear limits. For instance, one boy continued to make loud vehicle noises and insisted on returning to the shelves for more miniatures after the beginning of stories, when selecting time was over. Another boy in the group was telling his story, and clearly he wanted his peers to listen. After the counselor reminded the disruptive boy about playing quietly beside his tray during story time and he still continued his disruptive behavior, the counselor said, "Michael, making loud noises and going to the shelves during story time is not allowed here in this group because we want to listen to Daniel's story. If you continue, I'll take it to mean that you are deciding to end your playtime here with us today to go back to class. It is fine for you to play quietly by your tray while we listen." This is just one example of a clearly stated limit delivered with no blame. The statement includes what the child is doing that is not acceptable, what will happen if the behavior continues, and what the alternative acceptable behaviors are.

Skills in limit setting are essential for the success of sand tray group counseling. Many play therapy texts, play therapy videos, and training workshops provide opportunities for counselor skill development in this area. Without these skills, it is difficult to create the free and protected space necessary for sand tray group counseling.

STRUCTURING GROUP TIME FOR SAND TRAY PLAY AND STORYTELLING

The number of sessions for a sand tray group varies depending on the goals, therapeutic issues, and other constraining factors. It is difficult to observe measurable changes with fewer than 8 or 10 sessions. For children with severe emotional issues, 10 sessions are usually inadequate. For nonclinical populations, even one session is a treat. Most often, a group meets for 10 to 12 weekly sessions.

Table 13.2
Structuring Time for the Group Process

	One-Hour Group Grades 2–6	45-Minute Group Grades K-1
Building time	1:00 P.M.	1:00 P.M.
5-minute notice for ending building	1:35 P.M.	1:25 P.M.
1-minute notice for ending building	1:39 P.M.	1:29 P.M.
Story time	1:40 P.M.	1:30 P.M.
End session	2:00 P.M.	1:45 P.M.

Although sandplay therapy is essentially a nonverbal process, words often help children gain insight into their creative process, and words help them claim their experiences at a conscious level. Older children usually meet for one hour for the sandplay group; younger children in kindergarten and first grade usually meet for about 45 minutes. The last 15 or 20 minutes are for story time. Table 13.2 shows examples of how to structure the session time.

When storytelling time is near, children get a 5-minute notice from the counselor— "You have five more minutes for building"—and then again at one minute before story time. When the time is up for building, children may no longer go to the miniature collection to select figurines. They may, however, continue to play quietly in their trays while other children tell their stories. It is almost impossible for children not to play in their own trays while listening to other children. Children may not want to talk about their worlds, although usually, after the first two or three weeks, children want to tell stories and usually want a second or third turn to talk. Sometimes it is necessary to limit each child to the amount of time he or she may have for stories. It is very important to allow children to choose not to talk at story time, even if they choose to pass every session throughout the entire group process; this choice to talk or not talk is one of the defining features of the free and protected space.

It takes several sessions for children to catch on to being good listeners during story time. The most important way children learn to listen to others is through the modeling of their counselor, who demonstrates clear interest and good reflective listening skills during story time. The counselor can enhance the idea of holding a free and protected space by avoiding intrusive questions, by expressing interest in the stories, by inviting elaboration through reflective listening, and sometimes by just saying, "I see it," "I hear it," or "I feel it." To the extent possible, it is important for the counselor to give total attention to the children's building process and the story process. This is challenging, but children feel the difference when the counselor is paying full attention or is distracted by telephones, deskwork, other school personnel intruding during sessions, and so on. Children really appreciate it when others, both counselors and peers, listen to their stories. When others listen, it gives them a chance to express what is really important in their inner worlds.

CLEANUP ISSUES

Cleanup can make or break a good sand tray group process. It is essential for the counselor to schedule adequate time for cleanup between groups and to remember that it is more efficient to work with groups of children than individuals, even when cleanup time is added to the process. If there is not enough time for cleanup after the group leaves, it is very difficult to hold the space for children as a free and protected container.

Having adequate supplies for cleanup helps. The following items are useful: 1) sieves for sifting debris out of sand and clearing glass stones and treasures from the tray, 2) water container for children to rinse hands before washing their hands where plumbing might get clogged with sand, 3) strainers for drying out objects that are dipped in water for cleaning, 4) containers to hold the strainer as water drains off the objects, 5) paper or cotton towels, 6) several small brushes and dustpan sets, 7) combs for raking and smoothing sand, and 8) small tarps to protect carpeted areas or to contain sand spills.

In general, children do not clear their own trays. There is some controversy surrounding this issue, however. In individual sandplay according to the Kalffian tradition, the therapist always clears the tray. On the other hand, De Domenico (1999) notes there are times when it is appropriate for clients to clear their own trays, but that it should be done with care and perhaps with a sense of ritual or ceremony. Tibetan monks have special ceremonies for clearing and releasing the intricate sand mandalas they create over many hours and days as a reminder of the impermanence of life; Navajo Indians also have a ritual when clearing sand paintings used in healing ceremonies. If children help to clear their own trays, they should do it with respect and care under the supervision of the counselor.

Some counselors believe it is important for children to leave the session with their sand tray images intact. Children do think about their trays and plan from week to week what they will do next. It may be important for them to leave knowing the counselor will contain and then take care of the world they created.

PROTECTING CONFIDENTIALITY OF GROUP MEMBERS IN THE SCHOOL CONTEXT

Children need to know the policy on confidentiality regarding what they say or create in the counselor's office. Generally, their play and verbal expression are confidential, with the exception of legal limits of confidentiality. The counselor needs to explain the policy in clear, developmentally appropriate language. If the counselor intends to share information with the teacher or a parent, the child needs to know beforehand. If the counselor tells children that the counseling is confidential within stated limits, then the sand tray worlds also are confidential, even if children use no words to describe them.

PLANNING FOR EVALUATION OUTCOMES

Teachers, principals, and parents do not always understand how sand tray play therapy works. Although Lowenfeld (1979/1993) believed that normal development was not possible in the absence of play, society often regards play as a waste of time for children or at best an unimportant use of time. So the counselor faces many challenges in terms of articulating why play is essential for children's development, especially for children with social-emotional problems. Funding sources usually ask, "What is the science base of this program?" School mental health workers can help to build the science base of sand tray play by planning for outcome evaluation at the beginning of the process. Even the simplest measures, such as teacher rating scales, contribute to the body of data that helps to explain the crucial necessity of play in childhood. The focus of this section is on collecting data to assess outcomes.

QUALITATIVE DATA

Sand tray photographs are good sources of qualitative data. A photograph of each tray for each child on a weekly basis helps track individual and group progress for qualitative analysis. Many times, the counselor notices, via a series of photographs, progress that was not apparent during the actual building and storytelling process. Over time, the photographs often reveal consistent emerging themes. Digital cameras and computer printouts, after the initial investment, are an inexpensive way to track individual and group gains. Name-tags and dates of sessions in all the photographs will help with the management of photographic data. It is helpful to record teacher and parent comments and observations regarding a child's progress during and after the sand tray counseling sessions. Informal anec-dotal reports and clinical observations are important also; they provide the basis for exploring more formally the efficacy of sand tray group counseling. When sufficient in number, they become the basis of research questions and strategies for collecting more formal quantitative data.

QUANTITATIVE DATA

Obtaining quantitative data for experimental studies is difficult in the school setting because educational goals and protection of privacy are paramount. Teacher rating scales are fairly acceptable, however, and some provide good standardized data with national norms for comparison. The PMHP (Cowen et al., 1996) and the Behavior Assessment System for Children (BASC; Reynolds & Kamphaus, 1998) both offer a variety of rating scales with national norms (see reference list for information). The BASC has both clinical and adaptive scales to track children's progress in terms of teachers' perceptions. Both the PMHP and the BASC rating forms may be used as pre- and posttest measures.

HOLDING THE SPACE FOR GROUP EXPERIENCE: THE SCHOOL MENTAL HEALTH WORKER'S CHALLENGE

The most challenging part of the group sandplay process is learning how to hold the space for group experience. It is relatively easy to learn most of the organizational and management techniques that help groups run smoothly. Holding space for group experience, however, requires the counselor to use a focused, nonintrusive stance and to deal with transference issues that sometimes get stirred up more deeply because of the visual processing required by sand tray play. It also requires the counselor to track group process while letting go of many of the details of individual play, which can induce worries about not knowing what the children are doing when they play together.

TRACKING BOTH THE GROUP PROCESS AND THE INDIVIDUAL MEMBERS OF THE GROUP

Clinicians who follow the Kalffian tradition of sandplay therapy express caution regarding sandplay in the group context, concerned that group interaction of the clients will take precedence over the expression of the individual psyche (Mitchell & Friedman, 1994). De Domenico (1999), however, contends that there are appropriate times to work with the communal psyche as well as the individual psyche. Furthermore, she does not think the individual process is muted when clients work together in a sand tray process. Based on the developmental appropriateness of sand tray play for latency-age children discussed earlier in this chapter, there is a possibility that the group process actually enhances the potential for individual psychological growth as a child plays with peers.

Nevertheless, tracking the group process is a major challenge for most school mental health workers. One loses individual details in the service of holding the entire group process. It comes as a surprise to some that children still develop in positive directions even though the witness-observer misses many of the details. Children's resiliency comes through even in the group process, perhaps especially in the free and protected process of group play. The counselor must know how to extend the creation of the protected space to the group process as a whole. Experience, training, and good supervision are all helpful as the counselor develops this ability to hold group space.

THE ROLE OF THE COUNSELOR AS A WITNESS

One of the greatest challenges of sand tray group play is the counselor's need to take a nonintrusive stance while concentrating on the group dynamic and the activities of individual children. The counselor, as witness, needs to be willing to maintain focused attention without knowing exactly what will emerge. This is difficult for many counselors, yet it is this very sense of *not knowing* that allows children the freedom to move with their own creative energies. There is no need for interpreting worlds for children. Children need no direction on how to build their worlds. The mental health worker has to use all of his or her energy to hold the process as it emerges, rather than using energy to direct and manage the process. This means the counselor needs to organize the environment so that it is conducive to creativity and imagination and reduces the need for unnecessary limit setting. For instance, one counselor included a beautiful sailing ship in her collection; it was made of wood and had a fragile paper sail. When a child reached for it to put it in her tray of wet sand, the counselor said, "You can't use that one in the wet sand." This is an example of an unnecessary limit. If the counselor gives children wet sand or spray bottles to use in building their worlds, it is important not to have anything in the collection that cannot be in contact with water. This way, the counselor can concentrate on paying attention to the children's worlds and not on setting unnecessary limits.

Countertransference is another important challenge. In many instances, witnessing visual images is more potent than verbal therapy because, like the children, the counselor's own symbolic thinking processes become active. The children's trays can be deeply moving for the counselor. The counselor's capacity to join with children at the experiencing level is critical because it allows children to derive maximum benefit from their trays. When this joining happens, however, the counselor has to deal with countertransference issues that arise inevitably in response to the children's images and stories. Otherwise it is difficult to hold the group space so that children can open up more deeply to their own experiences that need to be played out. Witnessing children who are playing out painful experiences in the concentrated form of a miniature world is indeed very potent. Specific training for the role of witness is essential.

RECOMMENDED TRAINING AND EXPERIENCE

Following are some recommendations for preparation and training for using sand tray group counseling in the schools.

1. Do your own sand tray building process with a competent therapist so you know what it is like to use images that lead you into experiential processing.
2. Do your own sand tray group process to learn what it is like to share and process images at the community level.
3. Attend training seminars and workshops in both individual sandplay therapy and sandplay group counseling.
4. Attend training workshops that provide live presentations.
5. Review developmental needs of elementary school children.
6. Before starting sand tray groups, practice sandplay counseling with many individual clients until you are very comfortable with the process.

7. Organize your first group with just two children, and then increase the size of your next group to fit your level of comfort and training.
8. Obtain supervision from qualified persons who have used the group process, particularly the sand tray group counseling process.
9. Try to conduct your first groups with a trained colleague to help with post-session processing.
10. Read books and articles related to sandplay therapy and study relevant cases.

Group sandplay is relatively new, so it takes some effort to find good training opportunities. Training for individual sand tray therapy is available in many regions of the country, and, although less available, there also are some training situations for sand tray group work. Training for individual work is an important first step. Although general play therapy training benefits the sand tray group counselor, there are some elements of practice that are specific to sandplay therapy. Good preparation will help the counselor avoid a number of pitfalls that can easily occur with sand tray group counseling. When it goes well, however, it is a process like no other. It is a special gift for children when they can belong to a safe group where they can utilize symbolic language to deal with their innermost problems. They open up very quickly, and when they contact their own creative energies, they are astounding. Children are resilient; in the free and protected space their resiliency comes through, and they leap at the chance to develop themselves more fully.

REFERENCES

Cowen, E. L., Hightower, A. D., Pedro-Carroll, J. L., Work, W. C., Wyman, P. A., & Haffey, W. G. (1996). *School-based prevention for children at risk: The Primary Mental Health Project*. Washington, DC: American Psychological Association.

Damasio, A. (1999). *The feeling of what happens: Body and emotion in the making of consciousness*. New York: Harcourt Brace.

De Domenico, G. (1999). Group sand tray-worldplay: New dimensions in sandplay therapy. In D. Sweeney & L. Homeyer (Eds.), *The handbook of group play therapy: How to do it, how it works, whom it's best for* (pp. 215–233). San Francisco: Jossey-Bass.

Erikson, E. (1963). *Childhood and society*. New York: Norton.

Erikson, E. (1968). *Identity, youth and crisis*. New York: Norton.

Flahive, M. W. (2005–2008). *Group sand tray therapy at school with preadolescents identified with behavioral difficulties*. Unpublished doctoral dissertation, University of North Texas, Denton, Texas.

Ginott, H. (1961). *Group psychotherapy with children*. Northvale, NJ: Jason Aronson.

Hesse, E. (1999). The adult attachment interview: Historical and current perspectives. In J. Cassidy & P. R. Shaver (Eds.), *Handbook of attachment* (pp. 395–433). New York: Guilford Press.

Kalff, D. (1980). *Sandplay: A psychotherapeutic approach to the psyche*. Boston: Sigo Press.

Kalff, D. (1980/2003). *Sandplay: A psychotherapeutic approach to the psyche*. Cloverdale, CA: Temenos Press.

Kestly, T. (2001). *Sand tray project data 1999–2001*. Unpublished report. Corrales, NM.

Lowenfeld, M. (1993). *Understanding children's sandplay*. London: Margaret Lowenfeld Trust. (Original work published 1979.)

Mitchell, R. R., & Friedman, H. S. (1994). *Sandplay: Past, present and future*. New York: Routledge.

Reynolds, C., & Kamphaus, R. (1998). *Behavior assessment system for children: Manual*. Circle Pines, MN: American Guidance Service.

Siegel, D. J., & Hartzell, M. (2003). *Parenting from the inside out*. New York: Penguin Putnam.

CHAPTER 14

Play Therapy for Anger Management in the Schools

BARBARA A. FISCHETTI

INTRODUCTION

School mental health promotion has received increased interest during the past decade. Most recently, an inaugural issue of a journal addressing the importance of providing mental health services to children and youth, *Advances in School Mental Health Promotion* (Weist & Murray, 2007), has cited emerging literature that supports improved emotional and behavioral functioning for students who receive mental health prevention and intervention services. In spite of this, it has been reported that 75 to 80 percent of children and adolescents who require treatment do not receive it (Kataoka, Zhang, & Wells, 2002).

High-profile incidences of aggressive behavior such as school shootings have been featured prominently in the news media. Most recently, cyberbullying and bullying in general have been cited at alarming rates (Center for Mental Health in the Schools, 2006). This form of relational aggression and the cyberbully's inability to handle anger led to more than 13 million children becoming victims of cyberbullying (Fight Crime: Invest in Kids, 2006). The Fight Crime poll (2006) also found that one-third of teens and one-sixth of primary school-age children reported that they experienced aggressive actions on the Internet such as being threatened.

The literature suggests that there are approximately 6 to 9 million youngster in the United States with serious mental health problems (Friedman, Katz-Leavy, Manderscheid, & Sondheimer, 1996; Lavigne et al., 1996). The Surgeon General (U.S. Department of Health and

Human Services, 1999) reported that 21 percent of children and adolescents demonstrate *DSM-IV* symptoms and that in point of fact, 11 percent of all children experience significant impairment and 5 percent demonstrate extreme functional impairment. The literature is clear that children and adolescents are demonstrating significant social-emotional issues, and schools offer a viable alternative for treatment.

Youth violence and lack of anger management have been highlighted by the 1997 Youth Risk Behavior Surveillance System (YRBSS). This survey (Centers for Disease Control and Prevention, 1998) completed by 16,262 students across the nation indicated that 20.5 percent had seriously considered suicide, 15.7 percent had made a plan, and 7.7 percent had attempted suicide. The Surgeon General noted that suicide was the third leading cause of adolescent deaths. Additionally, the survey noted that 4 percent of students missed school because they felt unsafe, 8.5 percent had carried a weapon to school, 7.4 percent had been threatened or injured at school, 14.8 percent had been in a physical fight at school, and 32.9 percent had property stolen or damaged at school. The Mott Foundation (1996) noted that homicide was the second leading cause of death for 15- to 24-year-olds. These sobering statistics illustrate why the nation is concerned with youth's inability or difficulty with anger management.

Additionally, children are diagnosed with Attention Deficit/Hyperactivity Disorder (ADHD), Oppositional Defiant Disorder (ODD), and/or Conduct Disorder (CD). Behaviors commonly associated with these disorders include impulsivity and hyperactivity for the first disorder and aggression, disobedience, defiance, physical fighting, and loss of temper for the latter two disorders. Prevalence rates for ADHD range from 3 to 5 percent (Wolraich, Hannah, Pinnock, Baumgaertel, & Brown, 1996) and from 1 to 6 percent for ODD and 1 to 4 percent for CD (Shaffer et al., 1996). Surveys indicated that from 5 to 10 percent of children demonstrated significant aggressive behavior (Kingery, Coggeshall, & Alford, 1998).

More recently, the Annenberg Public Policy Center (2004) reported on a survey of more than 1,400 public school staff. The survey revealed that for middle school professionals, interpersonal conflict such as bullying (82 percent) and fighting (57 percent) was more concerning for them. For high school professionals, bullying (54 percent), fighting (37 percent), and carrying a weapon to school (6 percent) were areas of concern. Depression and drug use were viewed as more serious difficulties. In spite of these concerns and others, the survey revealed that only half of students who needed treatment received it outside of school and less than 25 percent received services in school (Annenberg Public Policy Center, 2004).

Schools are increasingly looked at as viable service delivery systems for mental health. Catron and Weiss (1994) found improved treatment access by providing mental health services in the schools. Schools have already been recognized as the primary mental health service delivery system (Rones & Hoagwood, 2000). In light of the research advocating mental health services in the schools and the prevalence of mental health issues involving anger management, play therapy presents the school clinician and children with a viable service delivery system to address anger management issues. Play therapy (Landreth, 1991) offers the school clinician (school psychologists, school counselors, and school social workers) a viable option as a treatment choice for children and adolescents experiencing anger management difficulties. Landreth (1991) noted that this treatment helped children become more available for learning.

Individual and group counseling of students by school psychologists, school counselors, and school social workers utilizing play therapy and play therapy techniques for anger management provides children the opportunity to work through issues, learn new skills, develop more effective social competencies, and meet with greater academic success. School clinicians also provide family treatment that can help the child and the family in the home environment. Due to staffing limitations, treatment is often short term and is directly related to the difficulties that impede learning. Play therapy interventions and techniques that are helpful to the therapeutic process with children and adolescents include but are not limited to child-centered play therapy; cognitive-behavioral play therapy; role playing; relaxation training; sandplay therapy; play utilizing the media of paint, clay, and balls; social skill training; and specific anger management activities.

UNIVERSAL PREVENTION SERVICES

A chapter on play therapy would be remiss if it did not advocate for schools to provide all students with programs that would help prevent mental health issues, promote prosocial behavior, and enhance resiliency. Commonly referred to as *universal prevention services*, these services are developed to lower the risk for children and adolescents in danger of developing mental health problems (Center for School Mental Health Assistance, 2002). These programs help students develop emotional competence and appropriate social skills. While the scope of this chapter cannot possibly cover prevention, it is important to understand that many preventative programs utilize play in delivering services. For example, Responsive Classroom (Northeast Foundation for Children, 2005) utilizes many play activities to encourage the social skills development of cooperation, assertion, responsibility, empathy, and self-control (CARES). Activities such as magic box and ball toss greeting are two examples. Of particular use for students with anger issues are the social skills curriculum conflict resolution protocols (Gootman, 1997). These protocols help children develop skills to solve conflicts in a respectful, effective way with others.

There are many other universal prevention programs that utilize play and play activities in their curriculum. These include but are not limited to I Can Problem Solve (http://www.thinkingpreteen. com/icps), the Skillstreaming Series (http://www.researchpress. org), and the PATHS curriculum (http://www.channing-bete.com/ prevention-programs/paths/). These programs have been recognized as making significant differences in the social and emotional competence of children and adolescents (Center for School Mental Health Assistance, 2002). In fact, rates of oppositional behaviors were reduced significantly with these programs. Referral for individual and/or group counseling interventions was, therefore, not required for many students. Violence prevention programs such as the Bullying Prevention Program (Olweus, 1993) is another example of an empirically supported program designed to reduce bullying and aggressive behavior. When universal programs are not successful with students, students are then referred for more intensive individual and group interventions.

REFERRAL FOR COUNSELING IN THE SCHOOLS

Children with anger management problems are usually easily recognizable in the schools. Referrals are frequently generated by teachers, parents, administrators, child study teams, discipline records, and special education teams. Behaviors commonly seen with anger management difficulties include, but are not limited to, physical aggression, poor social skills, poor conflict resolution skills, impulsivity, peer difficulties, and poor academic performance. These are the students often found in the principal's office, in time out, absent from recess, or absent from a fun or classroom activity. Prior to referral to a mental health clinician for direct services, teachers often employ behavior management interventions, consultation with mental health providers, instructional changes in the classroom, and parent conferencing. When these fail to bring about desired behavioral change, referral is often then made to counseling personnel for assistance.

Prior to intervention, the school clinician observes the student in the classroom and the general school environment. The clinician usually logs or charts inappropriate behaviors and includes in these logs antecedents and consequences of the behaviors. The goal of observation is to establish a baseline of the behaviors prior to school and counseling interventions. The clinician then reviews all available information relative to the presenting anger problems manifested in school. Interviews with the teacher, parents, and administration also provide invaluable information for the presenting issues. If needed, the school clinician may also help the parents with the development of a home program. Finally, the child is interviewed to obtain his or her perception of school and behavioral difficulties.

After all relevant information and observations are reviewed, the school clinician, with the assistance of the school team, generates an intervention plan for the student. The plan is always shared with parents and the referred student. If the plan includes counseling, written parental permission is obtained as well as verbal student permission. When play therapy techniques are to be utilized with elementary school children, books such as *A Child's First Book about Play Therapy* (Nemiroff & Annunziata, 1990), *Feeling Therapy: A Kid's Book about Therapy* (Rashkin, 2005), or *The Special Playroom: A Young Child's Guide to Play Therapy* (Gilfix & Heller Kahn, 1999) are read to or with the student. This provides for a smooth transition to the therapy process and encourages the student to ask questions relative to the therapy experience. For students at the middle or secondary level, a discussion is held regarding the treatment process to encourage their participation and ease their transition into counseling.

COUNSELING IN THE SCHOOLS

Many schools have a playroom that supports the school clinician's work with a child. Frequently, this room is the clinician's office and has been adapted to foster play as a therapeutic agent for children. A single standardized play therapy approach or technique for children is not effective in the schools. Time elements, client issues, and school structures significantly impact a clinician's ability to provide play therapy for students. A prescriptive approach enables the school clinician to specifically prescribe intervention(s) that address a child's social-emotional issues. This prescriptive approach to play therapy has been advocated by Dr. Charles Schaefer (James, 1997). The following approaches to play therapy are useful for planning treatment for children demonstrating anger management issues.

CLIENT-CENTERED PLAY THERAPY

For the clinician who has the opportunity to provide children the time to pursue their issues and personal growth, client-centered play therapy offers a viable choice of treatment. Axline (1969) highlighted the basic tenets of nondirective play therapy for use in the schools. Children are seen weekly for approximately 45-minute sessions. This approach can also be utilized in conjunction with group counseling and parent counseling.

Client-centered play therapy has as its core belief that children have the inner capacity for self-actualization. The therapist develops a relationship with the child that promotes and assists the child in his or her search for emotional growth. This therapeutic approach was originally introduced by Carl Rogers (1951) and further developed by Axline (1947) and Dorfman (1951). The play therapist needs to create a strong relationship with the child that is safe and secure. This fosters a therapeutic relationship in which the child can experience negative emotions and pursue growth. Three key features to this approach are limits, toys, and the therapist's role. Perry (1993) provided a complete description of this approach. Paone and Douma (2009) described an effective 16-session client-centered play therapy approach with a child diagnosed with intermittent explosive disorder. Of particular note was the improvement in behavior and academic performance.

CASE EXAMPLE

A boy who had been sexually molested was demonstrating aggressive behaviors in school. Classroom management techniques were not successful in ameliorating or reducing the aggression demonstrated in the classroom and in the general school environment. Coordinating with the outside therapist, the school clinician provided weekly client-centered play therapy sessions designed to allow the child to work through his anger. This student frequently utilized the Bobo doll, drawing, and other toys to displace his anger toward the perpetrator. After the initial sessions, he began to produce drawings depicting bombing the assailant. A reduction of aggressive behaviors was noted in the classroom and school environment. This child continued to participate in play sessions for the remainder of the school year. As the school year progressed, he expressed more positive themes and seemed to be experiencing all parts of the self. The aggressive behaviors previously noted were not evident the following school year.

RELEASE PLAY THERAPY

This type of play therapy was originally developed by Levy (1938) and extended by Hambidge (1955) as structural play therapy. The goal of this therapy is to assist the client in reenacting a stressful event. This fosters the child's ability to work through the event and to release the anger or pain associated with it. Landreth (1991) noted three forms of activities for release play therapy: "(1) release of aggressive behavior in throwing objects or bursting balloons or release of infantile pleasures in sucking a nursing bottle; (2) release of feelings in standardized situations such as stimulating feelings of sibling rivalry by presenting a baby doll at a mother's breast; (3) release of feelings by recreating in play a particular stressful experience in a child's life" (p. 30).

This type of play therapy can be selected for children who have experienced a stressful event that resulted in the demonstration of anger at school and home. The number of sessions is dependent on the youngster's ability to benefit from the therapeutic process. These sessions are offered weekly for approximately 45 minutes; sessions can be offered more frequently as needed.

CASE EXAMPLE

An elementary school child who witnessed the World Trade Center disaster repeatedly on television started acting out at home and school. Although not directly experiencing the death of a family member, the child also began to experience nightmares and became more oppositional. The student was seen individually, and the medium of drawing was utilized to begin the process of integrating the experience. Individual play sessions were planned for the student as necessary. The child spent the first three to four sessions reenacting the planes hitting the World Trade Center. The student also built towers of blocks and knocked them over with an airplane. For this student, the opportunity to reenact the disaster, and the discussion of the feelings associated with it, significantly helped to reduce the anger demonstrated in school and the nightmares at home.

COGNITIVE-BEHAVIORAL PLAY THERAPY

This type of play therapy is based on both cognitive and behavioral theories of emotional development (Knell, 1993). Behavioral therapy utilizes the concepts of antecedents, reinforcers, contingencies, and social learning theory; cognitive therapy helps children learn to change their own behavior, change cognitions, and become part of their own treatment. The therapist and the child develop goals for treatment. The therapist selects play materials and activities that will facilitate the meeting of the therapy goals. Braswell and Kendall (1988) described the methods utilized by this approach to include modeling, role-playing, and behavioral techniques.

Riviere (2006) described a short-term play therapy approach for disruptive children. He suggested these goals of treatment: have the interventions succeed, build self-esteem, teach on-task behavior, teach self-control, channel aggression appropriately, allow expression of anger through play, practice patience, and help problem solve through play. For each goal of treatment, Riviere (2006) listed a play activity or intervention designed to meet that goal. For example, the therapist can use therapeutic game playing to teach self-control.

For individual counseling of students with disruptive behaviors, Bodiford-McNeil, Hembree-Kigin, and Eyberg (1996) developed a 12-session model of short-term cognitive-behavioral play therapy. This approach utilizes behavioral and cognitive techniques that include systematic desensitization, positive reinforcement, shaping, differential reinforcement of other behavior, modeling, self-monitoring, recording dysfunctional thoughts, confronting irrational beliefs, and bibliotherapy. Play therapy process skills, as well as strategies for managing disruptive behavior, are also part of this therapeutic approach. The 12-session format contains a child's work and play activity as part of the therapy structure. Additionally, homework is assigned after each therapy session. Finally, parents are taught play skills and conduct special play sessions with their child on a daily basis.

CASE EXAMPLE

A child was referred for counseling due to impulsive behaviors demonstrated in the classroom and on the playground. The child's impulsivity resulted in disagreements with peers, temper tantrums when the child did not get his way on the playground, aggressive behavior, whining, and tattling on peers. The child's parents noted negative behaviors at home that included physical aggression with siblings and neighborhood children, frequent breaking of household rules, and sleep difficulties.

The child was seen for 12 treatment sessions; each session lasted approximately 45 minutes. In keeping with the previously described short-term treatment approach, each session contained a child's work and a child's play segment. An additional four sessions were held with the child and the parents to begin the process of teaching the parents play skills and providing coaching to assist in their development. Table 14.1 offers a description of each session.

Table 14.1
Sample 12-Session Play Therapy Treatment

Session	Description
1	Discussion of treatment goals with the child; read the book *A Child's First Book about Play Therapy.*
2	Week in review; began to identify feelings; played the Talking, Feeling, and Doing Game.
3	Week in review; practiced "I feel" statements; began to identify angry times and what happened at these times.
4	Week in review; read the book *How to Take the Grrrr Out of Anger;* played the Feelings game.
5	Week in review; made feelings thermometer; identified events or triggers of anger.
6	Week in review; learned the "Count to 10" and other anger management techniques; played the Anger Control game.
7	Week in review; completed the Who's Responsible for Feelings? activity; read the book *The Very Angry Day Amy Didn't Have.*
8	Week in review; learned the steps to decision making; played the game Exploring My Anger.
9	Week in review; role-played triggers or events that lead to anger management difficulties and utilized appropriate anger management techniques; played the Mad Game and a game of student's choice.
10	Week in review; student selected a play medium to demonstrate an understanding of feelings and an appropriate response to these; played a game of student's choice; began to discuss termination.
11	Week in review; taught the student progressive relaxation techniques; utilized the playhouse to share anger management issues at home and a resolution to them; read the book *The Mad Family Gets Their Mad Out.*
12	Week in review; review of previous sessions with an emphasis on steps to decision making, identification of feelings, anger triggers, and techniques to utilize in anger management situations; read the termination part of the book *A Child's First Book about Play Therapy.*

Table 14.2

Sample Additional Play Therapy Treatment Sessions with Parent(s)

Session	Description
13	Reviewed with parent(s) the concepts of developmental tasks and reflective listening; observed a 10-minute play session between parent(s) and child and provided feedback. Homework for the session: Play 10 minutes each day with the child and complete practice sessions 2 and 3 from manual.
14	Reviewed with parent(s) the concepts of reinforcement, parent messages, and structuring; observed 10-minute play session and gave feedback. Homework: Continue play sessions daily with child and complete practice sessions 4, 5, and 6. Began the discussion of termination with parent(s).
15	Reviewed play therapy techniques of limit setting, consequences, and rule setting with parent; observed 10-minute play session between parent(s) and child and provided feedback. Homework for the session: Play with the child daily for 10 minutes and complete practice session 8, Selecting the Proper Response. Continued the discussion of termination.
16	Reviewed previously taught play techniques; observed 10-minute play session between parent(s) and child and gave feedback to parent(s). Celebrated termination. Homework: Continue daily play sessions.

Four additional play sessions were designed to teach the parent(s) skills to work with the child at home in daily play sessions (see Table 14.2). Skill development emphasized reflective listening, parent messages, structuring, limits, rule setting, and consequences and was based on the work of Louise Guerney (1978). Exercises for homework were selected from the book *Parenting: A Skills Training Manual* (Guerney, 1978).

SUMMARY OF INDIVIDUAL PLAY THERAPY TECHNIQUES

Each referral for anger management difficulties requires the development of a treatment approach specifically designed to address the referral questions. When planning treatment interventions, there are a variety of play therapy techniques that can be helpful to the therapeutic process. Play therapy techniques useful for anger management difficulties can be found in *101 Favorite Play Therapy Techniques* (Kaduson & Schaefer, 1997). Examples of play therapy techniques described in this book include The Rosebush, Mad Game, Beat the Clock, Tearing Paper, The Anger Shield, and Knocking Down the Walls of Anger. Each technique offers the client an opportunity to address and work through anger management issues specific to his or her development. The therapist selects play activities that facilitate the therapeutic process.

Many of the aforementioned play therapy techniques, as well as others, can be useful for individual as well as group counseling. The school clinician selects appropriate techniques relative to the treatment goals of the child or children. Teachers are often helpful in assisting the student with generalizing new behaviors. Stop-and-think steps or steps to decision making are often posted in the classroom, and children are prompted to utilize these steps in situations that provoke anger difficulties in the classroom, in the cafeteria, and on the playground.

Games, toys, and books that are useful for practice of anger management issues are available from the Creative Therapy Store at (800) 648–8857 and Childswork/Childsplay at (800) 962–1142.

GROUP COUNSELING IN THE SCHOOLS

Many school systems offer group counseling to students demonstrating anger management difficulties. These groups are predominately skill-based, and play therapy is utilized as an adjunct to, and part of, the therapeutic process. Children are referred for groups by teachers, parents, and themselves. Group size ranges from six to eight students. Groups meet weekly for approximately 12 to 20 weeks for 45 to 50 minutes. Gumaer (1984) noted that groups need to meet at least 10 times to be effective for children. Parental permission is obtained for group counseling sessions. Students may participate in both individual and group counseling. Parent training and classroom social skills training may also be offered with group counseling.

COGNITIVE-BEHAVIORAL GROUP PLAY THERAPY

A number of curriculum-based counseling programs are available for use with children demonstrating anger management issues. Many of these programs contain play therapy techniques; if not, play therapy techniques are utilized as an adjunct to these groups. For children demonstrating impulse control issues, *Cognitive-Behavioral Therapy for Impulsive Children* (Kendall, 1992a) has proven effective for ameliorating impulsive behavior. This treatment modality was originally designed for individual therapeutic intervention and was adapted for group format. The treatment approach contains 20 sessions. Play therapy techniques incorporated into the sessions include role-playing, bibliotherapy, games, puzzles, drawing, modeling, storytelling, pretending, and making a commercial. Each student receives a *Stop and Think Workbook* (Kendall, 1992b). The group leader determines the appropriate sessions to teach the concepts. Some groups may require more sessions, and others may require fewer than the 20-session format.

This program teaches students specific steps to problem solving. These include the following:

What am I supposed to do?

1. Look at all the possibilities.
2. Pick an answer.
3. Check out your answer.
4. Tell yourself, "I did a good job!" (Kendall, 1992a, p. 3)

These steps are utilized throughout the counseling sessions. To improve generalization outside the counseling environment, these steps are posted in each classroom, and students are encouraged to employ them on a daily basis. The program has additional lessons (Kendall & Bartel, 1990) that can be used with an entire classroom to reinforce the concepts. The school clinician and the teacher may elect to co-teach these additional lessons to assist in the teaching of problem solving in the classroom. This approach helps students generalize the problem-solving techniques to other environments. Play techniques are also utilized with the classroom lessons and include role-playing, puzzles, and games.

For children exhibiting specific anger control difficulties, group counseling offers an opportunity to learn specific skills and the opportunity to utilize these skills with peers prior to doing so in other environments. For children ages 10 to 17, *Cognitive-Behavioral Therapy for Aggressive Children: Therapist Manual* (Nelson & Finch, 1996a) offers a 17- to 27-session group counseling series designed to teach anger management skills to students. Each student is given *Keeping Your Cool: The Anger Management Workbook* (Nelson & Finch, 1996b) for use in the counseling sessions. For students who demonstrate the need for additional instruction and intervention, the program has available *Keeping Your Cool Part 2: Additional Sessions for the Anger Management Workbook* (Nelson & Finch, 1996c).

This program integrates cognitive-behavioral therapy and utilizes play techniques for reinforcement of concepts. Nelson and Finch (1996a) noted that the program contains six basic components for anger training: cognitive change, arousal reduction, behavioral skill development, appropriate anger expression, moral reasoning development, and use of humor. Techniques utilized in the program include self-talk, relaxation training, role-playing, problem solving, assertion training, and humor. It is important to emphasize that the program is flexible and that additional play techniques can be integrated into the program as necessary for an individual and for a group of students. Anger management games such as Overheating or Breaking the Chains of Anger are often useful to play with students in the group during the course of treatment.

A problem-solving sequence is taught to the group of students:

1. Stop: What's the problem?
2. What can I do? Brainstorm solutions.
3. Evaluate: What's the best solution?
4. Act: Try it out.
5. React: Did it work? (Nelson & Finch, 1996a, pp. 42–43)

The problem-solving steps are posted in the classroom to assist with generalizing the new behaviors to other environments. This program is particularly useful as it can be utilized with elementary, middle, and high school students.

The Coping Power Program (Wells, Lochman, & Lenhart, 2008) is an empirically supported cognitive-social program that is useful for group counseling in the schools. It targets aggressive children in grades four to six and consists of both a child (34 sessions) and parent component (16 sessions). Additionally, each child receives 10 to12 individual counseling sessions during the course of the program. The program involves play therapy techniques such as role-playing, feelings identification, problem solving, developing social skills, and learning coping strategies. The parent component involves stress management, establishing rules and expectations, discipline and punishment, improving the parent-child relationship, giving effective instructions to children, academic support, family problem solving, family communication, family cohesion, and long-term planning.

Case Example

Five students were grouped for counseling due to anger management issues, impulsivity, and short attention span. The school psychologist chose to utilize the Stop and Think program for the group and the teacher's version in the classroom. Additionally, bibliotherapy, role-playing, and the therapeutic use of games were part of the counseling process. Games included Overheating; the Anger Solution Game; and the Talking, Feeling, and Doing Game. The book *Christopher's Anger* (Zuckerman, 2000) is an example of one used in group and individually with students.

Students were seen weekly for 45-minute sessions for approximately 20 weeks. Classroom lessons were co-led by the school psychologist and the teacher for 15 weeks. Students reported that the problem-solving techniques assisted them in delaying their need for immediate gratification. They frequently employed the techniques not only in school but also at home. At the beginning of the following school year, three students self-referred for an additional group, noting that they needed to review the problem-solving process to help them be successful in school. These students were allowed to participate in a review program of the skills, and therapeutic games were employed to practice anger management interventions.

CHILD-CENTERED GROUP PLAY THERAPY

As noted earlier, child-centered play therapy focuses on the child and the therapeutic relationship, rather than on the referring problem. Landreth (1991, p. 80) identified the objectives for child-centered play therapy:

1. Develop a more positive self-concept.
2. Assume greater self-responsibility.
3. Become more self-directing.
4. Become more self-accepting.
5. Become more self-reliant.
6. Engage in self-determined decision making.
7. Experience a feeling of control.
8. Become sensitive to the process of coping.
9. Develop an internal source of evaluation.
10. Become more trusting of self.

Children, therefore, are free to choose what they will work on during the play therapy sessions. The child drives to self-actualize, and the play therapist trusts that the child can chart the path. Limit setting, toys, and the role of the therapist continue to be critical to the therapeutic process.

Landreth and Sweeney (1999) discussed this approach to play therapy relative to group size, group selection, group playroom, and play materials. Additionally, they emphasized that the length, duration, and frequency of sessions are dependent on the age and needs of the children. In general, sessions can meet once or twice weekly and run approximately 45 minutes per session. This approach can be utilized in the schools but may be met with questions by teachers and administrators because the therapist is perceived as not directly teaching the students to control their anger in a planned programmatic way. It is important that the therapy sessions not be used as a reinforcer for appropriate behavior nor in a response-cost way for inappropriate behavior in school or in the classroom. Students are involved in counseling regardless of their behavior.

CASE EXAMPLE

A school psychologist assigned as a consultant to a preschool program was asked to work with three children referred for counseling due to conduct issues, withdrawn behavior, and school phobic reactions. These children were grouped and seen twice weekly for 30-minute sessions for 15 weeks. A child-centered play therapy approach was employed by the school psychologist. Additionally, the school social worker met with the parents to discuss child rearing and discipline issues at home. After the 30 sessions, the school psychologist noted a significant reduction in inappropriate demonstrations of anger; less anxiety was demonstrated; and positive social skills were noted in the classroom. The parents reported fewer discipline problems with their children at home; parents also noted more positive sibling relationships.

SOCIAL PLAY IN THE SCHOOLS

Classrooms provide an arena for encouraging the appropriate use of anger management techniques and socialization of students. Social play allows students to practice social behaviors in a controlled, supervised manner. *Social play* has been defined as "the technique of leading a group of people in a series of games, so that individuals experience, learn, and develop positive social attitudes and skills" (Aycox, 1985, p. 5). Social play helps students to be the center of attention, to get to know one another, to learn to cooperate with one another, and to resolve anger or aggression.

Aycox (1985) outlines more than 50 games that can be utilized in classrooms with students to encourage social skills, reduce anger and hostility, focus attention on students, encourage cooperation, and allow students to employ dramatic skills. Aycox (1985, p. 92) noted that social play will help students to:

1. Learn positive social behaviors.
2. Learn to increase self-control.

3. Be more socially organized.
4. Learn to develop gratification and control impulses.
5. Learn to enjoy the here and now and feel worthy of feeling pleasure.
6. Advance communication both verbally and nonverbally.
7. Foster a positive attitude toward writing and speaking as good ways to express feelings instead of acting out.
8. Learn the value of cooperating and supporting peers in the classroom community.
9. Learn to rely on intrinsic values and not prizes.
10. Increase use of mental imagery building.
11. Learn body coordination free of stressful performance anxiety.
12. Gain experience in social problem solving.
13. Be able to modulate shifting between active and calm state.
14. Adopt a happier and more respectful view of school, and eliminate name-calling, fighting, and vandalism.

The school clinician selects appropriate social games to introduce to the class. The goal of the early games is for the students to get to know one another; later games proceed to establish group cohesiveness. Games can also focus attention on individual students. Finally, games that focus on anger resolution can be introduced to the class. These games assist students in resolving anger and help them manage future anger issues. As stated by Aycox (1985), "The optimum resolution of anger takes place in the social realm, not in the individual, one-to-one mode and cultural, social activities (play, dance, and drama) are the most effective forms of controlling anger in humans" (p. 77).

There are a number of social games that are helpful for anger management: Alphabet Volleyball, Broom Hockey, Bull in the Ring, Caboose Dodgeball, El Tigre, Guard the Chair, How Do You Like Your Neighbor?, Line Tug O'War, Pris, Steeple Chase, Strideball, Swat, and Wave the Ocean. The school clinician visits the classroom twice weekly and leads the class in social games, which can often occur during recess time so that students will not miss instructional time. In many cases, social games can be used as an adjunct to individual and group counseling. As noted earlier, counseling interventions are selected based on individual and group treatment goals. Social games encourage the emotional growth of an entire class.

Leben (1999) developed 60 structured group games for children experiencing trauma, demonstrating low self-esteem, or diagnosed with attention deficit/hyperactivity disorder (ADHD). She organized her groups to include setting therapeutic objectives, a check-in, game play of approximately two to four games dependent upon duration of the session, and feedback time. Games particularly useful for anger management difficulties are Puppet Storytelling, Feelings Wheel, Copy Cat Circle, Family Picnic, Elephant, and Picture Projection.

Finally, for older children and adolescents, Ashby, Kottman, and DeGraaf (2008) offer Adventure Therapy. This experiential approach utilizes games and activities to facilitate group process, interpersonal relationships, personal growth, and therapeutic improvement. This therapy is noted for the movement inherent in the games and activities. The goals for Adventure Therapy include:

1. Improve communication and relationship skills.
2. Increase self-awareness and self-acceptance.
3. Develop and apply problem-solving and decision-making skills.
4. Increase understanding and valuing of diversity.
5. Demonstrate consistently responsible behavior.
6. Enhance positive attitudes and skills related to learning.

Activities that can be useful for adolescents include Cyclops Tag, Bump, Carry That Load, Flip Me the Bird, Gotcha, and Keypunch. Selection of the games and activities are based on the group participants' goals and objectives.

CASE EXAMPLE

A school psychologist was asked to consult with a teacher who was encountering multiple discipline issues in the classroom. At the point of referral, two of the students in this class were involved in group counseling for behavioral issues, and one student was involved in individual counseling due to anger management issues. The school psychologist helped the teacher develop a behavior reinforcement plan for the class and suggested that the class would benefit from structured social and adventure games to increase group cohesiveness and cooperation. These games and activities would also help the previously referred students improve their social skills and help them with anger resolution skills.

The teacher agreed to the new reinforcement plan and the introduction of biweekly structured social and adventure game sessions. The school psychologist led the games and activities; the teacher and class participated in the activities and games. Games and activities designed to help the class get acquainted were introduced initially; these were followed by those that encouraged group cohesiveness, empathy, problem solving, decision making, intimacy, being the center of attention, and anger resolution. Games were played with the class for the entire school year, and the teacher began to lead games as the school year progressed.

The teacher reported that the students had fewer discipline referrals, more group connectedness, and greater empathy toward each other after the introduction of the structured social and adventure games. The students noted less difficulty getting along with others and fewer anger resolution difficulties. The principal and playground monitors highlighted that the students demonstrated fewer verbal and physical disagreements on the playground, greater empathy toward students in other classrooms, and greater tolerance for frustration.

SUMMARY OF GROUP PLAY THERAPY TECHNIQUES

Group counseling integrating play therapy techniques provides students the opportunity to learn new skills, self-actualize, grow emotionally, and work through anger management difficulties. Group counseling in the schools often provides specific skill development and utilizes play therapy techniques to reinforce skills in the therapy session. As in individual counseling, the school clinician chooses counseling interventions specific to treatment goals and objectives. The student(s) may also participate in individual or family counseling if appropriate.

ADDITIONAL PLAY THERAPY INTERVENTIONS

Many programs and games are available that incorporate play in working with anger management issues. The reader is encouraged to review programs and games as to their usefulness in the schools and as a therapeutic agent for children. *The Anger Control Tool Kit* (Shapiro, Shore, Bloemker, Kahler, & Schroeder, 1994) and the *I Can Control My Anger Kit* (Shapiro, 1995) are two programs that incorporate a multi-modality approach to working with children with anger management issues. The former program includes 38 techniques for the school clinician to choose from when working with an angry child. It is recommended that the therapist choose techniques covering six different modalities: affective, behavioral, cognitive, developmental, educational, and social.

Techniques that incorporate play include storytelling, the turtle technique, the self-calming technique, feelings charade, the hot seat, substituting behaviors when angry, role-playing, and catharsis. The program also contains a videotape that reviews eight anger control techniques. The latter program also recommends that the clinician choose interventions from six treatment modalities: affective, developmental, behavioral, cognitive, educational, and social. Play activities include the Coping with Anger Target Game, Face It card game, Problem-Solving Cards, two story books, and Listen Up card game. The school clinician designs the treatment program for the individual child by selecting at least one treatment goal from the six modalities. Activities are chosen that will help the student work on these goals.

CASE EXAMPLE

An 8-year-old girl was referred to the school psychologist for anger management issues. Activities were chosen from *The Anger Control Kit* (Shapiro, 1994) that addressed the six treatment modalities. These included the feelings charade, the turtle technique, storytelling, self-calming technique, role-playing, bibliotherapy, a feelings thermometer, drawing, playing with clay, and others. The child was seen for 15 sessions. The teacher reported that the child demonstrated less impulsive and aggressive behavior. The child was observed to be less ostracized by her peers and more involved in play activities on the playground. The child was noted to be receiving invites for after-school play dates from peers.

SUMMARY

This chapter reviewed play therapy techniques and approaches useful for anger management issues. Individual counseling techniques suggested for therapeutic intervention included client-centered play therapy, release play therapy, cognitive-behavioral play therapy, and developing an individual treatment approach incorporating play therapy techniques based on individual student treatment goals. Group counseling techniques included client-centered play therapy, cognitive-behavioral play therapy, structured social games and adventure play, therapeutic games, and the use of specific programs designed to ameliorate anger management difficulties that incorporate play techniques. A prescriptive approach to play therapy was recommended for addressing a student's needs specific to anger management difficulties. Interventions may include individual play therapy, group play therapy, and family counseling. Additionally, special play sessions between parent and child were discussed to assist with anger management difficulties at home. Specific case examples were shared to illustrate the play techniques. Finally, specific play therapy techniques were identified for potential inclusion in a treatment program.

REFERENCES

Annenberg Public Policy Center (APPC) as part of the Annenberg Foundation Trust at Sunnylands' Initiative on Adolescent Mental Health. (2004). *School mental health professionals identify adolescent mental health conditions as more serious problems than violence and interpersonal conflict in high schools.* News release. Retrieved February 1, 2009, from http://www.annenbergpublic policycenter.org.

Ashby, J. S., Kottman, T., & DeGraaf, D. (2008). *Active interventions for kids and teens: Adding adventure and fun to counseling.* Alexandria, VA: American Counseling Association.

Axline, V. M. (1947). *Play therapy: The inner dynamics of childhood.* Boston: Houghton Mifflin.

Axline, V. M. (1969). *Play therapy.* New York: Ballantine.

Aycox, F. (1985). *Games we should play in school.* Byron, CA: Front Row Experience.

Bodiford-McNeil, C., Hembree-Kigin, T. L., & Eyberg, S. (1996). *Short-term play therapy for disruptive children.* King of Prussia, PA: Center for Applied Psychology.

Braswell, L., & Kendall, P. C. (1988). Cognitive-behavorial methods with children. In K. S. Dobson (Ed.), *Handbook of cognitive behavior therapy* (pp. 167–213). New York: Guilford Press.

Catron, T., & Weiss, B. (1994). The Vanderbilt school-based counseling program. *Journal of Emotional and Behavioral Disorders, 2,* 247–253.

Center for Mental Health in Schools. (2006). *Current status of mental health in the schools: A policy and practice anaylsis.* Los Angeles: Author.

Center for School Mental Health Assistance. (2002). *Empirically-supported interventions resource packet* (Project # U93 MC 00174). Baltimore, MD: Author.

Centers for Disease Control and Prevention. (1998). Youth risk behavior surveillance: United States, 1997. *CDC Surveillance Summaries,* August 14, 1998, *MMWR, 47* (No. SS-3).

Dorfman, E. (1951). Play therapy. In C. R. Rogers (Ed.), *Client-centered therapy: Its current practice* (pp. 235–277). Boston: Houghton Mifflin.

Fight Crime: Invest in Kids. (2006). *Cyber bullying.* Retrieved January 31, 2009, from http://www.fightcrime.org/cyberbullying

Friedman, R., Katz-Leavy, J., Manderscheid, R., & Sondheimer, D. (1996). Prevalence of serious emotional disturbance in children and adolescents. In R. W. Manderscheid & M. A. Sonnenschein (Eds.), *Mental health, United States 1996* (pp. 77–91). Washington, DC: U.S. Government Printing Office.

Gilfix, J., & HellerKahn, N. (1999). *The special playroom: A young child's guide to play.* Unpublished manuscript.

Gootman, M. E. (1997). *The caring teacher's guide to discipline: Helping young students learn self-control, responsibility, and respect.* Thousand Oaks, CA: Corwin Press.

Guerney, L. F. (1978). *Parenting: A skills training manual.* State College, PA: Institute for the Development of Emotional and Life Skills.

Gumaer, J. (1984). *Counseling and therapy for children.* New York: Free Press.

Hambidge, G. (1955). Structured play therapy. *American Journal of Orthopsychiatry, 25,* 601–657.

James, O. (1997). *Play therapy: A comprehensive guide.* Northvale, NJ: Jason Aronson.

Kaduson, H. G., & Schaefer, C. E. (Eds.). (1997). *101 favorite play therapy techniques.* Northvale, NJ: Jason Aronson.

Kataoka, S., Zhang, L., & Wells, K. (2002). Unmet need for mental health care among U.S. children: Variation by ethnicity and insurance status. *American Journal of Psychiatry, 159,* 1548–1555.

Kendall, P. C. (1992a). *Cognitive-behavioral therapy for impulsive children: The manual.* Ardmore, PA: Workbook Publishing.

Kendall, P. C. (1992b). *Stop and think workbook.* Ardmore, PA: Workbook Publishing.

Kendall, P. C., & Bartel, N. R. (1990). *Teaching problem solving to students with learning and behavioral problems: A manual for teachers.* Ardmore, PA: Workbook Publishing.

Kingery, P. M., Coggeshall, M. B., & Alford, A. A. (1998). Violence at schools: Recent evidence from four national surveys. *Psychology in the Schools, 35,* 247–258.

Knell, S. (1993). *Cognitive-behavioral play therapy.* Northvale, NJ: Jason Aronson.

Landreth, G. L. (1991). *Play therapy: The art of the relationship.* Bristol, PA: Accelerated Development.

Landreth, G. L., & Sweeney, D. S. (1999). The freedom to be: Client-centered group play therapy. In D. S. Sweeney & L. E. Homeyer (Eds.), *The handbook of group play therapy* (pp. 39–64). San Francisco: Jossey-Bass.

Lavigne, J. V., Gibbons, R. D., Christoffel, K. K., Arend, R., Rosenbaum, D., Binns, H., Dawson, N., Sobel, H., & Isaacs, C. (1996). Prevalence rates and correlates of psychiatric disorders among preschool children. *Journal of the American Academy of Child and Adolescent Psychiatry, 35,* 204–214.

Leben, N. Y. (1999). *Directive group play therapy.* Pflugerville, TX: Morning Glory Treatment Center for Children.

Levy, D. (1938). Release therapy in young children. *Psychiatry, 1,* 387–389.

Mott Foundation. (1996). *A fine line: Losing American youth to violence*. Flint, MI: Author.

Nelson, W. M., & Finch, A. J., Jr. (1996a). *Cognitive-behavioral therapy for aggressive children: Therapist manual*. Ardmore, PA: Workbook Publishing.

Nelson, W. M., & Finch, A. J., Jr. (1996b). *Keeping your cool: The anger management workbook*. Ardmore, PA: Workbook Publishing.

Nelson, W. M., & Finch, A. J., Jr. (1996c). *Keeping your cool: Part 2: Additional sessions for the anger management workbook*. Ardmore, PA: Workbook Publishing.

Nemiroff, M. A., & Annunziata, J. (1990). *A child's first book about play therapy*. Washington, DC: American Psychological Association.

Northeast Foundation for Children. (2005). *Responsive classroom*. Turners Falls, MA: Northeast Foundation for Children.

Olweus, D. (1993). *Bullying at schools: What we know and what we can do*. Cambridge, MA: Blackwell.

Paone, T. R., & Douma, K. B. (2009). Child-centered play therapy with a seven-year-old boy diagnosed with intermittent explosive disorder. *International Journal of Play Therapy, 18*, 31–44.

Perry, L. (1993). Audrey, the Bois d'Arc and me: A time of becoming. In T. Kottman & C. Schaefer (Eds.), *Play therapy in action: A casebook for practitioners* (pp. 5–43). Northvale, NJ: Jason Aronson.

Rashkin, R. (2005). *Feeling better: A kid's book about therapy*. Washington, DC: Magination Press.

Riviere, S. (2006). Short-term play therapy for disruptive behavior disorders. In H. G. Kaduson & C. E. Schaefer (Eds.), *Short-term play therapy for children* (2nd ed.). New York: Guilford Press.

Rogers, C. (1951). *Client-centered therapy*. Boston: Houghton Mifflin.

Rones, M., & Hoagwood, K. (2000). School-based mental health services: A research review. *Clinical Child and Family Psychology, 3*, 223–241.

Shaffer, D., Fisher, P., Dulcan, M. K., Davies, M., Piacentini, J., Schwab-Stone, M. E., Lahey, B. B., Bourdon, K., Jensen, P. S., Bird, H. R., Canino, G., & Regier, D. A. (1996). The NIMH Diagnostic Interview Schedule for Children Version 2.3 (DISC-2.3): Description, acceptability, prevalence rates and performance in the MECA study. *Journal of the American Academy of Child and Adolescent Psychiatry, 35*, 865–877.

Shapiro, L. E. (1995). *I can control my anger*. Plainview, NY: Childswork/ Childsplay.

Shapiro, L. E., Shore, H. M., Bloemker, M. A., Kahler, D. S., & Schroeder, J. M. (1994). *The anger control tool kit*. Plainview, NY: Childswork/Childsplay.

U.S. Department of Health and Human Services. (1999). *Mental health: A report of the Surgeon General—Executive Summary*. Rockville, MD: U.S. Department of Health and Human Services, Substance Abuse and Mental Health Services Administration, National Institute of Mental Health.

Weist, M., & Murray, M. (2007). Advancing school mental health promotion globally. *Advances in School Mental Health Promotion*, 2–12.

Wells, K. C., Lochman, J. E., & Lenhart, L. A. (2008). *Coping power*. New York: Oxford University Press.

Wolraich, M. L., Hannah, J. N., Pinnock, T. Y., Baumgaertel, A., & Brown, J. (1996). Comparison of diagnostic criteria for attention-deficit hyperactivity disorder in a countywide sample. *Journal of the American Academy of Child and Adolescent Psychiatry*, *35*, 319–324.

Zuckerman, D. (2000). *Christopher's anger*. Los Angeles: Western Psychological Services.

CHAPTER 15

Group Play Interventions for Children with Attention Deficit/Hyperactivity Disorder

LINDA A. REDDY

Attention Deficit/Hyperactivity Disorder (ADHD), a complex neurocognitive disorder, is one of the most common childhood disorders referred to school and mental health professionals. Current estimates suggest that 3 to 5 percent of all school-aged children have the disorder, translating to approximately two children with the disorder in an average classroom (DuPaul & Stoner, 2003; Reddy & De Thomas, 2006).

ADHD manifests in poor executive deficits in planning, attention, organization, monitoring, and self-control (e.g., Castellanos et al., 2002; Reddy & Hale, 2007). As a result, many children with ADHD exhibit severe and chronic academic (DuPaul & Stoner, 2003), social/emotional and/or behavioral symptoms (Clark, Prior, & Kinsella, 2002) in the home and at school. ADHD is confounded by high rates of comorbidity. Prevalence rates indicate that children with ADHD experience at least one (44 percent), two (32 percent), or three (11 percent) other disorders (Szatmari, Offord, & Boyle, 1989). Specific learning disabilities (SLD) affect about 31 percent of the ADHD population across studies (DuPaul & Stoner, 2003), with reading (8–39 percent), math (12–30 percent), and spelling (12–27 percent) SLD frequently reported (Barkley, 2005). Common comorbid psychiatric conditions include other disruptive behavior disorders (25–40 percent), mood disorders (10–30 percent), anxiety disorders (30 percent), and tic disorders (6 percent) (Barkley, 2005). Additionally, Rowland, Les-wesne, and Abramowitz (2002) found that prevalence rates for ADHD varied substantially based on presenting symptoms, assessment approaches used, and the setting in which the child was evaluated. Not surprising, the disorder's heterogeneous nature and sensitivity to context dependent factors (i.e., tests used, setting) challenge the identification, education, *and* treatment process for schools (Reddy & Hale, 2007).

SCHOOL INTERVENTIONS FOR CHILDREN WITH ADHD

The majority of school interventions for children with ADHD are individually based, focusing on techniques that allow school personnel to adapt their curricula to the needs of an individual child. Few programs include group-oriented interventions (e.g., developmentally appropriate games) that allow school personnel to target social, behavioral, and academic needs in schools (DuPaul & Eckert, 1997; DuPaul & Stoner, 2003).

School-based interventions for children with ADHD can be broadly conceptualized as falling into two categories, contingency management and cognitive-behavioral treatments. A contingency management program establishes positive and negative consequences for targeted behaviors. Rewards and punishments can be provided by teachers and/or parents for school behaviors, creating links between actions and consequences. Several contingency management guides for teachers exist (DuPaul & Stoner, 2003). Overall, contingency management programs are effective in improving individual classroom behavior, but gains tend to dissipate once treatment is withdrawn (DuPaul & Eckert, 1997). Daily report cards can foster collaborative parent-teacher partnerships by allowing teachers and parents to implement positive/negative consequences for school behaviors at home. Findings reveal that daily report cards can produce some improves in social behavior, hyperactivity, attentiveness, and self-control (Chafouleas et al., 2005).

Cognitive-behavioral interventions (e.g., self-instruction, self-monitoring) help ADHD children develop self-control and problem-solving skills by examining and correcting the thoughts that lead to actions (Kendall, 2000). They can be used in both individual and group formats for treating a broad range of behaviors including impulsivity, social skills, intrusiveness, and anger management. Cognitive-behavioral interventions in general are adult- rather than child-directed, in that adults initiate and guide the therapeutic process.

Research on the efficacy of school-based contingency management and cognitive-behavioral interventions has been inconsistent. While early studies have reported its effectiveness with this population (e.g., Douglas, 1980; Kendall & Braswell, 1985), the majority of the outcome literature reports modest gains that fail to generalize to the classroom (Barkley, 1998; Pelham, Fabiano, & Massetti, 2005). Pfiffner and O'Leary (1993) speculate that this failure to generalize may be due to differences between treatment goals and classroom expectations, as well as the brevity of the training provided. Treatment goals more relevant to the children, such as peer acceptance, sportsmanship, and making and maintaining friendships, may generate more motivation, learning engagement, and intervention success. Others assert that ADHD children lack the sustained attention (focus), self-control, and motivation for strict treatment regiments such as cognitive-behavior interventions (Reddy & Hale, 2007). Traditional cognitive-behavioral interventions may not be intrinsically appealing and motivating for ADHD children and may interfere with intervention success (Reddy, in press). To fill this important void in the outcome literature, new intervention models (e.g., group play interventions) have emerged that, in part, promote engagement and skill development of this population in schools.

PURPOSE

This chapter examines the clinical utility and efficacy of group play interventions for elementary school children with ADHD. The theoretical basis, value, and evidence for group play interventions or developmentally appropriate games (DAGs) for children with ADHD are presented. Considerations for designing DAGs are offered. An empirically supported ADHD child training group program and illustrative examples of DAGs from this program are described.

VALUE OF GROUP PLAY INTERVENTIONS

Group play interventions like developmentally appropriate games (DAGs) that are targeted, potent, and enjoyable to children can increase skill development and motivation for school-aged children. Scholars advocate that school interventions should focus on "the performance of particular behaviors at the *points of performance* in the natural environment where and when such behaviors should be performed" (Barkley, 1998, p. 65). Thus, interventions are most likely to be effective when skills are taught in contexts in which children work and play. Group-based DAGs are an effective way to capture ADHD children's interest while teaching them important skills in natural settings such as the school, home, and playground (Reddy, in press). DAGs provide children the opportunity to interact naturally with peers and learn appropriate behaviors in the context in which they will be used. DAGs offer school personnel valuable information on *when* and *how* social problems or opportunities occur among children. Treating children in a natural play setting also increases the likelihood of maintaining treatment gains over time and generalizing treatment gains to other settings, such as the school, home, or community (Hoag & Burlingame, 1997; Reddy et al., 2005).

School-based DAGs enhance children's socialization through group contact, increase self-confidence through group acceptance, and provide recreational and leisure time activities (Reed, Black, & Eastman, 1978; Reddy, in press). For ADHD children, DAGs offer an important means to acquire new skills, practice previously learned information, and experience a stimulating learning environment that enables peers and adults to share and practice new skills at school (Reddy, in press).

DAGs are gross motor activities that are based on four principles:

1. Each child has the opportunity to participate at his or her own ability level.
2. As each child plays the game, opportunities to participate increase.
3. Elimination of a group member is not possible and as a result, children become more active members of the group and exhibit greater cooperation, cohesion, and problem solving.
4. Children who vary in ability can interact positively with each other (Torbert, 1994; Reddy, Spencer, Hall, & Rubel, 2001; Reddy et al., 2005; Reddy, in press).

DAGs can build children's sense of accomplishment, creativity, and positive regard for themselves and others, while teaching them important life skills for learning and play (Reddy et al., 2001; Torbert & Schneider, 1993). Children who participate in school group games share an affiliation through which they can encourage other's growth in positive social interactions (Torbert, 1994). DAGs will also present social, academic, and behavioral/physical challenges that encourage children to persist and try alternative solutions (Bunker, 1991).

Despite the long and rich history of play therapy (Parten, 1932; Association for Play Therapy, 2001), some have questioned its clinical utility and efficacy (e.g., Lebo, 1953; Reade, Hunter, & McMillan, 1999). The main criticism of play interventions has been that the field in general lacks rigorous research designs and data analytic methods (Phillips, 1985; Ray, Bratton, Rhine, & Jones, 2001, 2005; Bratton, Ray, Rhine, & Jones, 2005). Similar to psychotherapy outcome literature, play interventions are generally based on anecdotal reports or case study designs and include small sample size, no-control and/or treatment-alternative groups, and limited or no generalizability of findings to natural settings such as school (LeBlanc & Ritchie, 1999; Files-Hall & Reddy, 2005). Despite these methodological shortcomings, new intervention programs that include group play interventions for children have emerged (for a detailed description of evidence-based models see Reddy, Files-Hall, & Schaefer, 2005).

Next, a synthesis of the evidence for group play interventions (DAGs) is presented. This review offers practitioners a glimpse of the scope of DAGs and group play intervention programs available for school personnel.

EVIDENCE FOR GROUP PLAY INTERVENTIONS

Research has shown that DAGs or group play interventions improve participation, cooperation, social skills, self-concept, and visual motor skills of regular education, emotionally disturbed, and perceptually impaired students more than traditional school-based games (Ferland, 1997; Reddy et al., 2005; Reddy, in press). For example, Baggerly and Parker (2005) examined the application of child-centered group play therapy with 22 African American boys in elementary school. Each group received from 9 to 11 child-centered group play therapy sessions, once or twice a week in groups of two, at the school the boys attended. Play materials in the sessions included: 1) real-life items, such as a bendable doll family, a cardboard boxtop with rooms indicated by strips of tape, a nursing bottle, plastic dishes, a small car, a small plane, and a telephone; 2) aggression-release items, such as handcuffs, dart gun, rubber knife, toy soldiers, and an inflatable plastic punching toy; and 3) items that could be used for creative expression, such as Play-Doh, a small plain mask, construction paper, crayons, and blunt scissors (Landreth, 2002). In addition, African American dolls were added to provide a more diverse, culturally sensitive selection of play materials. One of the goals of the play therapy sessions was to honor the African worldview and to facilitate self-confidence. Results revealed improvements in self-confidence, behavior, social skills, and expression of feelings and acceptance of self and others. Also, participants were found to progress from independence to a group identity and cooperation approach. In early sessions, children often hoarded toys, were overly dominant or submissive, and experienced conflict. As the sessions went on, the children began to use and value a "we" identity rather than a "me" identity. Children began to cooperate in their interactions and learned to trust each other for help (Baggerly & Parker, 2005).

Bay-Hinitz and Wilson (2005) examined the effectiveness of a cooperative-games intervention for 70 aggressive preschool children (ages 4 to 5 years). This intervention used teacher-directed cooperative board games and other cooperative activities to reduce aggressive behavior. It requires minimal training and can be used by parents, mentors, and paraprofessionals. Results indicate that children who participated in cooperative-games interventions exhibited more participation and prosocial behavior than those in traditional competitive games. Similar findings were also reported by Orlick (1988). Garaigordobil and Echebarria (1995) examined the effects of a cooperative-game program on the social behavior and self-concept of 178 mainstreamed children (ages 6 to 7 years). Twenty-two play sessions that included games designed to enhance children's cooperation, sharing, symbolic play, and feelings of self-worth were implemented. Significant improvements in classroom behavior (e.g., leadership skills, cheerfulness, sensitivity/respect to others, aggression, apathy, and anxiety) were found.

Schneider (1989) compared the effects of DAGs versus free-play (i.e., 15 to 20 minutes per session) on the self-esteem of 36 kindergarten students across 17 sessions. Teacher and child self-reported ratings of self-esteem improved more among students who participated in DAGs than those in free-play.

Shen (2002) investigated the effectiveness of short-term child-centered group play therapy in elementary school settings with Chinese children in Taiwan who experienced an earthquake in 1999. Thirty children ranging in age from 8 to 12 years old were assigned to an experimental group (15 children) and a control group (15 children). Children in the experimental group scored significantly lower on levels of anxiety and suicide risk after group play therapy than did the children in the control group.

Rennie (2000) compared the effectiveness of individual and group play therapy in treating kindergarten children with adjustment problems in comparison to controls.

Data for the group play therapy children, which served as the comparison group, came from 15 kindergarten children from McGuire's 1999 study with adjustment difficulties. Children received twelve to fourteen 45-minute group play therapy sessions for 14 weeks in Denton, Texas, between January 1999 and May 1999. Fourteen kindergarten children with adjustment difficulties (e.g., withdrawn, anxious, depressed, or inattentive) received ten to twelve 30-minute individual play therapy sessions in a 12-week period in an elementary school (serving as the experimental group). Control subjects consisted of 13 kindergarten children from the same population with adjustment difficulties who received no individual or group play therapy. Results revealed that children in group and individual play therapy exhibited significant reductions in total behavior problems and externalizing behavior problems as measured by the Child Behavior Checklist-Parent Form (Achenbach & Edelbrock, 1991). Also group and individual play therapy resulted in improvements in self-concept, while the control condition resulted in reductions in self-concept.

Hand (1986) examined the efficacy of group play interventions with children diagnosed as emotionally disturbed. Two groups of children ages 10 to 12 were systematically observed during recess. One group participated in traditional games where success was defined as the defeat or elimination of others, while the other group participated in DAGs three times per week for 16 weeks. Greater reductions in verbal and physical aggression and the use of time-out were found among children in the DAG group.

Reed, Black, and Eastman (1978) investigated the effectiveness of a parent-child group training program for perceptually disabled children (ages 6 to 12 years) who had limited peer group experience and were verbally and physically aggressive. The program consisted of 1-hour sessions held twice a week for 16 weeks and implemented games that enhanced social skills and perceptual motor abilities (e.g., visual-motor skills, visual acuity, and body awareness). Parent ratings revealed improved peer interactions at home and school, including greater group participation and rule following and fewer behavior problems.

Reddy and her associates (Reddy, in press; Reddy et al., 2005; Reddy et al., 2001; Springer & Reddy, in press) have conducted several investigations examining the efficacy of DAGs in a children's group training program as part of a Child Attention Deficit/Hyperactivity Disorder Multimodal Program (CAMP). CAMP is an empirically supported program that treats the social and behavioral needs of young children diagnosed with ADHD (ages 4 to 8 years). Grounded in social learning theory and behavioral principles, this developmental, skill-based program for children utilizes DAGs to develop social skills, self-control, and anger/stress management within a 10-week, structured group format. Parents receive concurrent group training focused on behavioral management techniques in the home, school, and community. Another unique feature of CAMP is that behavioral consultation services are offered to each child's parents and teacher in the home and school. Outcome evaluations of CAMP revealed statistically significant and clinically meaningful improvements in parents' functioning and child behavior in the home and school at program completion and follow-up (Reddy, in press; Reddy et al., 2005; Reddy et al., 2001; Springer & Reddy, in press).

Pedro-Carroll and Jones (2005) developed and examined the efficacy of a school-based prevention program, Children of Divorce Intervention Program (CODIP), that targets the needs of children of divorce. CODIP is implemented by specially trained and supervised mental health professionals and paraprofessionals. Developmentally sensitive, play group activities are used to help children address the stressful changes that divorce often brings. The authors reported that CODIP reduced (short- and long-term) children's stress related to the divorce and improved overall social, emotional, and school adjustment.

Another innovative model is the Denver Model developed by Rogers (2005). The Denver Model, a well-researched, school-based daily play intervention program, is effective in facilitating the development and growth of young children with autism spectrum disorders. The Denver Model is grounded in developmental theory and emphasizes the importance of symbolic, interpersonal, and cognitive aspects of play in the development of children with autism. Children who have participated in this program exhibit significant improvements in symbolic play and affective, reciprocal exchanges during play with their parents.

In sum, group play interventions afford children opportunities to learn new skills through participating in structured peer group activities that are socially, behaviorally, and cognitively challenging. DAGs are flexible, require minimum equipment, and can be easily modified to meet specific student, group, and/or classroom needs.

SHARED CHARACTERISTICS OF GROUP PLAY INTERVENTIONS

The literature reviewed provides practitioners an appreciation of the range of available group play interventions. Each intervention study has a strong theoretical basis and empirical support and uses targeted group play interventions/approaches. Collectively, these interventions offer practitioners an overview of the key play intervention components that *work* for children.

Shared intervention characteristics found across the outcome literature were: 1) strong cohesiveness, feeling of belonging, and ownership among group members; 2) skill-intensive group play interventions; 3) a highly structured, clear; and time-limited agenda for each group session; 4) coaching and positive corrective feedback for skill development; 5) use of structured homework; 6) use of developmentally appropriate interventions; 7) comprehensive outcome assessment approaches; 8) use of different treatment settings (e.g., school, clinic, shelter, home, medical facility, camp); 9) assessment of behavioral goals; 10) outcome success defined by statistical and/or clinically meaningful methods (e.g., effect sizes); 11) directive and/or non-directive play; and 12) varied treatment agents, such as school psychologists, social workers, teachers, and parents (Reddy, in press). The shared treatment characteristics provide a good foundation for designing DAGs for school.

CONSIDERATIONS FOR DESIGNING GROUP PLAY INTERVENTIONS

DAGs can be easily designed and adopted for the school, home, and playground. Ten considerations for designing school group play interventions are:

1. Identify the social, cognitive, academic, and behavioral needs of each student and the class as a whole.
2. Assess the skills (i.e., task demands) required of each student to successfully participate in each game.
3. Design/select games that allow each student to participate at his or her own ability level.
4. Design/select games that enable students who vary in skill level and experience to interact positively with each other.
5. Design/select games that provide students increased opportunities to play and interact with peers and adults.
6. Redesign existing games (see example of *Islands*) to meet DAG principles.
7. Evaluate the space and equipment (e.g., poster board, paint, balls) needed for each game, and identify available resources in the classroom/school.

8. Determine the number of adults and children required for effective and safe participation in each game.
9. Assess the skills and knowledge required for school personnel to successfully implement the game.
10. Provide school personnel with training and/or supervision as needed.

Children's needs and competencies must be carefully considered when designing games for ADHD children in a group and/or classroom context. For this population, users of group play interventions should consider the social, emotional, cognitive, *and* behavioral/physical competencies of the children. Examples of social competencies include the child's ability to share belongings, share information about himself or herself, play cooperatively, ask for help, and help others. Emotional needs include the child's ability to identify feelings in himself or herself and others, use words to express feelings, and manage stress and anger. Cognitive needs consist of the child's capability to understand and follow directions, identify personal and shared space, attend to details, and sustain effort during games. Possible behavioral/physical needs may include a child's ability to take turns with others; control his or her hands, feet, and mouth; move the body in a controlled fashion; and manage sensory input from the environment (e.g., visual, auditory, tactical, smell). Careful consideration of the unique individual child and group needs of children (classroom) are critically important for designing play interventions that *work.*

Example of Redesigning Existing Games   Schools use a number of traditional games that can be easily redesigned as DAGs. For example, the game Musical Chairs is a traditional game familiar to preschool and elementary school children. In looking at the objectives of Musical Chairs, the following is apparent: 1) the winner is the child who is fast enough to get to an empty chair and/or dislodge another child from a chair; 2) limited positive interactions take place between children who vary in ability level; 3) participants are not encouraged to help others, share personal space, and play cooperatively; and 4) as the game unfolds there are a decreased number of opportunities to participate, and once a child fails to secure a place on a chair, the chair and child are eliminated.

Following the four principles of DAGs and the ten considerations outlined, the game Musical Chairs can be redesigned as a cooperative training activity for children called *Islands.* For example, the same basic setup and game design can be used. Instead of chairs, towels or carpet squares can be randomly spaced on the floor in the area where the class meets (e.g., homeroom, library, gym). The game starts with one towel per child. The children are instructed, as in Musical Chairs, that the music signals the need to move off the towels into the general space and when the music stops each child must be on a towel. Controlled movements are required and encouraged. The use of imagery can also be added as needed. For example, the towels are described as *islands*, and the general space is described as *water*. The children can also be told that as they play the game *the tide* slowly comes in, making the area on the islands smaller. When the music starts, all children must *swim slowly* in the water (i.e., general area) and when the music stops, they must climb onto an island. Every time music stops, one towel is folded or removed, reducing the size of the islands. An island can hold as many children as is safe practice. These instructions encourage children to share personal space appropriately, to help others, and to practice self-control.

The first principle of DAGs indicates that each child has the opportunity to choose to participate at his or her ability level. Children who feel more confident in their ability to secure a place on an island may be observed moving further away from the islands. Conversely, children who feel less secure may stay close to the islands. Both options are acceptable. In addition, each child chooses how to move when the music plays. For example, one child might skip, another might crawl slowly, while another may pretend to float. All movements displaying self-control are allowed.

The second principle of DAGs requires opportunities to play, and practice skills increase as the game proceeds. The games offer children endless opportunities to participate because elimination of a player is not an option (i.e., the third principal). When the possibility of elimination is removed, children become active members of the group and exhibit greater cooperation, cohesion, and problem solving.

The fourth principle of DAGs indicates that children who vary in ability can interact positively with each other. In *Islands*, the game has been designed so that more than one child can safely be on an island. By knowing the individual child's and group's needs, school personnel can determine how many children can comfortably share one island. The children quickly learn that the islands must include more than one person for everyone to be out of the water. Children will invite others onto an island, create different ways to include children, and become enthused over trying to accomplish this goal as fewer islands become available. The game ends when all children are on a predetermined number of islands.

DAGs are usually as novel to children as they are to the adults who are presenting them. DAGs such as *Islands* become rewarding and successful learning experiences when children's needs are carefully considered. When first playing this game, children with ADHD may exhibit poor self-control and prosocial skills. This can be observed when some children are unable to safely share the islands with others. If this occurs, one may choose to increase the number of islands used at the beginning of the game. A ratio of two children per island helps orient the children to the game. As children become familiar with the rules and process of the game, their ability to participate in the game will flourish. For many children with ADHD, this is unlike any other experience they have had with peers, and it takes time for them to familiarize themselves with these new feelings and behaviors.

To further illustrate the utility of group play interventions, a brief overview of an ADHD Child Group Training Program that utilizes DAGs, in part, to train children with ADHD is provided next. The described children's group training program is part of the Child Attention Deficit/Hyperactivity Disorder Multimodal Program (CAMP; Reddy, 2000). CAMP is an empirically supported intervention that treats the social and behavioral needs of young children diagnosed with ADHD. CAMP includes children group training, parent group training, and parent and teacher behavioral consultation services (Reddy et al., 2005). For a detailed description of group play interventions, see Reddy (in press).

ADHD CHILD GROUP TRAINING PROGRAM

THEORETICAL BASIS AND OBJECTIVES

As mentioned, the ADHD child group training program is part of Child Attention Deficit/Hyperactivity Disorder Multimodal Program (CAMP; Reddy, 2000). The children's group training program is designed to promote three areas: 1) social skills, 2) self-control, and 3) anger and stress management. The children's program is based, in part, on the seminal work of Bandura's (1973) social learning theory and behavior-deficit model, Goldstein's (1988) Skill Streaming approach, and Torbert's (1994) cooperative games. Skill development is fostered through the teaching of skill sequences, a set of behavioral procedures designed to enhance social competence in children (McGinnis &

Goldstein, 1997; Reddy & Goldstein, 2001; Reddy, in press). Each skill is broken down into its behavioral steps, which are taught through didactic instruction, symbolic and in vivo modeling, role-playing, behavioral rehearsal, and coaching by adults in a group context. Collectively the behavioral steps illustrate the implementation of the skill. For example, the skill "follow directions" would consist of the following behavioral steps: 1) look at who is asking you to follow directions, 2) stop what you are doing and listen to what is said, 3) say the directions out loud, and 4) do it, follow what was asked of you.

Skill sequences are taught and reinforced through 1) *modeling*—adult therapists demonstrate behaviors and skills, 2) *role-playing*—guided opportunities to practice and rehearse appropriate interpersonal behaviors, and 3) *performance feedback*—children are frequently praised and provided feedback on how well they model the therapists' skills and behavior. A number of skill transfer and maintenance-enhancing procedures are used such as 1) *overlearning*—correctly rehearsing and practicing skills learned over time, 2) *identical elements*—children are trained in real-world contexts (e.g., schools, playground, peer groups) with children and adults they interact with on a daily basis, and 3) *mediated generalization*—teaching children a series of self-regulation skills such as self-evaluation, self-reinforcement, and self-instruction. In addition, skill acquisition is also taught and reinforced through the implementation of group DAGs.

GROUP SESSIONS

Children's training is run for approximately 90 minutes per session, once per week for 10 training sessions. Group sessions can be shortened (e.g., 60 or 30 minutes) by reducing the number of skill sequences and DAGs to fit any class or group need. A carpeted room that accommodates about 15 people is used. Approximately 8 to 10 children are in each group. For highly impulsive children, one adult for every two children is recommended.

CURRICULUM

Numerous skill sequences and DAGs are included to promote social skills, impulse control, and anger/stress management (see Reddy, in press). Examples of skill sequences taught include follow directions, share with others, help others, ask for help, use self-control, and manage stress and anger. Examples of DAGs are outlined.

BEHAVIOR MANAGEMENT APPROACH

A token economy system is used to monitor and reinforce positive behaviors during each training session. The children are given rewards for three goals: 1) follow directions, 2) use my words to express my thoughts and feelings, and 3) keep my hands, feet, and mouth to myself. Children are given one sticker/point for each of the three goals during each group session. A group sticker (point) chart is displayed and reviewed with the group for progress monitoring. At the end of each group, each child is asked to evaluate, with adult assistance, how well he or she achieved each goal during the session. Next, a star (point) for each goal the child attained is then placed by the child's name on the group sticker chart. The child then selects stickers (i.e., that correspond with the number of goals attained) and places them in his or her sticker book at the end of each session.

Time-out is used as a positive self-control technique in the group. Children are instructed that taking a time-out is not a punishment, but rather a positive technique for regaining self-control. In this program, children are not placed in time-out for a set period of time (e.g., 60 seconds times the child's age). Instead, children are to remain in time-out until they demonstrate positive control over their hands, feet, and mouth. For example, some children will be in time-out for 45 to 60 seconds, while others may remain in time-out for 2 to 3 minutes. Children are verbally praised for self-initiating time-out ("break time") and for compliance with adult direction to take time-out. Time-out is modeled by adult facilitators. Children are encouraged to monitor their behavior to self-initiate time-out. The procedure to take a time-out includes 1) raise your hand, 2) wait to be called on, 3) request a time-out, and 4) take the "time-out pass" to the time-out chair. A time-out pass is used to nonverbally communicate to others that the child is taking a break and needs to be left alone. After a few minutes (i.e., 1 or 2 minutes) in time-out, an adult facilitator approaches the child, validates him or her for taking a time-out, and then helps the child assess whether he or she is ready to return to the group.

Three levels of time-out are used. *Level one time-out* is designated by a specific chair placed on the far side of the group room. Level one time-out distances the child from being directly involved in the group's activity. *Level two time-out* is a chair located directly outside of the group room. Level two time-out further distances the child from the group activity and decreases the level of visual and auditory stimulation for the child. *Level three time-out* is a chair in a separate room. Level three time-out eliminates the visual and auditory stimulation of the group activity. A child is accompanied by a therapist when level two or three time-out is implemented. Children in level two or three time-out are required to return to the group activity gradually by spending a few minutes in each of the successively lower levels of time-out (e.g., the child in level two time-out must go to level one time-out before returning to the group activity).

At the beginning of each session the group rules (e.g., raise hand before talking) and the group structure (e.g., review of group goals, sticker awards, use of time-out or bathroom passes) are reviewed. The behavioral steps for each skill are written on an easel placed in front of the group/class. Each step is read out loud by a child or an adult and is then explained and discussed. Each skill sequence is role-played in three ways: 1) modeled by two therapists, 2) modeled by a therapist and child, and 3) modeled by two children who are assisted by an adult facilitator. Skills taught are role-played in three contexts: the home, school, and peer group. During role-plays, children are asked to evaluate whether the role-player demonstrated each skill step correctly.

Training

This program can be implemented by teachers, paraprofessionals, and/or professionals with appropriate supervision. Training focuses on the 1) behavioral, social, and neurocognitive features of ADHD; 2) structure of the group; 3) behavioral techniques to promote positive behavior and group cooperation; 4) implementation of skill sequences and DAGs; 5) time-out procedures; 6) token economy system; and 7) team building among the group therapists. It is recommended that all techniques and group sessions be discussed, modeled, and role-played (i.e., 40 minutes) prior to each session. In addition, it is helpful to conduct post-group process sessions (i.e., 30 minutes) to discuss the implementation process and the children's performance during the session.

EXAMPLE 1: GROUP PLAY INTERVENTION—*ALL MIXED UP*

Overview *All Mixed Up* is a game that involves learning a set of novel rules to respond to visual cues. Group play intervention skills taught include 1) follow directions, 2) impulse control (self-control), and 3) pay attention. Prerequisite skills include the ability to distinguish between playing cards, to attend and demonstrate self-control, and to follow simple verbal instructions.

Required Materials   Use several cards from an oversized playing deck of cards. An open space that is conducive to children moving around freely and in which they are able to easily see the playing cards when they are displayed in the front of the room.

Room Setup   Children should be sitting on the floor or in chairs facing the front of the room.

Game Synopsis   Children are taught behavioral rules corresponding to playing cards. As specific playing cards are displayed, children are to follow the associated rules.

STEPS FOR IMPLEMENTING *ALL MIXED UP*

1. Children are seated so that they have space around them to move freely in place. They are told that they are going to play a game that involves paying attention and following directions called *All Mixed Up.*
2. Children are told that for this game they will be taught rules instructing them to perform various behaviors corresponding to specific playing cards. Each card corresponds to a specific behavior. When a card is displayed, they are to quietly perform the corresponding behavior.
3. The rules corresponding to each card are provided, and a group facilitator should show the children how the game works, for example, 10-Put Hands on Head, J- Jumping Jack, Q- Touch your Feet, K-Sit Down, A-Turn Around. (The number of cards should be adjusted based on the childrens' abilities.)
4. Children are told to stand up in their spot, and one card is held up at a time for practice. Coaching is provided to correct mistakes and ensure proper acquisition of the information. This should be done until the majority of the children can recall and perform the behaviors corresponding to each card.
5. Children are told that the game will now formally begin. Once the game begins, if a child makes a mistake, they are to sit down and

become a judge, assisting group facilitators in identifying other group members that have made errors.

6. Group facilitators should start with a single card, then present two cards then three cards, and so on, simultaneously. Initially, cards should be held up until the commands are completed; however, as the game continues therapists should hold cards up for a shorter and shorter duration.
7. The round ends when only one child is left standing and performing the behaviors. This child is designated as the winner of the round.
8. Steps 3 through 7 are repeated for several rounds, until children have mastered the skills or until time allocated for the game has elapsed.
9. Group process—tell the children that the game is now over. Have them sit on their chairs or on the floor facing the front of the room, and tell them it is time to discuss the game.

GROUP PROCESS QUESTIONS

1. Ask the children what they needed to do to play the game. Emphasize the importance of following directions, paying attention, and learning to respond to nonverbal cues.
2. Ask the children what they needed to do when a card was displayed. Allow children to provide some specific examples of behaviors corresponding to playing cards.
3. Ask the children how they felt when they knew what to do in response to seeing a certain playing card.
4. Ask the children how they felt when they did not know what do in response to seeing a certain playing card.
5. Ask the children how they felt when they made a mistake.
6. Ask the children how they felt when they saw their peers make a mistake.

As mentioned, *Islands* is another example of a captivating group play intervention that fosters life skills such as following directions, impulse control, helping others, asking for help, sharing/respecting the personal space of others, taking turns, and controlling one's hands and feet. For a step-by-step description of *Islands* and other DAGs, see Reddy (in press).

EXAMPLE 2: GROUP PLAY INTERVENTION—*BEAN BAG TOSS*

Overview   Bean Bag Toss is a game that involves simulating a frustrating situation and encourages the use of an anger management technique to make oneself feel better.

Group play intervention skills taught include anger management, self-control, and following directions. Prerequisite skills include knowledge of various anger management techniques (e.g., pillow squeeze, turtle, controlled breathing, coloring, etc.) and the ability to utilize the techniques. Skill sequences should be used to demonstrate and practice various anger management techniques before playing this game.

Required Materials   Bean bag, small bucket or container, and props that can be used for anger management strategies (books, crayons, stuffed animals, pillows, etc.).

Room Setup   Children should be sitting in two single-file lines facing each other. A small bucket or container should be placed on the floor in the middle of the two lines. Props for anger management strategies should be placed behind each of the lines so that children can easily obtain them.

Game Synopsis   Children have to complete the difficult task of throwing a bean bag in a small bucket or container from a distance. When a child misses the task, they must perform an effective anger management strategy.

Steps for Implementing *Bean Bag Toss*

1. *Bean Bag Toss* should be introduced to children as an exciting game that involves throwing a bean bag into a container. If they get it in, a point is awarded. If they miss, they will have to perform an effective anger management technique to help them feel better.
2. Several anger management techniques are reviewed.
3. The first child in one of the lines attempts to throw the bean bag into the container. If the child makes it in, they receive two points and that child goes to the end of their line. If they miss, they must decide on an anger management strategy that has not already been used and perform it before proceeding to the end of their line. If

they are successful in coming up with a unique strategy, they receive one point.

4. The first child in the second line proceeds to go and follows Step 3. This alternation between the lines continues until all of the children have had the opportunity to observe/use a variety of anger management techniques.
5. Group process—tell the children that the game is now over. Have them sit, and tell them it is time to discuss the game.

GROUP PROCESS QUESTIONS

1. Ask the children what they needed to do to play the game. Emphasize the importance of appropriately coming up with and utilizing effective anger management strategies, following directions, and staying in control.
2. Ask the children how they felt when they got the bean bag into the container.
3. Ask the children how they felt when they missed the container.
4. Ask the children how they felt when they had to come up with an anger management strategy.
5. Ask the children how they felt after using the anger management strategy.

CONCLUSION

Children with ADHD exhibit unique social, behavioral, and cognitive strengths and difficulties that require specially tailored interventions. Group play interventions or DAGs are potent therapeutic experiences that can enhance learning, engagement, and motivation for this population. DAGs can be easily designed for classroom and playground settings. Group training curriculums that incorporate DAGs with behavioral skill training provide an effective, flexible, and rewarding learning experience for children with ADHD in schools.

REFERENCES

Achenbach, T. M., & Edelbrock, C. (1991). *Manual for the Child Behavior Checklist/4-18 and Revised 1991 Child Behavior Profile*. Burlington, VT: University of Vermont Department of Psychiatry.

Association for Play Therapy. (2001, June). Play therapy. *Association for Play Therapy Newsletter, 20*, 20.

Baggerly, J., & Parker, M. (2005). Child-centered group play therapy with African American boys at the elementary school level. *Journal of Counseling and Development, 83*(4), 387–396.

Bandura, A. (1973). *Aggression: A social learning analysis.* Englewood Cliffs, NJ: Prentice-Hall.

Barkley, R. (2005). *Attention-deficit hyperactivity disorder* (3rd ed.) New York: Guilford Press.

Barkley, R. A. (1998). *Attention-deficit hyperactivity disorder: A handbook for diagnosis and treatment.* New York: Guilford Press.

Bay-Hinitz, A. K., & Wilson, G. R. (2005). A cooperative games intervention for aggressive preschool children. In L. A. Reddy, T. M. Files-Hall, & C. E. Schaefer (Eds.), *Empirically based play interventions for children* (pp. 215–239). Washington, DC: American Psychological Association.

Bratton, S., Ray, D., Rhine, T., & Jones, L. (2005). The efficacy of play therapy with children: A meta-analytic review of treatment outcomes. *Professional Psychology: Research and Practice, 36*(4), 376–390.

Bunker, L. K. (1991). The role of play and motor skill development in building children's self-confidence and self-esteem. Special issue: Sport and physical education. *Elementary School Journal, 91,* 467–471.

Castellanos, F. X., Lee, P. P., Sharp, W., Jeffries, N. O., Greenstein, D. K., Clasen, L. S., et al. (2002). Developmental trajectories of brain volume abnormalities in children and adolescents with attention-deficit/hyperactivity disorder. *Journal of the American Medical Association, 288,* 1740–1748.

Chafouleas, S. M., McDougal, J. L., Riley-Tillman, T. C., Panahon, C. J., & Hilt, A. M. (2005). What do Daily Behavior Report Cards (DBRCs) measure? An initial comparison of DBRCs with direct observation for off-task behavior. *Psychology in the Schools, 42,* 669–676.

Clark, C., Prior, M., & Kinsella, G. (2002). The relationship between executive function abilities, adaptive behaviour, and academic achievement in children with externalizing behaviour problems. *Journal of Child Psychology and Psychiatry, 43,* 785–796.

Douglas, V. I. (1980). Higher mental processes in hyperactive children: Implications for training. In R. Knights & D. Bakker (Eds.), *Treatment of hyperactive and learning disordered children* (pp. 65–92). Baltimore, MD: University Park Press.

DuPaul, G. J., & Eckert, T. L. (1997). The effects of school-based interventions for attention deficit hyperactivity disorder: A meta-analysis. *School Psychology Review, 26*(1), 5–27.

DuPaul, G. J., & Stoner, G. (2003). *ADHD in the schools: Assessment and intervention strategies.* New York: Guilford Press.

Ferland, F. (1997). *Play, children with physical disabilities, and occupational therapy.* Ottawa, Ontario, Canada: University of Ottawa Press.

Files-Hall, T., & Reddy, L. A. (2005). Present status and future directions for empirically based play interventions for children. In L. A. Reddy, T. M.

Files-Hall, & C. E. Schaefer (Eds.), *Empirically based play interventions for children* (pp. 267–279). Washington, DC: American Psychological Association.

Garaigordobil, M., & Echbarria, A. (1995). Assessment of peer-helping program on children's development. *Journal of Research in Childhood Education, 10*, 63–70.

Goldstein, A. P. (1988). *The prepare curriculum: Teaching prosocial competencies.* Champaign, IL: Research Press.

Hand, L. (1986). *Comparison of selected developmentally oriented low organized games and traditional games on the behavior of students with emotional disturbance.* Unpublished master's thesis, Temple University, Philadelphia, PA.

Hoag, M. J., & Burlingame, G. M. (1997). Evaluating the effectiveness of child and adolescent group treatment: A meta-analytic review. *Journal of Clinical Child Psychology, 26*(3), 234–246.

Kendall, P. C. (2000). *Child and adolescent therapy: Cognitive-behavioral procedures.* New York: Guilford Press.

Kendall, P. C., & Braswell, L. (1985). Attention-deficit hyperactivity disorder. In P. C. Kendall (Ed.), *Child and adolescent therapy: Cognitive-behavioral procedures* (pp. 98–128). New York: Guilford Press.

Landreth, G. L. (2002). *The art of the relationship* (2nd ed.). New York: Brunner-Routledge.

LeBlanc, M., & Ritchie, M. (1999). Predictors of play therapy outcomes. *International Journal of Play Therapy, 8*(2), 19–34.

Lebo, D. (1953). The present status of research on nondirective play therapy. *Journal of Consulting Psychology, 17*, 177–183.

McGinnis, E., & Goldstein, A. P. (1997). *Skillstreaming the elementary school child: New strategies and perspectives for teaching prosocial skills* (Rev. ed.). Champaign, IL: Research Press.

Orlick, T. (1988). Enhancing cooperative skills in games and life. In F. L. Smoll, R. Magill, & M. Ash (Eds.), *Children in sport* (pp. 149–159). Champaign, IL: Human Kinetics.

Parten, M. B. (1932). Social participation among preschool children. *Journal of Abnormal and Social Psychology, 27*, 243–269.

Pedro-Carroll, J. L., & Jones, S. H. (2005). A preventive play intervention to foster children's resilience in the aftermath of divorce. In L. A. Reddy, T. M. Files-Hall, & C. E. Schaefer (Eds.), *Empirically based play interventions for children* (pp. 51–75). Washington, DC: American Psychological Association.

Pelham, W. E., Fabiano, G. A., & Massetti, G. M. (2005). Evidence-based assessment of attention-deficit/hyperactivity disorder in children and adolescents. *Journal of Clinical Child and Adolescent Psychology, 34*, 449–476.

Pfiffner, L. J., & O'Leary, S. G. (1993). School-based psychological treatments. In J. L. Matson (Ed.), *Handbook of hyperactivity in children* (pp. 234–255). Boston: Allyn and Bacon.

Phillips, R. (1985). Whistling in the dark? A review of play therapy research. *Psychotherapy, 22*, 752–760.

Ray, D., Bratton, S., Rhine, T., & Jones, L. (2001). The effectiveness of play therapy: Responding to the critics. *International Journal of Play Therapy, 10*(1), 85–108.

Ray, D., Bratton, S., Rhine, T., & Jones, L. (2005). The efficacy; of play therapy with children: A meta-analytic review. *Professional Psychology: Research and Practice, 36*(4), 376–390.

Reade, S., Hunter, H., & McMillan, I. (1999). Just playing . . . Is it time wasted? *The British Journal of Occupational Therapy, 62,* 157–162.

Reddy, L. A. (2000). *Early childhood ADHD child training program.* Piscataway, NJ: Rutgers University.

Reddy, L. A. (in press). *Group play interventions for children: Strategies for teaching prosocial skills.* Washington, DC: American Psychological Association.

Reddy, L. A. (in press). Group play interventions for children as an evidence-based practice. *International Journal of Play Therapy.*

Reddy, L. A., & De Thomas, C. (2006). Assessment of ADHD children and adolescents. In S. R. Smith & L. Handler (Eds.), *The clinical assessment of children and adolescents: A practitioner's guide* (pp. 367–387). Mahwah, NJ: Lawrence Erlbaum.

Reddy, L. A., Files-Hall, T. M., & Schaefer, C. E. (2005). *Empirically based play interventions for children.* Washington, DC: American Psychological Association.

Reddy, L. A., & Goldstein, A. P. (2001). Aggressive replacement training: A multimodal intervention for aggressive children. In S. I. Pfeiffer & L. A. Reddy (Eds.), *Innovative mental health prevention programs for children.* New York: Haworth Press.

Reddy, L. A., & Hale, J. (2007). Inattentiveness. In A. R. Eisen (Ed.), *Treating childhood behavioral and emotional problems: A step-by-step evidence-based approach* (pp. 156–211). New York: Guilford Press.

Reddy, L. A., Spencer, P., Hall, T. M., & Rubel, E. (2001). Use of developmentally appropriate games in a child group training program for young children with attention-deficit/hyperactivity disorder. In A. A. Drewes, L. J. Carey, & C. E. Schaefer (Eds.), *School-based play therapy* (pp. 256–274). New York: John Wiley & Sons.

Reddy, L. A., Springer, C., Hall, T. M., Benisz, E., Braunstein, D., Hauch, Y., & Atamanoff, T. (2005). Childhood ADHD multimodal program: An empirically-supported intervention for young children with ADHD. In L. A. Reddy, T. M. Files-Hall, & C. E. Schaefer (Eds.), *Empirically based play interventions for children* (pp. 145–167). Washington, DC: American Psychological Association.

Reed, M., Black, T., & Eastman, J. (1978). A new look at perceptual-motor therapy. *Academic Therapy, 14,* 55–65.

Rennie, R. L. (2000). A comparison study of the effectiveness of individual and group play therapy in treating kindergarten children with adjustment problems (Dissertation). International Section A: Humanities and Social Sciences, 63(9-A).

Rogers, S. J. (2005). Play interventions for young children with autism spectrum disorders. In L. A. Reddy, T. M. Files-Hall, & C. E. Schaefer (Eds.), *Empirically based play interventions for children* (pp. 215–239). Washington, DC: American Psychological Association.

Rowland, A. S., Leswesne, C. A., & Abramowitz, A. J. (2002). The epidemiology of attention-deficit/hyperactivity disorder (ADHD): A public health view. *Mental Retardation and Developmental Disabilities Research Review, 8,* 162–170.

Schneider, L. B. (1989). *The effect of selected low organized games on the self-esteem of kindergartners.* Unpublished manuscript. Temple University, Leonard Gordon Institute for Human Development through Play, Philadelphia.

Shen, Y. J. (2002). Short-term group play therapy with Chinese earthquake victims: Effects of anxiety, depression, and adjustment. *International Journal of Play Therapy, 11*(1), 43–63.

Springer, C., & Reddy, L. A. (in press). Effect of treatment adherence in a multimodal program for ADHD children: A preliminary investigation. *Child and Adolescent Mental Health.*

Szatmari, P., Offord, D. R., & Boyle, M. H. (1989). Ontario Child Health Study: Prevalence of attention deficit disorder with hyperactivity. *Journal of Child Psychology and Psychiatry, 30,* 219–230.

Torbert, M. (1994). *Follow me: A handbook of movement activities for children.* New York: Prentice Hall.

Torbert, M., & Schneider, L. (1993). *Follow me, too.* Menlo Park, CA: Addison-Wesley.

PART VI

SPECIAL POPULATIONS AND SPECIAL ISSUES

CHAPTER 16

Play Therapy for Children of Alcoholics

LAURA JACOBUS-KANTOR and
JAMES G. EMSHOFF

INTRODUCTION

It is estimated that over 17 million American adults meet the diagnostic criteria for alcohol abuse or dependence (Substance Abuse and Mental Health Services Administration, 2008). While the exact number of children of alcoholics in the general population is unknown, estimates suggest that approximately one in four children younger than 18 years old are exposed to alcohol abuse or dependence within their families (Grant, 2000). Our understanding of the effects of parental alcoholism on children continues to grow. Originally, many within the substance abuse field assumed that young children were unaware of parental alcohol abuse and were relatively unaffected by its presence (Anderson, 1987). However, more recent work within the field has acknowledged that alcoholism is a disease that affects the entire family system. Although recent work has highlighted the fact that there are many individual differences in the degree to which parental alcoholism affects children, it is also clear that there are many common vulnerabilities shared by these children.

Although there is wide variation in outcomes exhibited by children of alcoholics (COAs) (Carle & Chassin, 2004; Steinglass, 1979, 1981); alcoholic families tend to display a number of characteristics and processes that are associated with negative child outcomes (Keller, Cummings, Davies, & Mitchell, 2008). Alcoholic families have been shown to exhibit poor organization and low levels of cohesion (Bijttebier

333

& Goethals, 2006), and alcoholic parents and their spouses tend to display lower levels of sensitivity and have lower positive engagement with their children compared with their nonalcoholic counterparts (Eiden, Leonard, Hoyle, & Chavez, 2004). Despite a tendency for alcoholic parents to deal with their children in a rigid manner, children of alcoholic parents tend to receive less discipline (King & Chassin, 2004) and are subject to lower levels of parental monitoring (Chassin, Pillow, Curran, Brooke, & Barrera, 1993) than other children.

The above family characteristics and the concept of family systems have implications for the characteristics and behaviors exhibited by COAs. Children are often considered the most vulnerable of the family members to the adverse effects of familial alcoholism (National Institute on Alcohol Abuse and Alcoholism, 1981). Children of alcoholics have also been shown to be at an increased risk for a wide range of behavioral and emotional problems, including addiction to alcohol and other drugs, depression, low self-esteem, and anxiety (Bijttebier & Goethals, 2006; Chassin, Pitts, DeLucia, & Todd, 1999; Graber, 2004; Schuckit, 2000; West & Printz, 1987).

Although this brief review of the literature has suggested that COAs are at an increased risk for a wide variety of social, emotional, and behavioral difficulties, it is important to note that these findings cannot be generalized to individual children. Most experts agree that COAs are a heterogeneous population, and that substantial variation in outcomes is possible. Thus, counselors working with COAs must remain cognizant of the fact that knowing that a child can be labeled as a "COA" offers relatively little information about that particular child's adjustment or development. Instead, counselors must investigate and consider specific experiences and risk factors that may contribute to a COAs likelihood of experiencing a significant disturbance. Knowing that a child has experienced alcoholism within his or her family should not be used to label a child as "deviant" or even "potentially deviant." Instead, counselors should utilize this information in a responsible manner and use this classification as a challenge to gather more specific information regarding a particular child's experiences.

THE IMPORTANCE OF PLAY FOR COAs

Therapists have long understood the importance of play for the developmental growth of all children. Because of the many responsibilities and stresses that are associated with parental alcoholism, COAs are likely to be involved in a wide variety of experiences that may limit the amount and quality of play that they engage in. Play therapy can provide counselors with a set of tools that allows them to work with children in a manner that directly addresses many of the issues that these children face.

LACK OF POSITIVE ROLE MODELS

A significant amount of research suggests that alcoholic parents tend to demonstrate less competent parenting skills than their nonalcoholic counterparts. They tend to display lower levels of warmth and sensitivity toward their children than do other parents (Eiden, Edwards, & Leonard, 2007), and children of alcoholics tend to receive less monitoring and less discipline than other children (Chassin et al., 1993; King & Chassin, 2004). In addition, families in which one spouse is an alcoholic tend to demonstrate higher rates of interparental conflict and violence than other families (Quigley & Leonard, 2000). As a result of these experiences, COAs are likely to have experienced fewer adult role models for fun and play than have other children. Therapists using play therapy can serve as excellent adult role-models for COAs searching for healthy modes of play.

PARENTIFICATION

Although there are a wide variety of possible outcomes for children who grow up or live with an alcoholic parent, there are several symptom patterns that are frequently encountered among these children. One common symptom that is often witnessed among COAs is parentification. *Parentification,* or "role reversal," refers to the process by which children assume adult responsibilities within the family structure, such as taking responsibility for household chores, meal preparation, and caretaking of younger siblings. Because of these added responsibilities, COAs often seem older than they really are. While to the outside world, these children may appear to be successful and well-adjusted, they often suffer as a result of the extraordinary responsibilities that they assume within the family structure.

Alcoholic parents may be frequently unable to care for either themselves or others, leaving many COAs to assume these responsibilities themselves. While it is possible that taking on these added responsibilities may provide children with a temporary sense of control in an otherwise chaotic situation (Burnett, Jones, Bliwise, & Ross, 2006), they may leave children with fewer opportunities to engage in age-appropriate activities and may harm their ability to learn and practice socially appropriate behavior (Burton, 2007). Indeed, while these children may appear to the outside world to be successful high-achievers who are often praised for their maturity, parentification has been linked to a variety of negative outcomes. Research has suggested that parentified children tend to display higher levels of anxiety and depression than other children (Castro, Jones, & Mirsalimi, 2004; Mayseless, Bartholomew, Henderson, & Trinke, 2004). In addition, long-term parentification is associated with a variety of negative outcomes in adulthood, including narcissism (Jones & Wells, 1996), feelings of shame (Wells & Jones, 2000), and disturbed relationships with their own children (Jurkovic, 1998; Macfie, McElwain, Houts, & Cox, 2005).

Given the added responsibilities that these children face, play therapy can offer parentified children an opportunity to interact in an environment in which they can behave in an age-appropriate manner. Unlike other traditional forms of therapy, play therapy can provide children with a therapeutic outlet that can allow COAs to work through their problems in a safe, healthy environment while providing them with an opportunity to engage in the play and fun that they have likely been missing.

PERFECTIONISM AS A SYMPTOM

Another symptom that is frequently encountered among COAs is perfectionism. Perfectionist children learn very early that the easiest way to win approval within and outside the family structure is to demonstrate excellence in all areas of his or her life. Through this perfection, these children demonstrate to the world that their family is "OK."

This perfectionism comes with a heavy price. Perfectionist children are often wary of risk-taking and demonstrate elevated levels of depression and anxiety (Hewitt et al., 2002). Developmental research has consistently demonstrated that children need to be able to take risks and make mistakes if they are to learn normal, healthy coping strategies (Burns, 1989; Smith, 1990). Children who are too afraid or unwilling to take these risks are at risk of becoming rigid, unyielding adults.

Play therapy can help these children by offering them a safe environment in which *risks* can be explored with minimally adverse consequences. Because there are no *right* or *wrong* ways to play, counselors can help perfectionistic COAs to explore their environment in a setting that does not threaten their need for perfectionism.

Hammond-Newman (1994) suggests that these children often enter play therapy uneasy and uptight, choosing games that allow them to retain a sense of control over their environment. Through play therapy, these children can begin to give up some of this control and expose the pain and hurt that underlies their mask.

EXTERNALIZING SYMPTOMS

Research has also demonstrated that COAs are at high risk for a number of externalizing behaviors (Hussong et al., 2007; Sher, 1991; Windle, 1990). Although relatively little longitudinal research has examined the pathways by which COAs acquire these symptoms, there is considerable evidence documenting that externalizing behaviors are associated with a variety of negative outcomes, including future substance abuse. Hussong and colleagues (1997) have documented that externalizing behaviors may serve as a mediator in the transmission of heavy alcohol use from parent to child. Thus, therapy strategies that serve to reduce levels of aggression and antisocial behaviors among COAs may be able to influence the transmission of this disease between generations.

Wegscheider (1981) notes that although the majority of these children appear angry and defiant, they are actually using these behaviors to mask the more difficult emotions of rejection and inadequacy. Play therapy can prove to be an extremely beneficial tool for children who have demonstrated aggressive and delinquent behaviors. Play therapists can help these children to improve their self-image by offering them the positive attention and approval that they so desperately seek. Play therapy can also introduce these children to positive, healthy ways of coping with the stresses of living in an addicted household that can serve to replace the children's negative behaviors. Hammond-Newman (1994) suggests that these children may enter play therapy unwillingly and may demonstrate aggressive and destructive play strategies. However, through play therapy, these children can come to share the hurt and pain that is masked by these acting out behaviors.

INTERNALIZING SYMPTOMS

Another class of symptoms that are commonly witnessed among COAs are internalizing disorders. There is substantial evidence that COAs exhibit higher levels of internalizing behaviors than other children and that these symptoms may present in children as young as 18 months old (Edwards, Leonard, & Eiden, 2001). Older COAs have also been shown to have significantly higher levels of depression (Graber, 2004) and higher rates of anxiety (West & Printz, 1987). Children of alcoholics also tend to demonstrate lower levels of self-esteem than other children (Bijttebier & Goethals, 2006; Sher, 1991; West & Prinz, 1987). These children sometimes withdraw from both family and peer interactions. This withdrawal is somewhat functional for these children, in that they can remove themselves from many of the negative effects associated with parental alcoholism.

Many COAs learn to deny and minimize the effects of parental alcoholism on their lives. Because of this, some COAs have difficulty verbally expressing their feelings (Ficaro, 1999). While these children may enter therapy with difficulties trusting and sharing, Hammond-Newman (1994) suggests that play therapists can help these children by engaging in parallel play techniques. Slowly, these children can learn to trust their therapist and to reveal their inner pain.

SOCIABILITY AND SOCIAL SKILLS

Although COAs are often described in the literature as being isolated from their peer groups, some research suggests that these children may demonstrate similar levels of extraversion as their peers (Carle & Chassin, 2004; Sher, 1987). But while COAs may exhibit similar levels of sociability compared to other children, the quality of these interactions may be lower, with COAs engaged in fewer positive interactions than their non-COA counterparts (Carle & Chassen, 2004). Because these children are likely to demonstrate significant social skill deficits as a result of their association with other, delinquent peers, antisocial COAs children can often benefit from inclusion in a group play therapy program. Group play therapy techniques that allow these children to engage in supervised interactions with other children may prove beneficial to COAs and provide them with much needed opportunities to develop and practice healthy, competent social skills.

PLAY THERAPY: HOW IT CAN HELP

Play therapy provides counselors with an opportunity to assist COAs in a developmentally appropriate manner. The specific content of the play therapy session will vary considerably according to the needs of the individual child. Therapy should be guided by a desire to help COAs reduce their denial, abandon unhealthy coping roles, and release emotions and feelings related to their predicament (Hammond-Newman, 1994). An examination of how play therapy can accomplish these goals follows.

Whatever form of play therapy is utilized, counselors should remain sensitive to feelings of powerlessness experienced by COAs and utilize play therapy techniques that emphasize choice and foster a sense of empowerment among this population (Oliver-Diaz, 1998). Ficaro (1999) suggests that one way to allow children to retain a sense of control over the process is for practitioners to assure them that they are in control of the play therapy process and that they can terminate the sessions after a few meetings if they desire.

ESTABLISHING TRUST

An important goal of play therapy techniques should be to establish a sense of trust between the counselor and the client and to assist COAs in increasing feelings of trust in other settings. Because they have often experienced unreliable, inconsistent parenting techniques, COAs are likely to be distrustful of many individuals, especially adults. Play therapy offers practitioners an opportunity to connect to COAs in a manner that can serve as a foundation for trust building. Play therapy techniques that help children to make decisions on their own and practice problem-solving techniques can help COAs to trust in their own ability to make decisions (Giordano, Landreth, & Jones, 2005). In addition, therapists can utilize a number of exercises that foster trusting relationships (Landreth, 1991; O'Rourke,1990).

WORKING WITH CHILDREN'S AMBIVALENCE ABOUT DISCUSSING THEIR PARENTS' BEHAVIOR

Another important goal of play therapy should be to break through the denial and shame that many COAs experience as a result of their parents substance abuse problems. Group play therapy can often prove beneficial in this process. Group play therapy can facilitate the process of these children to understand that they are not alone in their dilemma and that they are not responsible for their parents inconsistent and, perhaps, abusive behaviors (Cable, Noel, & Swanson, 1986). Play therapists can also facilitate this process by displaying an understanding of the child's circumstances and reassurance that what the child is experiencing is a normal reaction to their parents' behaviors.

Allowing Children to Work Through Their Feelings in a Creative Fashion

Because many COAs learn to minimize and deny their feelings, they may have difficulty expressing themselves in traditional, talk-based therapy techniques (Ficaro, 1999). Play therapy offers these children an opportunity to express their feelings and emotions in a creative, emotional fashion that may prove more comfortable for them. Play therapy may additionally benefit children who appear to be rigid and perfectionistic. By allowing these children to explore their worlds in a setting in which the pressure to "succeed" has been removed, counselors may be able to help them learn to increase their flexibility and spontaneity.

Offering Children Education and Information Regarding Alcohol Abuse

Another goal of play therapy for COAs should be to help these children learn about alcohol-related issues in a developmentally appropriate manner. Although the amount and type of information that a child is able to handle will vary depending on a child's developmental level and maturity, counselors can use play therapy techniques in order to address some of these important issues with their clients. Therapists can provide children with information that helps to explain how alcohol affects individuals so that they are better able to understand behaviors exhibited by an alcoholic parent. In addition, therapists can construct and utilize games and techniques that teach and allow children to practice skills for living with an alcoholic parent. One situation that many COAs experience is driving in the car with an intoxicated parent. Practitioners can utilize play therapy techniques in order to address the dangers associated with driving under the influence and help children understand and practice skills that can help them avoid this situation.

Given estimates that suggest the risk of alcohol abuse among close relatives of alcoholics is between three to four times greater than that of the general population (Schuckit, 2000), another goal of play therapy should be to help COAs to understand their risk status in an age-appropriate fashion. And while it is important for therapists to stress that having an alcoholic parent does not ensure that a child will become alcoholic themselves, simply providing COAs with information regarding their risk status may prevent future alcohol problems. Some research suggests that children who are aware of their risk status drink significantly less (in both quantity and frequency) than do COAs who are unaware of this information (Kumpfer, 1989).

MODES OF PLAY THERAPY

Play therapy occurs in a variety of therapeutic settings and uses a variety of therapeutic techniques. Group therapy and family therapy represent two common settings in which play therapy techniques can be applied to COA populations. Although group play therapy techniques are easily applied to a school setting, family play therapy is infrequently used in school settings. Many schools believe that families are outside their scope of interest and prefer to restrict their focus to the child. However, schools may occasionally wish to conduct interventions that utilize family play therapy techniques. If this is not appropriate or feasible, schools may wish to refer families to an external therapeutic setting where family play therapy techniques are utilized.

GROUP PLAY THERAPY

Whereas many play therapists choose to work with children on an individual basis, there are several advantages to working with children in a group setting. Although many practitioners believe that children should be seen for several individual sessions initially, group-based play therapy can offer practitioners an ideal environment for children to learn and practice a wide variety of skills that can assist them with the difficulties of being a COA. Because these skills are learned and practiced in environments that are similar to those in which they may later be practiced, children may be more easily able to transfer these skills to other settings. Group play therapy is often considered the preferred treatment strategy for working with COAs. Group therapy can aid COAs by allowing them to break through many denial issues that are associated with having an alcoholic parent. By sharing their experiences and stories with other children, COAs can come to understand that they are not alone in their plight and can reduce feelings of shame, isolation, and guilt (Dies & Burghardt, 1991).

In addition, group play therapy can benefit children by offering them a number of additional sources of social support. Social support is a natural result of group participation. As children share common reactions and discover that they share similar coping mechanisms, group cohesion is built. This cohesion and support may be especially important for COAs who often face more than their share of problems with less than their share of support. Although individual play therapy techniques can offer children a considerable amount of support from their counselor, these are children who will generally benefit from as much support as possible. By offering these children a number of additional sources of support, group play therapy may assist these children in dealing with the difficult issues that they face on a daily basis. Furthermore, there is evidence that children may benefit not only from receiving support, but also from offering support. Some research demonstrates that programs that allow participants to both provide and receive support have the most positive outcomes (Maton, 1987), and there is some evidence that participants that are able to make social connections with other group participants exhibited the best outcomes (Pistrang, Barker, & Humphreys, 2008). Sweeny (1997) suggests a number of additional benefits that may be achieved through the use of group play therapy:

Group play therapy can encourage children to develop a therapeutic relationship with the counselor.   Withdrawn or unsure children can watch the other children participating in activities and building a trusting relationship with the counselor. By observing these activities, withdrawn children may be more likely to engage in the play therapy process and develop a trusting relationship with the counselor.

Children have the opportunity to develop and practice interpersonal skills in a group setting.   Many COAs may not have had the chance to develop and practice developmentally appropriate social skills, and group play therapy can prove to be an excellent opportunity for counselors to assist these children in this process. Counselors can utilize games and activities that allow children to learn and to practice these skills in a group environment. Group play therapy allows children ample opportunity to practice these skills, and the skills may be more likely to be transferred to other settings.

Group play therapy may offer children the opportunity to learn vicariously through others.   By allowing children to witness the play, growth, and insight of other children, group play therapy offers children increased opportunities to understand their own behaviors. In addition, by receiving feedback from other children, group play participants have increased opportunities to reflect and understand their own behaviors.

SCHOOL-BASED PLAY THERAPY

Most children affected by familial alcoholism will not seek or receive traditional counseling services for their problems. Given the potential difficulties that COAs face, school officials should consider instituting interventions such as play therapy programs that may assist these children with both their current difficulties and help to prevent future problems. Because of the large number of COAs in school, school-based play therapy programs typically occur in a group format. Parent involvement is typically not required or logistically feasible for this type of school-based intervention and may not be desirable for some youth. Although these programs acknowledge the importance of parental rehabilitation, school-based programs usually recognize that this goal lies outside the scope of their authority (Ackerman, 1983). Therefore, these programs typically work only with COAs, helping them build a set of skills and competencies that can assist them in dealing with issues surrounding parental alcoholism. If appropriate, school-based play programs can refer families to outside counseling services and treatment.

Virtually all young children are involved in the school system on some level. Thus, the school therapists and counselors represent an important opportunity in which to identify and intervene with children of alcoholics. In addition, schools are a logical point of intervention with this population because it is the environment in which problems relating to parental alcoholism may be the most consistently discernable (Dies & Burghardt, 1991).

BENEFITS

School-based programs may benefit children by offering them consistent, non-stigmatizing access to programs that they might not otherwise attend. Many children, particularly COAs, have limited access to out-of-school programs, especially when transportation is difficult. Additionally, children may resist attending programs that are based in traditional mental health settings because of the potential for stigma and embarrassment.

DETECTION ISSUES

Counselors working within this setting also face numerous challenges in detecting affected children. Because many of the symptoms exhibited by COAs are not unique to this population, identifying COAs, without overidentifying, often proves to be a difficult challenge without some type of referral (Ficaro, 1999).

Crowley (personal communication, 2000) suggests that counselors should use a "wide net" in identifying children at risk for these problems. By focusing their attention on children who are exhibiting school-related problems, children of alcoholics will ultimately come to the attention of counselors and school personnel. Because school counselors are not typically aware of family substance abuse problems within the home, counselors should focus their efforts on all children who are demonstrating behavior problems, attendance issues, or reduced academic performance. By assessing these children, counselors can ultimately detect and treat children who are suffering from family addiction problems. However, it should be noted that a large number of the difficulties associated with being a COA (e.g., depression, anxiety, perfectionism) might not be visible to many school personnel. Consequently, specific types of COAs may be systematically ignored if only external problematic behaviors are used as a screen. Teachers and other school officials should be given information and training on how to identify COAs as well as other at-risk children.

One way to ensure that interventions identify as many affected COAs as possible is to err on the side of overidentification. Emshoff (1989) describes a video technique that maximizes student awareness and participation, while minimizing stigmatization and threat. The technique involves exposing all children within a school to a video that dramatically portrays an alcoholic family. After the film, students participate in a brief discussion about the film, and interested students are invited to attend a longer discussion group later in the day. This longer discussion group at first focuses specifically on the film and then gradually moves to more personal issues surrounding the children's experiences with parental alcoholism. Toward the end of the discussion, children can be informed of, and invited to attend, an ongoing group to deal with issues surrounding alcoholism.

This recruitment technique allows school personnel to identify COAs with as little stigma as possible. Children participating in these groups are not clearly identified as COAs but rather as children who are interested in the subject. If asked, children can claim that they are participating in the discussion group out of curiosity or simply to skip class. In addition to this recruitment technique, there are several well-developed screening measures that can be used to identify COAs. Two of these measures are described below. For a more detailed analysis of screening measures for COAs, and issues surrounding detection, see Werner, Joffe, & Graham (1999).

The CAST One common screening device that is appropriate for school settings is the CAST (Jones, 1982). The Children of Alcoholics Screening Test (CAST) is a written, 30-item self-report questionnaire that asks children to report their feelings and experiences related to parental alcoholism. Youth respond to each question using a "yes" or "no" response format. The CAST is primarily useful with older children and adolescents but has also been used to screen adult COAs. The CAST is an extremely valuable tool in that it asks respondents to reflect not only on their parents drinking behaviors, but also on their reaction to and feelings about these behaviors.

The CAGE The CAGE is a screening device that is appropriate for use with younger children (Ewing, 1984). The CAGE questionnaire is a brief, four-question instrument that was originally designed to measure an individual's own alcohol problems. The CAGE instrument asks whether the respondent has ever "felt the need to cut down on your drinking," gotten "annoyed at criticism about your drinking," "felt guilty about your drinking or something that you've done during your drinking," or "had an eye-opener first thing in the morning." Although originally designed as a self-report measure, the CAGE has also been used to allow children to provide a report of another individual's drinking habits. By simply altering the wording of each question so that it refers to the behavior of other family members, school officials can quickly gain insight into the potential for alcohol problems in a child's home. When using this screening instrument with a younger population, many therapists have noted the utility of replacing the phrase "eye-opener" with another term, as many younger children are unlikely to be familiar with that wording.

While the CAGE has proven to be very useful in this capacity, school officials should be aware that because this measure is so brief and is designed to detect relatively severe forms of alcohol problems, it may fail to detect some children who are exposed to less serious, but also harmful, drinking patterns. Thus, schools should not use it as the sole diagnostic measure when identifying children affected by parental alcohol use. Instead, school officials should use positive responses on this measure as an indication to perform a more in-depth assessment and should use other behavioral cues to identify potentially affected children.

School officials should also remain cognizant of the fact that children who are exposed to parental alcohol problems are also at increased risk for exposure to other high-risk situations, such as parents with co-morbid mental illness or drug abuse (Kessler, Chiu, Demler,

& Walters, 2005) as well as exposure to domestic violence (Collins, Kroutil, Roland, & Moore-Gurrera, 1997; Murphy, Winters, O'Farrell, Fals-Stewart, & Murphy, 2005). Programs that serve children based on their COA status will likely identify a population that is experiencing multiple stressors.

Interventions working with this population should remain cognizant of other issues that these children may face and should decide how these issues will be addressed.

LABELING

Another important issue for counselors working within a school setting is the potential for labeling. Although it is well established that COAs are at increased risk for a number of difficulties, it is also clear that the majority of COAs are well adjusted and demonstrate no significant difficulties. In addition, research has demonstrated that mental health professionals are more likely to view a child as demonstrating pathological behaviors if they are aware of a family history of alcoholism, regardless of the child's actual behavior (Burk & Sher, 1990). Considering the dangers that exist for labeling to negatively affect COAs, mental health professionals should exercise caution in accepting referrals from school personnel. Mental health professionals should work closely with school personnel to explore the dangers of labeling to ensure that the proper children are being referred for treatment.

ETHICAL ISSUES

Confidentiality is another ethical issue that counselors working in a school environment must consider. School-based programs offer many advantages, but they also limit the degree to which confidentiality can be maintained. Although teachers and other school personnel will likely be aware of the purpose of school-based programs, counselors should take efforts to protect the confidentiality of children participating in these programs. Teachers and parents should be instructed that the content of such programs will remain strictly confidential and that the details of children's participation will not be divulged, except in cases where children pose a risk to themselves or others.

Another way to help ensure confidentiality is to refer to the program in vague terms, rather than as a "group for children of alcoholics." For example, counselors may wish to refer to the program as "a stress and coping group." By referring to the group in these terms, counselors are likely to include children in the group who do not have an alcoholic parent.

PARENTAL CONSENT

Crowley (personal communication, 2000) also suggests that counselors working within a school environment should carefully consider issues surrounding parental consent to participate in these programs. Although some researchers have argued that school-based interventions working with COAs do not require parental consent or notification, the vast majority of counselors working within a school setting are cautious of such claims and choose to obtain parental consent.

Obtaining such consent can present school mental health professionals with several difficulties. Because of the many disturbances that occur within an alcoholic family, it may be more difficult to secure consent for COAs to participate in school-related programs than other children. In addition, while some parents may recognize the necessity of these programs and may actually refer their child for treatment, some parents, especially actively addicted ones, may resent the school's involvement into what they consider "family business."

Crowley suggests that school counselors should emphasize to parents the fact that these programs can address specific symptoms presented by the child and should de-emphasize the fact that these programs also deal with the underlying cause of these problems— parental alcoholism. By helping parents understand how play therapy can help their child reduce anxiety, depression, anger, or shyness, rather than "deal with family substance abuse issues," school counselors are more likely to appeal to these parents and receive permission for the child's continued participation.

Another possibility offered by Crowley (personal communication, 2000) is to secure passive consent from parents for children to participate in such a program. School personnel using passive consent procedures often send out a "laundry list" of activities that children may be exposed to during the school year. Parents are instructed to inform the school of any program that they object to and do not want their child involved in. Parents who do not typically respond to information sent by the school are not likely to respond to this notification and will passively infer consent for their child to participate in any listed school activity. The use of such procedures remains somewhat controversial within the academic community, and each school must weigh the relative merits of instituting such a policy within its own school district.

SCHEDULING

Counselors working in a school setting must also carefully consider the scheduling of interventions working with children. Although many schools would desire that such interventions be scheduled after school hours so that children are not penalized academically or miss classes, this is not always feasible. Children, particularly COAs, may have limited access to after-school interventions, especially when transportation is difficult. Parentified COAs may also be unwilling or unable to take time away from their responsibilities at home to attend after-school activities. To ensure adequate participation in interventions targeted at COA populations, schools should consider conducting these activities during the school day. Interventions conducted during school hours can address concerns that children will suffer academically by rotating the day and time of the intervention. By ensuring that children do not systematically miss one class or subject more often than another, school officials can work to ensure that schools are adequately addressing children's academic and socioemotional needs.

STAFFING

School-based interventions working with COAs must also carefully consider staffing issues. Interventions are often conducted by a variety of school personnel, who may vary in terms of training and expertise on both play therapy techniques and COA issues. While some knowledge and training in these issues are important, play therapy facilitators from a wide variety of backgrounds have proven to be effective in working with children (Moore & Russ, 2006); and schools should carefully consider the characteristics of a proposed program when selecting appropriate personnel to staff it. Interventions that are highly structured and rely heavily on pre-designed programs may be less concerned with the specific training and supervision of their staff than are interventions that deal mostly with interpersonal issues. Instead, interventions that are highly structured can be less concerned with the official role and training that the intervention staff possesses than with the relationship and rapport that the staff has with the students.

Utilizing teachers in school-based interventions may also pose special problems. Intervention staff may wish to ensure that participants are not involved in interventions that are staffed by their regular teachers. Teachers may have a very difficult time separating their roles as teachers and therapists. In addition, labeling concerns may limit the utility of this approach. If this approach is chosen, schools must work carefully to emphasize confidentiality issues and techniques to minimize labeling. In order to minimize these concerns, schools may wish to institute a policy that states that regular teaching staff cannot operate interventions that are targeted to COAs.

TERMINATION

Counselors must also remain cognizant of the difficulties that the termination process may present to a COA. Because their own parents have often cared for them on an inconsistent basis, these children are especially vulnerable to feelings of abandonment at the termination of counseling. Therapists should explore the child's feelings about the process and allow the client to express fear and uncertainty at the prospect of termination. Benedict and Mongoven (1997) suggest that the termination process is often made easier by allowing the child to take something tangible home from the play therapy room. Often, counselors and children create a toy or game for the children to retain ownership over. This memento serves not only to remind the children of the progress that they have made in the course of their play therapy experience but also offers a mechanism for continuing the process of play after the sessions terminate.

Goldman and Rossland (1992) suggest that counselors working with COAs should discuss their own feelings of sadness at the termination of therapy and help children to model appropriate ways of expressing their emotions. They suggest that some children may experience a real sense of loss as the therapeutic relationship ends and may appear to "act out" during the final stages of therapy. Therapists working with these children should encourage them to discuss their feelings of loss and help the children to discuss ways to maintain the support that the therapeutic relationship provided.

School-based play therapy interventions must also be aware that the school calendar can strongly impact the termination of the play therapy process. School calendars are understandably rigid and do not take into account a child's progress in therapy when dictating the scheduling of the school year. Children may be forced to terminate play therapy at the end of the school year even if they are only beginning to make progress. Likewise, school-based interventions may be targeted toward children in specific grade levels; and children may be ineligible for participation in these interventions at the end of a school year, even if they are continuing to make progress. Counselors working in a school setting should carefully explore these issues with students and give the children considerable notice that the sessions may be terminated. If needed, counselors should consider referring children to outside agencies for assistance during the time period when school assistance is unavailable.

PLAY THERAPY: EXAMPLES OF HOW IT WORKS

The vast majority of play therapy techniques that are used in group play therapy can be used in school-based play therapy groups. In addition, school-based play therapists can incorporate play therapy techniques into academic and extracurricular subjects such as music and art that children participate in on a regular basis. Although the variety of play therapy techniques that can be adapted for use within schools is limitless, presented below are several techniques that lend themselves well to a school environment and specifically address some of the issues that are often faced by COAs.

One technique that can be used with a range of ages is the "feelings game." This technique is extremely popular within the play therapy literature, and numerous versions of the game exist. The purpose of the game is typically to help children to gain a better understanding of their feelings, specifically regarding alcohol-related issues. A simple version of the game involves children creating a series of masks or pictures that depict various emotions that children might experience. Children are encouraged to pictorially represent as many different emotions as they can name. Once the drawings are complete, children are encouraged to represent their own emotions according to the pictures that they have created. Children are also often asked to practice imitating facial expressions that mirror the emotions that they have chosen. This game is designed to aid children in understanding the sometimes complex emotions that they experience, as well as helping children to gain a more complex vocabulary for expressing such emotions.

Another technique that can be useful to help COAs deal with real-life problems that these children may experience is a simple card game that allows children to dramatize situations that may occur in alcoholic families. The counselor and children typically work together to create a series of situations that COAs may experience. The situations may run the gamut from the common (e.g., parents fighting) to the more serious (e.g., child sexual abuse). These situations are then transferred to cards, which are distributed to various members of the group. Children are then asked to work together with other members of the group to dramatize the situation that is depicted on their card. At the end of each dramatization, counselors should ask the group to respond to each situation. Special emphasis can be placed on responding to the complex emotions that are triggered by each scene, as well as increasing situational problem solving by having children offer a number of potential solutions to each of the depicted difficulties.

Play therapy techniques vary widely in structure. While the previous two examples are relatively structured and most suitable for use with older children and adolescents, there are a wide variety of less structured techniques that are appropriate for use with younger children. Many of these techniques, which often include items such as puppets, sandboxes, and art supplies, emphasize allowing children to use play therapy as a creative outlet for their shame, guilt, and anxieties related to their COA status. By offering these children a much needed opportunity to express themselves through play, therapists can provide these children with some relief from the stresses associated with being a COA, as well as gain a better insight into the difficulties plaguing these children.

FAMILY PLAY THERAPY

Although most school-based interventions for COAs will employ a group modality, occasionally it may be possible to engage the entire family in an intervention or refer the family for treatment elsewhere. Another form of play therapy that has been used with this population is family play therapy. Counselors widely accept the fact that alcoholism is a disease that affects the entire family and that the full effects of family alcoholism cannot be appreciated without examining the entire family system (Robinson, 1989). In a recent review of family treatment approaches for parental alcoholism, Copello, Velleman, and Templeton (2005) concluded that interventions that include family participation have proven effective in both alleviating child symptomology and reducing parent alcohol consumption.

Family play therapy may also be an attractive therapy option for working with COAs because a major focus of the family therapy process is strengthening the parent-child relationship (Van Fleet, 1994). COAs often develop distant, serious relationships with their parents, and family play therapy may be useful with these families. By offering families a supervised, healthy environment in which to engage in enjoyable and therapeutic games, family play therapy may strengthen the often difficult relationships that are created by substance abuse. Family play therapy also offers the advantage of allowing parents to witness and understand the consequences that their addictive behaviors have had on their family. Counselors can instruct parents on the importance of play for child development and ways in which play can be encouraged in the home environment. By involving the parents in the play therapy process, counselors may be able to increase the probability that these skills will be transferred to the home environment, where they are greatly needed.

However, family play therapy is clearly not appropriate for all families. Hammond-Newman (1994) suggests that family play therapy may be inappropriate for use with parents who are actively addicted. Parents frequently deny the effects of their addiction until they are at least six months into recovery (Hammond-Newman, 1994). Thus, parental involvement in the play therapy process may hinder its progress more than aid it. To this extent, counselors considering using family play therapy techniques should consider the specific dynamics of the family involved and whether they lend themselves well to this technique. Parents that are still in denial regarding their addiction and its effects on the family may not prove ideal candidates for this type of therapy. However, these children may still benefit from the play therapy process. Black (1982) argues that these children, who are living with actively addicted parents, may be the most in need of play therapy and the haven that it provides. One potential solution to this difficulty is to restrict family play therapy participation to the non-addicted parent if possible.

CONCLUSION

This chapter emphasizes the potential benefits of using play therapy with COAs. Because of the numerous responsibilities that are often associated with living in a substance-abusing household, COAs typically receive fewer opportunities to engage in this fun than do other children. Play therapy allows these children to participate in activities that not only provide them with a relief from the pressures of being a COA, but also address many of the risk factors that these children experience. As a result of the denial and shame that is often associated with living in an addicted household, COAs may initially feel uncomfortable expressing themselves verbally and may view play therapy as a more approachable, comfortable, and developmentally appropriate forum in which to discuss, and eventually heal, the many different trials that these children experience.

Schools provide counselors with an important environment in which to conduct interventions that utilize play therapy techniques. Schools are a logical point of intervention with COAs because many of the difficulties that are associated with parental alcoholism may be readily observed in a school setting. In addition, schools can provide counselors with consistent, non-stigmatizing access to children whom they otherwise might not be able to reach. By taking advantage of the many opportunities that schools provide, counselors can work to design and implement interventions that benefit this complex population.

REFERENCES

Ackerman, R. (1983). *Children of alcoholics*. Homes Beach, FL: Learning Publications.

Anderson, G. (1987). *When chemicals come to school*. Troy, MI: Performance Resource Press.

Benedict, H. E., & Mongoven, L. B. (1997). Thematic play therapy: An approach to treatment of attachment disorders in young children. In H. Kaduson, D. Cangelosi, & C. E. Schaefer (Eds.), *The playing cure: Individualized play therapy for specific childhood problems* (pp. 277–315). Northvale, NJ: Jason Aronson.

Bijttebier, P., & Goethals, E. (2006). Parental drinking as a risk factor for child's maladjustment: The mediating role of family environment. *Psychology of Addictive Behaviors, 20*(2), 126–130.

Black, C. (1982). *It will never happen to me*. Denver, CO: MAC.

Burk, J. P., & Sher, K. J. (1990). Labeling the child of an alcoholic: Negative stereotyping by mental health professionals and peers. *Journal of Studies on Alcohol, 51,* 156–163.

Burnett, G., Jones, R. A., Bliwise, N. G., & Ross, L. T. (2006). Family unpredictability, parental alcoholism, and the development of parentification. *American Journal of Family Therapy, 34*(3), 181–189.

Burns, D. D. (1989). *The feeling good handbook*. New York: Plume.

Burton, L. (2007). Childhood adultification in economically disadvantaged families: A conceptual model. *Family Relations, 56,* 1–17.

Cable, L. C., Noel, N. E., & Swanson, S. C. (1986). Clinical intervention with children of alcohol abusers. In D. C. Lewis & C. N. Williams (Eds.), *Providing care for children of alcoholics: Clinical and research perspectives* (pp. 64–79). Pompano Beach, FL: Health Communications.

Carle, A. C., & Chassin, L. (2004). Resilience in a community sample of children of alcoholics: Its prevalence and relation to internalizing symptomatology and positive affect. *Journal of Applied Developmental Psychology, 25,* 577–595.

Castro, D. M., Jones, R. A., & Mirsalimi, H. (2004). Parentification and the imposter phenomenon: An empirical investigation. *American Journal of Family Therapy, 32,* 205–216.

Chassin, L., Pillow, D. R., Curran, P. J., Brooke, S. G., & Barrera, M., Jr. (1993). Relation of parental alcoholism to early adolescent substance use: A test of three mediating mechanisms. *Journal of Abnormal Behavior, 102,* 3–19.

Chassin, L., Pitts, S. C., DeLucia, C., & Todd, M. (1999). A longitudinal study of children of alcoholics: Predicting young adult substance use disorders, anxiety, and depression. *Journal of Abnormal Psychology, 108,* 106–119.

Collins, J. J., Kroutil, L. A., Roland, E. J., & Moore-Gurrera, M. (1997). Issues in the linkage of alcohol and domestic violence services. *Recent Developments in Alcoholism, 13,* 387–405.

Coplello, A., Velleman, R., & Templeton, L. (2005). Family interventions in the treatment of alcohol and drug problems. *Drug and Alcohol Review, 24*(4), 369–385.

Cork, M. (1969). *The forgotten children.* Toronto, Ontario, Canada: Alcoholism and Drug Addiction Research Foundation.

Dies, R. R., & Burghardt, K. (1991). Group intervention for children of alcoholics: Prevention and treatment in the schools. *Journal of Adolescent Group Therapy, 1,* 219–234.

Edwards, E. P., Leonard, K. E., & Eiden, R. D. (2001). Temperament and behavior problems among infants in alcoholic families. *Infant Mental Health Journal, 22,* 374–392.

Eiden, R. D., Edwards, E. P., & Leonard, K. E. (2007). A conceptual model for the development of externalizing behavior problems among kindergarten children of alcoholic families: Role of parenting and children's self-regulation. *Developmental Psychology, 43,* 1187–1201.

Eiden, R. D., Leonard, K. E., Hoyle, R. H., & Chavez, F. (2004). A transactional model of parent-infant interactions in alcoholic families. *Psychology of Addictive Behaviors, 18*(4), 350–361.

Emshoff, J. (1989). A preventative intervention with children of alcoholics. *Prevention in Human Services, 7*(1), 225–253.

Ewing, J. E. (1984). Detecting alcoholism: The CAGE questionnaire. *JAMA, 252,* 1905–1907.

Ficaro, R. C. (1999). The many losses of children in substance-abused families: Individual and group interventions. In N. Webb (Ed.), *Play therapy with children in crisis: Individual, group and family treatment* (pp. 294–317). New York: Guilford Press.

Giordano, M., Landreth, G., & Jones, L. (2005). *A practical handbook for building the play therapy relationship.* Lanham, MD: Rowman & Littlefield.

Goldman, B. M., & Rossland, S. (1992). Young children of alcoholics: A group treatment approach. *Social Work in Health Care 16*(3), 53–65.

Graber, J. (2004). Internalizing problems during adolescence. In R. M. Lerner & L. Steinberg (Eds.), *Handbook of adolescent psychology* (pp. 587–626). Hoboken, NJ: John Wiley & Sons.

Grant, B. F. (2000). Estimates of U.S. children exposed to alcohol abuse and dependence in the family. *American Journal of Public Health, 90*(1), 112–115.

Hammond-Newman, M. (1994). Play therapy with children of alcoholics and addicts. In K. O'Connor & C. Schaeffer (Eds.), *Handbook of play therapy. Vol. 2: Advances and innovations* (pp. 387–407). New York: John Wiley & Sons.

Hewitt, P. L., Caelian, C. F., Flett, G. L., Sherry, S. B., Collins, L., & Flynn, C. A. (2002). Perfectionism in children: Associations with depression, anxiety and anger. *Personality and Individual Differences, 32*(6), 1049–1061.

Hussong, A. M., Wirth, R. J., Edwards, M. C., Curran, P. J., Chassin, L. A., & Zucker, R. A. (2007). Externalizing symptoms among children of alcoholic parents: Entry points for an antisocial pathway to alcoholism. *Journal of Abnormal Psychology, 116*(3), 529–554.

Jones, J. (1982). *Preliminary test manual. The children of alcoholics screening test.* Chicago: Family Recovery Press.

Jones, R. A., & Wells, M. (1996). An empirical study of parentification and personality. *American Journal of Family Therapy, 24*(2), 145–152.

Jurkovic, G. J. (1998). Destructive parentification in families: Causes and consequences. In L. L'Abate (Ed.), *Handbook of family psychopathology* (pp. 237–255). New York: Guilford Press.

Keller, P. S., Cummings, M., Davies, P. T., & Mitchell, P. M. (2008). Longitudinal relations between parental drinking problems, family functioning, and child adjustment. *Development and Psychopathology, 20,* 195–212.

Kessler, R. C., Chiu, W. T., Demler, O., & Walters, E. E. (2005). Prevalence, severity, and comorbidity of 12-month *DSM-IV* disorders in the National Comorbidity Study-Replication. *Archives of General Psychiatry, 62,* 617–627.

King, K. M., & Chassin, L. (2004). Mediating and moderating effects of adolescent behavioral undercontrol and parenting in the prediction of drug use disorders in emerging adulthood. *Psychology of Addictive Behaviors, 18,* 239–249.

Kumpfer, K. L. (1989). Promising prevention strategies for high-risk children of substance abusers. *OSAP High Risk Youth Update, 2,* 1–3.

Landreth, G. (1991). *Play therapy: The art of the relationship.* Muncie, IN: Accelerated Development.

Macfie, J., McElwain, N., Houts, R., & Cox, M. (2005). Intergenerational transmission of role reversal between parent and child: Dyadic and family systems internal working models. *Attachment and Human Development, 7*(1), 51–65.

Maton, K. I. (1987). Patterns and psychological correlates of material support within a religious setting: The bidirectional support hypothesis. *American Journal of Community Psychology, 15,* 185–207.

Mayseless, O., Bartholomew, K., Henderson, A., & Trinke, S. (2004). "I was more her mom than she was mine": Role reversal in a community sample. *Family Relations, 53*, 78–86.

Moore, M., & Russ, S. W. (2006). Pretend play as a resource for children: Implications for pediatricians and health professionals. *Journal of Developmental and Behavioral Pediatrics, 27*(3), 237–248.

Murphy, C. M., Winters, J., O'Farrell, T. J., Fals-Stewart, W., & Murphy, M. (2005). Alcohol consumption and intimate partner violence by alcoholic men: Comparing violent and nonviolent conflicts. *Psychology of Addictive Behaviors, 19*, 35–42.

National Institute for Alcohol Abuse and Alcoholism. (1981). *Fourth special report to the U.S. Congress on Alcohol and Health from Secretary of Health and Human Services* (DHHS Publication No ADM 81-1080). Washington, DC: U.S. Government Printing Office.

Oliver-Diaz, P. (1988). How to help recovering families struggle to get well. *Focus, 11*(2), 20–21, 49–50.

O'Rourke, K. (1990). Recapturing hope: Elementary school support group for children of alcoholics. *Elementary School Guidance and Counseling, 25*, 107–115.

Pistrang, N., Barker, C., & Humphreys, K. (2008). Mutual help groups for mental health problems: A review of the literature. *American Journal of Community Psychology, 42*(1–2), 110–121.

Quigley, B. M., & Leonard, K. E. (2000). Alcohol and the continuation of early marital aggression. *Alcoholism: Clinical and Experimental Research, 24*(7), 1003–1010.

Robinson, B. E. (1989). *Working with children of alcoholics: The practitioner's handbook*. Lexington, MA: Lexington Books.

Schuckit, M. A. (2000). Genetics of the risk of alcoholism. *American Journal on Addictions, 9*, 103–112.

Sher, K. J. (1987). *What we know and do not know about COAs: A research update*. Paper presented at the MacArthur Foundation Meeting on Children of Alcoholics, Princeton, NJ.

Sher, K. J. (1991). Psychological characteristics of children of alcoholics. *Alcohol Health and Research World, 21*(3), 247–254.

Smith, A. W. (1990). *Overcoming perfectionism: The key to a balanced recovery*. Deerfield Beach, FL: Health Communications.

Steinglass, P. (1979). The alcoholic family in the interaction laboratory. *Journal of Nervous and Mental Disease, 167*, 428–436.

Steinglass, P. (1981). The alcoholic at home: Patterns of interaction in dry, wet and transitional stages of alcoholism. *Archives of General Psychiatry, 8*(4), 441–470.

Substance Abuse and Mental Health Services Administration, Office of Applied Studies (2008). *Results from the 2007 National Survey on Drug Use and Health: National Findings* (NSDUH Series H-34, DHHS Publication No. SMA 08-4343). Rockville, MD.

Sweeny, D. (1997). *Counseling children through the world of play*. Wheaton: IL: Tyndale House.

VanFleet, R. (1994). Filial therapy for adoptive children and parents. In K. O'Conner & C. Schaefer (Eds.), *Handbook of play therapy. Vol. 4: Advances and innovations* (pp. 371–385). New York: John Wiley & Sons.

Wegscheider, S. (1981). *Another chance: Hope and health for the alcoholic family*. Palo Alto, CA: Science and Behavior Books.

Wells, M., & Jones, R. (2000). Childhood parentification and shame-proneness: A preliminary study. *American Journal of Family Therapy, 28*(1), 19–27.

Werner, M. J., Joffe, A., & Graham, A. V. (1999). Screening, early identification, and office-based intervention with children and youth living in substance-abusing families. *Pediatrics, 103*(5), 1099–1112.

West, M. O., & Prinz, R. J. (1987). Parental alcoholism and childhood psycho-pathology. *Psychological Bulletin, 102*(2), 204–218.

Windle, M. (1990). Temperament and personality attributes among children of alcoholics. In M. Windle & J. S. Searles (Eds.), *Children of alcoholics: Critical perspectives* (pp. 217–238). New York: Guilford Press.

CHAPTER 17

Understanding and Generalizing Communication Patterns in Children with Selective Mutism

LAURIE ZELINGER

THEORETICAL BASIS OF APPROACH

Selective mutism (SM) is a disorder of contrast, characterized by use of appropriate verbal and nonverbal communication in particular situations contrasted with a persistent reduction or absence of language in other settings. It is influenced by specific conditions that determine how a child will behave and whether he or she will be able to speak. The term *selective* is not meant to indicate that an individual makes voluntary choices about his or her conduct in certain situations (McInnes & Manassis, 2005). Rather, the environment and the people in it become the resolute factors in identifying the extent of the child's capacity to communicate. According to Ford, Sladeczek, Carlson, and Kratochwill (1998, p. 207), "Situations that most affected how often a person with SM talked were strangers (76.7%), school (72.7%), new settings (67.3%), family gatherings (60.7%), and stress/anxiety (53.3%)." This concept of labile language is difficult for others to understand, given the tendency to view selective mutism as willful or oppositional based on its changing position upon a sliding continuum. In truth, the determinants of the inability to communicate are likely found in environmental triggers that induce unmanageable levels of anxiety or tension that literally shut down the psychological apparatus necessary for communication.

According to some studies, as many as 30 to 50 percent of individuals with selective mutism have some sort of speech or language impairment

(McInnes, Fung, Manassis, Fiksenbaum, & Tannock, 2004; Shipon-Blum, 2007). *The Diagnostic and Statistical Manual of Mental Disorders, Fourth Edition, (DSM-IV-TR;* American Psychiatric Association, 2000) indicates that one of the criteria for the diagnosis of selective mutism is, "consistent failure to speak in social situations in which there is an expectation for speaking (e.g., at school) despite speaking in other situations (e.g., at home)." Other criteria indicate that the diagnosis be considered only when reduced speech is demonstrated within the context of a language with which the person is familiar and when speech or language delays are neither primary nor extensive enough to warrant a diagnosis of having a speech/language impairment instead. One might meet the criteria for selective mutism if "the disturbance is not better accounted for by a communication disorder by lack of knowledge of, or comfort with, the spoken language required in the social situation." The *DSM-IV-TR* further describes that diagnostic criteria require that "the disturbance interferes with educational or occupational achievement or with social communication, and that it must last at least one month." While the International Classification of Diseases: ICD-10 (World Health Organization, 1992) refers to this disorder as "elective mutism," most of the criteria in that classification system agree with those in the *DSM IV-TR*, except that the ICD-10 requires demonstration of symptoms for a six-month period rather than just one month.

Selective mutism can be one of the more intractable conditions of childhood (Dow, Sonies, Scheib, Moss, & Leonard, 1995), harboring the potential to create significant negative effects in many aspects of the child's life. It is often responsible for causing reduced social interaction, delayed acquisition of pragmatics and speech/language skill development, restricted involvement in daily school activities, and interference with the building of friendships and academic skills (Bergman, Piacentini, & McCracken, 2002; Kearney & Vecchio, 2007; Schwartz, Freedy, & Sheridan, 2006). It is conceivable that the inability to communicate could present serious consequences for a child who may require immediate assistance but is unable to alert someone to help. Children with selective mutism withdraw from interactive experiences, enveloping themselves in a metaphorical cocoon where their insulation keeps them safe and separate from the demands of the outside world. Understandably, it is then difficult to step outside of this protective retreat and relinquish their silence, since the silence is functionally adaptive. It successfully allows the child to escape the discomfort and anxiety caused by interpersonal contact and to avoid public opportunities for exposure.

The silence is further maintained by the child's awareness that if he or she started to speak, it would draw immediate and increased attention from others. Such children are especially afraid of being embarrassed by mispronouncing or miscommunicating words (Manassis, Fung, Tannock, Sloman, Fiksenbaum, & McInnes, 2003). Furthermore, many admit to disliking the sound of their own voice, especially when anxiety produces musculoskeletal tension and related vocal cord strain, resulting in a high-pitched, tense-sounding vocal production (Dummit, Klein, Tancer, Asche, Martin, & Fairbanks, 1997; Manassis, Fung, Tannock, Sloman, Fiksenbaum, & McInnes, 2003). Thus, a system of reinforcers serves to maintain this behavior (Anstendig, 1998), making it one of the more difficult behavioral chains to break.

REFERRAL PROCESS AND POPULATION BEING TREATED

The prevalence of selective mutism is difficult to gauge, but researchers agree that psychiatric clinic referral rates hover around 1 percent, with a slightly higher incidence of the disorder reported in girls than in boys and in immigrant children rather than in native speakers (McInnes & Manassis, 2005). Yet, only a minority of children meeting the *DSM-IV* criteria are formally referred for treatment as the children often get another diagnosis that may receive more attention in treatment owing to a lack of knowledge or experience with selective mutism among professionals. Standart and Le Couteur (2003) indicate that school assessments of selective mutism show much higher rates than those found in clinical samples, as school staff do not refer all children with symptoms. The authors report, "This may be due to the identification of children with so-called 'hidden selective mutism' where school staff find it difficult to rate the mental health of an affected child" (p. 155) and therefore may not make an outside referral for therapeutic intervention. Although onset of the disorder is often traced back to the preschool years, most children don't reach the attention of professionals until they are between the ages of 5 and 10, when feedback from teachers and school clinicians helps to elucidate the issue.

Low reported prevalence rates also reflect some caution in referring children who exhibit partial elements of the disorder but not enough to meet all of the criteria for diagnosis. The incidence of selective mutism is likely to be underreported and may really be closer to 2 percent in children at certain ages (Kumpulainen et al., 1998). In the study by Ford et al. (1998), it is posited that confirmation of the diagnosis has most frequently been made by psychologists (41.8 percent) and psychiatrists

(16.3 percent), followed by speech and language therapists (3.9 percent), social workers (3.3 percent), teachers (2 percent), neurologists (1.3 percent), pediatricians (0.7 percent), and counselors (0.7 percent).

Reduced parental referrals in the early years are often attributed to lack of awareness, particularly if the child had spent most of his time at home, the primary setting where expressive language is not likely to be affected. Frequently, parents also attribute the behavior to shyness, rather than to a psychiatric disorder. In all likelihood, other members of the family are probably exhibiting similar behavioral patterns, thereby following a familial pattern of reticence and selective speech that is customary for them. A closer look would probably reveal inhibited temperament and communication styles within other family members as well, with discomfort associated with change and novelty regarding people, places, objects, and situations.

By definition, children with selective mutism share characteristics of idiosyncratic body and language expression. They are most often comfortable in their own home and usually appear to be entirely typical in that setting. Videotapes of children with selective mutism while at home reveal that they are loud, feisty, uninhibited, and conversant (Moldan, 2005). However, when a stranger enters the home, the children are likely to begin to whisper to their parent in the presence of the newcomer. By comparison, outside the home, children with selective mutism appear shy, anxious, and withdrawn in the presence of others and are often described as "slow to warm up." In social settings, particularly school, restaurants, birthday parties, and family gatherings, they may cling to a parent, hide their face against their parent's body, avoid eye contact, and refuse to participate in efforts to engage them. The constellation of these behaviors is frequently misconstrued as oppositional or manipulative, especially because the child can behave typically under other circumstances, and the child who doesn't reciprocate a greeting is mistakenly seen as stubborn and rude. Rather, avoidant behaviors develop as a protective response to a perceived threat involving change or increased demands. The fierce resistance demonstrated is the child's expression of his or her seismic effort to exert control in order to prevent anticipated change or the pressure to perform. Transitions and novelty are usually not well tolerated.

Children with selective mutism are often terrified of being the center of attention, making mistakes, and being teased or ridiculed in public. They also avoid making decisions for fear of being wrong. Rather than taking that risk, it is safer for them to be nonverbal and noncommittal, allowing them to fly under the radar. When the pattern persists, teachers and classmates learn not to expect a response from the student, and the mutism becomes reinforced, eliminating opportunities for the child to say or do anything that could be criticized. A teacher might refrain from placing demands upon or referring the child for treatment, assuming that he or she needs a period of adjustment. These students are only too happy when teachers refocus their attention on disruptive students, allowing them to unintentionally but successfully recede in the classroom.

Comorbid disorders are commonly found among children with selective mutism and complicate the symptom profile (Cohan, Price, & Stein, 2006; Dummit et al., 1997; Kristensen, 2002; Kristensen & Oerbeck, 2006; McInnes, Fung, Manassis, Fiksenbaum, & Tannock, 2004; McInnes & Manassis, 2005; Omdal, 2007; Schwartz, Freedy, & Sheridan, 2006; Standart & Le Couteur, 2003). They include concomitant issues related to speech/language areas, auditory processing, developmental disorders, social phobia, anxiety disorder, oppositional defiant disorder, motor coordination, sleep disorders, eating disorders, and elimination disorders. In addition, descriptor phrases, including the concepts of withdrawal, submissive, dependent, aggressive, depressive, stubborn, demanding, manipulative, and sulky, have been reported in some children (Giddan, Ross, Sechler, & Becker, 1997; Kristensen, 2001; Kumpulainen et al., 1998).

In the largest study of individuals with selective mutism reported to date (Ford et al., 1998) where participants were recruited from the mailing list of the Selective Mutism Foundation, Inc., 135 children under age 18 provided information about their personal and school history. The researchers analyzed referral rates for support services among individuals in this sample and found that 45.1 percent of the research participants had been referred for special education, with a resulting 20.9 percent of students receiving services at the time of the survey. Classification data reveal that 18.8 percent of the children were classified under the rubric of Early Childhood, while another 18.8 percent were classified as having a Learning Disability. Students with a Speech or Language Impairment accounted for 44.9 percent of the population; students with an Emotional Disturbance explained 29 percent of the classification rate; students with a Cognitive Disability defined 5.8 percent; 18.8 percent of the students fell under the category of "Other" special education needs (Ford et al., 1998).

When these issues in isolation or combination produce substantial interference in a child's ability to learn, that student may require an educational classification in order to recognize and guarantee support under the Individuals with Disabilities Education Act (IDEA) or Americans with Disabilities Act (ADA). Following a comprehensive evaluation, the parents and school team will review the findings and determine whether the child meets the criteria for classification as a Student with a Disability. If so, an Individual Education Program or Section 504 Accommodation Plan will be developed, dictating the terms of the educational program and related service(s) that will be provided, (i.e., counseling, occupational therapy, speech/language, etc.) as well as curriculum or classroom modifications and test accommodations that are determined to be necessary.

VALUE OF PLAY THERAPY WITH THIS POPULATION

It is well-known that play is the natural language and expression of children. Even in the absence of toys or objects that can be reinvented as symbolic facsimiles, children use common interests and imagination as their primary tools of communication with one another. A child who is unable to generate or respond to overtures and invitations to participate in interactive exchanges will be robbed of the opportunity to develop the age-appropriate and necessary skills learned through play. Social skills, rules of order, alliances and friendship, frustration tolerance, pragmatics, self-esteem, and compromise are areas of development that are likely to be delayed.

The need to play has particular relevance to this population, as these students will have had limited social experiences based on their inability to tolerate them, even if offered the opportunity to have play dates. Instead, it is common for these youngsters to have developed ritualized play patterns with younger or older siblings, and seldom with children of their own age. Competitive situations with same-age peers are experienced as threatening, and fear of embarrassment will restrict participation in activities where they expect to lose or look foolish. Consequently, the child with selective mutism will remain perched on the sidelines, and seldom in the action. It is then the job of the counselor to introduce basic play opportunities within the confines of a setting that promises safety, acceptance, and positive responsiveness from the therapist.

The play therapist's first challenge will be setting the stage for a resistant and anxious student to feel safe enough to enter and remain in the playroom. The next step will focus on engaging the child in an activity where the therapist and the child share attention focused on the same object or activity, leading to the child's awareness and acknowledgment of the therapist. From there, the experience of play can begin. The play therapist will become the school professional to best understand and interpret the student's actions and behaviors. Her tacit understanding and acceptance of the child forms the foundation for an alliance that permits the student to take risks in spite of an extensive history of constriction. It is within this relationship that the child will experiment with new roles, behaviors, and even speech output. A play therapist who has successfully joined with the student will facilitate the child's process of acquiring skills and confidence in order to attempt new challenges. Her educated response to the child's posture, words, and behavior will influence the path the child takes toward venturing into new territory.

DESCRIPTION OF PLAY THERAPY MODALITY AND TECHNIQUE

Working with this population can be quite challenging for any therapist, suggesting that setting the stage for a successful relationship requires some forethought. The school counselor will need to take into account artifacts of the school situation, including characteristics of the physical setting and time allowances within the school schedule. She must also be prepared to do an assessment of the child's affective expression and social flexibility by considering when, where, how, how often, how spontaneously, how loud, and to whom the child speaks, in order to develop an effective program that will expand the boundaries of his or her communication. An observation of the child at home would also yield valuable information, with the expectation that home turf advantage will decrease discomfort. Increasing the number of people within his domain when he speaks provides a stimulus-fading experience that minimizes the anxiety surrounding the fear of speaking in the presence of others (Cook, 2004; Moldan, 2005).

The school therapist must be a team player, gathering, sharing, and coordinating information among teachers, family, and support staff (Mendlowitz & Monga, 2007). Before initiating the treatment process with the child directly, accurate information about the disorder must be shared and accepted by the team, with the play therapist acting in a consultation role. The parents need to adopt a counterintuitive approach, reducing pressure on the child to speak at school. The teacher will need to agree to accept alternate forms of communication, including gestures, nods, tugs, written notes, whispered speech, and pointing (Kryanski, 2003), and to inform classmates that they should not speak for the nonverbal child because the student will talk when he or she feels ready.

Communication boards have been used by nonverbal children to indicate what they need to express, while others have premade index cards with word choices they can hold up. To encourage participation in class activities and shape their behavior, some teachers have arranged a secret plan with the student, encouraging them to raise their hand in response to a question, with the understanding that they will not be called upon. Other children have behavior charts where rewards are earned for successive approximations toward verbal and nonverbal communication. In the Ford et al. study (1998), treatment strategies were analyzed and positive reinforcement was found to be the most effective modality at 31.4 percent, followed by behavioral contracting at 13.1 percent and psychotherapy at 9.8 percent. Professional assistance from teachers was found to be helpful 35.9 percent of the time, with intervention from psychologists following at 26 percent.

Of equal importance in the initial stages of developing a relationship in school with a child with selective mutism is the therapist's need to reflect upon her own personal traits and characteristics, qualities that can potentially facilitate or prevent a therapeutic relationship. A counselor who is calm, warm, patient, and understanding is the best fit for an anxious child who is afraid to take risks. Timid children need patient adults. By contrast, the therapist who may be struggling with her own feelings of anxiety or who is someone who is loud, intense, or intimidating will likely struggle to contain those elements of her nature when laying the groundwork for a relationship with this special kind of child. Ideally, the therapist should be prepared to make a commitment for the full school year, knowing that novelty and change are not well-received by children who thrive on predictability. It is important that the counselor be consistent and reliable about keeping appointments with the student. It will also be to her advantage if she is able to delay her own gratification, as progress can be slow, taking several months to over two years to approximate normal social mainstreaming.

It should be remembered that children who don't speak in front of others usually require warm-up time and may not get started as soon they enter the room. For this population, 45-minute blocks of time may be more productive than the commonly offered 30-minute school play therapy sessions. It is also recommended that the student receive at least one individualized session each week (1:1) and one session with just one other child and the counselor (2:1). Some children with selective mutism may not have any formalized individualized educational plan under the auspices of special education but will profit from these approaches if applied by a caring and consistent school worker.

The space or office used for counseling should be as inviting as possible. Toys and furniture that are well-used will convey to a child that he does not have to be extremely careful or vigilant and that mistakes will be tolerated. Toys don't have to be expensive or fancy. Those that elicit multiple uses lend themselves best to the imagination. Stocking the room with plenty of paper, markers, and stickers is a good start. Messy activities with play dough, glue and glitter, chalkboard, finger paint, or papier-mâché serve as a wonderful conduit to unlock the inhibited child.

Often, merchandise catalogues mailed to school counselors offer a variety of games and toys for specific student needs. While many of these may be appropriate for school settings, children with selective mutism may not be responsive to interactive therapeutic games at the outset. The counselor may want to engage the child in quiet activities that do not require language, or she may want to invest in toys that produce their own noise with little effort. Noise putty is a particularly favorite toy for many, many children. It elicits laughter when the child and therapist knead the warm putty with their hands until it produces flatulent sounds. Instruments, pots, wooden spoons, whistles, microphones, kazoos, and voice changers are great facilitators for affective expression as well.

The therapy room should have a table and at least three chairs, one for the student, one for the counselor, and an available one for a friend. The counselor should choose a smaller chair than the one provided for the child, in order to minimize the difference in their heights and to appear less authoritative. Timid children often feel more comfortable with adults who meet them at their eye level rather than looming above them, and sometimes prefer to sit in a side-by-side position rather than an opposite one, thereby reducing pressure to make eye contact.

It is common for children to engage in repetitive play during the process of getting acquainted with a therapist. Children may gravitate to the same warm-up activities at the start of each session for several consecutive weeks until they feel safe enough to explore beyond the reaches of the familiar. This behavior serves a purpose: It is very much like the child who reverts to baby talk when feeling anxious or the child who wants to have the same books read to him or her over and over again. Revisiting an activity or experience that the child enjoyed or accomplished at some point in the past brings comfort in its predictability, familiarity, and acquired mastery. There are no longer challenges associated with that experience, as the child has successfully overcome that hurdle and has moved on to face new developmental challenges in the process of growing up. Therefore, old demands no longer pose a threat. The ability to revert back to an earlier time in life is a frequently observed self-soothing technique utilized by children when they are about to face a challenge. It can be thought of as their warm-up routine. They regress to a period when they felt safe in order to reduce their anxiety, allowing them to rebuild their confidence before tackling new challenges that require courage and the application of yet unknown skills.

A therapist considering how to begin treatment with a child will do best to choose activities that do not require great physical skill or reliance upon verbal language. Activities should also avoid competition, knowing that these children are particularly sensitive to being or feeling evaluated. They are prone to experiencing embarrassment from even benign events and will likely withdraw from contact if they feel they are wrong, slow, stupid, or being laughed at. Taking risks and making even simple decisions are monumental events that could set them up for criticism or failure. The calm, unhurried, warm, engaging, patient, kind, and gentle therapist has the task of choosing a neutral but engaging noncompetitive activity, in a room that encourages play, with materials that are readily available in a school setting on a recurring basis in order to establish some consistency and routine. That's a tall order. But it can be done.

The very first goal of counseling should be to engage the child's interest and attention in a shared activity. Out of their element, children with selective mutism may appear "frozen" and unable to show variability in facial expression or body movement (McInnes & Manassis, 2005). Eye contact is likely to be accidental or fleeting. Children may have their fingers, hair, or sleeves in their mouth and will not adjust their body position in response to social nuances. The therapist should strive to provide a reassuring experience where it is clearly communicated that the child will not be coaxed to speak. Then, a task can be introduced where she and the child will share joint attention on the same object or activity.

ENGAGING THE RELUCTANT CHILD

Children with limited social experiences show a delay in reciprocal play skills. Their discomfort in social situations may have resulted in fewer play dates and inhibited behavior in large groups, whereby opportunities to learn and practice social pragmatics may not have existed. Therefore, the counselor needs to begin at a developmentally lower level of interaction and expectation, in order to create a setting where the child feels safe enough to take first steps and to break long-held patterns of behavior that effectively kept threats at a distance.

- One of the most basic elements of any relationship is the awareness of another person. In such a dyad, the play therapist would want to establish joint or shared attention with the child. This might be quickly accomplished with a storybook. Each session can begin the same way, with the reading of the same book to the child, preferably one about shyness or children who are afraid to speak. Cook (2004) discusses the success of using metaphorical stories with puppets and play figures. Repetition from week to week fosters familiarity and builds comfort. If the counselor sits next to the student rather than opposite him, the pressure to make eye contact is reduced. The play therapist must indicate to the student that there is no requirement for him to speak.
- The therapist should not ask questions. Instead, she should make simple comments about what she is doing (i.e., "Now I'm rolling my clay into a ball"). An option for the therapist is to take the play dough, a rolling pin, and some shape makers out in advance of the child entering the room and place them on the tabletop. She can begin by modeling for the child how to make a flat pancake and a long skinny shape. Cohan, Chavira, and Stein (2006) suggest that the therapist avoid targeting symptoms of selective mutism directly but instead use tracking techniques to describe how the child is using play materials in order to describe the symbolic meaning of the child's silence.
- If paper and markers are set out on the table, the counselor might announce that she is going to draw a rainbow. Since almost every child can draw one and usually doesn't feel that the order of the colors matters, this activity is usually accepted and may occupy the child for at least 10 minutes, allowing him or her time to warm up.
- Black scratch art has been very popular with many children. While commercially produced papers are available, the therapist and child can also make their own by using crayons to color a whole page of paper that is then covered over completely by black crayon. The fun part is scratching away the black top in order to reveal colorful layers underneath. No artistic talent is required.

- While experienced play therapists make productive use of sand tables and trays with miniature figures, a canister of baking flour or container of sanitized sand is inexpensive and can be used alone as a vehicle for reducing anxiety. Many children find it relaxing to immerse their hands into the depths of these materials while listening or talking to the play therapist. One should be careful, however, as flour and sand spills are often slippery afterward, and many schools have restrictions on the kind of cleanup products that can be used on floors and tables when the activity is over.

When the student begins to make eye contact or shows a change in facial expression, the therapist has succeeded in laying the foundation for a therapeutic relationship, preparing for the next level of engagement. It is far more critical to engage the child's interest and attention at the beginning and to develop affective expression than it is to elicit speech. Play can take place even in silence.

PROMOTING AFFECT AND EXPRESSION IN THE RELUCTANT CHILD

Expression can take many forms. Helping the child to unlock sound and movement will open the door to new levels of participation and interaction. Any intentional change in face or body position, sound, or production of air constitutes expression.

- A large freestanding mirror (or two small ones) can be set up on the tabletop in order for the therapist to model different kinds of facial expressions saying, "This is what my *happy, sad, scared,* and *surprised* face looks like. Let's see what yours looks like when you make a face."
- The therapist and the child can express air by blowing soap bubbles through a wand. After the adult makes an exaggerated *wind* sound when blowing her bubbles, the child should be encouraged to imitate the same sound. Other easily conquered sounds include those associated with the letters *h, p, wh,* and *n* (Ehrich Dowd & Jerome, 2008).
- The counselor can model how to mouth words silently and lip-read the child's attempts to do the same.
- With parental and school permission, the pair can blow bubbles with bubble gum and make chewing and popping sounds.

- Noise putty, while controversial, is a favorite activity of many children. A container of putty for each person is required. It is necessary to knead the material until it is warm and then return it to its container. Insertion of fingers into the container forms bubbles that when popped create different kinds of flatulent sounds. The laugher it elicits speeds the bonding process between child and adult. Mimicking those sounds (akin to "Bronx cheers" or "raspberries") effectively engages the child's oral mechanisms in the communication process.
- If a toy medical kit is available with a stethoscope, a doll or puppet can be instructed to "cough," "sneeze," "burp," or "stick out" its tongue.
- Simple musical instruments can be used to create a cacophony of sound. The parent might also send in a kazoo for the child's personal use in counseling sessions. Voice changers and toy microphones can be introduced to magnify and distort vocal sounds.
- Toy telephones of different sorts often capture the interest of children. Battery-operated phones with buttons that produce songs or prerecorded messages often intrigue the nonverbal child. At a later time, they can be used as a shaping device to help the child actually practice conversational skills. When ready, the child can be encouraged to use a real phone to call her parent at home, speaking to her mother from school in the presence of the therapist.
- The play therapist can promote the child's sense of control over her surroundings by allowing the youngster to turn the lights on and off in the office. Strategically placed glow-in-the-dark stickers in different places in the room will encourage exploration of his surroundings. If given a flashlight, the student can be asked to locate and shine the light on particular stickers. The therapist can give clues, such as "I spy a star the size of the button on your shirt and it's near the clock on the wall."
- For children in first grade or above, the game of "Hang Man" can be played on a chalkboard (Banotai, 2005). In the first round, the child would choose the word, while the therapist takes the role of asking about each letter. The child may nod or shake her head to communicate whether the letter is or is not in the word.

Signs that the child is beginning to relate to the therapist will be noticed when the child shows some interest in the play, awareness and increased eye contact with the therapist, brief physical contact with the therapist or his play materials when they are in use, less rigidity in body placement and posture, and a wider range of facial expression and emotion. When the therapist notices these subtle changes, she must resist the temptation to call everyone she knows, to reroute the school marching band through her office, or expect to be inducted into the Counselor Hall of Fame. Instead, it is wise to respond calmly and to downplay any awareness of this change in the child's behavior. Matter-of-fact responses that avoid any particular focus on the child will maintain the momentum of the communication. The child must see that the therapist is predictable and unchanged in spite of the risk he has just taken. The child should not be congratulated on this accomplishment. If he feels as though he is in the limelight, he will recoil and access to valuable progress will be lost. But if the child feels as though the therapist has enjoyed playing with him and is genuinely attuned to him (Moldan, 2005), the act of playing will begin to become reinforcing in itself.

PROMOTING PLAY SKILLS AND VERBAL INTERACTION

Many children with selective mutism may show immature or under-developed play skills since their discomfort in social situations may have resulted in fewer play dates and limited opportunities to learn and practice. Once they begin to acknowledge the therapist in play scenarios, they may be overwhelmed with giddiness or relief of pent-up tension, as this may be one of their first experiences playing with an outsider. Silly, regressive behavior may be reminiscent of a child who is much younger, requiring that limits be set to avoid having them become frightened by their own exuberance. Therefore, the counselor needs to begin at a developmentally lower level of interaction and expectation, in order to create a setting where the child feels safe enough to take first steps and to break long-held patterns of behavior that effectively kept threats at a distance.

It may be incumbent upon the counselor to model turn taking, giving a structure to the back and forth rhythms of game play. Sharing her thought patterns with the student, the therapist might wish aloud comments such as, "Oh I wish it was my turn already. It's so hard to wait," "Playing with friends is so much fun," and "Sometimes I just want to win." Comments such as these, offer the opportunity to learn social rules and interactive participation, while dealing with feelings and culminating acts of waiting, winning, and gracious losing.

When given puppets, many children with selective mutism often invent scenarios involving oral aggression. It is not uncommon for the child to engage the counselor's puppet in an approach/avoidance interplay that usually progresses to biting when the child curiously opens and closes the puppet's mouth. Children with selective mutism will not use the puppet's open mouth to have their puppet speak. Rather, they often cautiously approach the therapist's puppet, move toward it as though to kiss or touch, and then squeeze or bite, at first gingerly and then with more force and sometimes even glee. If the play therapist responds with sounds of pretend pain, the child will likely giggle and seek to continue the aggressive outlet, escalating to hitting and sometimes chasing after the other puppet. Children with difficulty in self-regulation may require the therapist to set limits in order for the child to feel safe in the context of this release.

When the child is ready to use sound and language in the office, it is suggested that this hurdle be met with an activity geared for a youngster at a lower developmental level. Chronologically, most 2-year-olds are able to produce animal sounds or identify the animal correctly when its characteristic sound is heard. For an older child with selective mutism, games or riddles that evoke these animal sounds are usually safe starts. Rhyming activities with simple word families and many possible answers are conducive to evoking speech. For example, the play therapist might say, "I'm thinking of a word that rhymes with, "cat" or "I'm thinking of a letter that rhymes with B." Since there are many possible choices that are correct, the child is taking less of a risk that he or she will be wrong.

The Zelinger Fortune Telling-er (ZFT) is a new spin on the timeless Chinese Fortune Teller (see Figure 17.1). In this cognitive behavioral technique, the student and the play therapist decide on the "therapeutic question." For a child with selective mutism, it is often a derivative of, "What are the different ways I can communicate in school?" The student is urged to write the therapeutic question on the outside of the ZFT and to decorate it. The medial interior flaps will contain a concept of the child's choice, usually numbers one through eight. The final interior panels provide the therapeutic value, as the student will use each one of the eight surfaces to write an acceptable response or solution to the therapeutic question beginning with the statement, "I can . . . " In a ZFT created by a 6-year-old girl in this psychologist's practice, each of the panels read "I can" and was followed by one of the following responses that the girl had chosen: talk, write, draw, cry, raise

Figure 17.1   ZFT photo

my hand, touch, use low voice, and shake my head. The client then reviewed her list and decided that she didn't want to include "crying" as a viable alternative, and changed that panel to read, "I can point."

CONCLUSION

Working with a child with selective mutism requires knowledge of the characteristics of the disorder, training in appropriate therapeutic techniques, the ability of the therapist to project personal qualities of patience and acceptance, and the therapist's ability to work as part of a team within the school. Behavioral contracting, use of classroom and curriculum modifications, determination of test accommodations, provision of parent and teacher training, and coordination of related services are all likely elements in an overall plan at one time or another and may fall within the play therapist's arena if she takes on a consulting role. Likewise, information from outside sources (i.e., psychotherapy or psychopharmacology) may filter through her.

The play therapist has the unique position of understanding the student and gaining his or her trust, as they work to minimize the impact of the disorder and facilitate typical social patterns. She will be the conduit for change in the child as well as the facilitator of generalization of these behaviors to the classroom setting. The play therapist's application of unique skills, position within the school team, knowledge of selective mutism, and personal involvement, will be the variables responsible for increasing mainstream social behaviors in the child who could not do it alone.

REFERENCES

American Psychiatric Association. (2000). *Diagnostic and statistical manual of mental disorders* (4th ed. text rev.) Washington, DC: Author.

Anstendig, K. (1998). Selective mutism: A review of the treatment literature by modality from 1980–1996. *Psychotherapy: Theory, Research, Practice, Training, 35*(3).

Banotai, A. (2005). Selective mutism: Creating a therapy program. *Advance for Speech-Language Pathologists & Audiologists, 15*(3), 7–9.

Bergman, L., Piacentini, J., & McCracken, J. (2002). Prevalence and description of selective mutism in a school-based sample. *Journal of the American Academy of Child and Adolescent Psychiatry, 41*(8), 938–946.

Cohan, S., Chavira, D., & Stein, M. (2006). Practitioner review: Psychosocial interventions for children with selective mutism: A critical evaluation of the literature from 1990–2005. *Journal of Psychology and Psychiatry, 47*(11), 1085–1097.

Cohan, S., Price, J., & Stein, M. (2006). Suffering in silence: Why a developmental psychopathology perspective on selective mutism is needed. *Journal of Developmental and Behavioral Pediatrics, 27*(4), 341–355.

Cook, J. (1997). Play therapy for selective mutism. In H. G. Kaduson, D. Cangelosi, & C. Schaefer (Eds.), *The playing cure. Individualized play therapy for specific childhood problems* (pp. 83–115). Northvale, NJ: Jason Aronson/ Rowman & Littlefield.

Dow, S., Sonies, B., Scheib, D., Moss, S., & Leonard, H. (1995). Practical guidelines for the assessment and treatment of selective mutism. *Journal of American Academy Child and Adolescent Psychiatry, 34*(7), 836–846.

Dummit, E. S., Klein, R., Tancer, N., Asche, B., Martin, J., & Fairbanks, J. (1997). Systematic assessment of 50 children with selective mutism. *Journal of American Academy of Child and Adolescent Psychiatry, 36*(5), 653–660.

Ehrich Dowd, K., & Jerome, R. (2008, February 18). Why Jacob Won't Talk. *People*, 109–112.

Ford, M., Sladeczek, I., Carlson, J., & Kratochwill, T. (1998). Selective mutism: Phenomenological characteristics. *School Psychology Quarterly, 13*(3), 192–227.

Giddan, J., Ross, G., Sechler, L., & Becker, B. (1997). Selective mutism in elementary school: Multidisciplinary interventions. *Language, Speech, and Hearing Services in Schools, 28*(2), 127–133.

Kearney, C., & Vecchio, J. (2007). When a child won't speak: They may be "chatterboxes" at home, but kids with selective mutism don't speak at all at school. Eight questions can help you assess, and address, this disorder. *Journal of Family Practice, 56*(11), 917–922.

Kristensen, H. (2001). Multiple informants' report of emotional and behavioural problems in a nationwide sample of selective mute children and controls. *European Child & Adolescent Psychiatry, 10*(2), 135–42.

Kristensen, H. (2002). Non-specific markers of neurodevelopmental disorder/delay in selective mutism: A case-control study. *European Child & Adolescent Psychiatry, 11*(2), 71–78.

Kristensen, H., & Oerbeck, B. (2006). Is selective mutism associated with deficits in memory span and visual memory? An exploratory case-control study. *Depression and Anxiety, 23*(2), 71–76.

Krysanski, V. (2003). A brief review of selective mutism literature. *Journal of Psychology: Interdisciplinary and Applied, 137*(1), 29–40.

Kumpulainen, K., Rasanen, E., Raaska, H., & Somppi, V. (1998). Selective mutism among second-graders in elementary school. *European Child & Adolescent Psychiatry, 7*(1), 24–29.

Landreth, G., Sweeney, D., Ray, D., Homeyer, L., & Glover, G. (2005). *Play therapy interventions with children's problems* (2nd ed.). Lanham, MD: Jason Aronson/Rowman & Littlefield.

Manassis, K., Fung, D., Tannock, R., Sloman, L., Fiksenbaum, L., & McInnes, A. (2003). Characterizing selective mutism: Is it more than social anxiety? *Depression and Anxiety, 18*(3), 153–161.

McInnes, A., Fung, D., Manassis, K., Fiksenbaum, L., & Tannock, R. (2004). Narrative skills in children with selective mutism: An exploratory study. *American Journal of Speech-Language Pathology, 13*(4), 304–315.

McInnes, A., & Manassis, K. (2005). When silence is not golden: An integrated approach to selective mutism. *Seminars in Speech & Language, 26*(3), 201–210.

Mendlowitz, S., & Monga, S. (2007). Unlocking speech where there is none: Practical approaches to treatment of selective mutism. *Behavior Therapist, 30*(1), 11–15.

Moldan, M. (2005). Selective mutism and self-regulation. *Clinical Social Work Journal, 33*(3), 291–307.

Omdal, H. (2007). Can adults who have recovered from selective mutism in childhood and adolescence tell us anything about the nature of the condition and/or recovery from it? *European Journal of Special Needs Education, 22*(3), 237–253.

Schaefer, C. (1992). *Cat's got your tongue?* Washington, DC: Magination Press.

Schwartz, R., Freedy, A., & Sheridan, M. (2006). Selective mutism: Are primary care physicians missing the silence? *Clinical Pediatrics, 45*(1), 43–48.

Shipon-Blum, E. (2007). Selective mutism and social anxiety disorder: Learning to socialize and communicate within the REAL WORLD (audio CD). www.sectivemutismcenter.org.

Shipon-Blum, E. (2008). Selective mutism anxiety research & treatment center. [Online] Helping our teachers understand selective mutism. Retrieved July 29, 2008, from www.selectivemutismcenter.org.

Standart, S., & Le Couleur, A. (2003). The quiet child: A literature review of selective mutism. *Child and Adolescent Mental Health, 8*(4), 154–160.

World Health Organization. (1992). *ICD-10: International statistical classification of diseases and related health problems*. Geneva, Switzerland: World Health Organization.

CHAPTER 18

Play, Create, Express, Understand
Bereavement Groups in Schools

RUTHELLEN GRIFFIN

THE NATIONAL CENTER for School Crisis and Bereavement (2008) states: "By the time children complete high school, most will experience the death of a family member or friend, with 5 percent of the children experiencing the death of a parent by 16 years of age." Despite these facts a reluctance to discuss death with children continues in school and at home. Tolerance for behavioral and academic changes occur early in the grieving process but decreases as adults believe it is time for the child "to move on with life" (Nelson-Feaver, 1996).

Schools can be the best setting to provide bereavement therapy groups to students. In this familiar environment, a large number of students can benefit from services. Schools can monitor students over time and make referrals for clinical services when necessary. Parents also may accept services more readily in school where stigmas about mental health are less (National Center for School Crisis and Bereavement, 2008).

The value of play therapy/creative arts bereavement groups are many. Children can experience emotional support and sharing. Mood changes, improvement in adjustment, and quality of life can be the result of these groups. When children grieve and express feelings about the deaths in their lives, a dialogue for healthy sharing and support among peers and adults evolves. The sessions, often educational, answer questions and honestly address concerns children have about illness, death, and related rituals. When we provide children with clear, correct information, anxiety may decrease. By participation in groups children begin to learn to cope and care for themselves. Body symptoms and behaviors connected to loss can disappear or decrease significantly.

Worden (1996) states that the task of mourning needs to be completed for equilibrium to be established. Incomplete grief can impair growth and development. Therefore, these programs are preventative and can only aid children in the future, when again skills will be needed. Together, children learn that their feelings and experiences are valued and heard. They begin to develop listening skills and have opportunities to hear and help others. Group members are encouraged to empathize, understand, and nurture one another. In these groups, children develop resilience.

Gurwitch's (2008) research looks at resilience in children, specifically the elements that build resilience in children who participate in groups. These factors include the need for connections, participation (especially active involvement), routine, support and nurturance, critical reflection, building coping skills, communication, and taking a break.

Finally, in this child-oriented forum, adults recognize and support children's and their own vulnerability. Together, all explore the universality of death and benefit from connection and empowerment instead of isolation and loneliness.

This chapter presents an approach that uses play therapy and creative arts therapy to facilitate child bereavement groups in schools. It presents ideas for group organization, facilitation, and recommendations for involvement and communication with staff and parents.

GROUP PHILOSOPHY

Wallace (2008) notes that art presents an opportunity to express powerful emotions and to facilitate discussion. It can say more through pictures than one is able to articulate in words. "Art creates association with the disconnected parts of the self." Visual images work on many levels and allow one to express contradictory ideas and feelings while it provides comfort and support.

Metaphors and symbols create an indirect, yet deep approach to death (Ward-Zimmer, 1999). Intense feelings may be experienced at times. When developmentally appropriate for children and used with play and other creative arts therapies, all create safe distance and nonthreatening language for exploration. They create art with words, art materials, play, and movement. All can sensitively and beautifully express their feelings about their experiences.

Our bereavement groups attempt to address the tasks of grief that Worden (1996) indicates are necessary for all mourners. These include accepting the reality of the loss, working through the pain of grief, adjusting to the environment in which the deceased is missing, and emotionally relocating the deceased, then moving on with life.

An indirect approach to the subject of death and related feelings is developmentally appropriate for children. Symbol and metaphor use in play and the arts can create safe distance and nonthreatening language for exploration. Piece by piece, children begin to make sense of the personal and universal experience of death. Exciting materials and playful interactions decrease fears as they experiment with the possibilities, impossibilities, wishes, and realities of their lives. Children are encouraged to participate in a supportive experience that provides the correct information and answers questions they have about death.

Ice breakers pave the way for serious work. Children connect and see similarities and differences between one another as they line up. Checking height, size of feet or hands, length of hair, even the length of their noses gives them a chance to look closely at everyone in the group. The categories are endless: color of clothing, birth marks, age, hobbies, pets. For example, when asked to line up according to height, size of feet or hands, or length of hair, the group constantly changes, and children discover that they have more in common with others than they realized, or everyone who is wearing white could stand in one area of the room, everyone wearing black in another part, and anyone who had a pet die could stand in yet another spot. Questions can be posed about the pets: What were their names? Did they die? How? Stories and names emerge as children begin to paint the stories of their lives. Children tell how families responded and how they responded to the deaths of their pets and friends. One boy recounts how upset he was when his mother flushed his fish down the toilet. Children nod their head in understanding and sympathy. In response to "Anyone who has had a death in their family, come stand here," the entire group moves to that spot. In this very powerful moment, children feel connected and literally see they are not alone in their grief. As one child said, "I don't want anyone to have to go through what I did, but it sure feels good to know that other kids know how I feel." Children want to share their stories.

As children become engaged, they process their world, manipulate concrete materials, and create symbols and metaphors. Each moves his or her body to develop an understanding of experiences and feelings that remain within, previously nameless and overwhelming. Kids are increasingly aware of their unconscious. Verbal processing is sometimes interwoven, but not necessary. Sometimes talking stops as the process that eventually will heal and promote peace, joy, and relaxation in many children unfolds.

This model supports individual and group expression. Therapists nonintrusively facilitate the group and the individual's unfolding experiences. Each moment is spontaneously acknowledged and is created by the group in its unique process (all groups are different). One needs to trust this process and with an open mind know that what is emerging has meaning and is important to the group. However, at times it may not be clear what is occurring. We help the children remain in unclear, uncomfortable, blank spaces, not knowing, and allow time for issues, feelings, and the creative to emerge. We don't jump in making choices, creating metaphors, or filling the space with words or questions. This approach can shut down individuals and the group. This literally gets you nowhere!

For example, a group of seven children were moving creatively in the room; they moved in different directions, at various tempos, stretching high and low. I waited, watched, and listened. A boy slapped his hands together, saying "I killed it"; someone stomped on the floor, saying "There, I killed an ant." I stopped the group, saying, "The ant is dead. What will we do?" Someone said, "We'll have a funeral for the ant!" How do we have a funeral? They dug an imaginary hole, put the ant in a box, lowered it, and filled in the hole with shovels full of imaginary dirt. All were involved. Some picked flowers to strew on the grave; some cried. "There," said a boy, "the ant is buried. Now we need a stone." They made a stone that they engraved with fingers swirling in the air and then had a ceremony and memorial for the ant. We stopped moving and sat in a circle on the floor. I asked the children about their experiences in the cemetery or at the funeral. Stories tumbled out as they eagerly contributed personal details and questions about the process. By gently guiding the group and individual ideas, I helped them develop a story that had personal and group meaning.

Honesty and openness are important aspects of this model (Carroll & Griffin, 1997, 2000). Children need to be given information that they understand. This should not be vague or misleading. Concise words need to be used when explaining death. Euphemisms such as "gone away" or "passed away" only confuse children. A story was told to me by the aunt of a 5-year-old whose grandmother had died. A little girl waited for her aunt to arrive at the wake. She refused to move or talk to anyone else until she came. Upon arriving, her aunt sat next to her and asked the child, who was quite distressed, what was wrong. The child said, "They said she has gone away, but she hasn't gone anywhere—she's right here!" An adult's choice of words did not help this child understand this experience. During these sessions, children are given permission to question and to express emotions.

The Children's Bereavement Center of South Texas (2008) enumerates "rules" that we also use in groups. They are the following: speak genuinely; use language appropriate (for the child's present stage of development); listen without judgment; respond with compassion and understanding; it's okay to say you don't know; and have patience with repetition.

The Baton Rouge Crisis Intervention Center (2008) states that death should be explained directly, using the deceased's name and using *death vocabulary*—not misleading expressions like "passed on," "expired," or "gone to a better place." They also suggest that we accept the way feelings are expressed and try not to alter these expressions. Adults must be role models and demonstrate honesty and openness about their feelings as well. Remember, this is an opportunity for children to share and to remember the deceased. By creating, participating, talking, and listening to others, they can begin to transform feelings and gain control over an uncontrollable experience. Always permit bereaved children to heal in their own time. Their growth is a personal process that requires support.

ORGANIZING GROUPS

Groundwork for the formation of school bereavement groups is important. Community and school counselors need to work together to support each other and ensure successful development of this project. Administrative support and approval are also needed. It is vital to find staff who will follow through and assure implementation of the group.

Initially an informal meeting, followed by a written proposal that outlines approach, theory, philosophy, goals, projected population, and a tentative outline of each group session, helps to clarify information. Encourage discussion and make recommendations for staff in-service. Education is paramount. During in-services, inform participants of the need to address grief and its related issues in school. School personnel need to be made aware of the way death can affect a child's ability to function academically and behaviorally. Staff need to know about the existence of groups. An explanation of the session's purpose, goals, and possible activities will help decrease anxiety about the appropriateness of groups. All are encouraged to make referrals to the school counselor (or social worker), who screen the children and create a list of possible group members. Children should not be ruled out if there are no apparent problems or if the death is not recent. Group leaders are classroom resources who answer questions and provide information and ideas when requested. These individuals also provide further support when necessary. Teachers are discouraged from handling these situations on their own.

A letter about the group should be sent to parents, with permission forms for involvement. Follow up with phone calls after one to two weeks (several calls may be necessary) after the mailing. Meetings for parents may be scheduled before the beginning of the group, although phone contact may be adequate to answer questions and concerns about the sessions.

The school counselor is responsible for screening children and gathering the basic history of those who attend the group. Intake forms can be developed or found in the literature (Fitzgerald, 1995). This includes a brief family history, information about the death/deaths in the family (who died, when, how, who told the child, whether the child attended the wake or funeral, and the nature of the relationship with the deceased). A short history with time frames related to other changes in the children's lives is helpful in determining the complexity of their grief. It includes other losses by death, separation/divorce of parents, moving, fires or thefts, job changes of parents, or deaths of pets.

A behavioral checklist (Fitzgerald, 1995) then pinpoints areas of concern or change since the death(s) occurred. The initial collecting of data is more accurate and informative for parents and counselors if gathered with the child, parent, and counselor before the initial group meeting. It can also serve as a record of progress at the end of eight sessions and is a springboard for further discussion.

SCREENING

The National Center for School Crisis and Bereavement (2008) notes that sometimes groups are not enough for hostile or withdrawn children. Children who exhibit excessive levels of guilt, denial, panic, or despair that interfere with daily functioning, an inability to cope, or a dramatic decline in functioning, may need individual counseling. Consequently, counselors need to scrutinize referrals made to the group to see if the child is capable at this time of being in a group. All concerned need to determine if any child would disrupt the group, making it unsafe for others. Are behaviors related to the deaths that occurred, or are they long-standing problems that need to be addressed elsewhere? Is bereavement a priority for this child? The maturity level of children also needs to be considered. Sometimes, 5-year-olds can participate in groups; sometimes, they need to wait until they are 6 or 7. These factors should be considered in conjunction with the number of referrals and possible configuration of group members. If a child requires more one-on-one help, you may find another staff member or volunteer to participate in the group. The group could be split into smaller groups and separate sessions. Experiment with possibilities, while being flexible and adventuresome. Be realistic, and tailor groups according to the children's needs.

LOGISTICS

In-school bereavement groups ideally occur at the end of the school day or after school. This way children do not have to return directly to class and focus on schoolwork. Groups at other times of the day may be necessary. Sessions should be 45 to 60 minutes for eight consecutive sessions during school. After school sessions are 1½ hours. Children may repeat sessions as many times as deemed necessary by staff and parents (sometimes, children do not want to leave the group). The ages of participants vary. Schools, now separated into grammar and intermediate levels, create a reasonably spaced chronology. Children who have experienced a recent or not so recent loss by death and are eligible are integrated into the group. Group size can vary from five to eight children with two adult facilitators. This size ensures the possibility of one-on-one intervention for behaviors, special work, or handling of unanticipated situations. Ongoing observations of group and individual processes can also occur from two adult perspectives.

Room Considerations

A large "Do Not Disturb" sign should be placed on the door. Intruders need to be confronted or escorted from the room when necessary to ensure safety and privacy. Ideally, the same room is used for all sessions, and the rooms should be organized with as few distractions as possible (i.e., toys, equipment). This decreases the need to constantly control disruptive, off-task behavior. Facilitators can restructure the space, if necessary. Large spaces with high, echoing ceilings are not conducive to groups and can be reorganized by determining clear boundaries, marking each child's spot with a carpet square, chair, or tape. The school counselor is responsible for finding the space and for communicating with staff and administration about the privacy of this group area.

MATERIALS

Basic materials for movement and games include balls of different sizes, textures, and weights; scarves; stretch bands; carpet squares; boom box; tapes; and CDs. Construction paper, glue, scissors, crayons, markers, paints, yarn, and decorative materials are needed for art activities. Other miscellaneous supplies include puppets, small toys, stuffed animals, pillows, books and story tapes about death, shoe boxes, large envelopes, equipment for pounding and squeezing, balloons, and plastic packing bubbles. Materials such as clay, blocks, figurines, and sand trays may be required if special projects are planned.

Feelings and memories may surface for group leaders and unprocessed feelings and issues may arise suddenly. When adults begin sharing too much of their stories or crying in the group, it interferes in the process. Personal issues need to be resolved before the adult can help others in this situation.

IMPORTANT CONSIDERATIONS

FACILITATOR CHARACTERISTICS

Group leaders must understand child development and child/adolescent bereavement in relation to grief theory. The leaders need to be able to identify the child's developmental process with regard to their understanding of death. An ability to develop groups that are nonverbal, using therapies such as movement/dance, art, poetry, drama, music, and play, is a must. Work with symbols and metaphors that arise and with nonverbal content that express issues and feelings helps counselors understand the child's present situation. Counselors need to be able to connect these aspects to theory in order to determine a therapeutic response. Facilitators also must be familiar with group process theory, its implementation, and how to follow group and individual processes. With an open-minded, accepting attitude the adults need to facilitate and support what arises. The ability to control behavior in groups is mandatory and usually learned through practice and experience.

PERSONAL EXPERIENCE

Personal experience with death, hospice programs, and the dying process allows one to empathize with a variety of death experiences. These experiences increase one's ability to feel comfortable with the subject. Our attitudes about death, as well as personal red flags that are raised when various issues arise, need to be processed before the group begins. They should be revisited on an ongoing basis and analyzed with an objective eye. Such preparation allows one to speak comfortably and directly about many death-related topics with children.

TALKING ABOUT DEATH

One needs to be familiar with and be able to answer questions about the dying process, types of death, medical terms, and procedures (e.g., murder, suicide, cancer, stroke, AIDS, bypass surgery, IV, radiation). If you don't know, find a resource that can provide you with the answers you need. In some groups you may decide to bring in an expert to share and answer questions posed by the children. Funeral directors, nurses, or adults or teenagers who have had someone die when they were children are good choices. A discussion of religious traditions and rituals related to death, such as wakes, funerals, cremations, and burials, provides new information to children. They often want to know more about processes performed by funeral directors. The questions children ask about these can be quite direct and make us feel uncomfortable. Often we don't know the answers! For example, one child asked, "What do you do with the blood?" Familiarizing yourself with death-related terms such as casket, vault, cremation, morgue, burial, gravestone, cemetery, and corpse allows you to present and explain some of the death vocabulary to children when the need arises. Various materials, books, resources, toys, and possible activities for bereavement groups makes the possibilities endless! Implementing appropriate activities allows the therapist to be spontaneous, creative, and flexible.

SELF-CARE

Finally, as we provide help to bereaved children, please remember that we can't take the children's pain away. We can only support them with their process. Remember that you must also take care of yourself in this process. Give yourself time to debrief, and incorporate activities and lifestyles that nurture and sustain you in this important and difficult work.

DIFFICULTIES

There is little space in our fast-paced society for grieving. Our culture does not always grant the time or energy needed for grieving. Allowing children to say what happened requires time. We have to create an openness despite desires to remain hidden on this topic. Children don't express feelings in the same way adults do, and often adults use or see this as proof that there are no reactions to, or feelings about, the death that has occurred. In the process of creating bereavement groups in school, there are issues that need to be dealt with and that may actually prevent the formation of groups. This includes an overworked and stressed staff who feel they cannot do another project. Often, one sees initial staff interest but with no follow-through. Staff appear enthusiastic, then ambivalent, sometimes evasive and then they begin not returning phone calls or responding to agreed time frames.

Some school systems prefer to handle bereavement issues themselves, denying the relief by, and need for, outside help. This resistance might be a reaction to grief, an unwillingness to broach this difficult topic, or an underlying belief that children should be protected from death ("Why open a Pandora's box?"). Some adults think if children say nothing, they are doing well. Staff may also believe that a bereavement program is not important, that this is not the role of school personnel, or that there should be a time limit to grieving and children "should get on with their lives." Resistance may be related to lack of experience and education about death or to unresolved personal issues or fears that shape attitudes and approaches to death.

Other glitches may occur, including lack of administrative support or lack of understanding of the system by the outside agency or counselor. Space and funding are ongoing problems to be resolved with a certain amount of persistence, grant writing, community support, and flexibility. At times, parents are resistant and refuse to become involved. Their resistance and attitudes are similar to those previously stated. Adults do have much of their own grief work to do, and this lack of acknowledgment can create barriers for children's growth!

CHANGING CONTENT

Group content varies according to the needs of individuals in the group. Each session lasts 45 to 90 minutes. The first two sessions are devoted to bonding, trust building, and introducing the topic of death and the person who died. Sessions three through six focus on issues, feelings, and stories connected to the deceased, death, and education about death. Finally, sessions seven and eight explore coping skills in the present and hopes for the future. Memorials are created, and participants say good-bye to each other.

For example, to help cope with fears, we make worry dolls. Clothespins, toothpicks, yarn, feathers, and other decorative materials for the children's use at home can create objects on which to displace their worries. Dolls can be named and given special powers of protection. We list worries people experience. What will happen to me? Who will take care of me? Am I safe? Some are afraid of the dark or of someone breaking into the house. The dolls created are often ancient, archetypical-looking; some are modeled after the superheroes seen on TV. All are unique with amazing abilities.

According to Corr (1995) and Schonfield (1993), much can be discussed about death. They suggest the following areas for exploration: death as universal, inevitable, unpredictable, irreversible, and nonfunctional; making sense of what happened; identifying, validating, expressing in constructive ways strong reactions to death; commemorating the life that was lived; to go on living and loving; coping skills; and considering some continued form of life.

DEATH

As we observe the group, its individuals, and their developmental levels, we are able to identify what to explore about death. After reading stories or folk or fairy tales about death, group art projects and puppet shows are utilized. They can be powerful. Some children create a story about a person who died suddenly in a car accident. They include how the family was told and responded and how the person was waked and buried. Puppets are named, with one aspect of each person's story included in this fictional puppet version. Many stories can be found that attempt to explain why death exists or the nature of death itself. Creative processes that conjure images of death may bring up many feelings for the children.

While moving creatively, children explore the meaning of death or life. They often play at being dead versus being alive. What does it mean to be dead? Some hold their breath for periods of time, only to realize that they are alive; some lie very still. We discuss the difference between being dead and alive. Being dead is not like sleeping.

Children create a drama about the struggle between life and death. They use scarves of various colors to represent characters. White represents life or God, red or black the devil and death. They choose metaphors and begin to create interactions between characters as they play at life and death. Many adults believe children don't think about death or life! After the session, counselors could introduce different thoughts about death for discussion with children. For example, is sleeping like being dead? Why is it different? The counselor may create and discuss, play and talk—all lead to more understanding.

Making sense of death is a long process. It is therapeutically important to repeatedly tell the story, play out the events, and put the experiences together to make a whole picture. One time is not enough! The group hears stories, and each member remembers his or her own. Part of our job is to help children break down these difficult experiences into digestible chunks. We ask them to remember a point in time during or after the death that sticks in their minds or when they were told about the death. Then they fold a piece of paper into six blocks, to create a cartoon format. They draw or write what they remember clearly or not so clearly. Showing the story and pictures to the group, they say one thing about the process or picture. This may help children experience an important beginning. They access pain, memories, or strong feelings. All are encouraged to be verbal or nonverbal; some may choose not to tell their story, but all are listening. The group leaders support all responses.

FEELINGS

We can validate strong feelings by making simple body drawings. Children draw their body and how it felt on the inside on the day of the person's death. The body knows what our consciousness does not. Body symptoms represent something that is not expressed consciously. Discuss the normalcy of symptoms as a reaction to events and point out similarities. This is important. What do these symptoms look like? If you became one symptom and it danced, how would it dance? What sound would it make? Take it out. What size is it? How do you take it out of your body? Show the group. What is its smell and taste? Now, what do you do with it? What color is it? How does it feel in your hands? Encourage interaction with the symptom. Explore it using different sensory channels. What does the symptom say to you? Does it have advice? During this activity, symptoms are pulled out of the body with much effort and affect. Symptoms are found in stomachs, hearts, heads, and throats. Grief is sometimes gooey, dark, and gray. It sticks to you when you touch it and then adheres to other parts of your body. Before you know it, you are covered with it and can't wipe it off. It is cold and sends chills through your body. It takes the group to unstick you. Some children want to flush it down the toilet, burn it, lock it in the closet, put it under the rug, or give it to people they don't like. Others save it to look at when they feel like it. Metaphors are rich in feeling and meaning.

Following the process always leads to the surprising, as demonstrated by "the man with a thousand hearts." Children began drawing their symptoms in a large communal body, adding headaches, stomachaches, jittery feelings, and broken hearts—many broken hearts. Several boys (whose fathers died suddenly from a heart attack) began drawing more and more hearts, saying "This man has a thousand hearts. That way, if one stops working every year, he will be able to stay alive for a thousand years"—wishes for their fathers. The group enthusiastically embraces this task, and all make hearts and support the children!

Commemorating the life that was lived can be difficult, especially after a long illness. How was life with that person? Lives can be commemorated in group sessions by making bricks out of cardboard and then painting them in memory of the person who died. Create a brick wall with names and dates, personality traits, interests, and feelings. A wall of styled fluorescent bricks can serve as a backdrop for a larger ceremony at the end of the group.

How do children cope? Many children have developed their unique forms of coping. Provide children with an opportunity to share their techniques. Try new ideas in the group. This supports the children's present and emerging healthy practices. Discuss, imagine, and draw individual places that children frequent at home or elsewhere. They draw pictures of themselves in their beds, at home under beds, in closets, or in forts they make in the woods. The children learn to center themselves in the present and during difficult times. What objects or activities make you feel better? Have them bring these to the group to share. You can also make dream catchers or emotional first-aid kits. Name people who help children through difficult times. Help them develop a list of dos and don'ts for adults (their advice to us is "Not so much kissing!").

If the group decides to explore some aspect of life after death, one needs to remember that all religious beliefs need to be supported. This is often the first time children are aware that others have beliefs different from theirs. Some children are shocked that people have different beliefs. Movement and dance aid in exploration of the concept of heaven. Questions may be posed to encourage creative, thoughtful yet spontaneous responses: Where is heaven? What does it look like? What's there? How do you get there? What do you do when you are there? How does it feel? Do you have questions about it? What are the answers? What advice does heaven have for you? Follow the flow; the group interest will take you through the varied terrains and experiences, perhaps to a heaven with water bubblers or cloud escalators. The final question, of course, is, How do we get back to Earth? We can't remain in heaven, and they can't return to Earth.

TRUST AND SAFETY

A creative and expressive climate is developed as we build a foundation of trust and safety. Bereaved children are generally anxious about their safety. The environment, with clear, group-made rules, sets the stage for safety and free expression. New group members are included up to the second session. Group membership needs to be as consistent as possible. Children create bonds, begin to respect each other's responses, and are encouraged to listen and question. They are not allowed to become physically or verbally abusive. This often occurs with siblings. Limits need to be enforced consistently.

The issue of trust is ongoing and tantamount to the development of the group process. Time must be taken with each group—but especially in the beginning of the session—for children to create group bonds and to become comfortable with each other as well as with adults in the group. The purpose of the group, topics that may be covered, and general format is made clear, along with the rules. Questions are encouraged and answered honestly.

Simply throwing a variety of balls of different sizes and weights or surprising objects (e.g., scarf, rubber chicken, stuffed animal) to people in the group, calling their names and making eye contact, develops bonds. Use sound, eye contact, and playful movement. During one group, we asked students to show us unique movements they could make with their faces. Children crossed their eyes, touched their tongue to their nose, giggled, and laughed. We all tried funny faces, laughed, and became closer. Asking personal and impersonal questions of each child while throwing the ball encourages spontaneous participation. What's your favorite food? Color? Hobby? What do you hate to eat? What is the name of the person who died? All break the ice/newness in the group.

Initially, children are told that their contributions are voluntary. If they would like to "pass," it's okay. This rule is usually tested very quickly in groups. For several meetings, two brothers chose to respond to most questions posed about their father's sudden death by saying "That's classified/top secret information." It was quite some time before they were able to express their pain outwardly.

Group trust temperament can be measured during trust-building activities in which children's reactions and interactions on a nonverbal level are assessed. If one or two children shove or disrupt group functioning, proceed cautiously. When trust is established, go forward. For example, in a trust circle, all were standing shoulder to shoulder; one at a time, each person, with his or her eyes closed, was passed around the group. An 8-year-old girl consistently shoved people into the middle of the circle and was unable to let the group pass her gently back and forth; another boy had no interest in supporting others in the group and would have let the child fall on the floor when passed to him. This lack of trust and ability to support need to be acknowledged, talked about in the group, and modeled for the children. Adults are actively involved in the group process and activity. They cannot sit and observe. The metaphors experienced in this activity are core elements of group support: helping to hold each individual through group support and cooperation by participating, listening, being attentive, respectful, and caring, while each individual allows the group to support his or her weight. The child doesn't have to stand up by himself or herself during this process.

Why proceed cautiously? Why trust? What happens when trust is not established and assured? Children withdraw and may begin off-task discussions and behaviors. Sometimes conflicts break out in the group. When this occurs, the group is not able to explore the topics effectively. In contrast, when too much is revealed too soon, anxiety in the group can increase. The result is a shutting down of group members and a decrease in the development of the group process. A girl of 7 years of age burst into the group during the first session and revealed everything about the very recent death of her grandfather. She repeated this the second session. She shut down in the third, after which she dropped out of the group. When she left, we had to begin again with the remaining fearful group members.

"Do Not Disturb" signs are posted on the door, and interruptions are discouraged. A consistent space (the same room) makes the group feel safer, and the children begin to take comfort in the predictable after having been in an out-of-control, unexpected situation connected to the deaths that occurred. Children love to repeat activities, and we do this by creating beginning or ending rituals.

The group and the individuals are encouraged to go to the edge of their difficulty. This can then be relieved by retreat into a place of safety and a less revealing or threatening activity. A 7-year-old was asked to draw a picture about the time she was told that her mother had died from cancer. She was able to talk about it for a short period but was unable or unwilling to draw what was said and her reactions. She could, however, draw a picture about things she did with her dad later that day, after she had been told about her mother's death: They played cards, checkers, and basketball. Too much anxiety in the group will decrease the likelihood of involvement and disclosure. Children also need to return home or to class in one piece, feeling in control of their emotions. At the end of especially anxiety-producing sessions, release activities can help shift the focus and relieve tension. Jumping on plastic packing pillows or breaking small plastic packing bubbles with hands and fists is fun and requires focus and use of one's whole body. The children love this activity, and it helps transition to leaving.

Ongoing awareness of the group's ability to feel safe needs to be gauged by the facilitators. Appropriately nurturing, less-threatening activities at different times may need to be introduced. An activity could reflect the group's reluctance to continue exploration of difficult topics. For example, a tug of war between the children and adults naming each side Yes or No may be an appropriate metaphor. The adults take the Yes side ("Let's talk about the deaths"). The children choose No. We switch sides. Each side wins, and we can change sides on this issue as well. This decreases fear in the group, and being less direct and requiring the use of the entire body releases tension. Do not forge ahead with blind determination.

RESISTANCE

Acknowledgment and support of resistance increases involvement in the group. It needs to be immediately addressed and explored. Ask children how they feel about attending the group, or simply ask them to anonymously write on a piece of paper how they feel about being in the group. Pieces are then wadded up, folded, placed, or thrown in the middle of the circle. A volunteer then reads the papers. Ask people to raise their hands if they feel that way. Children might not want to talk but will indicate feelings by raising their hands. Often, children say that they do not want to be present. This was obvious in the case of two brothers, who literally sidestepped into the room, their backs on the wall in the hall. In the room they proceeded to stand in a corner and refused to participate. They reported having headaches and stomach-aches. Some may not want to discuss painful experiences and refuse to respond in any way. In the case of two sisters, until we found a metaphor that reflected their unwillingness to share, little sharing was done. These girls responded to my request and metaphor that they make a fort to protect themselves. They proceeded to build a fort from furniture and blankets in the room. It was barricaded, and only they could see out through peepholes. No one could see in; they protected themselves. When people came too close to the barricade, the girls threw wads of paper at the "attackers."

Reluctance to be involved can be demonstrated in many ways: disruptive behavior, fighting, off-topic discussion, changing the topic, continued "passing," refusal to share or be involved, withdrawal or seeming bored, appearing not to hear, pairing with others to create conflict in the group, or seeing adults in the group as enemies.

MAINTAINING CONTROL IN THE GROUP

Euphoria is not an unusual reaction by children when they discover they are allowed to express their feelings. Euphoria can often escalate, making it hard for them to return to more difficult, focused responses (especially when they are moving or dancing). This creates an unsafe climate, where some can get hurt and others may withdraw; this does not encourage vulnerability. Environmental structures and activities can be easily applied within a larger space to help control the group. Let children choose their "spot" with carpet squares or masking tape boundaries. Children return to their spots as the group's energy begins to escalate and the counselor thinks things should slow down. Direct children to freeze into feeling statues, statues of the group, or statues on their spot. Ask them to move like lead, molasses, or a heavy weight. Using their entire body or just certain body parts, they can pretend to be stuck on the floor by glue or Velcro. This shifts the energy. These experiences can be translated into feelings related to the death in their family. Did anyone feel very heavy and tired after the person in their family died? What does this statue look like? How does it move? What feeling do you feel when you are heavy and slow? Does anyone feel this way today? Make a group statue. Move as a heavy, tired group, then freeze into a statue when the facilitator says to freeze. Part of the group can observe and learn that feelings can be expressed in different ways.

Containing the group in part of the room may be necessary in large spaces with high, echoing ceilings. At different times, the group can be broken into pairs or smaller groups that later return to the larger group. Do an activity on the floor. Elicit early developmental movement such as crawling or rolling. This literally grounds children. Movement from large to small shapes on the floor can be explored as a metaphor expressing how small they may have felt at the time of the death. Use pillows, stuffed animals, and blankets. Wrap them and make a safe, contained, nurturing space. Kids love playing baby, sucking their thumb, talking baby talk, throwing baby temper tantrums, and curling into a fetal position. In the group these are all acceptable ways to regress. They express feelings and return to their centers and a safer time. Punishment is not a way to control these groups, but specific rules need to be consistently reinforced with stated consequences (follow through consistently). Individuals may be requested to sit in a specific place in the room until they are able to return to the group.

STRONG FEELINGS

When children follow directions and listen, a climate of safety is developed in the group, and then we can begin to work with strong feelings. Clear guidelines (with the help of the group) need to be stated when implementing activities that could access anger. We create opportunities for children to express strong feelings in constructive and safe ways. The expressions need to be specific, focused, and contained. For example, ask children to write on pieces of paper what made them mad about the death in their families. Put each paper in a balloon into which the feeling is blown, and tie the balloon. The metaphor in this activity is obvious. Ask children to bat the balloons around and then, one by one, to jump on the balloons while thinking about the event that made them mad. All are asked to read what was written. A discussion on the topic or a general consensus about others who also felt this way can be determined by raising hands. Statements written on papers have included "I'm mad he didn't take care of himself"; "I'm mad he's dead"; "I'm mad the doctors didn't save his life like they are supposed to"; and "It should have been someone else."

RETURNING

Facilitators should take time to wrap up and to create a smooth transition to classroom or home. This helps children experience some control over their emotions. Cooldowns or predictable rituals developed by the group can be nurturing, expectable, and calming at the end of a session. For example, make a "hand sandwich" by stacking hands on top of each other; hands make contact, then float up and away to wave good-bye. Slow down breathing in the group or in pairs sitting back-to-back. Breathe slowly (children breathe together or focus on their breath). Both ways bring children to a calmer place. Acknowledge good-bye verbally or nonverbally, and use sound and creative waves that are mirrored playfully. Set the scene for leaving. Check in at the end of the group, and ask for one word that describes today's group. Children reflect their experiences of feelings, activities, and group process. We sum up the experience quickly and spontaneously. Sounds that express a feeling in the moment can be revealing. Create special group waves or handshakes that include ideas from the whole group. The focus changes from internal to external. Kids look at people and hold hands in a circle. They pass the squeeze. This signals the end of the session. Ask group members to talk about what they will be doing that night or in the next hour.

COMMUNICATION

The issue of confidentiality in children's groups arises repeatedly. How can one maintain contact with adults, and offer helpful ideas and information to be used with the children in other situations? Initial contact with parents is informative and clear. Parents need to be assured that this will be a safe situation (their child will not be traumatized). Provide parents with handouts containing a description of the group, the tentative plan for upcoming sessions, and an explanation of the group philosophy. Encourage questions, and answer them honestly. Brochures are also available that provide concise information. Inform parents that these groups are confidential and that, unless there are reasons for all to be concerned, they will not be told all the details. The child will be informed if facilitators will be speaking to parents.

Behavior intake forms that are pre- and post-assessments can be completed with the child and the parent.

"Homework" is given to group members, and parents are encouraged to become involved in this process. This could include making an Emotional First-Aid Kit (developed by Carroll, 1995, Camp Jonathon). What things do you need to comfort you after a death in your family? Children have included Harry Potter books, special quilts made by family members, their blankets, computer games, pictures of family members, and special objects given to them by the people they love. Ask children to wear an item of clothing or to bring in pictures or items that belonged to the deceased. One boy brought in his father's large T-shirt. He said he sleeps in it every night. If he smells it closely, it smells like his father. The presence of hands-on, concrete items again brings up feelings and stories for all involved.

Give parents explanations of activities done in groups. Home discussion is encouraged. The importance of parental involvement needs to be emphasized. This can be very difficult for parents, who are also grieving.

Weekly handouts to parents (and school staff) are short and informative. Include articles on bereaved children (Carroll & Griffin, 1997), the child's developmental understanding of death (Seager & Spencer, 1996), a brochure on children and grief (Carroll & Griffin, 2000), what to do on holidays, or special topics requested by parents and staff. There is information on the Internet.

Encourage an open, ongoing discussion of home and school behavior by voicing observations, hunches, and feelings. Counselors help parents by explaining child development related to grief and mourning. We make suggestions for home support by phone contact. Wrap-up meetings with parents, upon completion of the group, create closure and answers questions and concerns. At this time, make further recommendations or referrals. Complete and discuss post-screening tests at this time. Inform parents and staff that these groups are often just the beginning for children. Grief work has varying time frames because issues can emerge again in different ways as children mature.

INVOLVEMENT IN SCHOOLS

Death and grief are not popular topics in schools or in our culture in general. However, discussion needs to be more open, not hidden. Educating staff about child grief can help all move forward in life. Kids who have not been directly affected by death can learn; some day, death will be an experience for them. Large gaps in awareness and information can be filled with accurate and age-appropriate facts that can decrease fears as well as dissolve myths about death. For example, a 7-year-old boy was convinced that his father had been buried alive because he had been found by him with his eyes open after he had died. His 7-year-old friend confirmed this information. He did not believe adults who contradicted his friend. Staff in-services provide information in schools about grief and children's reactions and provide ways to interact with students who have experienced a death as well as how to involve their classmates. People are afraid that when they talk about this, they will do it the wrong way and make matters worse. Teachers can share what has been done in the past and in other schools. In-services should include staff's personal reactions to death and attempt to help staff reflect on their ability or willingness to provide support for grieving children.

Health classes in high school often include a section on life and death. Encourage students to openly share reactions, concerns, questions, and philosophies. Poignant collages have been created by high school students that reflect the distress they feel related to personal losses as well as to loss as a result of war, famine, and disaster. Education can be provided about funeral parlors, cremation, cemeteries, burials, and the dying process. Trips can be taken to funeral homes and cemeteries. This educates and stimulates discussion.

Individual counseling services should be provided to children who cannot function well in a bereavement support group. Counselors provide ongoing support for the children while explaining the process to counseling staff. Talks to PTAs aimed at parent education and support of programs such as these can begin to open this often avoided topic to more individuals. Encourage donation of books to school libraries.

CONCLUSION

Honesty, openness, and a lack of secrecy on the topic of death needs to be encouraged in school. The universality of death needs to be acknowledged and discussed. It is our duty to be a child advocate, to educate children about this important aspect of life. Discussion with schools and parents about the reluctance to broach these topics needs to be approached gently.

The presence of supportive adult role models is essential. Adults help children process grief and its experiences while providing information. Children should not have to rely on peers for support and information. Role models do not just have to be the parents, as grieving parents may not be emotionally available at this time.

Many difficult situations can be seen as opportunities for learning, the beginning of self-reflection, and creative expression. Protecting children is not helpful; it often confuses them and their perceptions of reality become distorted. Can we really prevent children from learning about death? Is there really an opportune time to discuss death? Why wait?

A young boy, whose father had committed suicide, was not told by his mother how his father had died. Several years passed, and he began making up facts about his father's death. His stories were quite distressing. All adults were upset, yet no one would tell him what happened. The child was criticized for what was not explained to him by adults. How will this continue to affect this child? Wouldn't the difficult truth have been better for everyone in the long run? Children are already familiar with aspects of death—from nature, TV, the news, and computer games. This is not an unfamiliar topic to young minds.

Finally, education, expression, and support lead to health and resilience. Children learn how to express difficult feelings (that they don't have to fear) in safe ways. Children learn about the facts related to death and as a result understand more. As adults, they will cope with and process difficult situations in communicative and successful ways. In short, educate parents, staff, and children, and all can continue to grow.

To do this, we need to be open to a number of difficult questions: Why aren't services being provided? What do we fear? What is our culture's influence on this dilemma? What is important in our lives? How does evading this topic actually affect one's ability to function and relate? And, most importantly, how can these services be provided?

Table 18.1
Sample 8-Week Bereavement Group

SESSION 1	"Getting to Know Each Other"
3:00–3:15	Snack (brought in by parents each week)
	Rules of the group (developed by children)
	Confidentiality
3:15–3:30	Warm-up
	Ice-breaker:
	Choose 2 toys, Name Game (name a word that rhymes with it— the group repeats the name, and the word that goes with it)
	#1 What do you like about yourself?
	#2 What do you not like about yourself?

3:30–4:00	Using blocks & Play-Doh
	-create a house that you would live in.
	-put your toy figures somewhere in or outside of the house.
	-create a path from one house to another.
4:00–4:20	"House Tour"
	-what are special features of your house?
	Share with the group.
4:20–4:30	Final group circle/Controlled breathing
	Pretend you are a balloon (expanding/contracting).

Homework: Bring in a picture of the person who died in your family. Bring in blankets/pillows/stuffed animals.

SESSION 2	"Safe Places"
3:00–3:15	Snack
3:15–3:30	Warm-up
	What kind of weather do you feel like today?
	Share photographs and items brought in.
3:30–4:15	Create safe place in room using blankets, chairs, boxes.
	Create artwork, signs to put on and in houses.
	Where does the picture of the deceased belong in the house?
	Place it there.
4:15–4:25	"House Tour"
	Say one word about our group today.
4:25–4:30	Close your eyes, "pass the squeeze" around the circle.

Homework: Bring in an object/piece of clothing that belonged to the person who died.

SESSION 3	"Connecting"
3:00–3:15	Snack
3:15–3:30	Warm-up
	What temperature are you today? Why?
	What about the person who died makes you feel good?
	What makes you feel bad?
	Draw a picture of/about the person who died.
3:30–4:00	Make one safe place for everyone. Bring in picture you made.
4:00–4:15	Share picture and object.

(Continued)

(*Continued*)

4:15–4:30	Pair up and sit back-to-back; stand up all at the same time.
	Stand in a circle, press palms together, everyone lean into the center.
	Hold on to each other's wrists and lean out, keeping the circle intact.
	Stand as circle, one foot leaning forward, then back.
	Standing together in circle or group, stay connected and walk slowly as a group to another side of the room.

Homework: Think of a story to tell us about the person who died.

SESSION 4	"Remember"
3:00–3:15	Snack
3:15–3:30	Warm-up
	Look in the box of toys (brought in by counselor); pick out one that reminds you of yourself and another that reminds you of the person who died in your life.
	Share.
3:30–4:00	Using toys, blocks, and Play-Doh, create a scene that is part of a story of the person who died. This can be done anywhere in the room.
4:00–4:15	Share your story with the group, if you want to.
4:15–4:30	Movement (with sound and movement)
	Shaking—all body parts with shaking sound
	Chopping with martial arts sounds
	Back to center, breath . . .
	Movement that opens body with sound—yes
	Movement that contracts body with sound—no
	Finally, large breath with long expulsion
	Holding breath expansion. Close eyes/open
	Balance on one foot

Homework: Bring in your favorite stuffed animal/blanket.

SESSION 5	"What Happened"
3:00–3:15	Snack
3:15–3:30	Warm-up
	Pass something invisible around the circle. Let it change as it passes from person to person. Show its "use" in some way.

3:30–4:00	Using clay, Play-Doh, or figures, create a moment in the "death" of that person in your life that sticks in your mind or that you find you will always remember. Give that moment a title.
4:00–4:15	Share with the group.
4:15–4:30	Telephone game (about the group today). Repeat several times.

Homework: Wear something that belonged to the person who died.

SESSION 6	"Change"
3:00–3:15	Snack
3:15–3:30	Warm-up
	Sit in your favorite seat in the circle, now change your seat. What does that feel like? Change again (go to a different place). What does that feel like? Now go back to your original seat. How's that? Can things always be the same? What's it like to change?
3:30–4:00	Draw a picture of your life whether before or after the person died using chalk/pastels and paper.
	Make a list of things that have changed. What do you like/dislike about it? What's easy? What's hard? What's better? What's worse?
4:00–4:15	Share.
4:15–4:30	Play Simon Says.

Homework: Bring in a list of what makes you feel better.

SESSION 7	"Coping"
3:00–3:15	Snack
3:15–3:30	Warm-up
3:30–4:00	Create one safe place for the group.
4:00–4:20	Share things and practice, if appropriate, what people do to feel better.
4:20–4:30	As a group, make a list of help and suggestions for other bereaved children.

Homework: Bring in objects/pictures to be used in a memorial for the person who died. Bring in a food that the person who died liked to eat. Bring in CDs with the favorite music of the deceased.

SESSION 8	"Memorialize"
3:00–3:30	Snack—Story of food that the people who died used to like to eat.
3:30–4:10	Give each family a grapevine wreath to decorate with objects and pictures brought by the family (counselor provides glue guns and other art supplies for decorations).

(Continued)

(*Continued*)

4:10–4:25	Share wreaths with the group.
4:25–4:30	Saying good-bye. Move together as a group.

Handouts for Parents (given out at different sessions):

- Children and Grief
- Developing an Understanding of Death
- Ways to Listen/How to Help
- The Process of Grief and Mourning
- How to Cope and Remember the Dead

REFERENCES

Baton Rouge Crisis Intervention Center. (2008). "Suggestions for Helping Children Through Grief." http://www.brcic.org.

Carroll, J. (1995). Nondirective play therapy with bereaved children. In S. Smith & M. Pennells (Eds.), *Interventions with bereaved children*. (1995). London: Jessica Kingsley Publishers.

Carroll, M. L., & Griffin, R. (1997). Reframing life's puzzle: Support for bereaved children. *American Journal of Hospice and Palliative Care*, *14*, 231–238.

Carroll, M. L., & Griffin, R. (2000). *Children and grief*. Litchfield, CT: Friends of Hospice.

The Children's Center of South Texas. (2008). www.cbst.org.

Corr, C. A. (1995). Children's understanding of death: Striving to understand death. In K. J. Doka (Ed.), *Children mourning, mourning children* (pp. 3–16). Washington, DC: Hospice Foundation of America.

Fitzgerald, H. (1995). Developing and maintaining children's bereavement groups: Part two. *Thantos*, *20*(4), 20–23.

Gurwitch, Robin H. (November, 2008). Building resilience in our children. University of Oklahoma Health Sciences Center. National Center for School Crisis and Bereavement. http://www.cincinnatichildrens.org/schoolcrisis.

Hill, M. (October, 2008). *Healing grief through art: Art therapy bereavement group*. http://www.drawntogether.com/healing.htm.

National Cancer Institute. *Children and grief*. http://www.cancer.gov.

The National Center for School Crisis and Bereavement. (2008) www.cincinnatichildrens.org/svc . . . /school-crisisdefault.html.

Nelson-Feaver, P. (1996). Be tolerant to grief in the classroom. *Thantos*, *21*(2), 16–17.

Schonfield, D. J. (1993). Talking with children about death. *Journal of Pediatric Health Care 7*(6), 267–274.

Seager, K., & Spencer, S. (1997). Meeting the bereavement needs of kids in patient families: Not just playing around. Waterlook, IA: Cedar Valley Hospice. *The Hospice Journal*, 0742-969x, *11*(4), 41–66.

Silverman, P., & Worden, W. (1992). Children's reactions in the early months after the death of a parent. *American Journal of Orthopsychiatry, 2*(1).

Wallace, K. (2008). *Art therapy bereavement group workshops. Healing grief through art therapy,* kwallace@islandnet.com.

Ward-Zimmer, D. (1999). *Grief as a metaphor for healing.* Paper presented at the Dying and Grieving Horizons of Hope conference, Springfield, MA.

Worden, W. J. (1996). *Children and Grief: When a Parent Dies.* New York: Guilford Press.

CHAPTER 19

Redrawing the Front Line

A Play Therapy Service for Meeting the Psychosocial Needs of Children and Families in School

GERALDINE THOMAS

"When a parent is able to respond to a child with empathy it teaches the child that emotional expressions will not overwhelm them and are sharable and tolerable experiences. Thus, the 'good enough' parent is one who does not become agitated, withdrawn, or disorganized by the child's display of strong affect, but rather is able to accept the child's expression of affect, while also modeling for the child new ways to express emotions" (Greenberg et al., 1991, p. 415).

T HIS SAME PRINCIPLE applies to the school where the child spends most of his waking hours. The play therapy in school program aims to contribute to the school's "good enough" ability to respond to and contain the child's most distressed expressions of emotion.

Pertinent issues, in relation to the role of significant others in the child's life, which have presented themselves during seven years of a play therapist's work in primary schools in London, are discussed, specifically those emphasizing the need to experience both physical and emotional security and the way in which the absence of these impedes learning and the ability to form healthy peer relationships.

The approach integrates work on nondirective and Filial play therapy (Axline, 1987; Wilson, Kendrick, & Ryan, 1998; Guerney, 1976; VanFleet, 2005), affect regulation (Stern, 1985), child attachment, (Bowlby, 1988; Bretherton & Munholland, 1999; Cichetti, Cummings,

Greenberg, & Marvin, 1990), early attachment and psychopathology (Cichetti & Toth, 1991), and adult attachment (Bifulco, Moran, Ball, & Bernazzan, 2002).

BACKGROUND

In the United Kingdom 10 to 20 percent of school-aged children experience emotional and behavioral difficulties (Office for National Statistics, 2004). Mental disorders among young people doubled between 1974 and 2009. Boys were shown to be more likely to have a mental disorder than girls, and the prevalence of mental illness was greater among children living within disrupted families and those in disadvantaged areas (Office for National Statistics, 2004).

A growing body of research shows that unresolved problems presenting in childhood can have enduring impact across the lifespan (Cichetti & Toth, 1991; Greenberg, Cichetti, & Cummings, 1990). The play therapist in the school is available at an early and, therefore, critical point of contact for children and their families.

Play therapy provides a setting in which the child can experience enough safety to gradually reveal the drama of his or her troubled inner world. In this therapeutic space the subjective attachment experiences, which guide children's behavior, are enacted and repeated, with their failures laid bare. It is here that the mechanisms that regulate attachment-related emotional arousal become available for change.

When this therapeutic space is set in an inner city primary school, the interface between the troubled child, the family, and the school requires a systemic collaborative and cooperative approach. The therapist, family members, teaching staff, and other professionals work together around the child. This clarifies the child's position within each network of adults and the impact that each system has on the child. It also provides early identification of the way in which the child's behavioral responses to complex interpersonal circumstances might progress to either internalizing or externalizing forms of dysfunction.

When children are referred for emotional and behavioral difficulties, what has been recognized are their failure to learn and inability to respond flexibly to the school situation. The school is often unaware of the extent to which the child's behavior and inability to learn or develop healthy peer relationships reflects difficulties in the home and attachment-related anxiety.

The approach thus requires a systematic gathering of information about the child, the family, and the presenting difficulties so that aspects of conflicts within each of the systems can be considered (Salzberger-Wittenberg, Henry, & Osborne, 1983). It is evident that the school, as referrer, often lacks knowledge of the complex family histories, individual and contextual factors and dynamics, as well as the risks associated with socioeconomic deprivation, cultural stigma, and trauma and what these bring to bear on children's behaviors and their affective states. Additionally, awareness is needed of the way in which school marks not only the beginning of the child's experience away from home, but also of the developmental shift in the child's way of relating to the world and in negotiating new stage-salient issues, such as self-regulation, peer relationships, and competence.

The developmental challenges of such a transition, of the wider systemic and attachment dynamics of the child within the family, and importantly the family's psychosocial safety and access to support are all integral to the play therapy work. In formulating a treatment plan within the school setting, the triangular dynamic among school, family cultural attitudes, and the child's difficulties is amplified and the process of healing within each system is accelerated.

Linkages Between Attachment, Experience, Behavior, and Learning

Research investigating the link between children's emotional and developmental performance at school has highlighted the association between poor scholastic performance and insecurity of attachment to mothers (Barret & Trevitt, 1991).

Investigation of how attachment experiences are organized in memory (Bretherton & Munholland, 1999; Bowlby, 1988) has exposed the important role these inner models play throughout life in the formation of social relationships and, more importantly, in behavior associated with relationship expectations. Children in receipt of insensitive care are likely to develop negative representations of their caregivers and of themselves and corresponding difficulties in regulating their emotions. Insensitive parental behaviors can be negatively arousing and interfere with the child's developing capacity to regulate arousal (Cummings & Davies, 1994). Conversely, research on dyadic regulatory systems has recognized the adult's emotionally attuned response to the child's attachment behavior as providing a "bio-social mechanism of homeostatic regulation" (Fonagy, 1999). In other words, the adult has the capacity to understand and to respond to the child's emotional reactions so that arousal can be regulated. In fact, the resultant reciprocity of early relationships is a precondition for normal development.

Children referred by their school for play therapy have in common failure to access the curriculum, inability to form healthy peer relationships, disruptive externalizing behaviors, or internalized withdrawal. Reasons for referral often include an inability to regulate emotion, poor development of the self-system, and poor development of attachments.

While these problems are usually reported individually, attachment theory provides an integrative model through which distinct attachment behaviors (developed through interaction with caregivers) are viewed as reflecting the child's predisposition to anticipate future relationships in terms of past experiences with important early relationship partners (Fonagy, 1999). If parenting is poor, it results in anxious ambivalence, with distress associated with need and anger at not gaining protection—or it results in avoidance, leading to fear and withdrawal because care-seeking signals are met with anger, harshness, and rejection. Whether through amplification or dampening of need, the strategy adopted by the child is tailored to the anticipated parental response.

Work with the child and the family is thus based on the premise that the child's coping, as reflected in behavior and internal regulation, is a function of his or her difficulty in either over-(internalizing) or under-regulating (externalizing) affect and frustration tolerance. Alongside provision of direct work for the child is the school's need to be aware of and to understand the functional and adaptive qualities of children's emotions and attachment related responses and the role they play in the regulation of individual, reciprocal, and classroom behaviors.

Fundamental to a child-centered and developmentally sensitive treatment plan for the child in school was the creation of a therapeutic setting in which the child could experience safety and healing in an environment otherwise associated with additional stressors. Thus it was necessary to shift from *controlling* and *managing* difficult and disruptive behaviors to an *attachment* approach in which behaviors could be understood as reflecting complex strategies for coping with environmental stressors that challenged the child's capacity for regulating emotional expressions.

The need for school staff to gain understanding of the importance of attachment throughout the child's life, in particular, school life, and the organized and disorganized patterns of relating that children bring with them into the classroom underpinned such an approach.

THE SCHOOL AS A HUB FOR PROVISION OF MENTAL HEALTH SERVICES

The integration of a play therapy service into London primary schools coincided with the long overdue acknowledgment at a government level that the risk and resilience factors that inhibit or promote emotional health have an inevitable impact on education and the school environment.

The publication of *Promoting Children's Mental Health within Early Years and School Settings* (DEFS, 2001) and of *Healthy Minds* (Ofsted Report, 2004) summarized findings indicating high rates of clinically defined mental health issues among pupils. With research demonstrating a high level of unmet need for child and adolescent mental health services and indicating a requirement for accessible therapeutic services for the child within an alternative nonstigmatizing setting (Meltzer, Gatward, Goodman, & Forde, 2000; Domitrovitch & Greenberg, 2000), schools were to be placed at the front line of service provision.

Responding to research evidencing the powerful influence of emotional and social competencies over and above cognitive abilities for scholastic success (Weare, 2000; Wells, Barlow, & Brown, 2003), the view that mental health in schools was essential to addressing barriers to learning became an integral component in schools having to demonstrate their contribution to the five outcomes stipulated in *Every Child Matters* (HM Government, 2004). These outcomes are: being healthy; staying safe; enjoying and achieving; making a positive contribution; and economic well-being.

The model of intervention introduced was aimed primarily at addressing the child's difficulties in school but also aimed to deliver a therapeutic service sensitive and appropriate to the needs of troubled children and their families within the community. In aiming to make significant changes for the child while also creating a trust between the child's familial and school contexts, the intervention was thought about in "much broader terms" (Ray, Muro, & Shuman, 2004). The cornerstone of play therapy was the linking of the children's behavior in the school to their life experience and engaging the school as a therapeutic setting in which emotionally intense social and interpersonal experiences could safely be expressed.

For many children therapy cannot be considered because of extreme parental dysfunction. For those for whom sufficient parental commitment enables involvement in the therapeutic process, direct work with a focus on family relationships and cultural history and beliefs is offered to help promote a systemic understanding of the child's difficulties. For the child the aim is to create more secure attachments, enhance self-concepts, strengthen the capacity to build healthy relationships, and increase resilience. For the family, the aim is to adopt a holistic attachment-based approach in which the therapist is able to provide a safe enough space within the school so that trauma, abuse, and discord at home can be addressed in a nonstigmatizing setting focused on the well-being of the child.

DEMOGRAPHIC CHARACTERISTICS

In North Kensington children's lives are often characterized by recent immigration from the Caribbean and North Africa and most recently from Balkan countries engaged in protracted conflict and war. For many of their families, poverty, exposure to violence, drug and substance misuse, and depression continue to challenge their experienced psychosocial security. Added to these early developmental risk factors are those that are common to many other populations such as disruptions in family relationships, trauma, alienation, and despair contributing to children's vulnerability and helplessness (Garbarino, 1995). Furthermore, intergenerationally transmitted patterns of relating (Fonagy, 1999), imported psychic trauma, and a deep mistrust of the values of the host country contributes to the risks of lower educational attainment and poor social adjustment. Research has demonstrated that children are able to withstand the presence of one risk factor. However, the accumulation of three, four, or more, particularly when these develop without parallel opportunity factors, erodes self-confidence and feelings of self-worth and contributes to increased vulnerability and lack of security (Garbarino, 1995).

For many of these children, school is a place of safety where they can seek refuge from their troubled home lives. For others, the inability to regulate arousal and inhibit feelings of frustration and the inability to respond to classroom imposed limits means that school becomes an extension of their conflict-laden homes. Conversely for those who inhibit all bad feelings for fear of a punitive or harsh response, the school also offers no respite.

THE TROUBLED CHILD IN SCHOOL

The well-documented increase in both aggressive and out-of-control behaviors in boys and internalizing behaviors in girls in the United Kingdom prevails in the primary school environments. Disruptive and acting-out behaviors seen in preschool and kindergarten have often been shown to be predictive of later disorders in adolescence and adulthood (Greenberg et al., 1991). By contrast, withdrawn children have been shown to be at-risk of depressive and anxiety disorders (Rubin & Mills, 1988).

From an attachment perspective the angry, acting-out child feels unable to engage the teacher. As he doubts his capacity to influence her, he feels compelled to maximize interactions. His deep anxiety about his lovability and self-value means that he is obsessively preoccupied with the interest others have in him and worries endlessly about his teacher's attention being lost. Such overactivation leads to ambivalence (need vs. anger) and lack of resolution to distress. His strategy is to amplify his behavior and be demanding and insistent. But once he has won the attention he has fought for, he resists and disengages. At the extreme end of this spectrum the ambivalent child becomes coercive in his control of his teacher, forcing her to attend to him through disarming, seductive, or punitive behavior. Such behaviors are also shown to be implicated in peer rejection (Coie, Belding, & Underwood, 1988).

For the avoidant child the expectation of rebuff and rejection contributes to displayed indifference, over self-reliance, and an inability to ask for help from his teacher when in need of support. This child's strategy is to minimize attachment behavior, keep his distance, and deny any feelings of distress. Anticipating that his negative feelings will lead to further rejection, this child distracts himself from interactions and expressions of emotion, and negative affect is inhibited. Extremes of this strategy are compulsive caregiving and compulsive compliance.

Angry ambivalent *externalizing* behavior—characterized by negativity, hostility, and defiance, including hyperactivity, noncompliance, and aggression—represents the largest reason for referring boys who exhibit aggressive and acting-out behaviors (Offord, Boyle, & Racine, 1991). Avoidant, or *internalizing*, behaviors, in which emotional arousal in situations of fear or anger is inhibited, result in anxiety, depression, and withdrawal. Nevertheless, withdrawn children equally experience difficulties with peer relationships (Rubin & Mills, 1988). Both threaten the ability to access the curriculum and, more importantly, get in the way of healthy emotional development.

Thus both externalizing and internalizing attachment behaviors challenge the two salient developmental tasks of this age: 1) the development and maintenance of positive relationships with peers within the school, and 2) the development of industry. Enjoyment, pride, and self-esteem reflect success in achievement and in making and maintaining positive peer relationships. Failure in these tasks results in resignation, terror, despair, frustration, and rage, which are then expressed as the predominant emotions (Erickson, 1963).

The *troubled child in school* is thus doubly troubled—a child at-risk of doing poorly at school and at-risk of failing to make peer relationships. In the achievement-orientated climate of the school, it is the child's behavior and academic failures that are likely to be negatively emphasized, often without the attenuating circumstances that show tolerance of the child's negative emotions or that help the child de-emphasize negative experience (Malatesta-Magai, 1991).

A shift in focus from the child's poor behavior and social failures to a more holistic view of *the troubled child in school* requires emphasis on the child's coping ability as a function of early developmental history; the degree of nurturance, sensitivity, and stimulation at home; as well as potentially experienced trauma (Greenberg, Kusche, & Speltz, 1991). Disruptive or withdrawn behaviors and the impediment these pose to academic success can be reframed to conceptualize the child's behavior in a way that links emotions and cognitions and learning and, more important, can link experience to behavior.

CRISIS INTERVENTION VERSUS PROMOTION OF POSITIVE SOCIAL AND EMOTIONAL DEVELOPMENT

Most referrals received are for 6- to 10-year-old boys who present with disruptive and angry behaviors. They are caught up in regular playground fights and have poor peer relationships. As a result referrals often tend to be crisis driven, with preadolescent boys facing expulsion and play therapy seen as a last resort. Referrals for girls, who tend to be more silent or withdrawn, are rare. These pupils are often not noticed because they present few challenges to teachers and are a welcome respite from those with angry and demanding behaviors.

Early on in the process preparatory work is undertaken with the school referrer to develop skills in identifying children who are at-risk of being "unseen" because they appear to have no special needs but who may have difficulties related to the stresses of the whole family system.

In referral meetings the play therapist needs to highlight internalizing difficulties as being equally demanding of therapeutic work because they potentially mask a threatening accumulation of risk factors and vulnerability. Such behaviors, conceptualized as avoidance, may not necessarily be perceived as problematic because the autonomy and self-sufficiency displayed is successfully masking the child's withdrawal from learning tasks and social situations. Prereferral procedures include the training of teachers to identify and assess early signs of anxiety, emotional distress, and behavioral difficulties that reflect the stresses of the whole family system.

Such was the referral of Salim.

CASE EXAMPLE

Salim, a 6-year-old Somali boy, was referred because he had never spoken at school. Except for brief expressions of need to his teacher, he had chosen to remain silent at all times.

Contrary to many children referred for therapeutic work in school, Salim was a high achiever. His refusal to speak had resulted predominantly in social difficulties—isolation, absence of age-appropriate communication, and positive peer relationships. His mother described him as "silent like his father," but she appeared to have little real concern because Salim did speak at home.

As with many selectively mute children, Salim's presentation suggested an inhibited temperament and difficulty in adapting to a socially stressful environment in contrast to uninhibited communication at home (Kolvin & Fundudis, 1981). In common with many other children who inhibit speech, Salim was born into an immigrant family who arrived in the United Kingdom shortly before his birth and he had been exposed to another language during formative language development between his second and fourth year (Zelenko & Shaw, 2000).

In the introductory meeting at the school, Salim's mother, Mrs. B., was initially mistrustful and reluctant to accept help for her son whom she perceived as being "so different from her other children." She felt persecuted by school staff who, in her view, had pathologized her son; she perceived both the school and play therapy to be "white middle-class British." She also believed that the work in school would further contribute to Salim being seen as disturbed and strange. Salim's father was not present, and I was informed that as a bus driver he could not take time off for such meetings.

Mrs. B. acknowledged that she felt unable to discuss the referral with friends because in the Somali community accessing a mental health service was seen as a sign of weakness and parental failure worthy of stigma. Speaking about her early experience as a mother, Mrs. B. shared that she had been depressed after the birth of her fifth child but was reluctant to explore further the impact of this on Salim and the family. She appeared concerned that I would make Salim speak. I emphasized that I would not be making suggestions nor would I ask him questions.

Salim, as expected, was silent when we met. He stood frozen in the corner of the room before tentatively exploring the toys in a solitary and detached way, as if oblivious of my presence. Toward the end of his first session he approached the dress-up toys and purposefully picked up the handcuffs, locked them around his wrists, and gazed up at me. "Look." he appeared to say, "My hands are tied, I cannot express myself as I would like." Several important themes emerged in his early sessions. Fear and aggression in relation to the dollhouse, barely suppressed rage, and sudden shifts from good to bad that suggested trauma and the likelihood of experienced or witnessed abuse. In puppet play, a crocodile's sudden change from lovingly stroking to savagely attacking the little pig suggested the experience of betrayed trust and confusion in relation to care that was both friendly and dangerous. Such enactments may arise from contradictory experiences of care or from denied or distorted accounts of observed or even directly experienced traumatic accounts (Hodges & Steele, 2000).

Salims's play was solitary and lacked reciprocity. However, the graphic detail with which he told his story was vivid and symbolically rich. He would lose himself in a trancelike Shamanic dance that suggested something ritualistic but also communicated his aliveness. Something more viscerally painful was also conveyed and the importance of my bearing witness to the magnitude of his hurt was not lost on me as he stabbed himself repeatedly in the face, thighs, and chest with the toy knife.

Soon afterward Salim started to make use of the doctor's kit. Careful examination of the inside of his mouth indicated a need for healing of the orifice that, later in an unexpected attack on the baby, would be violently twisted shut with pliers from the toolkit. Salim had shared with me a baby's trauma whose terror had included hearing terrible things that could not be repeated. The speechlessness imposed by the brutal twisting of the pliers lingered long after Salim had left the room making me complicit in his vow of silence.

As the sessions progressed Salim gradually started to emit small babylike noises. Starkly contrasted to the armoured warrior part he displayed was the vulnerability of the infantile mewling that came from deep inside him.

In preparing for the progress meeting with Salim's mother, I was mindful that she may have been victimized by aggression in the family and that I needed to present my views of Salim's play in a way that would be sensitive not only to her vulnerability, but also to her anguish that Salim may have revealed something of the family's private experience. Her customs and beliefs and her cultural perspective on therapy and what it meant to her to have a son who did not speak would also have to be approached delicately. I would also need to be sensitive to what emotions in her son she would be able to tolerate. I resolved to focus on the uniqueness of his personal difference and to convey my view that Salim's play displayed sadness in relation to having missed out on early infantile needs and some worry about other's vulnerabilities but also energy and wanting to be part of things. Mrs. B. listened carefully and was able to link Salim's need with his difficult place in the family between close siblings. She was able to share her memory of his early years having been hard due to their difficulty in settling in, her depression, and the arrival of a new baby. In the nonstigmatizing setting of the school, which Mrs. B. had initially perceived to be hostile to her child's demeanor, it had become possible to discuss Salim's difficulties and, more importantly, the issues that had affected the family and the shame she felt to disclose such weaknesses.

Review meetings with Salim's teacher further reinforced the concept of working within a network of those who cared for Salim and those who taught him. Work with his classroom teacher emphasized the need to focus on Salim's nonverbal expressions, to identify and name his actions and his feelings, and to ensure that she had a good understanding of the counterproductivity of pressurizing tactics to encourage Salim to speak.

In the second phase of Salim's therapy, his play took a turn from actively relating his experience in affective terms to an integration of his Arabic and British identities as he interlaced his Arabic name with his English one. Salim found release from his painstaking concentration in vigorous demonstrations of gymnastic skills. It was during such a display that Salim's tongue appeared, jutting out of his mouth in an explorative way, as a small baby might in imitating his mother's vocal communications or perhaps even as a precursor to speech.

Whenever play with the baby doll touched on intimate care, Salim requested a toilet break. Repeated acknowledgment of the baby being suddenly dropped gradually permitted Salim to show its need for tender and sensitive care. This soon developed into fully regressed behavior with Salim claiming the pacifier and baby bottle for himself and asking me to cover him with a blanket.

Salim's progress toward increased speech involved many frightening scenarios in which the baby was crushed by falling beds and telephones were urgently dialed to call for help. As Salim assaulted the bop bag, his quietly mouthed words gradually developed into loud grunting noises. In role-play Salim again tied his hands, lifted them up, and beckoned for me to cut him loose. As my sword came down on the handcuffs, Salim shouted "I'm free," now leaving me lost for words.

Mrs. B. had shared with me details of her depression when Salim was an infant and the enduring influence that the exposure to maternal depression has on the psychological adjustment of the child is well documented (Cummings & Davies, 1994). What Mrs B. had been unable to acknowledge was the likely trauma that had truly silenced Salim. His play suggested overheard and witnessed aggression and discord at home in reaction to which he had imposed on himself a code of silence for fear of betraying a family secret. Pertinent issues in Salim's therapy, it would appear, were a general lack of communication in the family and a secret that needed to be kept from the outside world. For Salim this had involved trauma of sufficient intensity to challenge self-organization and communication and that required social withdrawal to avoid a dysregulated aversive state (Fonagy, 1999).

Selective mutism is hypothesized to be a presenting symptom of unresolved problems that socially disadvantaged and marginalized families have with the outside world (Zelenko & Shaw, 2000). As the carrier of the family's problems, the child becomes the victim of such a conflict and family isolation exacerbates the child's symptoms. Because of the cultural stigma attached to mental health intervention, accessing a clinical service would have been ruled out. Over the course of therapeutic work with Salim, his mother had gradually come to trust the nonintrusive relationship that was offered to her and to her son through the school. She was no longer wary that this would lead to social services involvement, nor did she fear the stigma of support that would be perceived as taboo within the Somalian community.

RETAINING CONFIDENTIALITY WHILE RAISING THE STAFF'S AWARENESS OF THE EMOTIONAL EXPERIENCE OF LEARNING

Raising awareness among the teaching staff to the child's emotional difficulties, in the context of broader cultural and family factors, related to behaviors that interfere with learning without betraying the child's and family's confidentiality, requires careful consideration of what can and what cannot be shared.

Permission from the child and the family needs to be gained to share pertinent material sensitively without detailing personal and painful histories. The family's trust needs to be safeguarded above all. Yet, awareness of the underlying factors contributing to rising insecurity, aggression, or withdrawal needs to be raised among those key people who are engaged with the children.

The inseparability of emotional and social processes from cognitive functioning (Perry et al., 1995) needs to be understood, as does the child's difficulty in focusing on the task at hand when dominated by powerful emotions, especially negative ones. Children's classroom behaviors may be linked to anger and distress or fear and withdrawal because environmental triggers reactivate attachment-related anxiety. Or they may result from overwhelming terror because the environment is perceived as dangerous and frightening. Thus the troubled child in school displays a number of behaviors that not only impede its ability to learn but also can be bewildering to those who teach them if not understood in the context of safety seeking and self-regulating strategies.

Evaluation of how the child's experiences outside and inside the school may have contributed to negative outcomes in negotiating socio-emotional developmental tasks (Erickson, 1963) helps teachers conceptualize how the positive dimensions of this stage—such as curiosity, competitiveness, enjoyment, and pride in being industrious—have developed along a more negative trajectory, with guilt, jealousy, frustration, and rage as the dominant emotions. A more developmentally sensitive and holistic approach to the child in the classroom can thus be obtained.

Helping the child to address and manage powerful feelings in order to be free to learn (Greenhalgh, 1994) is a goal shared by the play therapist and the teacher or teaching assistant. The child's emotional experience and activated attachment behaviors can be responded to in the classroom in a way that is consistent with the principles of regulating emotional reactions so as to help him or her regain homeostasis.

Equally, awareness of the impact of potentially abusive relationships at home and the developmental consequences to the school environment needs to be raised among the school staff so that the potential markers and the different ways that these can be manifest in the child's presentation can be recognized. In the school setting educational underachievement, inattention, and withdrawal from peer relationships, as well as aggression in peer relationships, provide indicators of the child's distress; but also physical symptoms and failure to thrive in general are highlighted as potential manifestations of abuse (Erickson & Egeland, 1996).

PLAY THERAPY ASSESSMENT IN THE SCHOOL SETTING

The attachment framework also provides a useful conceptual frame in which to approach assessments to gain insight into children's attachment and care needs. Use of narrative story stems helps to gain a better understanding of what the child has made and continues to make of his or her experience. The internal representations elicited do not simply mirror experience but usefully illustrate how the child processes attachment-related information (i.e., negotiates the relationship with the caregiver in stressful situations, perceives others, anticipates reactions, sees the self in relation to others, as well revealing the child's strategy to gain access to the caregiver).

CASE EXAMPLE

Karina was referred for play therapy by her primary school due to concerns about her stealing, lying, and regressed behavior since arriving at the school. Nothing was known of the circumstances surrounding her separation from her mother and why she was cared for by her maternal grandmother. Lack of support for therapeutic work meant that play therapy could not be offered. However, as Karina's behavior continued to deteriorate, the school requested a play therapy assessment to gain further insight into her emotionally withdrawn, solitary, and sad behavior.

Six sessions of nondirective play therapy for the purpose of assessment were provided following an initial session during which a Narrative Story Stem Task was administered. The primary purpose of this work was to gain an understanding of Karina's unhappy and distressed presentation and to inform the school how best to approach her future developmental needs and ensure she was adequately cared for.

Narrative Story Stem Assessment   Each of the stories of the Narrative Story Stem Task (Bretherton, Ridgeway, & Cassidy, 1990) encourages representations of themes such as separation, conflict, distress, injury, or fear as indicators of the attachment figure's provision of comfort, reassurance, and encouragement; the way in which the child is directed or disciplined; and the way in which the child seeks proximity to the parent.

It was clear that Karina had experienced, and possibly continued to experience, care in which she felt unsafe. Her stories were characterized by themes of danger in which adults were portrayed as dangerous and frightening and children were bleeding, burnt, threatened, and would run away. Alarmingly, her response to the first stem was that the child died and was rushed to hospital by her sister. Themes of the child protagonist being endangered and victimized by aggressive adults and of children being cut by glass and eaten by monsters figured prominently in Karina's responses. Adults were typically depicted as aggressive and frightening, chasing the child into the bedroom and wrestling her to the ground. Conflict and aggression was also enacted between adults. Nevertheless, in some of the stories, the child's vulnerability and endangerment were acknowledged by siblings or other adults who provided both assistance and protection.

Such stories in which inexplicable and frightening events are enacted and the child portrays a sense of endangerment are usually told by children with a history of abuse. Interestingly, unlike many children who enact such disturbing scenarios, Karina was also able to resolve the stories in a satisfactory way, showing a safe resolution to the story, by demonstrating that others came to the child's rescue and provided her with protection. Nevertheless, the combination of catastrophic dramas in which the child died and representations of endangerment and violent frightening events suggested unresolved trauma and possibly ongoing abuse. Such fearful disorganized narratives, along with the suggestion that an adult is threatening and endangering, are suggestive of extreme insecurity in relation to distressing events that may or may not be historic.

Karina's presentation in the playroom corroborated this view of the girl's vulnerability and likely victimization in a caregiver-child relationship characterized by abuse. She was a wiry little girl whose anxious look, furtive glances, and above all her silence emphasized her fragmented sense of self and fearfulness. Avoiding close proximity to me, she also denied herself free exploration of the materials as she darted restlessly between areas of the room. She responded to my comments on her actions by suddenly freezing, her eyes widening in terror.

Karina appeared eager to come to the playroom but clearly had little sense of collaboration or of reciprocal enjoyment. She only occasionally laughed or spontaneously showed enjoyment. Her silent and diffident behavior suggested a difficulty in trusting me sufficiently to involve me in her play. Her poor ability to make use of the materials in the playroom extended to a similarly limited ability to make use of me as a person.

Throughout the six sessions she had an animated but unreachable quality that she carefully guarded by maintaining an inscrutable silence and distance that made her hard to get in touch with. Her play was solitary, and the expression and content of her play was impoverished and disturbed.

In her first session Karina's palpable anxiety was communicated by ringing the musical bells loudly and protractedly. Her wish to draw attention to feelings of alarm was repeatedly conveyed through her recourse to the mobile telephones, which she would approach purposefully and on which she would ring at length and with a sense of urgency. At times she was able to regulate her heightened arousal by blowing bubbles, moving quickly through the room to blow them onto the other toys or into the dollhouse. At other times her arousal could only be soothed by hungrily wolfing down the cookies I provided for her.

The following themes and feelings, in order of importance, were expressed in her play:

- *Lack of Permission to Express Herself.* Karina's attempts at producing music on the harmonica would be drowned out by her loud and alarming bell ringing. Her seemingly urgent wish to communicate a message to me by way of the mobile telephones was often followed by her picking up finger puppets with which she enacted aggressive interactions. Showing me that such cries for help would remain unheard, telephones were left to ring repeatedly as Karina maintained her silence.
- *Messiness, Stickiness, and Possible Sexual Abuse.* Mixing a slimy and gluey concoction occupied much of Karina's time in the room. She would become very focused on mixing glue into the water and blowing the bubble mix through a straw over the toys in the room. In one session she stood over the baby and dribbled the gluey substance over the baby's mouth.
- *Danger, Scariness, and the Likely Experience of Domestic Violence.* Karina's enactment of aggression and urgent need for help was repeatedly enacted with scary-looking finger puppets that picked at and bit each other, invariably leading her to look for the telephones so that she could activate their ring tones.

In the last session, having reiterated my reasons for seeing her in the playroom, Karina approached the dollhouse and showed three children being dropped down the stairs followed by a number of adults also crashing down to the floor.

- *Real Hunger and Deprivation.* Karina seemed happiest when she was reminded that the drink and cookies had been provided for her. She would quickly approach the table where the food had been placed and hungrily eat all the cookies and finish the juice. While the way in which children make use of the food provided is often indicative of their emotional hunger, in Karina's case she seemed physically hungry and pleased to find the offer of sustenance. On one occasion she hid a cookie under her jumper in an attempt to smuggle the food out of the playroom.

Family Life, Musical Beds, and Possible Sexual Abuse   In Karina's play with the dollhouse bizarre scenes were enacted with children placed in toilets or in sinks. A little girl shared a bed with a small boy or adult female figure surrounded by multiple doll-figures shown to be sleeping on the floor. Possibly suggesting her claustrophobic situation at home, such scenes may have represented a case of musical beds, however inappropriate, and possibly sexual adult–child relationships could not be ruled out.

Attachment   Karina's behavior with me and her responses to the story stems suggested fear and withdrawal as well as anticipation of danger and threat. Her relating style was generally characterized by both avoidance and disorientation and showed little anticipation of responsiveness to her actions or feelings. Instead, her inner world revealed a barrenness and high level of restriction with little capacity to approach others for help or allow for the experience of shared enjoyment. Clearly, she had learned to decrease any need for attachment, had minimized her needs, and knew how to keep her distance.

Summary and Recommendations   Karina's restricted play and inhibition conveyed an inner life characterized by anxiety, bleakness, and isolation. Through the evident disturbance and barrenness of her play she revealed an impoverished imagination, absence of symbolic play, a preoccupation with messy and, sticky feelings, and most importantly, a sense of endangerment and lack of safety. Unsurprisingly, she conveyed a strong sense of distrust in the availability of others and a strategy aimed at avoiding potential confrontation.

Her depressed affect and chronic sense of helplessness bore the hallmarks of neglect as did her anxiety about food and her inability to develop peer relationships or to ask for help.

While much of Karina's play was suggestive of something unpleasant that she wished to draw attention to but felt unable to express, nothing of a sufficiently concrete nature indicated with certainty a current threat to her safety. However, such disturbed play, in conjunction with passive and withdrawn behavior, frozen watchfulness, and real hunger, all contributed to a picture of inhibited/fearful and disorganized attachment, which can be indicative of experiences of trauma or abuse. Given these markers it was suggested that her progress should be carefully monitored.

It was recommended that Karina needed a facilitating environment in which she would be helped to express her feelings and be reassured that her physical, emotional, and security needs would be met. Her disturbed behavior and play indicated that a core assessment was required to determine her safety and well-being at home. While there was no real evidence that she was not safe, her play indicated that she continued to be disturbed and that she may have been the unwitting victim of neglect, domestic violence, and potentially past and ongoing sexual abuse. In every respect, it was clear that her emotional, and perhaps physical, safety was compromised by her environment.

ASSESSMENT OF THE RISKS AND RESILIENCIES OF THE FAMILY EMOTIONAL CLIMATE

The relationship dynamics revealed in the child's minimizing avoidance, hyper-activating anxious-ambivalence, or frozen and disoriented disorganization indicate the way in which the child-parent relationship has contributed to the child's inability to resolve difficulties within dyadic relationships. Such insight into the child's attachment dynamic, mirrored by the thematic content of the child's play, further emphasizes the need for enhanced assessment of the emotional climate in which these daily transactions take place. Even if the therapist emphasizes a security-inducing relationship in which emotional availability, empathic attunement, and provision of safety are predictable and reliable transactions, this relationship is not able to safeguard the child from the experience of anger, emotional distance, or engulfment by the parent.

In individual play therapy, efforts are made to increase the engagement of parents in the therapeutic process so that they can become more aware of the child's emotional needs and become actively focused on improving their parenting skills (Ryan, Wilson, & Fisher, 1995). Yet therapists often remain unaware of specific characteristics of the parent-child relationship when they endeavor to engage parents who are themselves resistant, angry, emotionally withdrawn, or fearful as well as mistrustful of the professional judgments perceived to be implicit in therapeutic work.

Parents of children with behavioral difficulties may show deficiencies in strategies for child control and discipline, but more fundamental may be their ability to be responsive to the child's needs if they themselves are either withdrawn or preoccupied. Research investigating preschool conduct problems (Speltz, 1990) found a strong correspondence between attachment of parents and behavior patterns of children. Thus in undertaking work with a child there is a need to focus on insight and understanding of the relationship between the parent and the child and the way in which this can become available for change.

A concern with the child's competencies, as well as weaknesses, is standard practice before embarking on direct work with the child. However, identification of dyadic and family strengths and weaknesses further allows for the development of an open and transparent therapeutic relationship in which both strengths and potential family dynamic dilemmas can be openly examined and discussed (Zeanah et al., 2001). Approaching work with the child by emphasizing the child-parent relationship is an accepted prerequisite for therapeutic work. Assessment of the child's behavior with the parent is made when the therapist first visits the child at home in preparation for the work to be started in school. To assess the child-parent relationship in the context of the child's development, a stringent developmental history of the child is taken as is the parents' evaluation of this. However, important questions can remain unanswered when such an assessment fails to reveal crucial domains of the family's emotional climate.

Fundamental to the assessment process is awareness and understanding of the degree to which the parent is able to provide the child with emotional and physical safety. As outlined by Bentovim et al. (1998), knowledge of extremes of disturbance in the family (i.e., psychiatric disturbance) is paramount, as is understanding of basic parental sensitivity to the child (i.e., how emotionally available is the parent, and how well the parent understands emotional and physical development and child care principles). Insight into the emotional climate in which the child resides can enhance and accelerate the therapeutic process.

Adult Attachment Style

The assessment of the emotional climate in which the child resides is fundamental to, yet often omitted from, the preclinical assessment phase. New developments of comprehensive assessment in the field of support needs and attachment style can usefully be linked to therapeutic work. Understanding parental attachment style provides important insight and understanding into how the parent behaves in relationships and how the child's attachment cues are likely to be perceived and responded to. Knowledge of the attachment style of parents of children engaged in the therapeutic process is thus pivotal for understanding the risks and resilience of the emotional climate within the family. *The Attachment Style Interview* includes a behavioral assessment of ongoing quality of relationship with partner, *Very Close Others* (VCO), and family of origin as the basis for a rating of ability to make and maintain relationships, which equates with degree of security or functioning in relationships (Bifulco et al., 2002). It identifies the presence or absence of positive adult supportive networks and partner relationships and provides an immediate window into how well-supported the parent is. It also provides quantified information on how supportive the relationships, are in terms of degree of confiding or active emotional support, how positive or negative social interactions are, and how much felt attachment is in the relationship.

Five distinctive attachment styles (Enmeshed, Fearful, Angry-Dismissive, Withdrawn, and Secure) and the degree of insecurity in each is determined by the poor quality of ongoing relationships and the intensity of negative attachment attitudes that characterize the way in which the individual conducts himself in relationships with others.

While there is no evidence that such attitudes in relationships are generalized from adults to children, it is possible to infer that a parent with an angry dismissive style is likely to provide parenting that is overly strict, potentially harsh, and possibly even punitive. Conversely, parents with a fearful style may find it difficult to be authoritative in their parenting and provide firm boundaries to contain the angry child behaviors that challenge their own fear of rejection. Importantly, those rated as *markedly* or *moderately* insecure, indicating limited or no support and highly negative attitudes, are shown to be vulnerable to emotional disorder (Bifulco et al., 2002).

Assessment of the parental support component of the measure alone has also proved invaluable in identifying the absence of support from partner and VCOs, which in itself determines insecurity. The absence of a partner or close others in whom the parent can confide and access emotional support is known to negatively impact the psychological factors of the individual's relating style.

Cursory analysis of the play therapy referral factors revealed that the two most common denominators were trauma resulting from domestic violence and being parented by a single parent with reduced coping capacity. This information was often belatedly shared with the play therapist due to parents feeling too ashamed to disclose abuse. A preoccupation with their own survival possibly also prevented full awareness of what was experienced by the child.

In addition to highlighting risks for psychological vulnerability and poor parenting, the ASI scale measuring positive and negative interactions with partner and VCOs can provide early insight into the level of conflict in the home as well as predict depression in the victim. Victims of violence in the home are known to have more difficulty in maintaining nondistressed relationships with children (Van der Kolk, McFarlane, & Weisaeth, 1996).

CLINICAL WORK

FILIAL THERAPY IN THE SCHOOL SETTING

Millie was a 7-year-old girl referred by the learning mentor at her primary school due to concerns about her temper tantrums and angry outbursts in the classroom but also her sadness, low self-esteem, and solitary behavior. Her withdrawal and gradual alienation from peer relationships had been noticed by her teacher, and she was reported to be increasingly less communicative with friends and with school staff. A very intellectually able child, Millie lacked confidence. Her teacher worried that in the classroom Millie would rather be invisible than make any contribution and was particularly worried that her behavior was impeding her ability to concentrate in the classroom.

Further referral information showed that Millie's parents had separated when she was 2 years old. Both had recently established new relationships, and Millie's father and his new partner were now expecting a baby. Millie's feelings about her mother's new boyfriend made her feel uncomfortable about leaving her mother, causing problems when separating from her at the school gate.

Millie's relationship with her mother appeared to be close, and her home life appeared stable; yet it was evident that her mother's new relationship, contributed to Millie feeling anxious and insecure. Such anxiety increased her feelings of protectiveness for her mother, but also heightened her anger at her role-reversed feelings of adult responsibility. Millie demonstrated all the hallmarks of controlling and punitive behavior. She alternately rejected and humiliated her mother and guided and encouraged her in an overly cheerful and solicitous way.

Millie's father continued to play a role in her life and, following many years of unpredictability, now offered her a more stable and dependable relationship. However the arrival of a new baby for his new family was evidently threatening and unsettling for Millie.

The meeting with Millie's mother, Mrs. W., corroborated the school's view that Millie's relationship with her mother, was characterized by Millie taking an inappropriate parental role with her in which she attempted to control her through punitive behavior (Solomon, George, & de Jong, 1995).

Mrs. W. shared details of a recent loss and her feelings of vulnerability in her on-and-off relationship with her boyfriend over the past few years. From her description, Millie's heightened emotional state and intense focus on her mother's needs indicated developmentally inappropriate negotiation of stage-salient issues relevant to middle childhood.

Millie's first session revealed her preoccupation with nurture, as demonstrated by a starving baby intent on preparing an elaborate meal for her mother. Verbally uninhibited, Millie told me she was lonely with no one to play with at home. The full range of her anger also lacked inhibition as it was released on the bop bag. Three clear themes ran through her sessions: anger and wish to hurt and dominate a man who upset her, her mother's failure to adequately nurture her, and her own invisibility. Each of these was seen as she wrestled with the bop bag, portrayed her mother with breasts dripping blood, and reiterated her invisibility as she noisily ran through the room.

In the second phase, the themes of anger and resentment at the invasion of her secret garden by strangers and her own marginalization as she floundered unseen and unheard in the muddy sea below the castle walls dominated Millie's sessions.

After eight sessions of nondirective play therapy Millie continued to struggle with feelings of marginalization of her own needs. Her role-reversed controlling care of her mother represented a distortion in the child-caregiver relationship at the expense of her own need for comfort and protection and, above all, visibility (Lyons Ruth et al., 1999).

Research has shown that Filial Therapy (Van Fleet, 2005; Guerney, 1997) can successfully provide a treatment plan where, through parents' involvement as therapeutic change agents, both children and parents can change together as increased parental understanding of the child's play expressions helps develop heightened empathy for and acceptance of the child.

I had earlier proposed Filial Therapy for Millie and her mother when I had assessed their relationship to be in need of repair. As role reversal is a dyadic construct, it seemed appropriate that the relationship, rather than only Millie's behavior and emotional state, should be taken into consideration. However, Mrs. W. had been unable to commit to the training due to work demands, and the school had felt that play therapy for Millie required some urgency.

Three months later Mrs. W. was able to acknowledge that she could no longer postpone addressing what was most important, providing Millie with the empathy, containment, and appropriate boundaries implicit in a secure attachment relationship. As I trained Millie's mother, I continued to see Millie for sessions in school so that she would not have the anxiety-provoking experience of feeling dropped by me as she anticipated a new and uncertain experience of therapeutic play with her caregiver.

In our final play therapy session Millie stumbled into the room with a wary smile. Initially placing the dinosaurs dangerously close to the little piggy, she rearranged three adult camels into a protective circle around the baby camel. Her anxiety about ending and her anger with me was shown as she repeatedly pretended to stab me in the heart and kill me. As the session approached its end, Millie made a small booklet on the cover of which she faintly wrote her name twice in pencil and twice in large glittered lettering. Sprinkling water over her name made the paint run and Millie added a clown face with a false smile and sad eyes from which large cascading tears turned into rivers. I congruently shared my sadness at saying good-bye and my understanding of her dread at not knowing what to expect of the sessions with her mother.

In the first Filial Therapy session with her mother that I observed, Millie carefully arranged the bedroom furniture and placed the little girl in her mother's bed. Mrs. W. had been quick to learn the skills and carefully reflected the little girl's pleasure and feelings of safety and comfort in being in close proximity to her mother. Millie nodded as she searched among the animals. Shattering the peace and serenity, a large tiger came charging through the window and chased the little girl out of her mother's bed. Jumping out of the window the little girl clung for some time before letting herself down into the uncertain area below the house walls.

Mrs. W.'s shock was palpable. She had not understood how profoundly persecuting her partner had been perceived to be and how alienated and despairing her daughter had felt in being chased from her mother's love and care.

It was through first engaging Millie by herself and then by involving her mother in the school setting that it was possible to address the underlying stresses underpinning what had become manifest in the classroom as poor achievement, low self-esteem, and withdrawal. In focusing on extending the trust built in the playroom into the child's wider existence, adverse future development resulting from disrupted secure attachment and role reversal with her parent could be sensitively addressed.

CONCLUSION

Erickson (1963) posits that the child's first task is the development of trust in the world. This is directly experienced in the care the child receives, both in terms of nurture and attitude. When the child enters school, the disruptive or depressed behaviors that interfere with the child's learning appear to have set the stage for adverse future development.

However, school provides a second chance for children to develop trust through the experience of care, the provision of which has been challenged by parental lack of security and support.

Play therapy in school approaches direct work with the child by taking the view that the key to effecting change for the child is to make significant changes in the child's wider environment. Educational work with the school to foster awareness of the impact of early experience on behavior and the empowerment of families to improve parenting responsiveness and skills through careful assessment and a consolidated therapeutic alliance enables the school to become the vehicle through which both child and family can become engaged with the school at a level available for change. In this way the *troubled child in school* can achieve emotional safety by being understood and helped both individually and within a wider systemic context.

REFERENCES

Axline, V. (1987). *Play therapy*. New York: Ballantine.

Barret, M., & Trevitt, J. (1991). *Attachment behaviour and the schoolchild: An introduction to educational therapy*. London: Routledge.

Bentovim, A. (1998). Significant harm in context. In M. Adcock & R. White (Eds.), *Significant harm: Its management and outcome*. Croydon, England: Significant Publications.

Bifulco, A., Moran, P. M., Ball, C., & Bernazzani, O. (2002). Adult Attachment Style I: Its relationship to clinical depression. *Social Psychiatry and Psychiatric Epidemiology, 37*, 50–59.

Bifulco, A., Moran, P. M., Ball, C., & Lillie, A. (2002). Adult Attachment Style II: Its relationship to psychosocial depressive vulnerability. *Social Psychiatry and Psychiatric Epidemiology, 37*, 60–67.

Bowlby, J. (1988), *A secure base*. New York: Basic Books.

Bretherton, I., & Munholland, K. A. (1999). Internal working models in attachment relationships: A construct revisited. In J. Cassidy & P. Shaver (Eds.), *Handbook of attachment: Theory, research and clinical applications* (pp. 89–111). New York: Guildford Press.

Bretherton, I., Ridgeway, D., & Cassidy, J. (1990). Assessing internal models of the attachment relationship: An attachment story completion task for 3-year-olds. In M. Greenberg, D. Cichetti, & E. M. Cummings (Eds.), *Attachment in the preschool years* (pp. 273–308). Chicago: University of Chicago Press.

Cichetti, D., Cummings, E. M., Greenberg, D., & Marvin, R. S. (1990). In M. T. Greenberg, D. Cichetti, & M. Cummings (Eds.), *Attachment in the preschool years: Theory, research and intervention* (pp. 3–49). Chicago: University of Chicago Press.

Cichetti, D., & Toth, S. (1991). A developmental perspective on internalizing and externalizing disorders. *Rochester Symposium on Developmental Psychopathology, 2*, 1–19.

Coie, J. D., Belding, M., & Underwood, M. (1988). Aggression and peer rejection in childhood. In B. B. Lahey & A. E. Kazdin (Eds.), *Advances in clinical child psychology* (Vol. 2; pp. 125–158). New York: Plenum Press.

Cummings, E. M., & Davies, P. (1994). Maternal depression and child development. *Journal of Child Psychology and Psychiatry, 35*(1), 73–112.

Domitrovitch, C., & Greenberg, M. (2000). The study of implementation: Current findings from effective programs that prevent mental disorders in school-aged children. *Journal of Educational and Psychological Consultation, 11*, 193–222.

Erickson, E. H. (1963). *Childhood and society*. New York: Norton.

Erickson, M., & Egeland, B. (1996). Child neglect. In J. Briere, L. Berliner, J. Bakley, C. Jenny, & T. Reid (Eds.), *The APSA handbook of child maltreatment* (pp. 4–20). Thousand Oaks, CA: Sage.

Fonagy, P. (1999). *Transgenerational consistencies of attachment: A new theory*. Paper Presented to the Developmental and Psychoanalytic Discussion Group at the meeting of the American Psychoanalytic Association, Washington, DC.

Garbarino, J. (1995). *Raising children in a socially toxic environment*. San Francisco: Jossey-Bass.

Greenberg, M. T., Cichetti, D., & Cummings, M. (1990). *Attachment in the preschool years: Theory, research and intervention*. Chicago: University of Chicago Press.

Greenberg, M. T., Kusche, C. A., & Speltz, M. (1991). Emotional regulation, self-control, and psychopathology: The role of relationships in early childhood. In D. Cichetti & S. Toth (Eds.), *Internalizing and externalizing expressions of dysfunction. Rochester Symposium on Developmental Psychopathology, 2*, pp. 21–55.

Greenberg, M. T., & Speltz, M. L. (1988). Attachment and the ontogeny of conduct disorder. In J. Belsky & T. Nezworski (Eds.), *Clinical implications of attachment* (pp. 177–218). Hillsdale, NJ: Lawrence Erlbaum.

Greenhalgh, P. (1994). *Emotional growth and learning*. New York: Routledge.

Guerney, L. (1997). Filial therapy. In K.J. O'Connor & L. M. Braverman (Eds.), *Play therapy: Theory and practice* (pp. 131–159). New York: John Wiley & Sons

HM Government (2001). *Promoting children's mental health within school and early years settings*. London: Department for Education and Skills.

HM Government. (2004). *Every child matters: Change for children*. London: Department for Education and Skills.

Hodges, J., & Steele, M. (2000). Effects of abuse on attachment representations: Narrative assessments of abused children. *Journal of Child Psychotherapy, 26* (3), 433–455.

Kolvin, I. & Fundudis, T. (1981). Elective mute children: Psychological development and background factors. *Journal of Child Psychology and Psychiatry and Allied Disciplines, 22*, 219–232.

Lyons Ruth, K., Bronfman, E., & Atwood, G. (1999). A relational diathesis model of hostile-helpless states of mind. In J. Solomon & C. George (Eds.), *Attachment disorganization*. London: Guildford Press.

Malatesta-Magai, C. (1991). Emotion socialization: Its role in personality and developmental psychopathology. In D. Cichetti & S. Toth (Eds.), *Internalizing and externalizing expressions of dysfunction. Rochester Symposium on Developmental Psychopathology, 2*, 203–224.

Office for National Statistics (2004). Mental Health of Children & Young People in Great Britain. www.statistics.gov.uk.

Office for Standards in Education, Children's Services and Skills (2004). *Healthy minds: Promoting emotional health and well-being in schools*. HMI 2457.

Offord, D. R., Boyle, M. C., & Racine, Y. A. (1991). The epidemiology of antisocial behavior in childhood and adolescence. In D. J. Pepler & K. H. Rubin (Eds.), *The development and treatment of childhood aggression* (pp. 31–54). Hillsdale, NJ: Lawrence Erlbaum.

Perry, B. D., Pollard, R. A., Blakely, T. L., Baker, W. L., & Vigilante, D. (1995). Childhood trauma: The neuro-biology of adaptation and use dependent development of the brain: How "states" become "traits." *Infant Mental Health Journal, 16*(4), 271–291.

Ray, D., Muro, J., & Shumann, B. (2004). Implementing play therapy in the schools: Lessons learned. *International Journal of Play Therapy, 13*(1), 79–100.

Rubin, K. H., & Mills, R. S. L. (1988). The many faces of social isolation in childhood. *Journal of Consulting and Clinical Psychology, 6*, 916–924.

Ryan, V., Wilson, K., & Fisher, T. (1995). Developing partnerships in therapeutic work with children. *Journal of Social Work Practice, 9*, 2.

Salzberger-Wittenberg, I., Henry, G., & Osborne, E. (1983). *The emotional experience of learning and teaching.* London and New York: Routledge.

Solomon, J., George, C., & de Jong, A. (1995). Children classified as controlling at age six: Evidence of disorganized strategies and aggression at home and at school. *Development and Psychopathology, 7*, 447–463.

Speltz, M. L. (1990). The treatment of preschool conduct problems: An integration of behavioral and attachment concepts. In M. Greenberg, D. Cichetti, & E. M. Cummings (Eds.), *Attachment in the preschool years: Theory, research and intervention* (pp. 399–426). Chicago: University of Chicago Press.

VanFleet, R. (2005). *Strengthening parent-child relationships through play.* Sarasota, FL: Professional Resources Press.

Van der Kolk, B., McFarlane, A., & Weisaeth, L. (1996). *Traumatic stress: The effects of overwhelming experience on mind, body and society.* New York: Guilford Press.

Weare, K. (2000). *Promoting mental, emotional and social health: A whole school approach.* London: Routledge.

Wells, L., Barlow, J., & Stewart-Brown, S. (2003). A systematic approach to universal approaches of mental health promotion in schools. *Health Education, 103*(4), 197–220.

Wilson, K., Kendrick, P., & Ryan, V. (1992). *Play therapy: A Nondirective approach to children and adolescents.* London: Balliere Tindall.

Zeanah, C. H., Boris, N. W., Heller, S. S., Hinshaw-Fuselier, S., Larrieu, J., Lewis, M., Palomino, R., Rovaris, M., & Valliere, J. (1997). Relationship assessment in infant mental health. *Infant Mental Health Journal, 18*, 182–197.

Zelenko, M., & Shaw, R. (2000). Case study: Selective mutism in an immigrant child. *Clinical Child and Psychology and Psychiatry, 5*(4) 1359–1045.

CHAPTER 20

The Nana's Model

School-Based Play Therapy with Children Who Are Homeless or Severely Impoverished

ANA MARIA SUTTON

FAMILY HOMELESSNESS IS a relatively new social problem. At any given time in the United States 1.35 million children are homeless. Working with this population becomes difficult due to the lack of verifiable data available (Institute for Children and Poverty [ICP], 2007).

With the exception of the Great Depression in the 1930s, women and children had not been on our nation's streets in significant numbers. However, the 1980s cutbacks in benefits and the current recession have jeopardized the stability of people with reduced or fixed incomes and even the middle and upper classes. During this time the number of households headed by single females dramatically increased. As a result, the nation's population of homeless families has swelled from almost negligible numbers to nearly 40 percent of the overall homeless population, young children being the fastest growing segment. The average age of a homeless child is six, and they comprise 39 percent of the overall population (National Coalition for the Homeless (NCH, 2008). During the late 1980s the McKinney Federal Act was passed by the U.S. Congress to provide, among other things, an effective way to identify and educate this population of "invisible" children. After several revisions over the years, it is now known as the McKinney Vento Federal Assistance Act, and it defines *homelessness* for purposes of education as "lacking a permanent nighttime residence, sharing a room with other families, living in a car, trailer, outdoors or in temporary shelter."

HOW HOMELESSNESS AFFECTS CHILDREN

HEALTH ISSUES

According to The Institute of Children and Poverty (2007), homeless children get sick twice as often, have lower birth weights, require special care four times as often, and have very high rates of acute illnesses. One-half of the children suffer from two or more symptoms during a single month. In 2007, 37 million Americans were living in poverty. The National Institute of Mental Health reports that low-income individuals are two to five times more likely to suffer diagnosable mental disorders than those of the highest socioeconomic group. Poverty also poses a significant hurdle in receiving help for those mental health problems (APA Monitor on Psychology, 2008).

EMOTIONAL WOUNDS

The constant barrage of stressful and traumatic experiences has profound effects on children's cognitive and emotional development. More than 20 percent of homeless preschoolers have emotional problems serious enough to require professional care. Forty-seven percent of homeless school-age children have problems such as anxiety, depression, or withdrawal. They suffer three times the rate of sexual abuse and twice the rate of physical abuse than that of housed children. And, 35 percent have been the subject of a Child Protective Service investigation (National Center on Family Homelessness [NCFH], 1999).

ACADEMIC ISSUES

Despite state and federal efforts to provide homeless children with improved access to public school, at least one-fifth of these children do not attend school. For many there is no transportation from shelters to schools, and duration of improvised living arrangements is too short to make enrolling in a new school worthwhile. Their parents' daily demands of finding food and shelter push their children's educational needs aside. Although 87 percent of school-age homeless children are enrolled in school, only about 77 percent attend school regularly. They are four times as likely to have developmental delays, have more academic problems, are underserved by special education, get suspended twice as often as other children, and are twice as likely to have learning disabilities. Because of frequent absences and moves to new schools they are twice as likely to repeat grade. This population has three times the number of students with emotional and behavioral problems than their poor housed counterparts. Homeless children often report that they are automatically placed in a lower grade level and are assumed to be poor achievers by virtue of their economic status. It is hardly surprising that teachers find their students' performance matches their level of expectation (Fletcher-Campbell, 2008).

Homeless children have deep-rooted and severe emotional issues due to lack of stability in their living conditions. The constant mobility inherent to their homeless situation proves detrimental to their education. Homeless students not only face the daunting task of keeping up academically despite extended absences, lack of learning materials, and multiple school transfers, but also have to face the challenges of these difficult transitions without any emotional support. A solid education offers the only way out of a seemingly hopeless situation (Institute for Children and Poverty, 2007). Homelessness is not just a housing issue; it is a community problem, multidimensional and complex, where drug and alcohol abuse, domestic violence, child maltreatment, and neglect are being constantly interplayed. Thus, no single service or intervention has been shown to treat effectively all the problems that ensue (Sutton, 2007). According to the Office for National Statistics (ONS; 2005), there is undeniable evidence that the situation is getting worse; and estimates are that one in ten homeless children suffer a diagnosable mental health disorder (Music, 2008). Much of the recent trauma literature is dedicated to research and treatment of trauma in adulthood. Invariably, research describes that childhood events of neglect, abuse, and chaotic lifestyle, such as homelessness, were present (Briere & Scott, 2008).

Although in recent years there has been an increasing awareness of mental health issues in children, attitudinal and organizational barriers are hard to break down when working with schools or school districts.

The time has come to implement a *holistic approach* to homeless education in a setting where children not only receive their basic needs of food, clothing, educational materials, and transportation, but also receive medical, dental, and mental health support, without ever leaving the security of their school.

The Nana's Model

A chance viewing by the author of a *Good Morning, America,* story featuring a school for homeless children in Phoenix, Arizona, resulted in a personal offering of play therapy treatment for homeless children at the school. Subsequently, the profound impact of the author's experiences resulted in the creation of a holistic program offering medical, dental, play therapy, and mental health and academic services within this school setting for homeless children. The Nana's Children Mental Health Foundation (MHF) Inc., was formed to deliver free play therapy (PT) services to homeless or severely impoverished children within the school setting. Its goal was not to treat severe pathology, but rather to reduce anxiety, diminish depression, increase self-esteem, and emotionally stabilize homeless children so they could learn, stay in school, and break the vicious cycle of homelessness and violence.

Since 1999, Nana's Children MHF, Inc., has provided services throughout school districts in Phoenix, serving over 1,200 children and delivered 7,000 sessions. Nana's has also been a training model and resource for programs in Europe and South America working with homeless and impoverished children. It has been the recipient of several national and international awards of excellence.

From Nana's beginning, we have conducted studies, supporting the efficacy of the program. By law, school districts must only allow evidence-based counseling programs in their schools to take place. While it was difficult at first to conduct scientific research with a treatment group, a control group, and a group that received other types of counseling by nonplay therapists—such as *anger management*—once several years had passed, we found that we had collected large amounts of clinical records/art production, group sandtray photos, and videotapes of sessions. Thus, different studies were designed by our Research Director and Nana's Advisory Board members. To date, we have conducted a longitudinal study of two years, where Boxall Profile outcomes of Nana's clients administered in different settings (classroom, lunch room, playroom, play yard) were administered by teachers and practicum students. Nana's administrative staff graphed the scores and placed those in the client's files. The *AIMS Reading Fluidity Test* (Shinn, 1989) was administered weekly, at the beginning of each PT session.

SETTING UP A SCHOOL-BASED MENTAL HEALTH PROGRAM

PRELIMINARY CONSIDERATIONS

Before a school-based program, such as Nana's, can be implemented, careful consideration must be given to how the program will fit into the school's culture. School personnel tend to lack an understanding of how mental health services relate to a child's successful education; thus, educating the educators becomes a priority. There are always frustrations encountered with some teachers, office staff, an IT person, or even a janitor who may not understand the therapeutic value of play. An important aspect of Nana's mission, as well as that of anyone modeling this program, is in making presentations not only to the local education agencies (LEAs) in charge of homeless education for the state but also to district administrators, boards, principals, designated liaisons, teachers, and staff. It is important to not only go "to the top" but to also be sure to start "from the bottom." Once teachers become aware of how a play therapy program helps students settle down emotionally and creates a better classroom climate, they themselves then promote the program to their principals, who in turn will promote it to their administrators.

USE OF VOLUNTEER DOCTORAL-LEVEL CLINICIANS

The use of volunteer practicum doctoral-level psychology/counseling students from local universities for delivery of services helps keep program costs down. However, it is important to not only communicate clearly to the practicum students what roadblocks they may face during their time working with homeless children, but also to be clear with their university supervisors. In particular, working in a school environment offers unique challenges for maintaining special procedures and confidentiality.

The selection process of graduate student applicants is critical. We look for candiates who are committed, emotionally mature individuals who will not become easily frustrated or become part of the problem rather than the solution. Group and individual supervision is given by a licensed psychologist and a registered play therapist–supervisor to deal with treatment and personal issues as they arise.

NANA'S MISSION

1. Delivery of free mental health services to students, within the school setting in the form of individual or group play therapy.

2. Provide a practicum site to doctoral psychology/counseling students from local universities.
3. Provide teacher training on how to work effectively with students and address the burn out factor that comes from working with this population.
4. Conduct research to evaluate and support the effectiveness of the program.

DELIVERY OF SERVICES

The first step is to identify school districts with large homeless populations. To get these statistics, the best way is to contact the state coordinator for education of the homeless (each Department of Education has a web site, where they indicate the name, phone number, and e-mail address of the person in charge). Educating this person on the need for, and availability of, services is of extreme importance. Yearly, the state coordinator is responsible for putting together a conference for all of the state's local educational agencies (LEAs) to find out about budgets and services available, as well as changes or modifications in the law. This is an opportune time for the introduction of the program's services. After this, districts with large numbers are identified, and their board is contacted by Nana's MHF. At the same time, schools are visited to check out the facility and to meet with teachers, social workers, and principals. If the school has enough students to justify the expense of building a model playroom, Nana's will offer to make a brief presentation to staff during an in-service meeting. Invariably, while the school may initially be reluctant for this initial contact, once they see the presentation they are responsive and invite us back. At this point questions about issues with students and the staff's own issues about needing ''new tools'' to teach these children come forward.

If the district (some of which may have as many as 32 schools) accepts the proposal, a written agreement is drawn up, clearly spelling out what Nana's duties are and what is expected from the school. If a playroom is to be created, the space must be dedicated to Nana's. That means cameras, video equipment, a one-way mirror, shelving, toys, sand tables, art supplies, computers for recordkeeping, and filing cabinets, although installed inside the school, remain the property of Nana's. The district/school also agrees to provide Nana's with a ''mental health liaison'' (school, district psychologist, or social worker) who will secure written consent for treatment (supplied by Nana's in English and Spanish) from the parent or guardian. No child is seen without first receiving the written consent. Although many schools want the program, most lack the space to dedicate two rooms for services. In those cases, arrangements are made to send one or two graduate practicum students a week with portable play therapy suitcases to offer mental health services. Consent forms and record keeping is maintained the same way, regardless if services are provided with portables or within a playroom.

REFERRAL PROCESS

Children are referred to Nana's PT program by teachers, parents, social workers, and school psychologists. At registration time for a new school year, packets are sent home containing consent forms for signature if either the child received services the year prior or the principal/social worker/district psychologist feels this child would benefit from services. We have found it most efficient if on parent's night Nana's staff is allowed to make a brief presentation where parents are able to ask questions, tour our playroom, or simply find why their child would benefit by receiving services. Sometimes, children are registered at a particular school by Child Protective Services (CPS), in cases where they removed the children from their residence and placed them in foster care.

Once a child has a signed consent (for homeless children under McKinney Vento only one signature is required), regardless if the child changes location where they are staying or guardianship, and continues to attend that school, the consent remains valid for the entire school year, unless revoked by the guardian who originally signed it.

The client is entered into our *Therascribe 5* network system, given an ID number, and assigned by the clinical supervisor to the caseload of a practicum student. Because of the high mobility of the homeless population, some children stay in the program for only a few weeks. If they leave the school, once we receive notification, they are moved to "inactive status" in *Therascribe* and a new client is assigned to that student therapist. Although we try to keep a large case load with each practicum student, sometimes a child moves from one of the schools where we deliver services to another. In that case, the child will have the same ID number but with a different two-letter code ending (which identifies the school) and is assigned to a new therapist.

By keeping computerized records in the *Therascribe* network encrypted, Nana's is APA and HIPPA compliant. We are able to print and send records when requested with verified signed release to a new school or mental health provider. Having this network program facilitates access to records and/or consultation with Nana's personnel.

PRACTICUM STUDENTS AND THEIR PARTICIPATION IN THE PROGRAM

In order to deliver service to as many schools as possible and keep costs down, local universities were tapped for graduate students. It was a mutually beneficial arrangement, as universities were looking for good practicum sites to place their students and Nana's needed student clinicians. After contacting heads of departments in the graduate schools of psychology or counseling and presenting our program, agreements were developed and signed with local universities. Nana's provides one week of intensive training prior to starting services, along with weekly supervision by a licensed clinical psychologist, who is also an RPT-S. Students receive one hour of individual and one hour of group (with no more than four students per group) supervision per week. The practicum lasts for 37 weeks, a full academic year, following the school's schedule. This schedule allows the required hours of practicum.

The students must travel to different schools within districts. Each practicum student is supplied with a carry-on–sized wheeled suitcase at the beginning of the practicum. All suitcases are standardized with the same contents arranged the same way. Students are also provided with a soft blanket (rolled up and attached to the suitcase) to place on the floor to define and cover the space where the child will play (see addendum for a list of specific items).

It is important that the student maintains the portable play therapy kit in "inspection-ready condition" at all times. For the child, having the playroom/portable maintained in perfect order provides a measure of stability and consistency; it also lets the child know that he or she is valued as a client. Practicum students are given forms in a folder, together with Nana's policies and procedures, at the beginning of their practicum, which allows them to request supplies from Nana's head office as needed.

Flexibility and the ability to accept change and to always keep a "playful attitude" (not always easy to achieve) are critical components constantly reminded to our practicum students.

TRAINING

A full week of training prior to working with the children in therapy is conducted. Training covers the essentials of nondirective, child-led therapy, responsiveness to the child's comments, note keeping, confidentiality, duty to report, and ethical issues. One full day is dedicated to the supervision process and to how they must prepare to meet with their supervisor, forms that need to be filled out, treatment plans, and teacher or social worker contacts. *Therascribe* is utilized for client records. In-depth training is given to students on how to use the program correctly. Each student is assigned a password, so only that student can access the program from his or her site. Confidentiality is assured, as once they place information into the computer, they cannot remove or change records. Supervisors may access the program from any location and can edit or "sign off" on the student's work. The American Psychological Association requires that 95 percent of all clinical notes be reviewed by a supervisor.

We try to help practicum students understand the time-limited nature of the children's placements, as the homeless population frequently moves around and the child may only attend school for brief periods of time. Thus, issues of transference, loss, and the need to be flexible are also addressed in the training and subsequent supervision sessions.

PLAY THERAPY MATERIALS USED

Playroom toys are arranged by themes, and are placed on shelves and in bins that are clearly labeled to simplify the cleanup and prevent the need to rearrange the playroom after each session. The playrooms are 11 feet by 20 feet in size, painted a soft yellow color, with light blue, commercial-grade carpeting, different from what is found throughout the schools or classrooms. Because homeless children have particular issues about lack of housing; incarceration; and lack of money, food, and clothing, Nana's has developed a list of toys that are included in each playroom or portable in exactly the same place. During training, it is explained that toys have been selected for therapeutic value and to elicit and facilitate expression of emotions and conflict. We have a large number of "families" of different ethnicities and age groups, different types of houses, a cash register, sand table, art supplies, dress-up clothes, pots, pans, play food items, and rescue vehicles. Every single "theme" is found in smaller amounts in the portable play bag (see addendum).

Because schools in Arizona have *zero tolerance of weapons*, we are not allowed to have toy guns or play knives in our portables. We do have a couple of brightly colored water pistols in the playrooms, as allowed by the school district.

Before bringing any type of toy that may be considered a weapon to school, it is a priority to check with the school administrators about policies (American Psychological Association Zero Tolerance Task Force, 2008). Also, practicum students must be familiar with the lockdown and fire drill policies of each of the schools we service. If during a session the fire alarm goes off, there are signs posted in the room as to how to proceed. During lockdowns, no one is allowed to use the school phone system; therefore, all therapists must carry a charged cell phone with them, turned off, with instructions on where to call for more information.

Because schools must know at all times who is on the premises, our therapists are issued badges by the districts with their photo, and they must sign in and out every time they go to a site.

ADDITIONAL SERVICES OFFERED

Nana's not only provides individual and group sessions but also is available for schoolwide crisis intervention. Some examples of school-wide interventions include children being shot, a school bus that caught fire, or another bus that hit a pedestrian and kept on going, which the children witnessed. In addition, due to one year of having unusually cold weather in Phoenix, pipes froze and broke resulting in the destruction of the school-based playroom. Of all the crises faced, the most difficult was the sudden death of a beloved social worker at the start of the school year.

Teachers and staff are also offered regular in-service training on how to understand the special needs and behaviors of homeless and impoverished children. The director of clinical services, the program director, and the clinical supervisor give these trainings.

RESEARCH

As required by the Department of Education, all public school counseling programs must be evidenced based. Nana's has been careful, as required by law, to keep data and to design studies that would support our effectiveness. In early studies we successfully researched our population's characteristics and play therapy outcomes. We were able to show a statistically significant correlation between number of play sessions received and reduction of acting out in the classroom. A study titled "The Effectiveness of Child Centered Play Therapy on Developmental and Diagnostic Factors in Children Who Are Homeless" was conducted and accepted for publication by the *International Journal of the Association for Play Therapy*. The study's authors are Dr. Jennifer Baggerly (University of South Florida), an Advisory Board Member of Nana's Children, and Dr. William W. Jenkins, Nana's Children clinical supervisor and research director. It was published in 2009.

In 2008, Dr. Jenkins completed a "pilot study" looking at progress and supervisory notes to assess how the supervisor can influence trainee's tasks or behaviors in play therapy. He used the 2006–2007 year's notes. The notes were analyzed to examine key provider observations of therapist's levels of therapeutic connection and engagement. Research questions were related to supervision's influence on the therapist. Information emerged regarding the efficacy of using standard Likert-Type indicators in process notes as well as closed-ended questions. Numeric ratings, emergent narrative themes, issues, and emotive responses extracted from notes were congruent with research on the analysis of children's play content. The findings indicated analysis of children's play content and that themes found in child-centered play therapy are related to goals required for therapeutic progress. This study is in the process of being submitted for publication.

CASE STUDIES

All information has been modified to protect the identity and confidentiality of the children and families presented. The case studies of Susana and Joey were seen in therapy by graduate practicum students. The case study of Pat was seen in therapy by the author.

CASE 1: SUSANA—AN OPPOSITIONAL DEFIANT CHILD

Susana, a Mexican American girl of 11 years of age, was continuously acting out in class to such an extent that she was disrupting her classmates and not learning anything. She would fly into temper tantrums, hit other students, or defy her teacher. Yet, at other moments, she would appear very near despair, often before lashing out again. The school staff was concerned about her disruptive behavior and referred her to individual play therapy, after securing written consent from her grandmother.

BACKGROUND INFORMATION

At first Susana would barely play, often in silence. As sessions progressed and her therapist established a relaxed relationship by reflecting on her limited play, she began exploring and explaining her life situation through her play. She was now living with her grandparents, following a period of homelessness with her mother. She had also been previously placed in foster care due to her mother's drug addiction and neglectful behavior, prior to going to her grandparents. Her father had been violent with her mother, which she witnessed, and he was a heavy user of drugs and alcohol. Her father had been incarcerated for a while, and Susana had no idea if she would ever see him again. Susana was allowed supervised visits with her mother once a month. It was noted that after such visits her behavior would become more extreme at school with staff and peers and with her grandmother.

Additional information was obtained by the practicum therapist through the school social worker. Susana's maternal grandfather had been diagnosed with a terminal illness. The grandmother was distraught and admitted to being at the end of her rope with taking care of two sets of grandchildren, one from Susana's mother and the other from a younger daughter who was HIV positive. The doctors had prescribed the grandmother antidepressants, which she could not always get, and Susana was getting very little attention at home. In fact, the grandmother expected Susana to help with chores and take care of the younger children, and then she would become very frustrated when Susana would refuse to obey. Susana's teacher reported that Susana was always defiant and ready to strike out at the least provocation.

PLAY THEMES

Her play themes were quickly identified as "nurturing, but punitive." She would play with dolls but when they would "cry" because they missed their mommy or they were hungry, she would hit them, shake them, or send them away "without anything to eat." Every now and then she would show a little empathy and get them a bottle or change their diapers.

The theme of money (or lack of it) and the need to get some money for drugs or medication also was evident. Susana would frequently interchange the words *drugs* and *medication*. The therapist would reflect on how some medicine makes you better, but some drugs can make you get sick. When this was mentioned, Susana would make immediate eye contact with the therapist and ask for clarification between drugs and medication.

During weekly supervision, it was decided that this child would benefit from more directive play therapy, where an activity would be prepared ahead of time, to help her address following directions without having meltdowns. At first she seemed not to respond well at the lack of control in the play, but after a couple of sessions, she would come into the playroom and ask, "What are we going to do today?" At around the same time, reports from her teacher indicated that she was doing much better in class, had started making friends with some children, and was even engaging with peers in the playground.

To help facilitate peer interactions, Susana was placed in "Nana's Friendship Group Sandplay." Although ideally children would benefit from individual and group at the same time, district policy does not allow for a child to be removed from class more than once a week, unless mandated by CPS or the courts. Nana's Group Sandplay is time-limited to eight weekly sessions where four students, in the presence of two practicum students as facilitators, build individual sand trays with miniatures and are allowed time to share a story about their tray, while the others listen. Children are given the freedom to share or to pass the "talking stick." Although for the first two sessions Susana passed and did not talk about her tray, in sessions three through eight not only did her trays became organized, but she was able to tell a story about a girl who was not a "bad girl," but rather she just behaved badly because she was so lonely. By the end of that year, Susana had received 28 individual PT sessions and 8 group sandplay sessions. She never missed a single appointment. According to her teacher, she was now able to complete assignments and follow directions and was promoted to the next grade.

As with most of the students we see, she was not at the school the following year, but it is the hope of this author that the level of empathy, structure, and limit setting she received in the playroom will allow her to continue her school work with more confidence and self-worth.

CASE 2: "MY NAME IS PAT." A WITNESS TO HER MOTHER'S SUICIDE

At age 7 Pat was referred to Nana's Playroom. She was confused, depressed, and extremely thin. Pat had been the sole witness to her mother's suicide, and she was left alone with her mother's body for two days before the police intervened and Child Protective Services placed her in foster care. When her estranged father returned to remove Pat from foster care, *he made matters worse by changing her name from Pat to Sandi.* He did this so he would not be reminded of his late wife, who bore the same name as their daughter.

When play therapy first started, Sandi did not know how to describe in words what she felt or why. Due to her young age, she had extreme difficulty verbalizing feelings of fear, anger, despair, and grief. She only knew that she wasn't happy, that she had no friends, that she was constantly tired, and that she felt no trust toward adults.

Her father had expressed suspicions of sexual abuse on the part of Mom's boyfriend. Much of Sandi's art production was consistent with his concerns. She would draw very large men with their genitals exposed, while the females were very small and with expressions of fear in their faces.

After Sandi had participated for approximately seven months of twice-a-week individual PT (the school approved this due to the severity of the case), it became apparent that she was dealing not only with emotional issues but also with physical issues as well. The "all homeless school" licensed medical clinic was able to schedule a full physical exam with the onsite head pediatrician. After several tests, results came back that Sandi suffered from a severe foot infection, had a bad case of head lice, and was dangerously underweight. A plan was developed to provide her with a combination of antidepressants; food supplements administered at the school twice daily; antibiotics for her foot infection; and treatment for head lice. Individual play therapy sessions were increased from once to three times a week. The school psychologist had tried to treat her unsuccessfully, but she refused to work with a male. It was decided that this author/therapist would gradually introduce the school psychologist for a few minutes into the sessions, so he could administer all of the evaluations for her Individualized Education Plan (IEP) as required by the district. While at first Sandi seemed uncomfortable with this new arrangement, she adjusted quickly and would even approach the school psychologist from time to time to include him in her play.

Within a few weeks a remarkable change took place. Her teacher came to our office to report a very important shift. On that particular day, the teacher had asked her a question referring to her as "Sandi," since that was the name she had been going by. Surprisingly, the child looked at the teacher and corrected her by saying, "My name is Pat."

Pat continued play therapy for the rest of that year and half of the following school year. She was never placed in Special Education. She then moved out of the homeless school but, like so many other homeless children, eventually returned again to the homeless middle school.

Today, Pat no longer attends PT, but according to her teachers she is doing well in school, has many friends, and fully embraces her identity as Pat. The few times we have crossed paths, she has acknowledged me with a big smile.

CASE 3: JOEY—SELECTIVE MUTISM

At age 9, Joey, a girl in fourth grade, was referred to the playroom by the school psychologist and by her mother Suzy. Joey lived in a homeless shelter with her mother and two younger sisters. She also had an older sister and a brother who attended the same school but lived elsewhere. She had attended the homeless school since kindergarten. Her referral was due to learning disabilities and her lack of speaking in school. According to her mother, Joey was quite vocal at home. In all the years she had spent at the school, she had been placed in special education class and received weekly visits from the district's speech pathologists without any noticeable improvement.

As soon as she was accepted into Nana's program, a battery of tests was administered to assess learning disabilities and speech impediments. Although her scores were on the low side, Joey suffered from selective mutism, whereby she would elect when to speak and when to remain silent. Currently it is well understood that this condition has nothing to do with speech impediments or voluntary withholding of verbal communication. It is a social phobia: The more the person is asked to speak, the higher the anxiety level, and the less likely the person will be able to do it (Giddan et al., 1997). In Joey's case, once a diagnosis ruled out any physical or mental difficulties, a treatment plan was developed for individual weekly play therapy sessions to address her social phobia and anxiety.

Once Joey became familiar with the playroom environment, she started exploring and experimenting. While at first she played alone, little by little she invited the therapists to participate in her play. Although Joey played silently at first, the therapists would reflect and make comments on her activity and label the feelings that were perceived, such as fear, frustration, anger, or happiness. As the sessions progressed Joey started to speak, at first in whispers and later in a normal tone. Today, Joey is no longer in therapy and attends junior high school. Recent reports are that she is able to speak and is doing well in class.

Below are detailed notes, from *Therascribe*, that help to show the development and changes in this case study.

PSYCHOSOCIAL HISTORY

Joey lives in a Phoenix shelter with her mother and two younger sisters. It is uncertain if Joey parents are divorced or separated at this time. All that is known is that her father does not live with them, as her mother did not address the situation while filling out the evaluation forms. Joey has three sisters (Kristina, Amber, and Samantha) and a brother named Jeremiah. Joey's sister Kristina is also currently in play therapy. There is no known substance abuse in the family history. At the IEP meeting, Nana's representatives, the school psychologist, the speech pathologist, the special education teacher, and Joey's mother Suzie, were present. At this meeting Nana's representatives discussed the uniqueness of selective mutism.

DEVELOPMENTAL HISTORY

Joey's mother was in good health during her pregnancy with Joey. Her mother did not report use of drugs or alcohol during that time. Joey was a full-term pregnancy and was born during a natural vaginal delivery. Forceps were used in assisting the delivery, and no known complications occurred or followed the delivery.

Joey was described as a quiet infant and child. Her language skills developed at 18 months. No growth or other developmental problems were noted or described by her mother. The only medical problem was at four years of age when Joey developed chicken pox. According to her mother, Joey is verbal at home with her siblings. A vision screening at age 6 indicated that Joey required glasses. Although in the fourth grade at the time of referral, she had been attending the homeless school since Kindergarten. Attendance has been sporadic, with Joey having missed 24 days of school since September during her initial year in therapy.

Concerns arose about her expressive language skills during her first year at the school. She did not volunteer to speak on her own nor to participate in groups. When she spoke, it was in a voice just slightly above a whisper. Joey was referred for and began speech therapy that same year. She was re-evaluated after 6 months and showed some progress, demonstrating that she had learned some basic concepts. She scored 45 out of 50 (90 percent) on spatial/direction concepts and 26 of 30 (87 percent) on quality concepts. She also showed improvement with articulation skills. When referred to Nana's she was showing a weakness in verbalizing and rarely spoke to adults or peers while at school. When she did speak, she used as few words as possible and preferred to answer multiple-choice questions to open-ended ones.

SOCIOECONOMIC

Joey is homeless. She and her family are currently living in a shelter.

MEDICAL

Joey has had a yearly physical evaluation since her enrollment at the homeless school. Her health was described as generally good with the exception of vision and dental problems. At her first physical she was fitted for glasses. Her vision was 20–50. Her corrective lenses, provided by the Lion's Club, were soon lost and she now has no glasses. The physical also noted that she has dental cavities and speech delay. She is in special education and receives speech therapy but has not received any dental care.

THERAPY

Joey was seen in the play therapy room for a total of 29 individual sessions. She participated in nine sandplay group sessions.

ASSESSMENTS

All assessments were administered, scored, and interpreted by Nana's practicum students under the supervision of a clinical licensed psychologist, RPT-S.

Boxall Profile Joey scored within the average range for the majority of the developmental strands. She showed a slight deficit in "engages cognitively with peers" and "responds constructively to others," but not enough to be considered significant. On the diagnostic profiles she once again fell into all of the average areas except for "self-negating," "craves attachment," and "avoids attachment." Once again the differences were not enough to be significant in these areas.

Woodcock Johnson Test of Achievement, 3rd edition (WJ-III) Joey worked hard and did not appear to be distracted by outside influences. She made good eye contact when appropriate, though she whispered many of her answers. Her ability to comprehend what she was reading appeared to be low. She appeared to be guessing in areas that required reading a sentence before she responded. Her English oral language skills are low when compared to others who are at grade level. Joey's academic skills, her ability to apply those skills, and her fluency with academic tasks are all within the very low range. Also, when compared to other students at her grade level, Joey's performance was low in mathematics, math calculations skills, written language, and written expression—and very low in broad reading

Standard Scores Grade Equivalent

Broad Reading 62 1.6
Broad Math 82 2.5
Broad Written Language 73 2.0
Oral Language 82 1.7
Math Calculation Skills 81 2.6
Written Expression 80 2.4
Academic Skills 77 2.2
Academic Fluency 65 1.5

Child Depression Inventory (CDI)   Joey endorsed many items suggesting depression, negative mood, anhedonia, and negative self-esteem. She also endorsed the item that states, "*I want to kill myself.*" A suicide risk assessment was completed immediately, and the supervisor was notified. It was established that no immediate danger existed. She had no plan to carry this out. She just circled the item.

California Verbal Learning Test (CVLT-C)   Testing observations: Joey recalled items between lists that never appeared on either list A or list B. The CVLT-C measures strategies and processes involved in learning and recalling verbal material within the context of an everyday shopping task. Joey's ability to repeat a list of words the first time she heard it indicates a low-average initial attention span for auditory-verbal information. On her fifth learning attempt, her performance was average. Joey's use of semantic clustering, where words from the same category are remembered together, which is usually more effective than serial clustering, where words are remembered in order, was low-average compared to others her age. Because she tended not to recall words with similar meanings together, she did not use the learning strategy that typically is best for remembering verbal information. Taken together, the findings suggest that Joey can encode verbal information into memory adequately, but she has mild difficulty retrieving information from memory. When presented with a second interference list, Joey's recall was high-average. Joey actually recalled fewer words when provided with the category cues than when recalling words on her own. This again suggests that she has difficulty using semantics strategies to remember verbal information. Joey had a mild difficulty learning verbal information. Compared to other students her age, she may need more repetition of material to learn it. Care should be taken not to frustrate her by presenting too much information too quickly. Joey exhibited a problem in auditory attention span when she was first attempting to learn the word list. She may benefit from shorter periods of learning, longer breaks between periods of learning, and/or behavior modification programs designed to reinforce her ability to sustain attention for progressively longer periods of time. Joey would likely benefit from learning more effective strategies for remembering verbal information. Specifically, she should be taught to think about the meaning of words when trying to remember them and to recall words together that are close in meaning. She should be encouraged to *chunk* information, that is, group individual units of information into smaller number of groups. Joey can encode information into memory adequately, but she has difficulty retrieving information from memory. In order to test how much Joey really knows, she should be given classroom exams that require recognition memory, such as true-false and multiple choice items.

Joey will likely struggle on exams such as essay and short-answer tests that require her to retrieve information herself; these latter types of exams should be avoided whenever possible.

Other Measures

Children's Apperception Test (CAT)
Vineland
Reynolds Child Manifest Anxiety Scale (RCMAS)

Joey scored high on anxiety but was willing and focused to answer all questions, either by scribbling on a white board but mostly with a nod of her head or a very soft whisper.

ASSESSMENT SUMMARY

Strengths   Joey has a disarming manner and uses nonverbal cues such as facial expression and good eye contact to substitute for her lack of verbal communication with others. Joey is attentive to her environment and appears to attend to the cues of others. This interest and attention to her environment is valuable and will enable her to communicate more effectively with others especially when she chooses to do so in a verbal manner. Joey's IEP (Individual Education Plan) reflects that she no longer qualifies as MIMR (Mild Mental Retardation) and instead is eligible for SLI (Speech/Language Impairment).

Areas of Concern   Joey's IEP indicates that she has learning disabilities in math reasoning, reading, written language, and expression language. Joey does not communicate with teachers and other students verbally. Instead she uses nonverbal cues. Although the homeless school environment may attempt to adapt to Joey's communication style, this lack of verbal communication likely precludes typical development in academics, emotional, and social areas. Joey's awkwardness is likely exacerbated by her lack of practice using reciprocal conversation skills. As her peers progress, Joey may feel an increasing sense of anxiety about her inability to communicate with others.

Diagnosis
Axis I 300.23 Social Phobia (Selective Mutism)
Axis III Unknown
Axis IV Housing: Homelessness, Educational Deficit
Stress Severity Rating: 5 High
Axis V: Current 51–60 Prior 51–60

Treatment Plan   Because selective mutism is an anxiety disorder, successful treatment focuses on methods that lower anxiety, increase self-esteem, and increase confidence and communication in a social setting. Emphasis should never be on "getting a child to talk," nor should it be the goal of treatment for the child to speak to the therapist. Initially all expectations for verbalization should be removed. As the child's anxiety is lowered and confidence increases, verbalization will usually follow. Individual nondirective, child-led PT at this time is recommended, with the hopes of eventually moving this child to participate in group sandplay.

PROGRESS NOTES

Joey was seen in the playroom for a total of 29 individual sessions. This author has copied "verbatim" clinical notes placed into *Therascribe 5* network by practicum student therapists involved in this case.

These are just three instances of progress notes that represent important shifts in the treatment.

Session 6: First Time She Plays a Game   Joey came into the playroom and walked around the perimeter of the room looking at the toys and games, but not selecting anything. The therapist reflected, "There is so much to look at . . . sometimes it is difficult to decide what to play." She seemed to ignore the comment. After a few more minutes she took out a game of checkers and holding the box looked at the therapist, making good eye contact.

The therapist reflected, "You picked a game . . . . you are looking for a place to play the game." Joey motioned to the small table and sat down, putting the game on the table and looked up at the therapist as though saying, "Sit opposite to me." The therapist reflected, "You want me to sit down?" Joey nodded her head. She opened the box, and then she set up the board . . . she knew how to play the game, and the therapist joined her in playing. The therapist won, but this did not seem to disappoint or discourage Joey. After the game was over, she carefully put everything back in the box and placed it on the shelf. She then moved to the sand table and started running her fingers through the sand. The therapist commented that she enjoyed running her fingers through the sand, because she was smiling. She nodded yes.

This was the first time that Joey has engaged in any type of play. Although she did not speak, she nodded her head twice yes, and when it was time to leave she moved her mouth as though saying, "Bye."

Session 15: First Time She Attempts to Speak but Changes Her Mind   Joey came into the playroom with a smile on her face and went directly to the *Talking Feeling Doing Game* and pulled it off the shelf. The therapist commented, "You know exactly what you want to play with." Joey nodded, "Yes." She sat at the table and motioned to the therapist to sit opposite to her. She did not know how to play the game but tried to read the directions. She passed the box to the therapist, who said, "You want me to read how to play this game?" Again she nodded, "Yes," but this time her mouth also said, "Yes" without sound. The therapist explained the game and asked who should go first. Joey pointed to the therapist. She moved the dice, read the card, and told a story of a time when she was happy. Now it was Joey's turn; she rolled the dice, pulled the card, read it, shook her head "No," and picked up the entire game and put it neatly away. The therapist commented, "You decided you did not want to play this game after all." Joey looked at her for what seemed like a long time and let out a big sigh nodding her head, "yes!" After that she moved over to the sand table and placed some small animals inside and played there in silence until it was time to go.

Session 17: Suicidal Ideation   Joey entered the playroom for testing. The therapist administered the CDI and the RCMAS (see above scoring in the assessment section). She endorsed an item on the CDI, noting that she had wanted to kill herself within the last two weeks. She looked up at the therapist for a response when she circled the item. Once the test was completed, I inquired about that specific item. I went over the item with her and repeated it to her. She gave a gentle head nod and shoulder shrug to indicate that she understood what the item meant. I asked her if she had anyone to talk to or spend time with when she felt this way or had ideas about it. She shook her head, "yes." I asked her to show me with her fingers how many people she knows that she can go to talk to or spend time with when she feels this way. After about a minute she held up four fingers. Next, I asked her to play a game or make a rule that whenever she feels this way that she goes to one or more of these people to talk or spend time with them. Also, the therapist reassured her that the play friends and therapist are available while she is here at school if she feels like this. She was allowed to pick out a stone to remind her of her friends at the playroom and of the therapist. She was assured that she could come to the therapist or any other therapist whenever she had feelings or ideas of killing herself. When the session ended, the therapist felt confident that Joey would stick to the rule and contact someone should she entertain these thoughts or feelings.

When Joey had been picked up from class, she had just been dropped off by two other women; one may have been the speech therapist, so it is possible that she spent some of the morning being tested and her level of anxiety increased. The therapist's supervisor was immediately contacted and notified of her statement and that a suicide risk assessment had been completed.* (See below at end of notes)

Session 22: First Time Joey Speaks   Joey came into the playroom, took the cash register to the sand table, got a small chair, and said to the therapist, "Sit down" (in a very low voice). She sat opposite the therapist. Next Joey opened the register and said, "I'm going to sell you ice cream. . . . Do you have money?" (She speaks in a clear and loud enough voice to be picked up by the camera's microphone.) The therapist replied, "Yes, I want to buy ice cream . . . How much does it cost?" Joey replied, "A lot, but I'm going to let you buy it cheap." The therapist answered, "Thank you," and Joey replied, "You are welcome"! After that she spent a long time counting and arranging the money in silence. She then went over to the corner where the babies are and said "They are hungry . . . we should feed them." The therapist reflected on the fact that babies should be fed when they are hungry. Joey stated, "Yes, they should be fed and not cry!" During the remainder of the session there are several moments when Joey speaks and looks into the eyes of the therapist to see any reaction or surprise on her part. Since the therapist does not make any comments, Joey seems to relax and play with the doctor's kit. When she leaves she says . . . "BYE!"

*Practicum students are trained to follow Nana's special protocols whenever there is disclosure of suicidal ideation or when any type of abuse or neglect is identified. In cases where the supervisor deems it necessary, either Child Protective Services (CPS), a district psychologist, parents, or guardians are contacted immediately. Practicum students must document in the logbook the ID number of the child, the date, what occurred, who was notified, and what actions were taken. No child is ever left unattended, even if there are delays in getting CPS to respond to the call. Practicum students receive, during training, a three-ring binder with Nana's policies and procedures. Before starting delivery of services they must sign a document stating that they have read and accept to adhere to said policies and procedures or face immediate dismissal from the program.

After session 29, when Joey had started to speak during individual sessions, it was decided during supervision that she should start participating in Nana's Sandplay Groups with three peers from her class, along with two practicum students. Because at Nana's therapists are switched, she was familiar with the practicum therapist conducting the groups as she had been one of the therapists that treated her in individual PT. At first she was guarded and would build a tray but pass on the story, but after a few sessions, she started telling brief stories about monsters living together and being best friends. Although at times she still appeared anxious and guarded and tended to whisper, her peers made an effort to engage her and were patient with her process. Joey looked around at her peers and the therapist/facilitators for direction and possible approval. Her self-esteem seemed to have increased, and her physical appearance changed from being disheveled to being neat and clean.

TRAINING FOR TEACHERS AND STAFF

Ideal Classroom for SM Child   It is crucial for teachers and school administrators to understand selective mutism (SM). The ideal teacher for an SM child must clearly understand the behavioral characteristics of his or her student. A nurturing and comfortable environment is key for the SM child to build a sense of comfort within the classroom. Teachers should use strategies specifically developed for the treatment of SM children, such as visual aids and manipulative materials for a hands-on experience; allow adequate time for verbal and nonverbal responses; emphasize and complement creativity, imagination, and artistic expression; and understand that in testing situations and with time limits SM children will perform poorly (Shipon-Blum 2003). It is easy for a teacher to misinterpret the SM characteristics and assume that the child has a lower than average intelligence. Teamwork in cases such as this one is of extreme importance (Goetze-Kervatt, 1999).

CONCLUSION

Homelessness in the United States has become a serious concern in the past 20 years. The largest and fastest growing segment of the homeless population are families with young children. These children face many challenges to fit into the current education programs. The McKinney-Vento Homeless Assistance Act provides funding for in-school services. The intent of this act is to ensure that all homeless children and youth have access to the same free and appropriate public education. The act calls on all states to eliminate barriers to enrollment and attendance and to promote success in school. Local education agencies (LEA) are to ensure that these children and their families receive services and referrals to health, dental, and mental health care that are appropriate.

Nana's Children MHF was established in 1999 by a group of concerned citizens and mental health clinicians to provide free mental health services, in the form of play therapy, within the school setting. To accomplish this goal, Nana's relies on practicum students from local universities to deliver services under the supervision of a licensed clinical psychologist, who is also an RPT-S.

Whenever possible, Nana's builds model play/observation rooms, where video cameras are set up and record sessions. When space is not available, practicum therapists visit school sites with portable play cases.

All student clients participating in the program must have a signed and dated consent form. All clinical records are kept in *Therascribe 5* network, which is APA and HIPPA compliant. As required by law, the provider must keep the client's clinical records until the minor reaches age 21.

In March of 2009, Nana's became a licensed mental health provider, nationally and with the state of Arizona. After 10 years of delivery of play therapy services in schools, we have been able to compile ample data supporting the effectiveness of a holistic approach to educate the homeless student where not only transportation, food, clothing, and educational needs are met, but also the emotional and physical as well.

Nana's Children's mission is not only to provide services to children who are homeless and suffer from emotional and behavioral difficulties, but also to maintain an approved practicum site, provide in-service training for teachers and school administrators, and conduct research to assess the effectiveness of the program as mandated by law. Although most clients stay with Nana's for only brief periods of time, teachers and principals report remarkable changes in the student's behavior and improved academic achievement. The Nana's model is easily replicable and is currently being implemented in four schools in Phoenix, Arizona, and two schools in Buenos Aires, Argentina.

ADDENDUM

Parent Consent Form

Your child has the opportunity to participate in counseling services through play therapy at Nana's Children Mental Health Foundation, Inc., located within Manzanita and Orangewood Elementary Schools. This method is used with children in numerous schools, and early results indicate improved school behavior as well as improved academic work for many children.

Play therapy provides a safe, therapeutic environment in which children express/release their emotions about their life experiences. Children have opportunities to create, build, and/or tell stories about their creations if they so choose. Each session is videotaped for two purposes: 1. To ensure a safe, therapeutic environment for the child and therapist, and 2. To develop training materials and research that may be used to educate other professionals in the use of play therapy. Please be assured that your child's name and confidentiality will be maintained at all times.

Play therapy is scheduled with your child's teacher so that your child misses as little class time as possible. Children are scheduled for counseling services depending on the child's particular needs.

Your child's name or any other identifying information will not be used. You may discuss the results of your child's overall progress with the Director of Clinical Services at Nana's Children Mental Health Foundation, Inc., at any time.

Please sign the consent form below and return to your child's teacher to authorize your child's participation.

If you have any questions or concerns at any time regarding your child's progress or this study, please contact Dr. William Jenkins, the Clinical Supervisor of Nana's Children Mental Health Foundation, at 480–946–6262 or Administrator of Social Services at the school district of attendance.

I give my child permission to participate in the counseling services through play therapy at Nana's Children Mental Health Foundation located at the XXX Elementary School. I understand that my child's work in session may include videotape/photograph/artistic production/sandtray work that may be used for educational and training purposes only. I agree to the use of testing and evaluation for research purposes, and I understand that my child's teacher may fill out a rating scale to help assess my child's progress. I also understand that my child's name and confidentiality will be maintained at all times. I also understand that my child's participation is voluntary and that he or she may withdraw from counseling at any time with no penalty.

Please Check One:

_____ I give my consent for my child to participate in this counseling program

_____ I do not give my consent.

Child's Name_____

Parent/Guardian Signature X_____

Parent/Guardian Name (Please Print)_____

Child's Date of Birth_____Grade_____

Date of Consent_____

Formulario de Consentimiento Paterno

Su hijo ha sido seleccionado para participar de los servicios de asesoramiento psicológico (counseling) a través de Terapia de Juego en Nana's Children Mental Health Foundation, Inc., ubicada en la escuela elemental que mi hijo/a atiende. Este método es utilizado con niños de numerosas escuelas, y ya sus primeros resultados han demostrado una evidente mejora en la conducta escolar así como en el trabajo académico de muchos niños.

La terapia de juego provee un ambiente seguro y terapéutico en el cual los niños expresan y sueltan sus emociones sobre sus experiencias de vida. Los niños tienen la oportunidad de crear, construir y/o de contar historias sobre sus creaciones si así eligen hacerlo. Cada sesión es filmada con dos objetivos: 1. Para asegurar un ambiente seguro y terapéutico para el niño y su terapeuta y 2. Para desarrrollar material de entrenamiento e investigación que puede ser utilizado para el entrenamiento de otros profesionales en el uso de la terapia de juego. Por favor tenga la absoluta certeza que el nombre de su hijo y la confidencialidad serán mantenidos en todo momento.

La Terapia de juego será coordinada con la maestra de su hijo a fin de que no pierda mucho tiempo de clases. Los horarios de asesoramiento psicológico de los niños dependerán de las necesidades específicas de cada uno.

No se utilizarán el nombre del niño ni cualquier otra información que lo identifique. Ud. puede discutir los resultados del progreso general de su hijo con el Director de Children's Therapy a Nana's Children Mental Health Foundation, Inc., en cualquier momento. Por favor firme el formulario de consentimiento adjunto y devuélvalo a la maestra de su hijo para autorizar su participación.

Si tiene alguna duda o preguntas en cualquier momento respecto del progreso de su hijo o sobre este estudio, por favor contacte a Dr. William Jenkins, Supervisor de Servicios Clinicos de Nana's Children Mental Health Foundation, al 480–946–6262 o a la, Administradora de Servicios Sociales en el distrito escolar que corresponde.

Autorizo a mi hijo a participar de los servicios de asesoramiento psicológico a través de la terpaia de juego en la Fundación Nana's Children Mental Health Foundation ubicada en la Washington Elementary School District. Entiendo que el trabajo que mi hijo realice durante las sesiones puede ser grabado en video/fotografia/produccion artistica/mesa de arena y tuilizado y entrenamiento únicamente para fines educativos. Estoy de acuerdo que esas grabaciones sean utilizadas para supervisión y evaluación y por motivos de investigación, y entiendo que la maestra de mi hijo puede completar un cuadro de evaluación para ayudar a determinar el progreso de mi hijo. También comprendo que el nombre de mi hijo así como la confidencialidad serán mantenidos en todo momento. Asimismo, comprendo que la participación de mi hijo es voluntaria y que él o ella pueden retirarse del programa de asesoramiento psicológico en cualquier momento sin apercibimiento alguno.

Por favor marque lo que corresponda:

_____Doy mi consentimiento para que mi hijo participe en este programa de asesoramiento Psicológico

_____NO doy mi consentimiento

Nombre del Niño:_____

Firma del Padre o tutor:_____

Parent/Guardian Name (Please Print)_____

Fecha de Nacimiento_____**Grado**_____

Fecha de Consentimiento_____

ARTICLE I.   PORTABLE PLAY THERAPY KIT MATERIAL

Animals

Baby bottle

Baby doll

Bubbles

Bugs

Cars

Cell phones

Construction paper

Crayons

Dishes

Doctor toys

Farm animals

Feathers

Football

Glue

Handcuffs

House toys

Jewelry

Markers

Money

Paper bags

Paper plates

Pebbles

Pipe cleaners (fuzzy and sparkly)

Play-Doh

Popsicle sticks

Preemie diapers

Puppets

Sand box

Scissors

Scotch tape

Small dolls

Snakes

Toy food

Toy soldiers

Trees

Wand

Watercolors

White box

White drawing paper

Ziploc baggies

NANA'S CHILDREN

MENTAL HEALTH FOUNDATION, INC.

February 19, 20XX

███████████

Superintendent

███████ Elementary School District

███████████████

Dear ████████:

Nana's Children MHF, Inc. (Nana's Children), and ████████ Elementary School District (District) agree to the following procedures:

Play Therapy Services:

1. Nana's Children will provide portable play therapy services to children in a designated place decided by the District. All services are referred by means of Nana's Children consent forms provided in English and Spanish (copies included). Referrals will be reviewed and approved by the Administrator of Social Services.

2. Nana's Children will provide two Supervised Practicum Students, each at two days per week, with portable play therapy bags to two locations designated by the District. In order for services to begin, a minimum of 20 signed consent forms must be given to Nana's Children. Nana's Children will provide services from March 3, 20XX, to May 30, 20XX (depending on school calendar), and provide 240 play therapy sessions for $5,000. The Nana's Children play therapy program is providing the additional funding needed to complete this agreement.

3. A safe and confidential environment will be provided by the District to provide play therapy services. The School staff will be instructed that play therapy sessions are not to be interrupted while in progress for any reason. Nana's Children will follow protocol for fire drills and lockdowns as provided by the District.

4. Therapists provided by Nana's Children are required to have fingerprint cards and insurance statements on file at Nana's Children. Nana's Children shall require all therapists to comply with all policies, regulations, and procedures of the district. The ████████ Elementary School District should provide to Nana's Children all policies, regulations, and procedures.

5. The District will provide Nana's Children with protocol or policies and procedures for crisis situations. Nana's Children will follow said protocol, policies, and procedures in any crisis. Nana's Children will provide the District with its established protocol for crisis intervention. Nana's Children staff may be contacted at any time to support and assist in any situation deemed necessary by designated School staff.

6. Nana's Children will provide and maintain proof of comprehensive general liability insurance with a limit of not less than $1,000,000 per occurrence and $2,000,000 aggregate coverage with a deductible of not more than $5,000 and naming the ████████ Elementary School District as an additional insured party (see attached Certificate of Liability Insurance). If Nana's Children hires employees as determined under federal law, they will provide proof of Workers Compensation and Employer's Liability Insurance. At this time Nana's Children only hires contract employees.

Training:

1. Nana's Children will provide training at a reduced cost to the District. The District will decide which type of training to be given, listed below:

   a. **2 Day** – 9:30am to 3pm PowerPoint training, experiential with sand tray and session, and assessment instruments **for one group**.

   b. **1 Day** – 9:30am to 3pm PowerPoint training with no experiential **for two groups**.

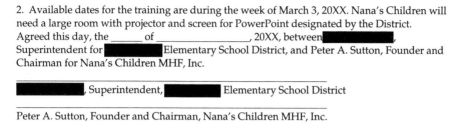

2. Available dates for the training are during the week of March 3, 20XX. Nana's Children will need a large room with projector and screen for PowerPoint designated by the District. Agreed this day, the _____ of _____, 20XX, between███████████, Superintendent for ███████ Elementary School District, and Peter A. Sutton, Founder and Chairman for Nana's Children MHF, Inc.

_____

████████████, Superintendent, ██████████ Elementary School District

_____

Peter A. Sutton, Founder and Chairman, Nana's Children MHF, Inc.

6210 East Thomas Road, Suite 104, Scottsdale, Arizona 85251,
Phone 480–946–6262, Fax 480–874–4167
www.nanaschildren.org

REFERENCES

American Psychological Association Zero Tolerance Task Force. (2008). Are zero tolerance policies effective in the schools? An evidentiary review and recommendations. *American Psychologist, 63*, 852–862.

APA, *Monitor on Psychology, 39*(10) November 2008, www.apa.org/monitor.

Baggerly, J., & Jenkins, W. W. (2009). The effectiveness of child-centered play therapy on developmental and diagnostic factors in children who are homeless. *International Journal of Play Therapy, 18*(1), 45–55.

Baggerly, J. N, Jenkins, W., & Drewes, A. (2005). *The effects of play therapy on academics, development, and mental health of homeless children: Research conducted at Nana's Children MHF, Inc.* Paper presented at the annual meeting of the Association for Play Therapy, Nashville, TN.

Bassuk, E. L., & Friedman, S. (2009). *Facts on trauma and homeless children,* National Child Traumatic Stress Network, Homelessness and Extreme Poverty Working Group. Retrieved January 10, 2009, www.NCTSNet.org.

Bennathan, M., & Boxall, M. (1998). *The Boxall Profile: A guide to effective intervention in the education of pupils with emotional and behavioural difficulties.* London: The Nurture Group.

Briere, J., & Scott, K. (2008). *Principles of trauma therapy.* Thousand Oaks, CA: Sage.

Fletcher-Campbell, F. (2008). *Safeguarding children and schools.* Philadelphia, PA: Jessica Kingsley.

Goetze Kervatt, G. (1999). *The silence within: A teacher-parent guide to helping selectively mute and shy children.* Oak Ridge, NJ.

Institute for Children and Poverty. (2007). *Back to the future, the brownstone and future link: Afterschool Programs for homeless children.* Retrieved July 1, 2007, www.icpny.org/index.asp?CID4&PID=105.

Jenkins, W. (2007). Evaluation of Nana's Program 2006–07. Nana's Children Mental Health Foundation, Inc. Unpublished manuscript.

Jenkins, W., Reuter, E. F., & Krech, P. R. (2009). Exploring structured supervision and progress documentation in play therapy (in press).

McKinney-Vento Homeless Assistance Act of 1987, P.L.100-77, reauthorized as Title X, Part C, of the No Child Left Behind Act in January 2002; 34 CFR Pt.200. http://www.ed.gov/policy/elsec/leg/esea02/pg116.html.

Moses, D. (1999). *Homeless children: America's new outcasts*. Fact sheet. Newton Centre, MA: The National Center on Family Homelessness Publications: www.familyhomelessness.org.

Music, G. (2008). *Safeguarding children and schools*. Philadelphia, PA: Jessica Kingsley.

National Center on Family Homelessness—NCFH, State Report Card on Child Homelessness. www.homelesschildrenamerica.org/report.php.

National Coalition for the Homeless. (2008). *Education of homeless children and youth, NCH Fact Sheet #10*, http://www.nationalhomeless.org.

Shinn, M. R. (1989). *Curriculum-based assessment: Assessing special children*. New York: Guilford Press.

Shipon-Blum, E. (2003). *The ideal classroom setting for the selectively mute child*. Philadelphia, PA: SMART-Center Publisher.

Sutton, A. M. (2007). Play therapy and children who are homeless. *Play Therapy*, 2(4), 12–13.

CHAPTER 21

Better Playtimes

A School-Based Therapeutic Play
Intervention for Staff and Children

ALISON WOOLF

Playing in education settings is often considered an important cognitive learning tool. But through considering the needs of children and the functions of play we can build a model for re-creating essential early experiences. The attuned playmate can facilitate change in perceptions and ways of relating, while the time and space for supported playful exploration may offer the wounded child a chance to heal. (Woolf & Austin, 2008, p. 39)

BETTER PLAYTIMES

IN 2005, WOOLF and Austin developed the *Better Playtimes* model, informed by Kinder Training research (Hess, Post, & Flowers, 2005). Training of school staff began in therapeutic play skills to prepare them for introducing individual play sessions with identified pupils. Initial work began in one school in England for pupils aged 5 to 11 years. Now, in 2009, *Better Playtimes* is being used in schools throughout England and Wales for pupils aged 3 to 16 years.

Better Playtimes are weekly half-hour play sessions, typically offered for 12 sessions (the length of a school term in England) for an identified child with a member of school staff—either the teacher or classroom assistant—who has training in attending to children through the medium of play. The staff member working with the child is an adult who either currently has the child in his or her class, or has, through previous contact with the child, an important relationship that endures over time. The rationale for staff-led play sessions is based on the belief that play is a therapeutic and reparative experience (Erikson, 1995; West, 1996) and that the presence of an attuned and nondirecting adult can enhance and facilitate this process (Axline, 1969; Cattanach, 1992). *Better Playtimes* has "a quality that is outside of everyday experience and it is the ingredients chosen to create this special time that make it uniquely a vehicle for healing and growth" (Woolf & Austin, 2008, p. 7).

THEORETICAL BASIS

Attachment theory (Bowlby, 1979; Karen, 1998; Gerhardt, 2004) informs the training and the practice of the model.

In nondirective play therapy, conditions are created that are similar to the optimum socialization processes that occur between an infant and a caregiver during normal development (Ryan & Wilson, 1996, p. 64).

Staff are introduced to "attachment" and its relevance to early childhood development and adult choices and reactions. The inclusion of theory gives school staff an opportunity to learn more about the basic underpinning science of learning (Shore, 1997; Klein, 1997; Gerhardt, 2004)—an area not often covered from an ethological perspective in teacher training courses. Adult understanding of primary attachments and patterns, which then form in subsequent relationships (Klein, 1997), may mean new responses can be chosen and habitual reactions recognized and acknowledged. The training program can be taken as either 10 weekly 2-hour sessions or as a block of 4 full days (Woolf & Austin, 2008).

The goal of school staff training is an alternative but parallel process to parent training in which the therapist works "to help parents to help their children, with a focus on strengthening the parent-child relationship" (Ford-Sori, 2006, p. 139). Strong teacher-pupil relationships may offer some reparation for insecure attachments at home (Shore, 1997; Chaloner, 2001). The Filial therapy (VanFleet, 2000; Guerney, 2003) parent training program is adapted for the training of school staff rather than parents. The enhancement of an attachment relationship remains core to the process. Just as in Filial therapy, where

> the therapist trains and supervises parents as they hold special child-centered play sessions with their own children, thereby engaging parents as partners in the therapeutic process and empowering them to be

the primary change agents for their own children. (VanFleet & Kaduson, 1999, p. 33)

So in *Better Playtimes* interventions, the therapist trains and supervises school staff to be key to healing and growth through therapeutic playtimes.

The model of involving school staff works because:

Bringing the educators directly into the process maximizes the chance that the teachers and children will work through their difficulties. (White, Draper, & Flynt, 2003, p. 332)

The "Kinder Training" program (White et al., 2003) and other staff-led therapeutic play sessions in schools have been introduced where a child, or a group of children, may need the support of attuned adult attention and opportunities for exploration and communication through play (Chaloner, 2001; White et al., 2003; Peabody, 2006). Play therapists working in education services train school staff in "active listening skills" (Geldard & Geldard, 2000) and child-centered play skills. These skills can then be used either during individual play sessions (White et al., 2003; Woolf, 2008), group work (Sweeney & Homeyer, 1999; Woolf & Austin, 2008), or in whole-class playtimes (Chaloner, 2001). As the child learns about himself or herself through the developmentally appropriate medium of play and learns to trust in the relationship with the facilitating adult, he or she can explore his or her internal world in a safe environment, before being asked to learn about a wider world in directed teaching and learning sessions.

CLIENT POPULATION AND REFERRAL PROCEDURES

The *Better Playtimes* program was first introduced to a primary school for children with social, emotional, and behavioral difficulties. All pupils attending the school are aged between 4 and 11 and have a Statement of Special Educational Needs. This statement provides guidelines for the program that the school must provide to meet the needs of the child. This includes individual remedial, therapeutic, and additional provisions. Pupils have higher than average incidence of extended family care and Local Authority placements. Many have diagnoses of ADHD; some have diagnoses of ODD and/or Autistic Spectrum Disorder (ASD). Often children in SEBD (Social, Emotional, and Behavioral Difficulties) schools also have specific or nonspecific learning difficulties as well as developmental delays. Children who have experienced moves, losses, family breakdown, and repeated exposure to risk and to inadequate care are likely to find mainstream expectations, large-group situations, and academic demands particularly stressful and threatening.

> When the child feels threatened, the attachment system is activated and the child's capacity to engage in other activities is reduced or rendered non-existent. (Ryan & Wilson, 1996, p. 150)

Behaviors in school that lead to referral to SEBD provision include inability to concentrate or to comply, aggressive reactions to peers and to staff, and persistent distraction of self and of others from the task at hand (Kellmer-Pringle, 2000; Dreikurs, Grunwald, & Pepper, 1971). Persistently infringing school rules, unruliness while waiting, and lack of concern for others were among the behaviors noted by teachers as being disruptive to lessons in a survey carried out by the Welsh Office (DES & WO, 1989).

> A child's skittish vigilance to everything in the environment—often judged to be nothing more than an unfortunate impediment to learning—may serve a higher and invaluably adaptive need for survival. (Bromfield, 1997, p. 133)

The behaviors that are inappropriate for the child are not helpful within the group and make maintaining a placement in a mainstream school setting unlikely. School then becomes another negative experience and a source of rejection for children already experiencing their needs not being met by the adults in their world. These difficulties may sometimes be accompanied by a lack of support for, and cooperation with, school from parents and caregivers. The adults' own negative experiences of school are often confirmed by their child's school staff seeming to say that neither their child nor they as parents are good enough.

So children starting at the school where the *Better Playtimes* project runs may be unable to "achieve real social or academic success because they are caught in the throes of their struggle for self-integration" (Burton, 1968, p. 7). Without providing reparative experience, addressing attachment needs, and being the secure base needed for moving away to explore and moving forward to recuperate, it is "unlikely" the child will "make progress on other fronts, in particular in his intellectual development" (Ryan and Wilson, 1996, p.151). The *Better Playtimes* project grew out of a recognized need for school staff to have increased knowledge and understanding of attachment theory, the importance of play, and effective communication skills for supporting the child at play. The use of an already established relationship in providing therapeutic play sessions was also acknowledged as being the way to provide an intervention for children whose parents were unable to engage in "Filial Therapy Training" (VanFleet, 2000; Guerney, 2003). It was seen as a potential program for those children whose attachment relationships at home were unable to support an individual intervention with the school play therapist.

TYPES OF THERAPEUTIC PLAY SERVICES

Within the school there are four services for children to access therapeutic play experiences. These play interventions developed from the initial service of play therapy. Play therapy was offered to children following discussion among teachers, the play therapist, and parents. As the play therapy service became established, Filial Therapy was offered to parents and caregivers where the head-teacher and play therapist felt it was appropriate, following referral from the Child and Adolescent Mental Health Services (CAMHS) team or when a parent or caregiver requested the training for himself or herself. The individual *Better Playtimes* was offered to children when play therapy with the specialist was not deemed appropriate (West, 1996) or when using an existing attachment relationship was felt to be more appropriate.

Play sessions with school staff were felt to be a fundamentally different service to play therapy, relying as they do on an already established relationship rather than on introducing a new person into the school life of the child. For this reason, while play therapy is an "opt in" intervention, *Better Playtimes* is offered as an "opt out" service. The fourth way of providing therapeutic play experiences is through *Better Playtimes* for whole-class groups—called "Everyone Playing in Class (EPIC)" (Woolf & Austin, 2008). EPIC, when used by whole classes, is treated as Circle Time (Mosley, 1996) and other class activities such as anger management and drama. Parents are informed of the sessions but, as the group dynamic is core to the process, they are not invited to opt out. However, like school assembly, religious education, and other sensitive areas of the curriculum, parents are welcome to approach the school to talk through any concerns or to make a case for their child's exclusion from the session. Designated children are removed from class for their individual work with teachers and classroom assistants, focusing on additional training in providing targeted interventions. In the school where *Better Playtimes* was first introduced, classroom staff provided physical and occupational therapy, sensory integration work, anger management sessions, and reading recovery work. Parents know of all the school's specialist interventions before they enroll their child in the school. Written consent is required for play therapy sessions or for work with the play therapist, but not for therapeutic play sessions or for special work with school staff. An opportunity to refuse permission for these interventions is essential.

THE RATIONALE BEHIND THE APPROACH FOR THIS CLIENT POPULATION

> Research clearly suggests that having a secure attachment with a teacher can partially compensate for an insecure one with a parent. . . . In summary, interventions for at-risk children should . . . utilize developmentally appropriate methods including play, address attachment needs, and be, at least in part, school based. (Chaloner, 2001, pp. 370–371)

The relationship established over the course of play therapy sessions is core to the efficacy of the intervention. Enhancing a teacher-pupil attachment can have positive effects in the classroom as well as for the child in a wider context. Having a teacher in class as an attachment figure provides the safe base from which exploration becomes possible. "Securely attached infants maintain balanced and flexible deployment of attention to both the caregiver and the surrounding environment" (Goldberg, 2000, pp. 154–155). But

> insecure children will concentrate on one area of information to the exclusion of the other. The impact of this in the classroom is seen in the child who attends to, and seeks attention from, the adult in the room and is unable to settle to independent exploration or work. Another child may seem unable to attend to the adult in the room and to avoid contact with him, preferring to engage with materials and more solitary activities. (Woolf & Austin, 2008, p. 6)

As the teacher learns to better understand the "drivers" (Chaloner, 2001) of the child's behaviors, he or she may have greater tolerance for these behaviors and, at the same time, have a new knowledge of how to respond in order to be the "thermostat" (Landreth & Bratton, 2006) that regulates feelings and actions.

> As a social being, each child wants to belong. His behavior indicates the ways and means by which he tries to be significant. (Dreikurs et al., 1971, p. 12)

Understanding this—and that in behaving as he does, the challenging pupil is in fact "fighting to save himself as an individual, despite the tremendous odds that he faces" (Burton, 1968, p. 7)—changes how the teacher feels about the child and how he or she creates a benign environment in class. Frustrations often arise when adult and child are unable to communicate—this inability sometimes seen by the adult as unwillingness on the part of the child. Playing together offers a new medium for communicating, an appropriate vehicle for expression for the child, and a powerful symbolic language for the adult to listen to what the child is saying.

> In my view, the need to acknowledge and understand children's communications is crucial in providing a school environment that is safe enough in which to learn. (Watt, 2000, p. 67)

THE BETTER PLAYTIMES PROGRAM

The core elements of play therapy and therapeutic play interventions are (Axline, 1969; Ryan & Wilson, 1996; West, 1996; VanFleet, 2000):

- The relationship between adult and child
- Play
- Attunement
- Containment
- Consistency

The *Better Playtimes* training, using as it does the Filial Therapy Training program, teaches child-centered play skills (VanFleet, 2000; Guerney, 2003). The eight basic principles of Axline (1969) underpin the approach. The training sessions for school staff cover the following.

Learning how to *be* in the play sessions:

- Developing listening skills
- Practicing the use of reflection and summarizing
- Attending to children and the communication in their play
- Matching, mirroring, and amplifying the child's verbal and non-verbal communications

Learning what to *do* to structure and provide the play sessions:

- Setting up a time and a place
- Starting and finishing the session
- Equipping a play box
- Deciding which limits to set and the consequences to limit breaking

Staff need to "unlearn" much of their previous knowledge and expertise. New skills are taught in the *Better Playtimes* training, while ongoing supervision is a space for "unlearning old ideas and learning new ways of thinking and doing things" (Garburo & Rothstein, 1998, p. 1). Teaching is about setting the pace, seeking answers, correcting mistakes, and working toward aims and objectives. Therapeutic play is about being with the child, following at the child's pace, staying with the child, and accepting and living with uncertainty.

> In therapy I was not expecting him to achieve a particular result as I might in the classroom. . . . In therapy, by contrast, the focus was on him learning about himself, in his own time and at his own pace. (Adams, 2000, p. 87)

Children have to learn that play sessions are different than the rest of the school day and that usual limits and structures will stay as they always have been. Also, staff must believe that the differences can create a powerful learning environment and that not knowing what just happened, why it happened, and what will happen next does not mean the event is meaningless or of no value.

> The purpose of the session is accomplished when the adult can be what the child needs her to be. The adult does not need to know the purpose of the child's chosen play. The child does not need to know the purpose of her choices. (Woolf & Austin, 2008, p. 36)

PROGRAM GOALS

Better Playtimes are included in school provision in the hope that:

- Children will be able to process and express their needs, feelings, and beliefs (Chaloner, 2001).
- Staff will be able to develop insight into relationships and aware-ness of their responses and reactions and those of the child.
- The school will be able to offer an appropriate intervention to meet the emotional needs of the particular pupil cohort.

It truly is an intervention for both staff and children. In choosing Filial Therapy (VanFleet, 2000; Guerney, 2003) as the intervention most likely to facilitate positive change for a child, it is the anticipated change in the parent or caregiver who undertakes the training that is key to the outcome. So staff learning and development in *Better Playtimes* is key to the changes for the child.

CONSIDERATIONS IN PROVIDING THERAPEUTIC PLAY WITH PARAPROFESSIONALS IN SCHOOLS

The dual role of teacher and therapist in the life of the child needs addressing (Adams, 2000) in order for both adult and child to feel safe in both situations.

> It was made clear that what took place in the sessions would not be referred to outside of the therapy room. (Adams, 200, p. 87)

In schools where circle time (Mosley, 1996) is part of the class experi-ence, the understanding of confidentiality and its limits when informa-tion needs sharing in order to keep a child safe is already in place. In play sessions the permissiveness and the supportiveness of the environment allow a child to go emotionally where they would not normally go, to be who they would not normally be, and to risk what they would not normally risk. The child needs to feel that these experiments in being and doing can be left behind the closed door of the therapeutic play room.

COMMON PROBLEMS ENCOUNTERED

> A common problem facing an elementary school counselor is an over-whelming caseload. (Allen, 1988, p. 178)

There are different ways to address this issue that will be school or service-provider specific. Group work can be a means to provide therapeutic sessions in schools to a greater number of children (Geldard & Geldard, 2001). The use of teachers as paraprofessional session providers is another (White et al., 2003). Having sufficient adults in school trained to work therapeutically with children is one of the issues facing schools where the need for addressing a sizeable population of children with emotional difficulties can feel "overwhelming."

> First there are the constraints of the timetable which face any new course which is being established in the existing curriculum pattern adopted by the school. (Coppock & Dwivedi, 1993, p. 267)

Time in school is a precious commodity for everyone. And finding staff time for one-on-one individual work means using class teaching time, which requires the need to find class cover or using staff non-contact management time. School assembly time, lunch breaks, or, in some schools, "Choices" reward time may be used. Supervision for the therapeutic play provider adds to the time demands of introducing this new school provision. Space is the next important consideration along with the need for privacy, consistent availability, and appropriateness to the activity.

RESOURCES

Resources for providing play experiences in schools may seem to be an issue that is easily addressed. However, even those schools that seem to have generous supplies of play materials and opportunities, on closer examination, may have toys that are chosen for learning outcomes and for educational purposes rather than for therapeutic goals. Resources are not often chosen for symbolic importance and for emotional expression.

> In order for the child to maintain contact with the inner world of symbols and feelings, . . . some form of symbolic expression or outlet is needed. (Allen, 1988, p. 7)

Additional finance may be required to supply a play box that allows for exploration across the developmental continuum (Jennings, 1999) and that will only be used in *Better Playtimes.*

Financial considerations include the issues of staffing, curriculum time, and appropriate space and resources. They also involve choices about cohesion and integration of services (Gray & Noakes, 1997). In SEBD schools there may be tensions with other services, such as Health and Social Welfare, over who funds and provides vital noncurriculum provisions to children whose most pressing special needs are social and emotional, rather than educational. For some, providing support for mental health and well-being can be felt like they are doing the work another agency is funded to cover.

The restraints in school settings on time, space, and money and the requirements of *Better Playtimes* on resources will put demands on the goodwill throughout the school. The inclusion of any teacher-and-child therapeutic play service will require not only wide cooperation across the staff group, but also a belief in the value of the work.

CASE STUDY

Carl is an 8-year-old boy attending a school for children with social, emotional, and behavioral difficulties. His first two years at the school were spent in the infant classroom with Suzanne. Two years in one class with two staff members and between 3-to-8-year-old children meant that some powerful relationship dynamics were created. Whether they were negative or positive, the relationship between the teacher and each child can have significant impact on both. When Carl moved up to the next class in the school, Suzanne felt that maintaining her relationship with Carl could be a helpful part of the transition for him and would give the message that he continued to be important to her despite the move.

For children where losses and moves have perhaps not been planned, have not been explained, and have been sudden and final, this message can be a reparative experience. Having play sessions with Carl after the "separation" also created a situation where, when sessions were to end, Carl could be part of choosing how and when to end within the parameters given by the teacher. Having control in a situation that hitherto has been totally outside of the control of the child is empowering and affirming.

Carl was receiving input from the Young Offenders Team, and introducing another new relationship with the play therapist did not feel appropriate. He was receiving directed work on developing strategies for keeping himself safe and had a relationship with a male role model who offered support and time to talk. No service, including school, was offering Carl time to engage in meaningful play. Therefore, continuation with Suzanne was recommended. He was seen for a total of 12 sessions over 13 weeks in weekly 30-minute sessions.

> A child experiencing adjustment problems can become better adjusted and more socially and emotionally competent when allowed to engage in the developmentally appropriate activities of play. (Peabody, 2006, p. 20)

Before the intervention started, Carl was interviewed as part of the assessment process. In addition to pre- and post-intervention questionnaires, the program used information from drawings and visual representations to provide a nonverbal means of communication of feelings and perceptions. The child was asked to create a picture of himself in his school environment and to identify and color figures representing himself and his staff playmate on a pre-drawn sheet.

Before the sessions began, Carl's responses to the questionnaire included:

> Can you tell me 5 words to describe yourself?
> "Sometimes good."
> Can you tell me one thing you wish was different about you?
> "Stop being naughty every time."
> Can you tell me 5 words to describe your school?
> "Good."
> Can you tell me 5 words to describe Suzanne?
> "Nice, kind."
> Can you tell me 5 words she might use to describe you?
> "Don't know."
> Can you tell me one thing you think she might really like about you?
> "Being good."
> Can you tell me one thing you think she might wish was different about you?
> "Don't be naughty."

Carl seemed to feel that either he was, or was thought by others to be, "naughty." He seemed to have little confidence about how Suzanne might feel about him. "Good" seemed to be the positive adjective in his value system.

During sessions, Carl often struggled to engage in play. Suzanne was very attuned to his feelings in the room. She felt that he was both drawn to and wary of approaching the dolls' house. She recognized this ambivalence as a theme (Chaloner, 2001) throughout his sessions. Knowing Carl's home situation from her long involvement with him, her hypothesis was about the house being a powerful symbol of where his feelings were often overwhelming, where his needs were not being met, and about which his beliefs had to be denied (Chaloner, 2001). The playroom house was a stark contrast to Carl's real-life house. A house with window boxes, no broken glass panes, a tidy garden, and perfect paint work did not represent the reality of the housing estate Carl knew as home. As he became more comfortable in sessions, Carl was able to take the house apart, thereby recreating possible feelings about his life at home and probably creating a visual representation of a house that felt more like his own. He said of the house, "It's not real." Suzanne was able to see that this could be a literal statement—no house really looks like that—or that it could be Carl's way of making the play feel distanced and safe.

Another theme of Carl's play that Suzanne recognized as it presented itself and tracked and acknowledged as it changed, was his ability to persevere and to be effective. Touching base with Erikson's (1995) developmental model helps paraprofessionals to recognize possible ages and stages in children's play themes. An 8-year-old boy may not yet have worked through the crises of "Initiative vs. Guilt" with the potential strength of a "Sense of Purpose" (Erikson, 1995, pp. 229–232) and of "Industry vs. Inferiority" with the potential positive outcome of "Competence" (Erikson, 1995, pp. 232–234). Carl appeared to be working on both of these issues in parallel. Suzanne supported his development in her new and different role by allowing him to learn what she could not teach him (Frank, 1982). Her affirmations of these developing strengths ("You thought that through really well," "You've got that sorted out now!" and "You've got another plan—you have different ways of sorting problems out") strengthened the development of a new, more confident, competent, and effective Carl.

Another theme that was played out during the sessions was Carl's feeling, need, or belief (Chaloner, 2001) that he had to tidy up any play materials he got out. Suzanne also picked up on the related theme in their relationship ("You feel it's important to help me," "I think you wanted to save me then"). This theme of needing to be the caregiver of those who are in the position of caring for him was symbolically communicated by Carl in his penultimate session. In session five

Carl approached Suzanne with a large furry spider, which she felt was him "wondering how I feel about the spider, thinking it might scare me." Carl got the spider out again in session ten and told Suzanne, "This is me, I have to clean up all the house, get rid of all the flies, and make it nice for everyone." Carl again demonstrated his ambivalent feelings to Suzanne. This time those feelings are about himself. He seemed first to wonder if the spider might scare or repulse Suzanne, then to demonstrate his understanding of the useful role a spider fulfils. Asking a child how it is for him at home could never elicit such an informative response. The trusting relationship and the medium of play created a space where Carl could "speak" and be heard.

After the sessions were ended, Carl's responses to the questionnaire included:

> Can you tell me 5 words to describe yourself?
> "A good boy."
> Can you tell me one thing you wish was different about you?
> "Be even more nicer."
> Can you tell me 5 words to describe your school?
> "Good and happy."
> Can you tell me 5 words to describe Suzanne?
> "Kind, nice, happy."
> Can you tell me 5 words she might use to describe you?
> "Kind, good, happy."
> Can you tell me one thing you think she might really like about you?
> "Getting to come in here [the playroom] with me."
> Can you tell me one thing you think she might wish was different about you?
> "Don't know."

"Good" still featured as a positive description in Carl's responses, but now "happy" appears alongside it as an element of his experience of himself and others. "Naughty" was not given as an answer to any post-intervention questions. Carl's replies seemed to have moved from negatives—"don't" and "stop"—to positives—"be nicer." This suggests a powerful shift in his perception of himself and in his belief in his potential. Another shift in perceptions is suggested in Carl's view of what Suzanne might like about him. He no longer feels he has to be "being good" to be valued, and just being together is now valued. His inability to name how Suzanne might prefer him to be now could mean Carl is starting to believe "Perhaps I am 'good enough' just as I am."

Post-intervention, Suzanne described the program as "interesting," "quite challenging," and "a thought provoking reflective experience, both on a personal and professional level." She described Carl as "more able to persevere," more likely to "have a try," more relaxed, and less "needy for contact and reassurance." Her conviction that supervision was "vital" to the effectiveness of the intervention was evidenced by her "continual commitment to self-development and learning" (Garburo & Rothstein, 1998, p. 8).

CONCLUSION

When learning is divorced from human values, the persons involved in the process are alienated from each other and from themselves. (Moustakas & Perry, 1973, p. 9)

Relationships between adults and children in schools and the provision of appropriate play experiences help to create an optimal environment for learning (Geddes, 2006) the activities the school is required to support and develop. After experiencing *Better Playtimes*, school staff may find their new skills and new way of communicating so effective that they adopt them as standard practice before generalizing is introduced. The practice of using session skills in classroom situations for managing conflict, giving limits, and acknowledging feelings is explicit in session recording under "Skills I want to focus on this week in class," being the last section of the sheets. The benefits of training and supporting staff to provide *Better Playtimes* enhances the adult-child relationship, enhances the adult-class relationship through the generalizing of skills, and enhances education provision by creating a more secure learning environment (Geddes, 2006).

Teachers need to learn to communicate better with their students so they can be more successful in their classwork. They need to use more reflective methods of instruction and evaluation so that children receive a more relevant and vibrant classroom experience. (Garubo & Rothstein, 1998, p. 88)

Better Playtimes is a program that benefits both children and paraprofessionals in schools. It enhances relationships, empowers participants, and strengthens schools.

REFERENCES

Adams, S. (2000). Combining teacher and therapist roles: Making the space and taming the dragon. In N. Barwick (Ed.), *Clinical counselling in schools*. London: Routledge.

Allen, J. (1998). *Inscapes of the child's world: Jungian counseling in schools and clinics*. CT: Spring Publications.

Axline, V. (1969). *Play therapy*. New York: Ballentine Books.

Bowlby, J. (1979). *The making and breaking of affectional bonds*. London: Routledge.

Bromfield, R. (1997). *Playing for real*. Northvale, NJ: Jason Aronson.

Burton, L. (1968). *Vulnerable children*. London: Routledge & Keegan Paul.

Cattanach, A. (1992). *Play therapy with abused children*. London: Jessica Kingsley.

Chaloner, W. B. (2001). Counselors coaching teachers to use play therapy in classrooms: The Play and Language to Succeed (PALS) early, school-based intervention for behaviorally at-risk children. In A. A. Drewes, L. J. Carey & C. E. Schaefer (Eds.), *School-based play therapy*. New York: John Wiley & Sons.

Coppock, C. & Dwivedi, K. N. (1993). Group Work in Schools. In K. N. Dwivedi (Ed.), Kingsley. *Group work with children and adolescents: A handbook*. London: Jessica Kingsley.

Department of Education and Science and the Welsh Office (DES & WO) (1989). *Report of the committee of enquiry into discipline in schools* (Chair: Lord Elton). London: HMSO.

Dreikurs, R., Grunwald, B., & Pepper, F. (1971). *Maintaining sanity in the classroom: Illustrated teaching techniques*. New York: Harper & Row.

Erikson, E. (1995). *Childhood and society*. London: Vintage.

Ford-Sori, C. (2006). *Engaging children in family therapy*. New York: Routledge.

Frank, L. (1982). Play in personality development. In G. Landreth (Ed.), *Play therapy: Dynamics of the process of counseling with children*. Springfield, IL: Charles C. Thomas.

Garburo, R. C., & Rothstein, S. W. (1998). *Supportive supervision in schools*. Westport, CT: Greenwood Press.

Geddes, H. (2006). *Attachment in the classroom*. London: Worth Publishing Ltd.

Geldard, K., & Geldard, D., (2000). *Counselling children*. (2001) London: Sage.

Geldard, K. & Geldard, D. (2001). *Working with children in groups: A handbook for counsellors, educators and community workers*. Basingstoke, England: Palgrave.

Gerhardt, S. (2004). *Why love matters*. Hove, England: Brunner Routledge.

Goldberg, S. (2000). *Attachment and development*. London: Arnold.

Gray, P., & Noakes, J. (1997). School Support: Towards a multi-disciplinary approach. In D. A. Lane, & A. Miller, *Child and adolescent therapy: A handbook*. Buckingham, England: Open University Press.

Guerney, L. (2003). The history, principles, and empirical basis of filial therapy. In R. VanFleet, (Ed.), *Casebook of Filial Therapy*. Boiling Springs, PA: Play Therapy Press.

Hess, B., Post, P., Flowers, C. (2005). A follow-up study of Kinder Training for pre-school teachers of children deemed at-risk. *International Journal of Play Therapy, 14*(1), 103–115.

Jennings, S. (1999). *Introduction to Developmental play therapy*. London: Jessica Kingsley.

Karen, R. (1998). *Becoming attached*. Oxford, England: Oxford University Press.

Kellmer Pringle, M. (2000). *The needs of children* (3rd ed.). London: Routledge.

Klein, J. (1997). *Our need for others and its roots in infancy*. London: Routledge.

Landreth, G., & Bratton, S. (2006). Child-Parent Relationship Therapy (CPRT) treatment manual. New York: Routledge.

Mosley, J. (1996). *Quality circle time in the primary classroom*. Wisbech: LDA.

Moustakas, C., & Perry, C. (1973). *Learning to be free*: Prentice Hall.

Peabody, M. A. (2006). Play therapy for prevention—A Pound of Cure. *Social Work Today, 6* (4): 20.

Ryan, V., & Wilson, K. (1996). *Case Studies in Non-directive play therapy*. London: Balliere Tindal.

Shore, R. (1997). *Rethinking the brain: New insights into early development*. New York: Families and Work Institute.

Sweeney, D., & Homeyer, L. (1999). *Group play therapy*. In D. Sweeney, & L. Homeyer, *The Handbook of Group Play Therapy*. San Francisco: Jossey-Bass.

VanFleet, R., Lilly, J. P., & Kaduson, H. (1999). Play therapy for children exposed to violence: Individual, family and community interventions. *International Journal of Play Therapy, 8*(1), 27–42.

VanFleet, R. (2000). *A parent's handbook of filial therapy*. Boiling Springs, PA: Play Therapy Press.

Watt, F. (2000). Is it safe enough to learn? In N. Barwick, (Ed.), *Clinical counselling in schools*. London: Routledge.

West, J. (1996). *Child-centered play therapy*. London: Arnold.

White, J., Draper, K., & Flynt, M. (2003). *Kinder training: A school counselor and teacher consultation model integrating Filial Therapy and Adlerian theory*. In R. VanFleet, (Ed.), *Casebook of Filial Therapy*. Boiling Springs, PA: Play Therapy Press.

Woolf, A. (2008). Better Playtimes training: Theory and practice in an EBD primary school. *Emotional and Behavioural Difficulties, 13*, (1, March 2008): 49–62.

Woolf, A., & Austin, D. (2008). *Handbook of therapeutic play in schools*. Chester: A2C Press.

Author Index

Subject Index